Professional Web Graphics

Matt Slaybaugh

COURSE
TECHNOLOGY
™
THOMSON LEARNING

Australia • Canada • Mexico • Singapore • Spain • United Kingdom • United States

COURSE TECHNOLOGY
™
THOMSON LEARNING

Professional Web Graphics
by Matt Slaybaugh

Senior Product Manager:
Jennifer Muroff

Managing Editor:
Jennifer Locke

Senior Acquisitions Editor:
Christine Guivernau

Development Editor:
Lisa Ruffolo, The Software
Resource

Associate Product Manager:
Tricia Coia

Editorial Assistant:
Janet Aras

Production Editor:
Elena Montillo

Manufacturing Coordinator:
Alec Schall

Cover Designer:
Christy Amlicke, Black Fish
Design, Inc.

Compositor:
GEX Publishing Services

BRIEF

Contents

CHAPTER 5
Creating and Using Background Images   **183**

CHAPTER 8
Creating Thumbnail Galleries

CHAPTER 9
Creating Animation for the Web

Preface

Web graphics are an important part of all professional Web sites. Not only do they decorate pages, but they also establish an identity and make the site more useful. *Professional Web Graphics* will familiarize you with how to create and use Web graphics in professional Web sites. The book introduces common terms and guides you through the process of creating and optimizing graphics for the Web. This book focuses on the types of projects that Web graphic artists and designers encounter every day, including creating images such as backgrounds, buttons, icons, and thumbnails. It also provides detailed explanations of creating more complex Web graphics, such as animations, rollovers, image maps, and image slices.

This book takes a goal-oriented approach toward teaching Web graphics creation, which is different from many other graphics tutorials. Most books that attempt to cover Web graphics focus on the tools used to create images, rather than on the images themselves. *Professional Web Graphics* focuses on the end-results required in real-world Web design projects, and along the way explains the tools necessary to achieve these results.

Because Adobe Photoshop is the standard for creating computer graphics, this book uses Photoshop as the software for creating basic Web graphics. It also uses ImageReady to create Web-only graphics such as animations, image maps, and rollover buttons. However, you can apply the concepts and guidelines presented in this book using any commercial or shareware image editors.

The Intended Audience

Professional Web Graphics is intended for anyone who wants to create effective, useful, high-quality Web graphics. You should be familiar with the desktop interface of either Mac OS or Windows. Most chapters require only the use of Photoshop or ImageReady, and full explanation of the features used is included. Some chapters require simple coding of HTML and Cascading Style Sheets (CSS), so basic familiarity with these languages is required. For the projects that use HTML and CSS, you can use either an HTML editor such as Dreamweaver, or a basic text editor such as BBEdit or TextPad. Some exercises at the end of the book require simple JavaScript programming. Although familiarity with JavaScript is not required, it is recommended.

The Approach

This book is organized into three major sections: basic, intermediate, and advanced Web graphics. The basic section covers general topics about computer graphics and issues about Web graphics that apply to every project you work on. These chapters introduce Photoshop, and explain how to optimize images, display graphics in Web pages, and acquire images to use on the Web. The intermediate section guides you through creating and using Web graphics that do not require special HTML coding or special Web graphics software, such as background images, icons, buttons, and thumbnail images. The advanced section shows you how to create and use graphics that require special coding to display on the Web, including animations, rollover effects, image maps, and image slices.

Each chapter provides a thorough explanation of the topic, concrete examples from professional settings, and opportunities for applying principles and practicing skills in hands-on tasks. Each chapter concludes with a summary, review questions, Hands-on Projects, and a Case Project. The summary and review questions highlight and reinforce major concepts. The Hands-on Projects are guided activities that let you practice, reinforce, and extend the techniques presented in the chapter. They also enhance your learning experience by providing additional ways to apply your knowledge in new situations. The Case Project lets you use the skills that you have learned in the chapter to solve real-world problems.

Overview of This Book

The examples, steps, projects, and cases in this book will help you achieve the following objectives:

- Use Adobe Photoshop and ImageReady to create and edit Web graphics
- Optimize graphic files to reduce their size as much as possible without compromising the quality of the image
- Generate and use HTML to display images on a Web page
- Acquire images for the Web by creating, scanning, or photographing them
- Create, use, and tile background images
- Create and use icons that convey meaning in a small space
- Create buttons and enhance them with 3-D effects such as shadows and highlights
- Create a thumbnail gallery of miniature images that link to full-sized images
- Create GIF animations and understand the pros and cons of other animation formats, such as Flash and Shockwave
- Make Web pages interactive by including rollover effects
- Create splash screens with image maps that invite viewers to explore your Web site
- Create sliced images positioned with HTML

Chapter 1 introduces you to the basic concepts of Web graphics and the tools and techniques used to create them. In **Chapter 2**, you learn how to optimize Web graphics, which means making the image file size as small as possible without compromising the quality of the image—your major goal in creating graphics for the Web. After you optimize your images, you incorporate them into a Web page and preview them in a browser so you know how they will appear on users' screens. **Chapter 3** explains how to use HTML to include images on a Web page. Whether you are creating graphics for print, the Web, or other electronic media, you need to acquire images on your computer before you can edit them. **Chapter 4** covers all your options for acquiring images. **Chapter 5** explains how to create background images, which are the simplest images to design and use in Web pages. The most common type of Web graphic is the icon, which is used to express identity and information with a small image. **Chapter 6** covers the creation of icons. Buttons are covered in **Chapter 7**. Buttons are a specific type of icon that are designed to be clicked to take the user to another page. **Chapter 8** explains the fundamentals of creating thumbnail galleries, and shows you how to write a script in Photoshop to save you time when creating multiple images. In **Chapter 9**, you will learn how to create simple, effective animations. **Chapter 10** teaches the complexities of JavaScript rollover effects. Image maps are images that can link to multiple pages and are useful as splash screens that introduce users to a Web site. Image maps are covered in **Chapter 11**. Another type of graphic used for splash screens is the sliced image. Sliced images are really many images placed next to each other. They can contain animations and rollover effects, and are one of the most advanced types of Web graphics. Sliced images are covered in chapter 12.

Each chapter in *Professional Web Graphics* includes the following elements to enhance the learning experience:

- **Chapter Objectives:** Each chapter in this book begins with a list of the important concepts to be mastered within the chapter. This list provides you with a quick reference to the contents of the chapter as well as a useful study aid.

- **Step-By-Step Methodology:** As new concepts are presented in each chapter, tutorials are used to provide step-by-step instructions that allow you to actively apply the concepts you are learning.

- **Tips:** Chapters contain Tips designed to provide you with practical advice and proven strategies related to the concept being discussed. Tips also provide suggestions for resolving problems you might encounter while proceeding through the chapter tutorials.

- **Chapter Summaries:** Each chapter's text is followed by a summary of chapter concepts. These summaries provide a helpful way to recap and revisit the ideas covered in each chapter. They include a list of common sample code techniques that were presented during the chapter that can be used for review or reference while proceeding through the chapter tutorials.

- **Review Questions:** End-of-chapter assessment begins with a set of approximately 20 review questions that reinforce the main ideas introduced in each chapter. These questions ensure that you have mastered the concepts and understand the information you have learned.

Hands-on Projects: Along with conceptual explanations and step-by-step tutorials, each chapter provides Hands-on Projects related to each major topic aimed at providing you with practical experience. Some of the Hands-on Projects provide detailed instructions, while others provide less detailed instructions that require you to apply the materials presented in the current chapter with less guidance. As a result, the Hands-on Projects provide you with practice creating Web Graphics in real-world situations.

Case Project: The case project builds from one chapter to the next, providing you with a portfolio of Web graphics. The case is designed to help you apply what you have learned in each chapter to real-world situations. It gives you the opportunity to independently synthesize and evaluate information, examine potential solutions, and make recommendations, much as you would in a professional situation.

Resources for Instructors

The following supplemental materials are available when this book is used in a classroom setting. All of the teaching tools available with this book are provided to the instructor on a single CD-ROM.

Electronic Instructor's Manual. The Instructor's Manual that accompanies this textbook includes:

- Additional instructional material to assist in class preparation, including suggestions for lecture topics.
- Solutions to all end-of-chapter materials, including the Review Questions and Hands-on Projects.

ExamView®

This textbook is accompanied by ExamView, a powerful testing software package that allows instructors to create and administer printed, computer (LAN-based), and Internet exams. ExamView includes hundreds of questions that correspond to the topics covered in this text, enabling students to generate detailed study guides that include page references for further review. The computer-based and Internet testing components allow students to take exams at their computers, and also save the instructor time by grading each exam automatically.

PowerPoint Presentations. This book comes with Microsoft PowerPoint slides for each chapter. These are included as a teaching aid for classroom presentation, to make available to students on the network for chapter review, or to be printed for classroom distribution. Instructors can add their own slides for additional topics they introduce to the class.

Data Files. Data Files, containing all of the data necessary for steps within the chapters and the Hands-on Projects, are provided through the Course Technology Web site at *www.course.com*, and are also available on the Teaching Tools CD-ROM.

Solution Files. Solutions to end-of chapter review questions, exercises, and Hands-on Projects are provided on the Teaching Tools CD-ROM and may also be found on the Course Technology Web site at *www.course.com*. The solutions are password-protected.

Distance Learning. Course Technology is proud to present online courses in WebCT and Blackboard, as well as at MyCourse.com, Course Technology's own course enhancement tool, to provide the most complete and dynamic learning experience possible. When you add online content to one of your courses, you're adding a lot: self tests, links, glossaries, and, most of all, a gateway to the twenty-first century's most important information resource. We hope you will make the most of your course, both online and offline. For more information on how to bring distance learning to your course, contact your local Course Technology sales representative.

ACKNOWLEDGMENTS

Dedicated to Lisa Feigenson, for her patience and encouragement.

Thanks to Murad Mirzoyev for the photographs used in Chapter 4.

Thanks to Colleen M. Case, Schoolcraft College; Christi Ward-Walter, Atkins-Behham, Inc.; and Kas Aruskevich, University of Alaska Fairbanks, who provided invaluable comments and suggestions during the development of this book. Thanks also to the reviewers of the proposal: Ann Carter, Rock Valley College; Michael Day, Sheperd College; and John Purcell, Castleton State College.

Matt Slaybaugh

Read This Before You Begin

To the User

You can use your own computer to complete the tutorials, Hands-on Projects, and Case Project in this book. To use your own computer, you will need the following:

- **A Web browser,** such as Microsoft Internet Explorer version 5.0 or later, or Netscape Navigator version 6.
- **Adobe Photoshop 6.0 and ImageReady.**
- **An HTML editor,** such as Dreamweaver, or a text editor such as BBEdit or TextPad.

Visit Our World Wide Web Site

Additional materials designed especially for you might be available for your course on the World Wide Web. Go to *http://www.course.com*. Periodically search this site for more details.

1

INTRODUCTION TO WEB GRAPHICS

Understanding the Basics of Web Graphics

In this chapter, you will:

♦ Learn the basics of Web graphics
♦ Understand the difference between vector and bitmap graphics, and the software you use to create and edit them
♦ Get started with Adobe Photoshop and ImageReady
♦ Learn to manipulate images
♦ Learn the concepts, terminology, and methods involved in working with Web graphics

Twenty-five years ago, computer graphics were of interest only to scientists, programmers, and other professionals who had access to high-end, powerful computers. When desktop computers with graphical interfaces became popular in the mid-1980s, the mainstream population was exposed to computer graphics for the first time, and they responded enthusiastically. Now that the World Wide Web, Windows, and other graphical user interfaces are so widespread, many people view and use computer graphics on a daily basis—whenever they turn on a computer.

Adobe Photoshop is the most popular program used to create computer graphics. Adobe also publishes graphics software called ImageReady, which is similar to Photoshop, but has special features for creating Web-only graphics such as animations, image maps, and rollover buttons. This chapter introduces you to these programs.

When you are familiar with the basic tools of Adobe Photoshop and ImageReady, you will be ready to manipulate images. You also will have a chance to practice navigating and editing images, and learn some techniques to use for creating professional Web graphics.

The expanding Internet industry will likely continue to provide job opportunities for professionally trained, skilled Web graphic artists.

APPRECIATING THE VALUE OF WEB GRAPHICS

Web graphics are sometimes dismissed as mere decoration, but effective graphics enhance a Web site, and make it easier to use and understand. As people surf the Web, viewing one page after another, they quickly decide whether to stay and explore a site or move on. According to Nielsen/NetRatings, Inc., the average user in September 2000 spent between 50 and 55 seconds viewing a Web page before clicking away. Users quickly leave unattractive, uninformative sites, but stay at useful, well-designed ones.

As a Web designer, you must make your images count—they must be appealing, informative, and easy to interpret. When viewed on a standard monitor, Web pages have a fixed, limited size, and every square inch of those pages needs to be used efficiently. A well-designed graphic often uses less space than a full paragraph of text, yet can be more informative and functional.

Understanding Web Graphics

Although Web graphics did not even exist ten years ago, for many of us, they are now an integral part of our lives. Without graphics, the Web would be much less informative and interesting. Before you start creating Web graphics, you must first understand the terminology that describes graphics for the computer in general, and for the Web in particular.

The quality of Web graphics also affects viewers' perceptions of a Web site. A background image that obscures text, or an image with jagged edges, gives an impression of amateur or careless work. Poor-quality graphics can negatively affect the rest of the site, and make the content and services seem unprofessional as well. On the other hand, high-quality graphics reassure users that the site is worthy of their trust and time, and users are more likely to believe that the products and services the site offers will also be high-quality.

Understanding Common Computer Graphics Terms

A computer graphic is different from a drawing on a piece of paper because a drawing is an actual image, while a computer graphic is an **image file** and an **image display**. The image file is a set of instructions that tells the computer what to show on the monitor; the image display is the image that consequently appears on the monitor.

To edit a paper drawing, you physically add or remove pigment. However, to edit a computer graphic, you edit the instructions in the appropriate computer file. When you use a graphics program, you have the illusion that you are directly manipulating an image, but the process is actually more indirect. The signals from your mouse and keyboard tell the software to change the image file; the edited image then appears on your monitor.

Image displays are grids of tiny squares of colors. Each square is called a **pixel**, which is short for picture element. The grid of pixels is called a **bitmap**. An image file that produces a grid of pixels is called a bitmap file. Paint-type graphics programs typically let you create bitmap images, and treat images as collections of dots, not shapes.

Another type of image file is a **vector**. A vector file is a small program that describes the position, length, and direction of lines. A vector file contains instructions on how to draw pixels, rather than information about the pixels. Draw-type graphics programs typically let you create vector images, which are collections of lines, not patterns of individual dots or pixels.

When a vector file is executed, the graphics software renders a new bitmap image display. Rendering produces a graphic image from a data file to an output device such as a monitor. The act of rendering a vector image file into a bitmap image display is called **rasterizing**. Bitmap images that are created from vector images are sometimes called **raster** images, or rasterized images. Figure 1-1 shows the bitmap image created after rasterizing a vector image.

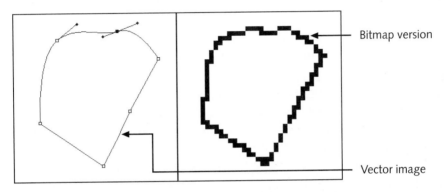

Bitmap version

Vector image

Figure 1-1   A vector image and its rasterized bitmap version

The grids of pixels in bitmap images are measured in terms of **resolution**, or how many pixels the monitor can display in an inch. Resolution is measured in pixels per inch, **ppi**; or in dots per inch, **dpi**. Most monitors have a display resolution of 72 ppi, so a bitmap image that is 72 pixels high and 144 pixels wide appears one inch high and two inches wide. Bitmap images are **resolution-dependent**, because the resolution of the monitor determines the size of the image. If the bitmap image in the previous example appeared on a monitor with a resolution of 96 ppi, it would be only three-quarters of an inch high and one and one-half inches wide.

In contrast, a vector image is not measured in pixels, and can appear at any size, regardless of the monitor's resolution. Vector images are **resolution-independent**—their size is not affected by the resolution of the display device. However, when a vector image is rasterized into a bitmap image, the raster image *is* resolution-dependent.

WORKING WITH GRAPHICS SOFTWARE

Adobe Photoshop is the software most often used for creating graphics for the Web and for other media such as print. You can use Photoshop to create vector images, but its main function is creating and editing bitmap images. After you work with an image, you should preview it in a Web browser such as Internet Explorer or Netscape Navigator. You can preview images in Photoshop, but most of the time you should preview them in a Web browser, where the images ultimately will appear. Browsers can display Web pages and graphics, but cannot be used to edit the graphics.

Working with Vectors

A vector is a line segment with a specific length and direction. A vector-based image is composed of lines, curves, and geometric shapes. These lines have no thickness, only length, direction, and degree of curvature. (Pixels, on the other hand, have a uniform size and a specific color and position in the bitmap grid.)

The lines and shapes of a vector image can be either **stroked** or **filled** to make the lines and shapes in the final image. Vectors themselves do not appear in the final image, but they do determine where colors will appear. When a line is stroked, it is given a thickness and color. A line can be filled only when it loops on itself to form a complete closed shape. A shape can be filled with a solid color, a color gradient, or a pattern. Figure 1-2 shows a raster image created from a vector file.

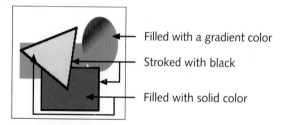

Figure 1-2   A raster image

To create complex images with vectors, you must separately define every area of solid color so that the image looks like a cartoon or a paint-by-numbers kit. Vector images are limited because they cannot reproduce rich texture very well. Photographs are never represented as vector images because a separate vector shape has to be defined for every spot of detail in the image. Vector images are appropriate for simple images, such as line art and graphs.

As mentioned earlier, one advantage to using vector images is that they are resolution-independent, so changes to the image dimensions do not affect the image quality. Because vector images are resolution-independent, they also can be scaled to any size without changing the image quality or the size of the image file. This is not true for bitmap images, which are resolution-dependent. When you increase the dimensions of bitmap images, the resolution decreases accordingly, resulting in jagged edges instead of smooth lines. The size of bitmap image files also is linked directly to the image dimensions, so a larger image means a larger file. Figure 1-3 shows a vector image and a bitmap image that have been doubled in size.

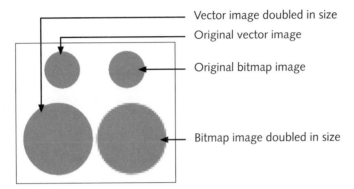

Vector image doubled in size
Original vector image

Original bitmap image

Bitmap image doubled in size

Figure 1-3 A scaled vector image and a scaled bitmap image

While vector images tend to have smaller file sizes and scale better than bitmaps, Web browsers do not display vector images. Browsers display only bitmap images, so any vector image must be rasterized before a browser can display it. Browsers use small programs to rasterize vector images into bitmaps on the user's computer; these programs are called **plug-ins**. Plug-ins have other functions, but one of the most common is converting vector images to bitmaps to display those images in a Web browser.

Dissecting a Vector Image

In Photoshop, vectors are referred to as **paths**, and vectors that form complete loops are called **shapes**. Recall that vector images are simple programs—line-by-line commands that tell the computer what to display. A sample vector file might contain the following code, and produce the image shown in Figure 1-4.

```
create background {
    width=4;
    height=4;
    color=white;
}
create square {
    upper-left corner: x=1, y=1;
    lower-right corner: x=3, y=3;
    color=red;
}
```

The code tells the computer to draw a white background that is four pixels wide and four pixels high. The second instruction is to draw a red square two pixels wide and two pixels high in the middle of the background.

To add more shapes, you add instructions to the file, and specify the shapes you want. Adding instructions makes the image more complex and increases its file size. The preceding code has only eight lines of commands, so the file is less than one kilobyte in size.

The vector file size, however, does not reflect the actual size of the image. For example, if you change the image in Figure 1-4 so that the background is 400 x 400 pixels, the dimensions of the image change, but the file size remains about the same. The size of a vector image file is directly related to the complexity of the image—how many shapes the image contains. This is the primary advantage of vector images: changing the dimensions of the image has no effect on the quality of the image.

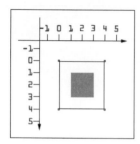

Figure 1-4   A vector image

Using Software Tools with Vector Images

When you work with vector images, you do not edit the instructions directly. You use an illustration program such as Macromedia FreeHand, Adobe Illustrator, or CorelDraw for editing. The tools in these programs act as an interface between you and the image file. As you work with an on-screen image, the illustration program makes the appropriate changes to the file. These drawing programs also work with lines and shapes and create vector image files, which can then be rasterized into bitmap images and displayed on a Web page. Additionally, illustration programs let you perform common vector-editing tasks, such as creating simple line art or technical diagrams.

Rasterizing Vector Images

Vector images were perfect for old-style line printers. Those printers had a mechanical arm with a stylus that drew shapes according to the instructions in the image file. Modern printers and computer monitors, however, do not print or display images that way. They work with grids of pixels and display one pixel after another in a horizontal row, and line by line vertically from top to bottom. Look closely at your computer screen, and you can see the individual pixels that make up every desktop icon, character, window, and graphic.

To display a vector image on the screen in this pixel-grid style, an illustration program has to render, or rasterize, the image by executing the vector image file and generating a map of pixels, known as a bitmap. The vector image is composed of lines and geometric shapes, as mentioned earlier, and rasterizing the vector image converts these lines and shapes onto a grid of pixels. The new bitmap image file contains none of the vector information in the original file. The bitmap file simply lists the color value of each pixel in the grid. Figure 1-5 illustrates how a program rasterizes a vector image by converting it to a bitmap image.

Figure 1-5   Rasterizing an image

Working with Bitmaps

Bitmap images have two advantages over vector images: They display texture better and do not need to be rasterized to appear in a Web page, so they do not require the use of a plug-in.

The amount of detail in a vector image is limited by the number of shapes the image has, but the detail in a bitmap image is limited by the number of pixels. A small bitmap image that appears as a one-inch square on a standard monitor has over five thousand separate pixels. A vector image with many shapes is so complicated that the process of rasterizing it into a bitmap image takes several seconds to place each shape. The level of detail possible in bitmap images has a cost, however. Bitmap files tend to have much larger file sizes than do vector images. Although bitmap files can contain more texture and visual information, they take longer to download.

Vector images and bitmap images are fundamentally different in the way they store information. Whereas a vector image file is a list of the shapes included in the complete image, a bitmap image file is simply a list of pixels, each one with its own color. To define the shape in Figure 1-4 using a bitmap, the image file might contain the following code, and then create the image shown in Figure 1-6.

```
0,0 = white
1,0 = white
2,0 = white
3,0 = white
0,1 = white
1,1 = red
2,1 = red
3,1 = white
0,2 = white
1,2 = red
2,2 = red
3,2 = white
0,3 = white
1,3 = white
2,3 = white
3,3 = white
```

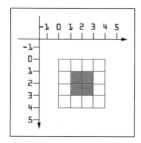

Figure 1-6   A bitmap image file

Notice that the axes are centered in the upper-left corner of the image. This is how Web graphics are always defined. The pixel grid numbers the columns from left to right, starting with zero, and numbers the rows from top to bottom, also starting with zero.

The image in Figure 1-6 is not complex, and the dimensions are small, so the vector image in Figure 1-4 is not noticeably different from the bitmap version shown in Figure 1-6. Imagine doubling the width of each image. To do so, you change only a few numbers in the vector image file—set the width to eight instead of four. In the bitmap image, however, you must define the color for twice as many pixels—the new image has the same number of rows but twice the number of columns. That doubles the information in the image file, and thus doubles the file size.

As explained earlier, the file size of a vector image is affected by how complex the image is, not how big it is when it appears. Figure 1-7 shows what happens if the image in Figure 1-4 is scaled, or resized, to double its original width. This new image has larger dimensions but does not have a larger file size.

On the other hand, because bitmap images are resolution-dependent, the dimensions of a bitmap image affect the size of the bitmap file. Doubling the width or height of a bitmap image roughly doubles the file size. Figure 1-8 shows what happens if Figure 1-6 also is scaled to double the original width. The number of pixels doubles, making the file size larger.

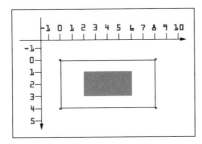

Figure 1-7　A scaled vector image

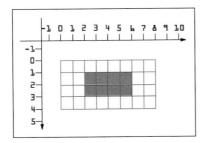

Figure 1-8　A scaled bitmap image

All Web graphics must be transferred over networks, from the Web servers where they are stored to users' computers and Web browsers. Images with smaller file sizes are transferred more quickly than are image files with larger sizes. Much of your work in creating Web graphics involves keeping file sizes as small as possible.

When you choose to use either vector or bitmap images, first determine which type produces the image that you desire, and then decide which type is most convenient for the user to view.

Printing and Viewing Graphics

Although you do most of your graphics work with a paint-like editor such as Photoshop, occasionally you will use a drawing program such as FreeHand or Illustrator to create a vector-based logo or figure. A printed vector image usually is much cleaner than a printed bitmap image. You've seen this if you've ever printed a Web page; the bitmap graphics were probably fuzzy instead of crisp.

To display the vector images on the Web, however, you must **export** the image into a bitmap. This is the same process as when a drawing program rasters the drawing, converting it into a bitmap. Although it's easy to convert a vector image to a bitmap image, it's nearly impossible to convert a bitmap to a vector image. As shown in Figure 1-9, you can rasterize a vector image so you can display it on a computer monitor, in a bitmap graphic, or on a printer. You can display a bitmap graphic on a monitor or printer, but you cannot convert it to a vector image.

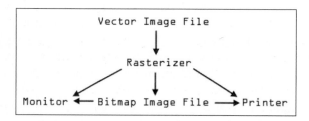

Figure 1-9 Relationship between vector and bitmap images

In general, vector images download quickly, but do not display texture detail as well as bitmap images. Always use bitmap images for photographs.

Web browsers cannot display vector images; they display bitmap images only. A browser uses a plug-in to rasterize vector images into bitmap images that can be shown in the browser. Because browsers require plug-ins to display vector images, you use bitmap images for almost all Web graphics.

GETTING STARTED WITH ADOBE PHOTOSHOP AND IMAGEREADY

The most recent version of Adobe Photoshop, version 6.0, comes bundled with Adobe ImageReady, version 3.0. ImageReady and Photoshop both are used to create and edit computer graphics, but ImageReady has fewer features and is designed specifically for creating Web-only graphics such as animations. Photoshop has more general features and can be used to create graphics for print, software, or the Web. To complete the steps and exercises in this book, you must use Photoshop and ImageReady.

Choosing Web Graphics Tools

Software that works with vector images are typically called **drawing programs**, while software that lets you manipulate bitmap images are called **image editors**. Some examples of drawing programs are Adobe Illustrator, CorelDraw, and Macromedia FreeHand. Because drawing programs produce vector images, and because vector images have better print quality than bitmap images, you usually use drawing programs for print projects such as magazine ads or letterheads. You also can use them to design graphics such as logos that appear in print and on the Web.

However, image editors are what you will most often use to create Web graphics, such as Adobe Photoshop and Macromedia Fireworks. You also can use many freeware and shareware programs such as PaintShop Pro or The GIMP to edit images. (Most editors can open image files created in other editors.)

Becoming Familiar with Your Work Environment

Before you can become fully proficient with any software, you first must become familiar with the software's features and how they work. Every Photoshop version has more features than the last, and can overwhelm new users. Many features are redundant, and simply provide different ways to do the same thing. Take some time to investigate Photoshop and ImageReady, and learn which tools you will use frequently, and which you will use only in special circumstances. Not only is Photoshop an excellent tool for designing and creating graphics, but it also provides a well-designed interface, with easy-to-access features. The following sections introduce you to the Photoshop and ImageReady palettes, tools, and menus. Figure 1-10 shows the Photoshop environment components—the menu bar, Options bar, Image window, toolbox, status bar, and all palettes.

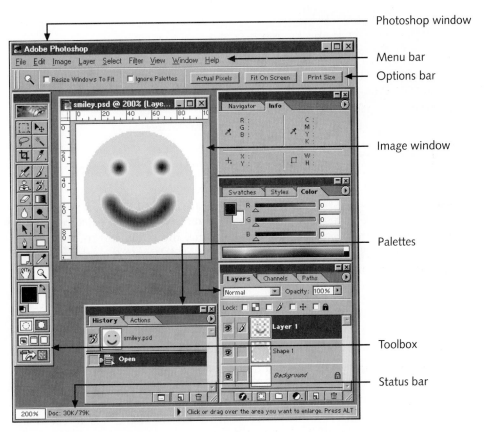

Figure 1-10   The Photoshop environment

Using Palettes

The Photoshop work area contains several windows in addition to the window that displays the image. These additional windows are called **palettes**, and they contain tools, commands, and settings. You use palettes to select options for tracking and editing images. You select colors from the Color palette, parts of images from the Layers palette, tools from the toolbox, and so on.

Most palettes are grouped together to save space on the desktop, but you can open a single palette by dragging its tab. The palettes contain a triangle in the upper-right section of the palette window. Click the triangle to open a menu of options for the palette. These options change depending on which palette you select. For example, click the triangle on the Swatches palette and you see a menu of options for creating and editing color swatches. Figure 1-11 shows options for working with the Channels palette.

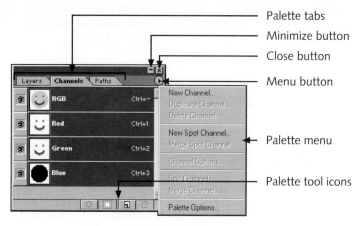

Figure 1-11   Channels palette options

To save room on your desktop, you can minimize or close the palettes. To re-open them, click Window on the menu bar, and then click the command to show the palette you need. For example, to open the Color palette, click Window on the menu bar, and then click Show Color.

Info Palettes   The Info palettes provide general information about the image in the Image window, and include the Navigator palette and the Info palette itself. The Navigator palette shows you a small version of the opened image. You use the Navigator palette to change the scale of the image display in Photoshop. The Info palette, shown in Figure 1-12, shows you information about colors and dimensions of the image. You use the Info palette to see information about the color value and position of individual pixels in the image. ImageReady includes an additional Info palette called the Optimize palette. The Optimize palette shows information about the size of the image file, and allows you to shrink the image file without affecting the quality of the image.

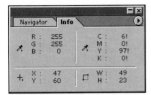

Figure 1-12   The Info palette

Color Palettes   The Color palette shows you the selected color and lets you select new colors by sliding bars or entering numerical color values. The Swatches palette, illustrated in Figure 1-13, shows a table of commonly used colors. You use the Swatches palette to select colors without having to indicate their numerical values. The Style palette contains effects you can add to images. ImageReady uses the Color Table palette, which shows information about the colors used in the image. ImageReady also uses the Layer Options/Style palette, which shows information about effects used in the image.

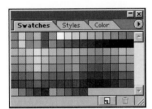

Figure 1-13   The Swatches palette

Action Palettes   The Action palettes include the History palette, which lets you track your actions, and the Actions palette, which lets you create and edit a series of commands, which you then can play back on one or more files. The History palette, shown in Figure 1-14, lists recent edits made to the image. You can undo commands and reverse most edits you have made to an image by selecting different states in the History palette. The Actions palette contains sequences of edits that you can run as scripts. The Actions palette allows you to automate certain processes so that you do not have to perform the same sequence of edits manually on multiple images.

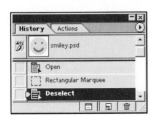

Figure 1-14   The History palette

View Palettes   A number of palettes, including the Layers, Channels, and Paths palettes, let you work with different parts of the image. The Layers palette shows information about layers used in the image. Layers are like sheets of transparent film laid on top of each other, each containing different parts of an image. You use layers to manipulate individual pieces of an image. The Layers palette is shown in Figure 1-15. The Channels palette shows information about colors used in the image. You can modify color channels independently to create interesting visual effects. A color channel is the set of all shades of a particular color. A full-color image has three color channels, one for all shades of red, one for green, and one for blue. A color image is the combination of the color channels. The Paths palette shows information about vectors used in the image.

Figure 1-15   The Layers palette

Web Effects Palettes (ImageReady Only)   Photoshop is an all-purpose image editing program that lets you create images that can be displayed in print, on the Web, or in digital video projects. ImageReady is primarily used to create images for the Web. It shares many features with Photoshop, but does not contain some tools that are appropriate for print projects only. However, ImageReady does contain some Web-only features that are not available in Photoshop.

The following four ImageReady-only palettes are generally used for creating Web-only graphics such as image maps, and buttons that change when rolled over with the mouse.

- The Animation palette is where you compose animated images. You usually save these files as simple animations that play on a Web page, though you can also save them as complicated movies that users can download from a Web site.

- The Rollover palette lets you create **rollover effects**. Rollover effects involve dynamically replacing one image with another when the user's mouse rolls over the image, for example, when you point to a button and it changes color or position. The Rollover palette is shown in Figure 1-16.

- The Image Map palette shows information about images being used as **image maps**. Image maps are normal images that can link to multiple destinations.

- The Slice palette shows information about **slices**, which are pieces of a single image that are saved as separate images.

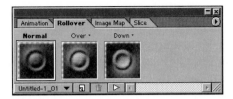

Figure 1-16   The Rollover palette

Text Palettes   You use the Character and Paragraph palettes to manipulate text in your images. The Character palette lets you control settings for fonts. The Paragraph palette lets you adjust the alignment and justification of text. The Character palette is shown in Figure 1-17.

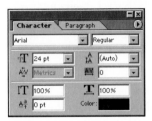

Figure 1-17   The Character palette

Tool Palettes   The toolbox and Options bar are considered tool palettes because they let you work with the Photoshop and ImageReady tools. The toolbox contains the tools you use to edit images, and is shown in Figure 1-18.

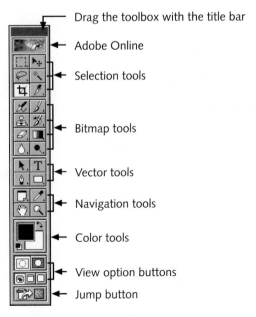

Figure 1-18   The toolbox

The Options bar contains settings for the toolbox tools, and is shown in Figure 1-19. For example, when the Magic Wand tool is selected in the toolbox, the Options bar displays options for tolerance and when the selection should be anti-aliased. When the Paintbrush tool is selected in the toolbox, the Options bar displays options for the size of the brush and the quality of the mark produced by the brush.

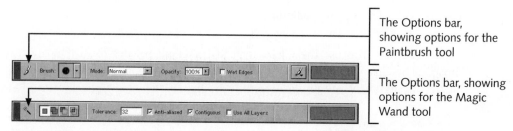

The Options bar, showing options for the Paintbrush tool

The Options bar, showing options for the Magic Wand tool

Figure 1-19   The Options bar

Using the Toolbox

You often use the toolbox when working with Photoshop and ImageReady. The toolbox contains most of the tools you use to manipulate images. For example, you use tools to select parts of the image, add color, magnify, and move images. Each tool has its own pointer to indicate how it affects the image. Some buttons on the toolbox are not tools, but are quick ways to adjust settings. The following sections briefly describe each tool in the toolbox. They are described in more detail in following chapters.

Adobe Online

Click the Adobe Online logo in either Photoshop or ImageReady to visit the Adobe Web site where you can access online help and find software upgrades.

Selection Tools

The selection tools let you select a specific group of pixels, or divide the image into separate pieces. See the Acquiring Images chapter for more details about using the selection tools listed below:

- The Marquee tools create elliptical and rectangular selection areas.
- The Move tool lets you drag selected areas to other parts of the image.
- The Lasso tools let you create selection areas of any shape.
- The Magic Wand tool lets you click a pixel and then select pixels in the image that are similar in color to the pixel you clicked. You can then manipulate all of these pixels at once with a tool, filter, or command.
- The Crop tool selects an area of an image. Double-clicking the selected area discards all of the image area outside the currently selected area.

- ImageReady includes one selection tool not offered in Photoshop—the Image Map tool. You use this tool to define linked areas in image maps. Image maps are single images that can link to different destinations.

- The Slice tool is similar to the Crop tool, but instead of selecting one area and discarding the rest, you can use the Slice tool to split the entire image into many slices that are all saved as separate images.

Bitmap Tools

The Bitmap tools listed below allow you to change the colors of pixels in an image by adding patterns, and by adding, removing, lightening, or darkening colors. See the Acquiring Images chapter for more details about using the Bitmap tools.

- The Airbrush tool lets you paint over the image using the foreground color, creating a spray paint effect. Holding the pointer over one area increases the intensity of the painted line.

- The Paintbrush tool is similar to the Airbrush, but holding the pointer over an area does not affect the painted line. The edges of lines painted with the Paintbrush tool are not as soft as those painted with the Airbrush tool.

- The Pencil tool also is similar to the Airbrush, but lines created with the Pencil have a hard edge.

- The Clone Stamp tools let you copy area in the image and use that area as a texture with which to paint. These tools are useful for retouching photographs.

- The History Brush tools let you change the patterns of pixels in your image. As you make changes to an image, Photoshop keeps a copy of the original. When you use the History Brush tool to paint over an image, instead of applying color, it applies the pixels which have been retrieved from the original version of the image. The Art History Brush applies random patterns to the image as you paint across it and creates soft, pseudo-Impressionist style effects.

- The Eraser tools let you erase pixels instead of adding them when you drag the pointer over an image. The Magic Eraser tool works like the Magic Wand tool; first you click a pixel containing the color you want to delete, and then, only pixels that are similar in color to the pixel you clicked are erased.

- The Gradient tool covers the entire image with both the foreground and background colors, fading from one color to the other.

- The Paint Bucket tool fills an area with the foreground color. It also affects pixels of similar color to the one you click.

- The Blur tool softens the edges in images, while the Sharpen tool exaggerates them. The Smudge tool lets you drag pixels across an image, creating a smeared effect.

- The Dodge tool lightens the area you paint over, and the Burn tool darkens them. The Sponge tool lets you remove color from an area without affecting the shapes and contrast in the image.

Vector Tools

Vector tools allow you to create and edit vector paths and text, or type. Photoshop is not considered a vector program because it is used primarily to generate bitmap images. However, the newer versions of Photoshop contain tools that create vectors within bitmap images. These vectors are called **paths** in Photoshop and ImageReady, and must be rasterized into bitmap information before the image can be saved as a bitmap file. A list of vector tools in Photoshop and ImageReady follows:

- The Path Selection tool lets you select individual paths to modify or reposition.

- The Type tool adds text to images.

- The Pen tools do not draw lines the way the Paintbrush or Pencil tools do. Pen tools allow you to create and edit vector paths.

- The Shape tools create closed paths such as ellipses, rectangles, and polygons.

Navigation Tools

Use the navigation tools listed below to find out information about an image, or to navigate around an image.

- The Documentation tools let you add text or audio notes to images.

- The Eyedropper tools let you sample the color value of a given pixel and set the foreground color to that color value.

- The Measure tool gauges the distance between any two pixels.

- The Hand tool lets you navigate to different parts of the image. If the image is larger than the Image window in which it appears, you can adjust the visible part of the image by moving the scroll bars on the right and bottom of the Image window.

- The Zoom tool is also called the Magnifying Glass tool and allows you to change the scale at which the image appears. Using this tool does not change the dimensions of the image, only how it appears in Photoshop or ImageReady.

Color Tools

You use the color tools to control the foreground color used by the Painting tools, and the background color used by the Eraser tools. The Photoshop and ImageReady Color tools are listed below:

- Set Foreground Color

- Set Background Color

- Default Foreground and Background Colors

- Switch Foreground and Background Colors

View Options

You use the View Option buttons listed below to switch between different view settings. Normally, you will work only with the default settings, but occasionally you will need to preview your work in a different way, using one of the following:

- Toggle Image Map Visibility (ImageReady only)
- Toggle Slices Visibility (ImageReady only)
- Rollover Preview (ImageReady only)
- Preview in Browser (ImageReady only)
- Selection View Mode
- Screen Mode

Jump

You click the Jump button to open the current image file in the alternate Adobe image editing program. For example, clicking Jump in Photoshop opens the image in ImageReady, and clicking Jump in ImageReady opens the image in Photoshop.

Using Menus

The menus in Photoshop and ImageReady contain commands that affect the image file and/or the image display. According to Macintosh and Windows standards, most of these commands have keyboard shortcuts which are indicated next to the commands in the menu. Many commands open dialog boxes where you choose related settings and options. For example, you choose Image Size from the Image menu to open the Image Size dialog box, where you then can specify the width and height of an image. You also can point to many commands to open submenus that list related commands. A list of each Photoshop and ImageReady menu follows, with a brief description of the most commonly used commands.

- The File menu lists commands that work with image files. Among those commands are Open, Close, Save, and Print images.

- The Edit menu includes the Copy, Paste, and Undo commands. It also includes the Preferences submenu, which lists options, such as saving files or using units of measurement, to set your preferences for working with Photoshop.

- The Image menu lists commands to adjust the colors in an image as well as commands to change the dimensions of an image.

- The Layer menu lists commands to rasterize vector image information into bitmap information, and commands to work with layers in an image.

- The Slices menu is included in ImageReady only. This menu lists commands that manipulate separate pieces of an image, known as slices.

- The Select menu lists commands that work with the Marquee, Lasso, and Magic Wand tools to control the selection areas in an image.

- The Filter menu lists 14 submenus of filters, that affect entire images or selections of images. You use filters to create special effects, such as blurring or adding texture in images.

- The View menu includes commands that affect the way the image appears in the Photoshop window, but do not change the image file itself. This menu contains an option to Show Rulers, which displays a pair of rulers above and to the left of the image. Rulers are helpful because they let you see the dimensions of your images. Figure 1-20 demonstrates an image with rulers showing.

Figure 1-20   An image with rulers showing

The Window menu lists commands that affect the appearance of the windows and palettes used by Photoshop.

The Help menu contains links to information about Photoshop, ImageReady, and Adobe.

Documenting Images

Photoshop has two tools that allow you to add comments to an image. The Notes tool lets you add a text box to an image. The text box is associated with a particular spot on the image and can be useful when collaborating on an image. The Audio Annotation tool allows you to add a spoken message to the image. This tool requires that you have a microphone on your computer. Both of these types of documentation can be saved only in the special Photoshop PSD format, and cannot be viewed over the Web. Figure 1-21 shows the Notes and Audio Annotation tools in the toolbox.

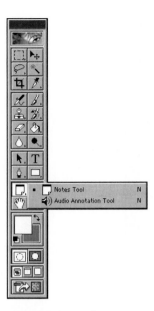

Figure 1-21   The Notes and Audio Annotation tools

Setting Preferences

You can set a variety of preferences to customize your work on Photoshop and ImageReady. On the File menu, point to Preferences to see a submenu of ten options. Choose a Preference option to open the Preferences dialog box, where you can change general settings, such as the units used on rulers and in measurements. Before you begin working with Photoshop to create Web graphics, you need to change the Units & Rulers setting. Graphics intended for print output are usually measured in inches. Graphics used on a Web page, however, are usually measured in pixels. Therefore, you must make sure that the rulers on the Image window use pixels as the measurement unit.

To change the measurement units used in Photoshop:

1. Click **Edit** on the menu bar.

2. Point to **Preferences**, and then click **Units & Rulers**. You see the Preferences dialog box, as shown in Figure 1-22.

3. In the Units area, click the **Rulers** list arrow, and then click **pixels**.

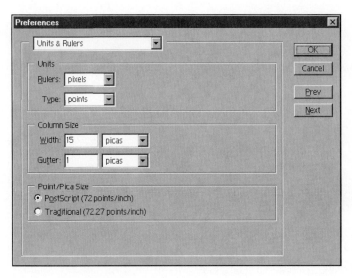

Figure 1-22   The Preferences dialog box

MANIPULATING BITMAP IMAGES WITH PHOTOSHOP

Most of your work creating Web graphics involves editing bitmap images, probably using Photoshop or a similar graphics program. While you use some features of Photoshop only in special circumstances, you use other features for your work with almost every image. The features you use most often change the scale and dimensions of an image, and reverse edits you make to an image. Each of these frequently used features is discussed in the following sections.

Changing the Scale of Bitmap Images

You often will want to change the scale of an image without changing the actual image file. You need to be able to magnify (zoom in) and reduce (zoom out) your view of the image without altering the actual dimensions of the image.

The easiest way to zoom in and out is with the Magnifying Glass tool, also called the Zoom tool.

To change your view of an image using the Zoom tool:

- To zoom in, click the **Zoom** tool, and then click the **image**; to zoom out, hold down the **Option** key on the Macintosh, and click the **image**.

 In Windows you can zoom out by clicking the Zoom tool, holding down the Alt key, and then clicking the image.

You also can drag the Zoom tool across the image to zoom in to the selected area, as shown in Figure 1-23.

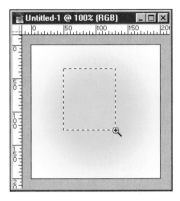

Figure 1-23   Dragging the Zoom tool across an image

Besides using the Zoom tool, you can also change magnification using menu options and the Navigator palette.

To change magnification using menu options:

1. Click **View** on the menu bar, and then click **Fit on Screen** to zoom in on the image so that its outer edges reach the edges of the Photoshop work area.

2. To return the magnification to 100%, click **View** on the menu bar, and then click **Actual Pixels**; you also can double-click the **Zoom** tool.

To change magnification using the Navigator palette:

1. To control magnification in the Navigator palette, shown in Figure 1-24, use the slider at the bottom of the palette. Drag the **slider** to the left to reduce magnification, and to the right to increase magnification.

2. The area of the current image is surrounded by a red border. Drag the **red square** to change which part of the image you view in the Image window. You also can use the Hand tool to drag the image in the Image window.

The status bar at the bottom of the Photoshop window indicates the current percentage of scale. For example, 100% indicates that the image appears at its true size. A scale of 200% means the image appears twice as large as it really is, with half the resolution. A scale of 50% means the image appears only half as large as its true size. You can type directly on the status bar to change the scale.

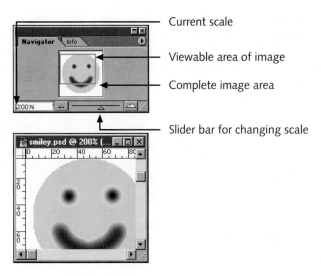

Current scale

Viewable area of image

Complete image area

Slider bar for changing scale

Figure 1-24   Using the Navigator palette for zooming

Changing the Dimensions of Bitmap Images

Changing the scale of an image means altering the height and width of how the image appears in Photoshop. Changing the scale does not affect the image file and does not affect how the image appears in a browser. Changing the dimensions means changing the actual height and width of an image. In Photoshop, the term **canvas** refers to the dimensions of an image. An image's canvas size is its height and width in pixels.

In Photoshop you alter image dimensions with the Image Size and Canvas Size tools. Image Size lets you stretch or shrink the image, while Canvas Size lets you pad or crop the image. When you select the Canvas Size tool, you see the Canvas Size dialog box, shown in Figure 1-25, where you can specify how much you want to pad or crop the image.

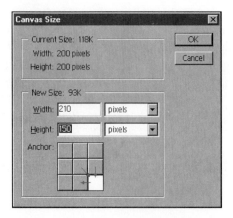

Figure 1-25   The Canvas Size dialog box

When you pad or crop, you change the size of the canvas, but not the image itself. For example, you could crop an image of a cloud over a tree to remove the cloud. The dimensions of the cropped image are smaller, but the size of the tree stays the same. Stretching and shrinking with the Image Size tool affects both the canvas size and the image size. For example, if you shrink the image of the cloud over a tree, you reduce the size of the cloud and the tree, as well as the amount of space they take up in the window.

Figure 1-26 illustrates the effect of using the Image Size command in Photoshop. To familiarize yourself with these tools, use the Image Size option to stretch and shrink an image, and use the Canvas Size command to change an image's viewable area, while maintaining the size of the elements within that image.

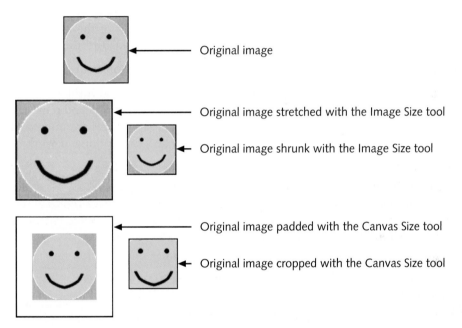

Figure 1-26   Padding and cropping

Padding means increasing the width or height of an image, and includes filling the new space with background color, while cropping actually cuts away from the image to fit a new size. By setting an anchor point in the Canvas Size window, you can control the direction of the padding or cropping. For example, if you select the center anchor point, padding or cropping occurs evenly on all sides of the image. If you select another anchor point, padding or cropping occurs on the opposite side of the image.

The Canvas Size dialog box illustrated in Figure 1-25 has settings that pad the selected image by adding 10 pixels to the left side, and crop the image by cutting 50 pixels from the top.

The following steps show you how to pad and crop an image using the Canvas Size tool.

To pad and crop an image using the Canvas Size tool:

1. Open the image file **pad.tif** from the Data Disk.

2. Click **Image** on the menu bar, and then click **Canvas Size**. The Canvas Size dialog box illustrated in Figure 1-25 appears and shows the current dimensions of the image.

3. Set the Width to **100 pixels** and the Height to **150 pixels**. Select the top-center **anchor box**. Click **OK**. When you see a confirmation dialog box, click **Proceed**.

4. Review the image, which should appear narrower, but taller. The image itself has not been stretched or shrunk, but the right half of the image should be gone, and an extra 30 pixels of space should be added to the bottom.

5. Save the image as **pad.tif** in the Chapter 1 folder on your hard drive.

Besides using the Canvas Size dialog box, you also can crop with the Crop tool, or use the Trim command to crop away the background. The Trim command removes the margins around an image, based on similar colors. If the color edges are uneven, the image is cropped at the point where a new color starts. The Trim command works only if an image's background is a uniform color.

To pad and crop an image using the Crop tool:

1. Open the image file **crop.tif** from the Data Disk.

2. Select the **Crop** tool.

3. Drag the pointer over the **object** in the image. A selection box appears.

4. Drag the **selection tabs** to adjust the selection area.

5. To set the crop, double-click inside the selection area, or click **Image**, and then click **Crop**. The image is cropped to the specified size.

6. Click **Edit** on the menu bar, and then click **Undo Crop**.

7. In the Options bar, set the Width to **50** and the Height to **75**.

8. Drag the pointer over the image again. This time the ratio of height to width is constrained. Adjust the selection tabs to completely enclose the figure.

9. Double-click inside the selection area. The image is cropped and resized to 50 × 75 pixels.

10. Save the image as **crop.tif** in the Chapter 1 folder on your hard drive.

Changing Your Mind

Photoshop and ImageReady contain several ways for you to change edits you have made to an image. Like most software, Photoshop and ImageReady have an Undo command that reverses your most recent edit, whether it is running a filter, making a selection, or using a tool. You can specify a maximum number of steps the Undo feature can reverse.

To set the maximum number of steps Undo can reverse:

1. Click **Edit** on the menu bar, point to **Preferences**, and click **General**.

2. The General dialog box opens. In the History States text box, enter the maximum number of steps you want Undo to reverse. The default number of history states for the Undo command is 20. If you increase this number, Photoshop runs more slowly.

You can see all the past edits made to an image in the History palette, where you also can review recent changes and delete multiple edits. The history is deleted, or purged, when an image is closed. After saving an image, you cannot use the Undo command to reverse changes made before the save. You can, however, use the Step Backward command to view the image without the most recent edit. The Step Backward command is available on the Edit menu, and from the History palette. This command does not delete the edits, it only lets you see the image without them.

To delete your changes, perform one of the following activities:

- In the History palette, select the changes you want to delete, and then click the trashcan icon.

- Drag the changes you want to delete to the trashcan icon.

- Click the History palette list arrow, and then click Delete.

- To quickly delete all the changes you made to an image, click File on the menu bar, and then click Revert. Using the Revert command returns the image to the way it was when it was last saved, or last opened if you did not save it.

PULLING IT ALL TOGETHER: AN OVERVIEW OF PROFESSIONAL WEB GRAPHICS

This chapter introduced you to the basic concepts of Web graphics and the tools and techniques you use to create them. In the remaining chapters, you will learn more detailed methods for creating graphics for the Web.

There are several distinct types of Web graphics, and a number of concepts associated with each type. This book is structured so that each remaining chapter covers one type of graphic or one concept. The chapters are grouped together into three main sections: Basic, Intermediate, and Advanced Web Graphics. The following sections provide an overview of Web graphics so you know what to expect as you work through the book.

Basic Web Graphics: Optimizing, Displaying, and Acquiring Images

The first third of this book covers general topics about computer graphics and issues about Web graphics that apply to every project on which you work. These general topics include an introduction to Photoshop, optimizing images, displaying graphics in Web pages, and acquiring images to use on the Web.

An Overview of Optimizing Images

Optimizing refers to making the image file size as small as possible without compromising the quality of the image—your major goal in creating graphics for the Web. Currently, the limiting factor on the Web is bandwidth. Regardless of the size or quality of your computer or your Web server, most users have to wait a few seconds before your Web page is downloaded and rendered on the page. In the next five to ten years, broadband technology should remedy this. Until then, every Web page must be as small as possible to minimize the download time.

Most Web files, whether HTML, image, or other format, have extra space in the file that is not used for anything crucial. Just as a sponge has pockets of air inside it that contribute to the volume of the sponge without contributing to the mass, computer files often have unused space that does not add any value. Optimizing means squeezing out this unnecessary space from the files. Every graphic you create, whether it be a logo, an animation, or an image map, must be optimized.

An Overview of Displaying Images

After you optimize your images, you incorporate them into a Web page and preview them in a browser so you know how they will appear on users' screens. To include images on a Web page, you need to use and understand HTML code. Graphic artists often use editors such as DreamWeaver to generate the HTML they need to display graphics in a Web page. However, you should understand the HTML code itself in case you need to modify an image's appearance in a way that cannot be done with HTML editors. This book assumes you have a working knowledge of HTML.

You must preview your images because display devices show images differently. The size and color of images on your screen will not match those on all of your users' screens. Monitors have variations in color, so an image can look one way on your computer, but different on another. Screens also vary in size, so images can look too big or small on other systems, even if they are just the right size on yours. You need to be aware of the variations so that you can design images that look good on all systems. The best way to do this is to test your images on a variety of systems and on a variety of browsers.

An Overview of Acquiring Images

Whether you are creating graphics for print, the Web, or other electronic media, you need to acquire images on your computer before you can edit them. You can acquire images by using graphics software or by using a drawing tablet to create them yourself.

1

You also can draw images on paper, and then scan them with a flatbed scanner. You can take pictures with a digital camera and import them into Photoshop, or you can take pictures with a film camera and then develop the film on slides, prints, or CDs. You can scan slides with a slide scanner, and scan prints with a flatbed scanner. You also can open images on a CD, just as you open image files on your desktop.

Regardless of how you acquire images, you often need to fix defects on an image. Some defects are the result of poor quality in the originals. A photo might include flaws, such as stray marks or inadequate lighting. A drawing might have weak colors or crooked lines. Other defects are the result of the scanning process. You must repair these defects before using the images in a Web page.

Intermediate Web Graphics: Using Background Images, Icons, Buttons, and Thumbnail Galleries

The middle third of this book covers creating and using Web graphics that do not require special HTML coding or special Web graphics software; you can create them with any image editor. These Web graphics include background images, icons, buttons, and thumbnail images. You can apply the skills covered in the intermediate section of this book to graphics that are used on or off the Web.

An Overview of Creating and Using Background Images

Web pages can display images either as single elements on a page, laid out with blocks of text, or as backgrounds behind text and other images. Background images normally tile, or repeat, across and down a page. You should create background images so that the edges match and the tiling is seamless.

You can use any combination of tools in Photoshop to create background images, but you almost always will use layers, filters, and painting tools. A new image in Photoshop has a single layer called the background layer. Other layers are transparent except where you create part of an image. You apply layers on top of the background layer to create a complete image—where the layer is transparent, you can see through it to any image part below. Web pages can include background images, and images in Photoshop and ImageReady can include background layers, although background images and background layers are not related.

Most Photoshop filters work by scanning through an image, pixel by pixel, performing a mathematical transformation as they go. The Blur filter, for example, combines the values for every pair of adjacent pixels to reduce the contrast of edges and make the image appear softer. You use painting tools to apply a color to an image.

An Overview of Creating and Using Icons

Icons include bullets, symbols, and small pictures, and are some of the most common types of Web graphics you will create. The main difference between icons and other Web graphics is that icons are generally small, and working with small graphics requires special consideration. It can be difficult to see the edits you make, for example, and small graphics also must convey meaning in a small space.

To create icons, you need to use the various selection tools in Photoshop. You also can use vector drawing tools to create specific shapes because icons often appear in shapes other than rectangles. Icons also can have transparent backgrounds. Transparency allows rectangular images to have clear areas that let background colors or images show through.

An Overview of Creating and Using Buttons

Buttons are a special type of icon. While most icons help identify information on a page, buttons are meant to be clicked, taking users to new Web pages. Buttons and icons may both include text, which you create using the Type tool in Photoshop.

Buttons need to look specifically as if they can be clicked, and often use 3-D effects such as shadows and highlights to make them appear to pop out of the page.

An Overview of Creating Thumbnail Galleries

A gallery of images is a common type of Web page used especially to show a portfolio of products, services, or artwork. A gallery includes miniature versions of each image, called thumbnails, which link to the full-sized versions. To create many small versions of images, you could perform identical operations on all of the full-sized versions, or you could write a script that includes those operations, and then instruct Photoshop to run the script with all the images. Running a script saves time, particularly if you have hundreds or thousands of images to process. Photoshop and ImageReady include commands to generate scripts that you can use to process batches of images. At the core of batch image processing in Photoshop or ImageReady are actions, which are displayed in the Actions palette.

Whether you are creating graphics for the Web or another medium, you often need to perform the same sequences of edits on multiple images. Batch processing and scripting help you do this quickly and simply.

Advanced Web Graphics: Creating Animations, Rollover Effects, Splash Screens, and Sliced Images

The last third of this book covers advanced Web graphics. These are graphics that require special coding to appear on the Web. They include animations, rollover effects, image maps, and advanced layout.

An Overview of Creating Animation for the Web

Animation is one of the more sophisticated types of Web graphics. You can include animations in Web pages by using Flash, Shockwave, Java, SVG, MPEG, or other formats. The easiest and most common way to add animation, however, is with the GIF format. GIF files can contain single images or multiple images called frames that play in sequence like a slide show. If the sequence of images in a GIF file plays quickly, it creates the illusion of movement similar to television or cinema. Unlike the frames of video or film, however, GIF animation frames each can play for a different duration.

You can adjust the number of frames in a GIF animation, the duration of each frame, and how many times the animation repeats. One of the most common applications of GIF animation is in the banner ads that appear at the tops of pages of most commercial sites.

An Overview of Creating Image Rollover Effects

The Web is considered an interactive medium, especially when compared to other media, because you can click links to visit one page after another. This interactivity is similar to using a magazine, where you can turn to the page you want, or to watching television, where you can tune in to any channel you want.

Web page interactivity, however, can include more than letting users click links. Using Dynamic Hypertext Markup Language (DHTML), you can create additional opportunities for user interaction, such as rollover effects, which cause images on a page to change based on user actions. DHTML is the combination of JavaScript, Cascading Style Sheets (CSS), and advanced features of HTML that work together to give Web pages true interactivity. You also can create rollover effects using JavaScript or CSS, and use JavaScript in other ways to control how images appear.

An Overview of Creating Splash Screens

Splash screens are large images or sets of images that usually appear on the home page of a site. They are similar to the splash screens on most software packages, including Photoshop and ImageReady. Splash screens can invite your viewers to your site and provide information about its contents while other images preload on the other pages of your site. Splash screens often appear on informational and personal sites.

Splash screens, however, are not very common on commercial sites. Most professional sites must show relevant information, such as a list of products and services, as soon as possible, rather than nested one click away.

A common way to create a splash screen is to use an image map. An image map is any Web graphic that relies on special HTML code to link to multiple destinations, rather than being able to link only once.

An Overview of Creating Sliced Images

While image maps are often used for splash screens, it is more common to use sliced images. You can take any image, cut it into smaller images, and position them in HTML tables. This allows you to optimize each slice separately. It also allows you to add animation or rollover effects to individual slices. Splash screens using sliced images will represent the culmination of all your knowledge of Web graphics. These types of splash screens can include backgrounds, buttons, icons, animations, and rollover effects.

CHAPTER SUMMARY

❑ A Web graphic is a computer file that is interpreted by software to create an image display.

❑ Every computer graphic file is defined either as a vector image or as a bitmap image. Bitmap images reproduce better texture detail than vector images and are the most common type of Web graphic.

❑ Vector images have smaller file sizes but must be rasterized before they can appear in a Web page. To use a vector image in a Web page, the Web browser must use a plug-in to convert the vector image into a bitmap image.

❑ Photoshop and ImageReady are the most popular programs for creating graphics for the Web. They share most features, though Photoshop has more general features, and ImageReady has more features for Web-only graphics.

❑ Most of the work you do in Photoshop and ImageReady involves using palettes, tools in the toolbox, and menu commands.

❑ You can change the scale and dimension of bitmap images and reverse your recent edits as you work with images.

❑ Basic work with Web graphics includes optimizing, displaying, and acquiring images. You can use Photoshop to create common Web graphics such as background images, icons, buttons, and thumbnail galleries. You also can create more advanced graphics, such as animation, rollover effects, splash screens, and sliced images, using Photoshop or ImageReady.

REVIEW QUESTIONS

1. What defines a vector image, as compared to a bitmap image?

   a. Small file size, high detail, resolution–independence

   b. Small file size, low detail, resolution–independence

   c. Large file size, high detail, resolution–dependence

   d. Large file size, low detail, resolution–dependence

2. What is rasterizing?

   a. Converting a bitmap image to a vector image

   b. Converting a pixel to a bitmap image

   c. Converting a vector image to a bitmap image

   d. Converting a vector image to a pixel

3. What can cause jagged edges in an image?

   a. Changing the dimensions of a bitmap image

   b. Changing the dimensions of a pixel

    c. Changing the dimensions of a vector image

    d. Converting a vector image to a bitmap image

4. What is the purpose of plug-ins?

    a. Photoshop uses plug-ins to convert images from one type to another.

    b. Some images must be rasterized into plug-ins before they can be viewed.

    c. Some plug-ins work with browsers to display vector images.

    d. The graphic artist uses plug-ins to convert images from one type to another.

5. What determines the size of an image file?

    a. For vector images, it is the dimensions of the image; for bitmap images it is the number of pixels.

    b. For vector images it is the number of pixels; for bitmap images it is the amount of texture detail.

    c. For vector images it is the number of pixels; for bitmap images it is the number of shapes and lines.

    d. For vector images it is the number of shapes and lines; for bitmap images it is the number of pixels.

6. What kind of software is Adobe Illustrator and when would you use it?

    a. It is a drawing program and is used for creating bitmap images.

    b. It is a drawing program and is used for creating vector images.

    c. It is an image editor and is used for creating bitmap images.

    d. It is an image editor and is used for creating vector images.

7. Which palette in Photoshop displays a small version of an image?

    a. Actions palette

    b. Info palette

    c. Navigator palette

    d. Options bar

8. Which tools help you navigate an image?

    a. Airbrush tool and Eraser tools

    b. Hand tool and Zoom tool

    c. Move tool and Crop tool

    d. Path Selection tools and Shape tools

9. Where do you find the option to Show Rulers?

    a. On the File menu

    b. On the Select menu

    c. On the View menu

    d. On the Window menu

10. Where do you find the dialog box that lets you change the measurement units used in Photoshop?

    a. Choose Preferences from the Edit menu, and then choose General.

    b. Choose Preferences from the Edit menu, and then choose Units and Rulers.

    c. Choose Settings from the Edit menu, and then choose Units and Rulers.

    d. Choose Preferences from the File Menu, and then choose Units and Rulers.

11. If you change the scale of the image display without changing the image file, what are you doing?

    a. Changing the image size

    b. Changing the canvas size

    c. Cropping the image

    d. Zooming in or out

12. What happens when you double-click the Zoom tool in the toolbox?

    a. The image becomes twice as large.

    b. The image reverts to its state the last time it was saved.

    c. The image scales to 100%.

    d. The Zoom tool options window opens.

13. What happens if you increase the numbers in the Canvas Size dialog box?

    a. The image is cropped by that amount and stretched to the new size.

    b. The image is padded to the new size.

    c. The image is stretched to the new size.

    d. The image is scaled to the new size without affecting the image file.

14. What happens when you drag the Crop tool over an image?

    a. A selection area appears and defines the area to be cropped.

    b. The image is cropped.

    c. The image is cropped, then stretched to the original size.

    d. The image is trimmed.

15. Which command does not delete the most recent edit made to an image?

    a. The Revert command

    b. The Step Backward command

    c. The Undo command

    d. None of the above

16. What are layers?

    a. Layers are areas of an image that can link to different destinations.

    b. Layers are like sheets of transparent film that each contain different parts of an image.

    c. Layers are separate channels that each contain different color information about an image.

    d. Layers are slices of an image which can be saved as separate image files.

17. What tool is not used to create vector shapes in Photoshop?

    a. Lasso tool

    b. Pen tool

    c. Shape tool

    d. Type tool

18. What tool would you use to create a line with a hard edge?

    a. Airbrush tool

    b. Paintbrush tool

    c. Pen tool

    d. Pencil tool

19. What does the Magic Wand tool do?

    a. Erases pixels of similar colors

    b. Fills areas with the foreground color

    c. Lets you define selection areas of any shape

    d. Selects pixels in the image of a similar color to the pixel clicked with the tool

20. What tool or palette cannot tell you the numerical color value of a pixel?

    a. Color palette

    b. Eyedropper tool

    c. Info palette

    d. Swatches palette

HANDS-ON PROJECTS

Project 1: Looking at Bitmap Images

Find a Web graphic that you like and zoom in on it to see individual pixels.

1. Use your Web browser to visit a site you like that uses graphics.

2. In your browser, point to one image and hold down the mouse button (click the right mouse button in Windows). A shortcut menu appears.

3. On the shortcut menu, click **Save As** or **Save Image As**. A dialog box appears where you can specify the name and location of the saved image. Save the image as **WebImage** on your desktop.

4. Start Photoshop and open **WebImage**.

5. Enlarge your view of the image to see the individual pixels.

6. Return to your original view of the image.

Project 2: Adding Documentation

You use Photoshop's documentation features when collaborating with others on a project.

1. Open the image file **1-2.tif** from the Data Disk.

2. Select the **Notes** tool. Make sure your name appears in the Author field in the Options bar.

3. Click the image. In the text box, type a brief message, and then close the text box by clicking the small square in the upper-right corner.

4. Save the image as **1-2.psd** in the Chapter 1 folder on your hard drive. The documentation is saved with the image.

Project 3: Setting Preferences

You often need to edit the way Photoshop works with images.

1. Change the Photoshop measurement units from inches to pixels.

2. Display the rulers in the Image window.

3. Decrease the maximum number of steps the Undo feature reverses from 20 to **10**.

Project 4: Create a New Image

Practice creating new images.

1. Click the **File** menu, and then select **New**. A dialog box will appear.

2. In the **Name** text box, type **MyImage**.

3. Set the image size to **200** pixels in width and **150** pixels in height. Set the Mode to **RGB Color**. The Resolution matters only for images that are to be printed. You can ignore this option.

4. Specify that the contents are **white**.

5. Save the new image as **MyImage** in the Chapter 1 folder on your hard drive.

Project 5: Use the Image Size Feature

Stretch and shrink an image.

1. Open the image file **1-5.tif** from the Data Disk.

2. Open the Image Size dialog box.

3. Make sure that the **Constrain Proportions** check box is clear.

4. Set the Width to **88 pixels** and the Height to **400 pixels**.

5. Review the image, which should be half as wide and twice as high as the original image. You have shrunk the width and stretched the height.

6. Save the image as **1-5.tif** in the Chapter 1 folder on your hard drive.

Project 6: Use the Trim Command

Trim an image.

1. Open the image file **1-6.tif** from the Data Disk.

2. Open the Trim dialog box.

3. Set options to trim the bottom and left parts of the image, based on the lower-right pixel color.

4. Review the image, which should be cropped only on the bottom and left.

5. Open the Canvas Size dialog box.

6. Set options to pad the bottom and left sides of the image by **5** pixels each.

7. Review the image, which should have a 5-pixel margin on the bottom and left, and a larger one on the top and right.

8. Save the image as **1-6.tif** in the Chapter 1 folder on your hard drive.

Project 7: Examine Web Sites

Determine how different Web sites use images.

1. Use your Web browser to open pages from three different sites you use often.

2. Answer the following questions:

   ❑ Are these sites content sites, commerce sites, service sites, promotional sites, or combinations of sites?

   ❑ How do the sites use graphics? Are graphics an integral part of the design, or are they used only for decoration?

   ❑ Imagine that you work on creating these sites. What sort of images would you be asked to create for each site?

Project 8: Examine Online Portfolios

Learn how others design their online portfolios.

1. Use your Web browser to do an online search for graphics portfolios.

2. Visit at least three different online portfolios.

3. Answer the following questions:

❑ How are the portfolios similar? How are they different?

❑ What are the portfolios doing well? What are they doing poorly?

❑ How would you design your own online graphics portfolio?

CASE PROJECT

Over the course of this book you will be completing different projects that will become the elements of your final project, an online portfolio. This portfolio will include a home page, your autobiography, and a gallery of work you've accomplished. In future chapters, you will learn techniques for creating original Web graphics, and for including them in a Web page. For now, you should collect images to use in your portfolio. Begin with an image of yourself to use in your autobiography, and continue by making a list of Web sites or original illustrations or photographs you've created. Additionally, look at other online portfolios and think about ways you could imitate the design or graphics that you like.

2

OPTIMIZING GRAPHICS FOR THE WEB

Preparing to Transfer Graphics Across the Web

In this chapter, you will:

- ◆ Understand the effect of color on file size
- ◆ Change color depth
- ◆ Select a file format
- ◆ Save files as Web graphics
- ◆ Optimize images with Photoshop and ImageReady

Web graphics are different from other computer graphics because they must be transferred across the Internet. Large files take a long time to transfer, forcing users to wait while the images download on their computer. Your goal is to make graphics files as small as possible while still illustrating the content you intend. Most graphics files contain unnecessary data that can be discarded without affecting the appearance of the image. Eliminating unnecessary data is called optimizing, and results in small image files that users can download more quickly from the Web to their computers.

You can optimize an image file either by reducing the number of colors used by the image, or by compressing the data stored in the image file. The color-reduction method is better for images with solid color, and the compression method is better for images with gradations of color.

You should optimize every Web graphic you create. Learning how to optimize computer graphics for the Web is the focus of this chapter.

UNDERSTANDING THE EFFECT OF COLOR ON FILE SIZE

Like all files that make up Web pages, graphics files should be as small as possible so they download quickly. Images with more colors tend to have larger file sizes than images with very few colors. The trick is to reduce the number of colors in an image without reducing the quality of the image.

Understanding File Size

The smallest unit for measuring the size of an image file is the bit. A bit is a BInary digiT and is basically a tiny space in a computer's memory that acts like a switch that can be turned on (set to 1) or off (set to 0). A byte is a more common unit, and is equal to 8 bits. The next largest unit is the kilobyte, which is equal to 1,024 bytes. A kilobit is 1,024 bits, or one-eighth the size of a kilobyte. Kilobits are usually used when measuring network transfer speeds. Modems are characterized by their transfer rate, measured in kilobits per second (Kbps).

File size is measured in kilobytes. The term kilobyte is often shortened to KB or just K, as in "Keep the animated ad banner under 12 K." Operating systems and other software usually display file size in terms of block sizes instead of kilobytes. Think of an ice cube tray as a block of memory, with each of the 16 wells being a kilobyte. If you have a file of 40 kilobytes, you need three trays, but do not fill all of the wells. All the same, your operating system detects that the file uses three trays and lists the size as 48 kilobytes (three full blocks of 16 kilobytes each) instead of the true number, 40. This rounding up is misleading, and indicates the file is bigger than it really is. In Figure 2-1, the blue area shows 40 kilobytes being used, although the computer counts three blocks, or 48 kilobytes, in use.

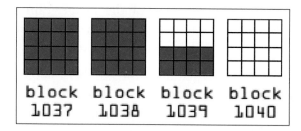

Figure 2-1   File using 40 kilobytes, but three blocks

 To see the true size of a file on a Macintosh computer, select a file and choose Get Info from the File menu. On a Windows computer, right-click the file in Windows Explorer or My Computer, and then click Properties to see the file size.

The number of bits in an image file is set by the three dimensions of height, width, and color depth. If two images show rectangles, but one rectangle is wider and taller than the other, the larger image has a larger file size. The size of an image file is also based on color, as explained in the following section.

Understanding Color Depth

As defined in the previous chapter, a bitmap image is a grid of pixels. You can easily see that an image has a certain width and height. What is not so obvious is that an image has a specific depth as well. The **color depth** of an image is the number of available colors for each pixel. Color depth is sometimes called bit depth or pixel depth. Just as increasing the height or width of an image increases the file size, increasing the color depth of an image also increases the file size.

The color depth does not indicate how many colors are actually used in an image. It only tells you how many colors are available for the image. You cannot calculate the color depth of an image by looking at it. The images in Figure 2-2 all use the same number of colors, but have different color depths. The images with greater color depths have more memory allocated to them, increasing their file size. Image 1 is the original, unoptimized image and uses about 6 KB. Image 2 has a color depth of 256 colors and uses about 2.3 KB. Image 3 has a color depth of 128 colors and uses about 1.8 KB, while Image 4 has a color depth of 64 colors and uses about 1.4 KB. Yet these images are identical; — images 1, 2, and 3 do not need the extra depth to show all their colors. The extra memory is wasted and makes the image files unnecessarily large.

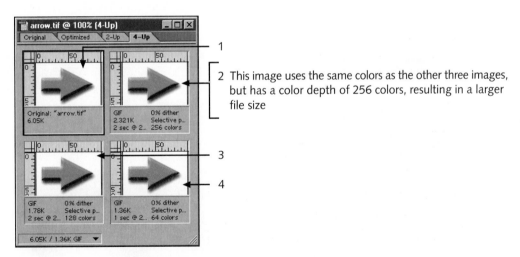

Figure 2-2   The same image using different color depths

The number of colors actually used in an image is called the **color palette**, also called the **color table**. (This is unrelated to the Color palette in Photoshop and ImageReady.) The color palette of an image cannot be larger than the color depth, but can sometimes be smaller. For example, in Figure 2-2, image 2 has a color depth of 256 colors, but a palette of 64 colors. An image with a color depth of 256 colors can have a palette of any size up to 256 colors.

As discussed in the "Understanding File Size" section, each pixel is associated with at least one bit of computer memory. For a black and white image, each pixel has exactly one bit associated with it. If the bit is set to 1, the pixel is white; if the bit is 0, the pixel is black. This is called 1-bit color depth and yields a palette of two colors. The word bitmap is often used to describe these 1-bit, black and white images.

 The term bitmap can mean two things. As noted in the "Introduction to Web Graphics" chapter, a bitmap refers to a computer graphic that is not vector based. All rasterized images are bitmaps. Bitmap also means an image with 1-bit color depth.

Figure 2-3 shows the color table of an image with a 1-bit color depth that yields two colors: black and white.

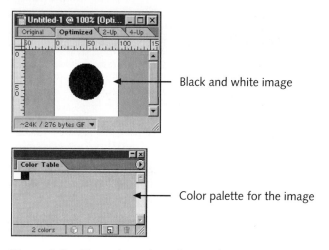

Black and white image

Color palette for the image

Figure 2-3   The color palette for a 1-bit image

An image with 2-bit color has two bits associated with each pixel, giving four colors in the palette ($2 \times 2 = 2^2 = 4$). Table 2-1 shows the possible combinations of bits and colors in a 2-bit color image.

Table 2-1   Two-bit color depth provides a palette of four colors

Bit 1	Bit 2	Color
0	0	Black
1	0	Color a
0	1	Color b
1	1	White

Colors a and b could be any color: two shades of gray, red and blue, green and dark green, and so on. Figure 2-4 shows the color table of an image with 2-bit color depth that yields four colors: black, white, and two shades of gray.

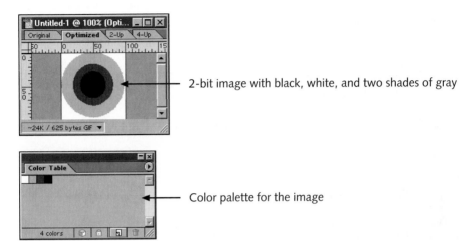

— 2-bit image with black, white, and two shades of gray

— Color palette for the image

Figure 2-4 A possible color palette for a 2-bit image

Adding another bit doubles the possible colors again, so that 3-bit color yields eight colors in the palette ($2 \times 2 \times 2 = 2^3 = 8$). Table 2-2 shows the possible combinations of bits and colors in a 3-bit color image.

Table 2-2 Three-bit color depth provides a palette of eight colors

Bit 1	Bit 2	Bit 3	Color
0	0	0	Black
0	0	1	Color a
0	1	0	Color b
0	1	1	Color c
1	0	0	Color d
1	0	1	Color e
1	1	0	Color f
1	1	1	White

Figure 2-5 shows the color table of an image with 3-bit color depth that yields eight colors: black, white, and six other colors.

An image with 4-bit color adds another bit for each pixel, and doubles the number of colors again to create a maximum of 16 colors in the palette ($2 \times 2 \times 2 \times 2 = 2^4 = 16$). With each additional bit, the color depth doubles, and the size of the file roughly doubles as well. Changing the color depth does not necessarily affect the color palette. If an image uses

10 colors in its table, and you change the color depth from 4–bit (16) to 5–bit (32), the table does not change. It still contains 10 colors with several unused colors available. If the depth changes from 4–bit (16) to 3–bit (8), however, the color palette loses two colors.

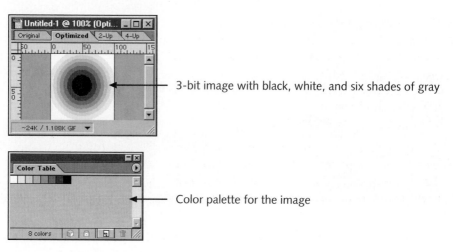

3-bit image with black, white, and six shades of gray

Color palette for the image

Figure 2-5   A possible color palette for a 3-bit image

Color depth can be any power of two, up to 2^8, or 256 colors. Although 256 seems like a lot of colors, some images, such as those with smooth gradations of color require far more than 256 colors to look realistic. Figure 2-6 shows an image with 64 colors, clearly not enough to replicate the transition from one color to another.

Figure 2-6   An image with inadequate color depth

You can use 16-bit color in Photoshop, which produces 2^{16}, or 65,536 colors. However, 16-bit images do not display on many browsers because they use 16 bits per channel.

If 8-bit color depth is not enough, you can increase the depth to 24 bits. A color depth of 24 bits divides the color information of the image into three **color channels**, one for red, one for green, and one for blue. Each channel is an 8-bit color table containing only shades of one primary color. This creates a much larger color table, with 16,777,216 different colors. This number, usually called millions of colors or 16 million colors, is the result of multiplying the color depths for each color channel, $2^8 \times 2^8 \times 2^8 = 256 \times 256 \times 256 = 2^{24} = 16,777,216$.

When you decide which color depth to use, keep in mind that increasing the depth sometimes increases the quality of the image, and always increases the file size. Keep the color depth as small as possible without sacrificing image quality. For example, you can convert some 8-bit images to 7-bit color and roughly halve the file size without hurting the detail in the image.

Table 2-3 shows all the color depths you can use in computer graphics and their corresponding color palette. It also lists appropriate uses for some palettes.

Table 2-3   Table of possible color depths

Color Depth	Maximum Color Palette	When Used
1-bit	2 colors	Line art, black and white
2-bit	4 colors	
3-bit	8 colors	Good for most scanned black and white drawings and figures
4-bit	16 colors	
5-bit	32 colors	Minimum depth for most color images
6-bit	64 colors	
7-bit	128 colors	
8-bit	256 colors	Maximum color depth for GIF and PNG-8 images One full-color channel
24-bit	16,777,216 colors	Only depth available for JPEG and PNG-24 images RGB Color Three full-color channels
32-bit	16,777,216 colors, plus a fourth 8-bit transparency channel	RGB plus alpha

Using Color Modes in Photoshop and ImageReady

In Photoshop and ImageReady, color depth is referred to as **mode**. To choose color depth, click Image on the menu bar, and then point to Mode. You will see a list of color modes, including Bitmap, Indexed, and RGB; most of the modes are meant for print projects and are not appropriate for Web graphics. The two color modes you use for Web graphics are RGB color and indexed color. Indexed color has a depth of between 1-bit and 8-bit. RGB color is 24-bit color.

Using RGB Color

In RGB mode, the color depth is 24 bits; each of the three color channels has a value between 0 and 255. Recall that combining the three channels produces over 16 million possible colors.

You should use RGB color mode to edit images because many filters work only with this mode. RGB color creates large files, however, so save images with this mode only when they have rich color gradients, or when they are photographs with many colors.

When you create and save Web graphics, always start with 24-bit RGB color as you edit the image. If necessary, reduce the color depth later, when you are ready to save the image. If you need to edit an existing image, increase the color depth to RGB before you edit. All painting tools, filters, and other editing tools produce better results when you use them in RGB mode.

To increase the color depth to RGB color, select an image and then follow the steps below.

To increase color depth to RGB color:

1. Click **Image** on the menu bar.
2. Point to **Mode**.
3. Click **RGB Color**.

You will not see a change in the image, because the actual colors used in the image have not changed. What has changed is the number of available colors. This improves the results when you edit the image.

Using RGB Color to Control Jagged Edges

Hundreds or thousands of colors in a palette might seem like more than enough, especially for a simple black-and-white image. But, when you use all the colors, they fill in the feathered areas between the image's foreground and background. You can see the difference when you reduce the color palette of an image containing a diagonal or curved line. What was a straight, soft line becomes a ragged staircase. This rough line is described as being **jaggy**, and has an abrupt transition from foreground to background. As you can see in Figure 2-7, reducing colors too much results in jaggy edges.

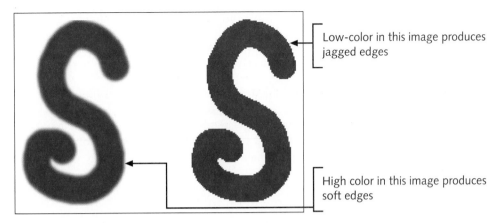

Low-color in this image produces jagged edges

High color in this image produces soft edges

Figure 2-7   The same image in a jagged low-color version and a high-color version

When you resize an image or use a paint tool, Photoshop adds pixels to fill in the gaps created when the original pixels are spread out. Photoshop fills in the missing spaces by **resampling** or interpolating, that is, calculating the proper colors to use between the original pixels. Figure 2-8 shows an image resized in 8-bit and 24-bit color depth.

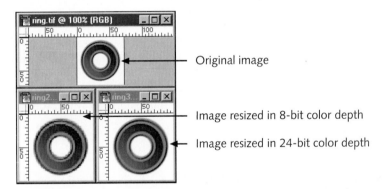

Original image

Image resized in 8-bit color depth

Image resized in 24-bit color depth

Figure 2-8   Resizing in different modes

As you learned in the Introduction to Web Graphics chapter, to resize an image in Photoshop, you click Image on the menu bar, and then click Image Size to open the Image Size dialog box, where you can specify the width and height of the image. When resizing an image, Photoshop resamples the image to interpolate the missing pixels. You can resample pixels in one of three ways: **Nearest Neighbor**, **Bilinear**, or **Bicubic**.

The Nearest Neighbor method produces jagged edges, while the Bicubic method produces smooth edges by interpolating pixels. The Bilinear method produces edges that are somewhat less smooth than the Bicubic method. The first two methods, Nearest Neighbor and Bilinear, are faster when you are working on very large images, but Bicubic interpolation, the default method, produces the smoothest results, and is your best choice for Web graphics.

The effects of interpolation are visible only when an image contains curved lines or gradients. You should save these images in 24-bit RGB color. You can safely use indexed color to save images that contain only vertical or horizontal lines and have no gradations of color.

Using Indexed Color

If 24-bit color is more than an image needs, or produces a file that is too large, you should reduce the color to Indexed Color mode. While RGB color must have exactly 24 bits of color in the palette, indexed color images can have any number of colors, up to 8-bit, or 256 colors.

Using the Color Look-up Table with Indexed Colors

Recall that an 8-bit color palette devoted to a specific primary color is called a color channel. The color palette for an indexed color image is called a **clut**, or **color look-up table**. An indexed color image can have a color depth of three bits, which means the color palette holds up to eight different colors, one in each cell of the palette. But the image might have only some of these colors. If it uses five colors, for example, it leaves the other three cells in the palette empty. When software, such as Photoshop or a Web browser, opens the image, it also opens the associated color table and looks up the proper color for each pixel.

The clut can list up to 256 colors, and each color has a unique ID. To see the clut for an indexed color image in Photoshop, you click Image on the menu bar, point to Mode, and then click Color Table. In ImageReady, the clut has its own palette. Open the image, and then to show the Color Table palette you click Window on the menu bar, and then click Show Color Table. The clut can have a maximum of 8 bits of color (256 colors), but often uses fewer to reduce file size. The Color Table palette in ImageReady is shown in Figure 2-9.

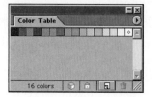

Figure 2-9   The Color Table palette

Some cluts are preset and always have the same colors in the same order. Among these pre-set color tables are the system color tables for Macintosh and Windows and the **Web-safe** color table, which has only 216 colors. Different browsers and operating systems use different default color palettes. The 216-color Web-safe color table provides a standard for Web pages, which is viewed on different types of browsers and platforms. These 216 colors are the only ones guaranteed to look the same on every viewing environment.

With indexed-color images, different images can have different cluts. When you paste an image selection into an image with indexed color, the colors of the pasted areas are different in the new image. For example, in Figure 2-10, the colors in the image named go.tif contain shades of red and green, but the image named bevel.tif uses a color table with only six shades of gray. When the full-color image is copied and pasted into the image with reduced colors, the pasted selection automatically matches the existing palette, resulting in undesired colors. To solve this problem, you increase the colors in the destination image. This is a potential difficulty in Photoshop, but not in ImageReady. ImageReady automatically converts every image to RGB mode.

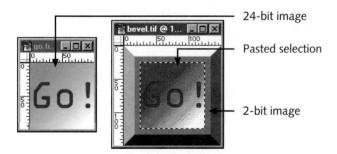

24-bit image

Pasted selection

2-bit image

Figure 2-10   Pasting into an indexed-color image with a reduced clut

If you edit images or copy and paste between images in 24-bit color, all possible colors are available, and mismatching of colors in the table does not occur. This is why you should use 24-bit color while editing and manipulating files, even if you plan to save the image in a lower color depth.

CHANGING COLOR DEPTH

The process of reducing file size by reducing the number of colors is called optimization through color-reduction. If you reduce color depth from 8-bit (256 colors) to 7-bit (128 colors), you halve the number of available colors in the color palette and reduce the file size by almost half as well. An image with 5-bit color depth has roughly one-quarter the file size of an image with 8-bit color depth.

You can reduce many color images to 5-bit color before they show any negative effects. You also can reduce grayscale images (those with up to 256 shades of gray) to 3-bit color without losing any vital image data. Figure 2-11 shows a color drawing, a photograph, and a black-and-white drawing with different color depths. The color drawing uses the most colors in its smooth gradations from one tone to the next. The quality deteriorates at depths below 7-bit. The photograph also uses many colors, but no tonal variation, and the quality deteriorates with a depth below 5-bit. The grayscale drawing tolerates color depth as low as 3-bit.

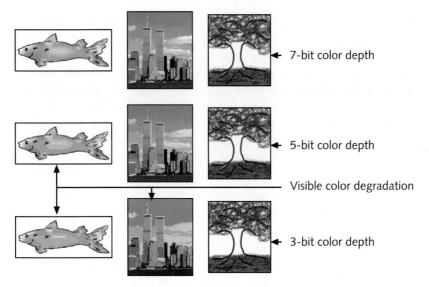

Figure 2-11 Different images require different color depths

Large high-quality images, such as photographs or 3-D images, often lose image data even at 8-bit color depth. These images should remain at 24-bit color.

To reduce the color depth to 8-bit color in Photoshop, select the image and then follow the steps below.

To reduce color depth to 8-bit:

1. Click **Image** on the menu bar.

2. Point to **Mode**.

3. Click **Indexed Color**. This option lets you set any number of colors from 1-bit (2 colors) to 8-bit (2^8= 256 colors). You see the Indexed Color dialog box, illustrated in Figure 2-12.

4. Set the palette to **Local (Perceptual)**.

5. In the Colors text box, set the number of colors, from **2** to **256**, if necessary, and then click **OK**.

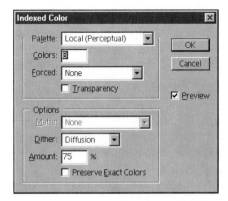

Figure 2-12   Adjusting the color depth

Choosing a Palette

When you reduce the color depth of an image, you reduce the number of available colors in the color table. If the image uses more colors than are available in the new color depth, some colors are eliminated.

When you reduce colors from the roughly 16 million available in 24-bit images to 256, for example, Photoshop finds the 256 most commonly occurring colors and uses those in the palette. To do this, Photoshop uses a **color reduction method**, which is a formula for counting the most common colors.

To select a color reduction method, open the Indexed Color dialog box shown in Figure 2-12, and then click the Palette list arrow. You see the following list of options:

- *Exact:* Creates a clut based on the colors currently used in the image. If the image has 256 or more colors, the clut contains the 256 most commonly used colors. You should use Exact only if the image uses very few colors and does not need to be reduced.

- *System* (Windows or Mac OS): Uses the Windows or Macintosh system 8-bit palette. This option is seldom used for Web graphics.

- *Web:* Uses the Web-safe palette of 216 colors. This palette reduces the amount of dithering (explained later in this chapter) that occurs in certain monitors.

- *Uniform:* Creates a palette of uniformly sampled colors. Most images do not have uniformly distributed colors, so this reduction method usually produces poor results.

- *Perceptual:* Creates a customized palette, giving weight to colors to which the human eye is more sensitive.

- *Selective:* Is similar to the Perceptual color reduction method, but also gives weight to colors in the Web palette. This method usually produces the best color reduction results.

- *Adaptive:* Creates a table with colors from specific areas of the color spectrum, based on which colors exist in the image.

- *Custom:* Lets you create your own customized palette, or load a previously saved one.

- *Previous:* Uses the color table from the last image you converted. This is useful for some print projects, but is not so useful for Web graphics.

The three methods you use most often when creating Web graphics are Adaptive, Selective, and Perceptual. These methods produce similar results.

When you select the Uniform, Adaptive, Selective, or Perceptual color reduction method, you can specify how many colors to use in the final color table. Because the bit depth of indexed color images has a maximum of 8-bits, the maximum number of colors you can use is 256. Using fewer colors results in an image with smaller file size.

Setting Other Color Reduction Options

In creating the color table, you can force certain colors to appear, regardless of how often they appear in the image. Some software requires all images to have black and white in the color table.

To include black and white in the color table:

1. Select the **image**, and then to open the Indexed Color dialog box, click **Image** on the menu bar, point to **Mode**, and then click **Indexed Color**.

2. Click the **Forced** list arrow, and then click **Black and White** so that the image can be edited later in other image software. (You do not need to use the other options in the Forced list for Web graphics.)

When you create a new image, you can choose whether the background is white, is based on the background color in the toolbox, or is transparent. When you add colors to the image, the transparent areas are covered, as shown in Figure 2-13. You can preserve transparency so that the final image allows background colors to show through when displayed in a Web browser. (Transparency is discussed in detail later in this chapter.)

Figure 2-13   An image with a transparent background

To set the background color of an image:

1. Select the **image**, and then to open the Indexed Color dialog box, click **Image** on the menu bar, point to **Mode**, and then click **Indexed Color**.

2. To make the parts of the image with no color values transparent, click the **Transparency** box to check it, if necessary.

3. To fill any existing transparent areas with the matte color, click the **Transparency** box to clear it. Then click the **Matte** list arrow and select a color, which is white by default. You can specify a matte color even when you select the Transparency box. The matte color then affects how feathered edges blend with the background color. If your images will appear in a Web page that has a colored background, make sure to set the matte color to the background color of the page.

Figure 2-14 shows an image with transparent areas and a white matte against a colored background. You can see how the edges of the image do not match the background color. The figure also shows an image saved with the proper matte color.

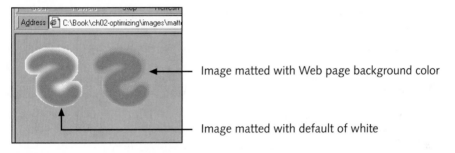

Figure 2-14   Incorrect and correct matte colors

Using Dither

Unless you use the Exact color reduction method (see the "Choosing a Palette" section earlier in this chapter), the color table probably will not exactly match the colors used in the image. As you experiment with different color depths, you will notice that areas of gradient color develop stripes of color where there should be a smooth transition.

When you reduce the color palette from 24-bit to 8-bit, even for images with simple gradations of color, **banding** often results. **Banded color** has thick stripes of color, instead of imperceptible color changes. Even though the 8-bit color palette has 256 colors, it isn't enough to prevent banding. Figure 2-15 shows that banding is most noticeable in areas of gradient color.

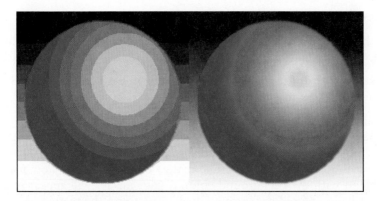

Figure 2-15   A banded low-color version and a high-color version of the same image

To prevent banding, try leaving the color depth at 24-bit. You also can simulate colors not in the color table by **dithering** existing colors. Dithering is a procedure used in many types of graphics in print and on the Web to simulate colors when the actual colors are not available. Instead of finding intermediate shades of color the way interpolating does, dithering creates patterns of color to simulate other shades. In print, for example, often the only available colors are the white of the page and black ink. To simulate shades of gray in images, the black ink is dithered, as shown in Figure 2-16, creating tiny dots of black in varying concentrations. These dots give the illusion of being shades of gray when viewed from a distance.

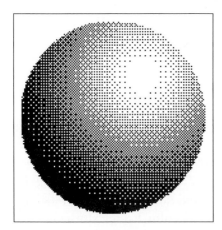

Figure 2-16   Dithering to simulate intermediate tones

To dither gradient colors:

> 1. Select an **image** with reduced colors, and then to open the Indexed Color dialog box, click **Image** on the menu bar, point to **Mode**, and then click **Indexed Color**.

2. To prevent banding of gradient colors, click the **Dithering** list arrow and choose one of the dithering options described below:

- *None:* Uses no dithering and causes banding of graduated colors.

- *Pattern:* Uses a pattern of squares to dither the colors in the image. The pattern is unsightly and noticeable. You could use this for some print projects, but not for Web graphics.

- *Diffusion:* Produces a pattern that is not as obvious as the Pattern dither.

- *Noise:* Produces a random pattern. For Web graphics, use this or the Diffusion dither.

Figure 2-17 shows an image reduced to 4-bit color using the four different types of dither. The diffusion dither pattern usually produces the smoothest gradations.

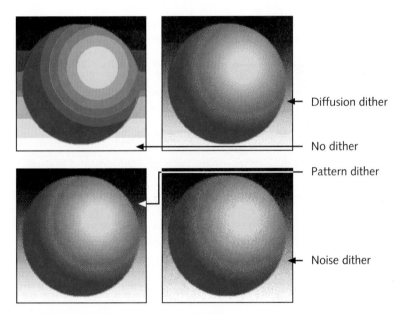

   ← Diffusion dither

   ← No dither

   ← Pattern dither

   ← Noise dither

Figure 2-17   The four dither options

When you choose the diffusion dither pattern, you also can select the amount of dither to use, as a percent from 0 to 100. A higher percentage dithers more colors, but increases the size of the file.

Normally, dithering affects all colors in the image, whether they are in the final color table or not. To dither only the colors that are not in the table, select the image, open the Indexed Color dialog box, and then click the Select Preserve Exact Colors box to check it. This prevents thin lines, such as text, from being dithered.

Dithering is appropriate for images with a lot of visual texture, such as photographs. The dither patterns are more noticeable in images without texture. Figure 2-18 shows images with different amounts of visual texture and the effect of dithering. The center image has no gradients, so little dithering occurs. The images on the left and right both have dithering, but the effect is concealed by the texture in the image on the left. The image on the right has noticeable dithering because of the smooth color gradations in the original image.

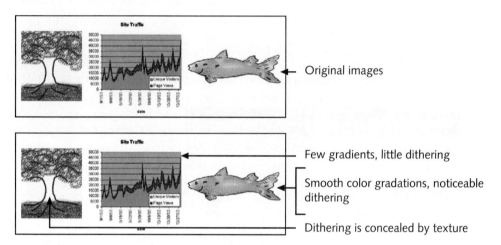

Figure 2-18   Dithered images with different amounts of gradients and texture

Controlling Color Reduction

If reducing colors using the Indexed Color dialog box does not give you the control or results you want, you can use other Photoshop and ImageReady options. You can reduce colors by posterizing them or setting a threshold, and then convert the image to indexed color.

Using the Posterize Command

A quick way to change the number of colors in an image is to **posterize** the image. In Photoshop, this means reducing the colors used in an image without changing the colors in the color palette.

To posterize an image in Photoshop:

1. Open an **image** and then click **Image** on the menu bar.

2. Point to **Adjust**.

3. Click **Posterize**. You see the Posterize dialog box and your image, as illustrated in Figure 2-19.

4. In the Levels text box, enter the number of colors you want to use in the palette, and then click **OK**.

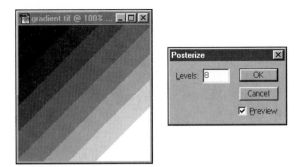

Figure 2-19   Posterizing an image

The Posterize dialog box lets you define the number of colors used in the palette. Although this reduces the palette, it does not affect the color depth. After you posterize an image, make sure to convert the image mode, for example, to Indexed or Grayscale. You can posterize an 8-bit image with 256 colors in its palette, and reduce it to use only two colors. The palette then contains the two colors in the image, plus 254 unused colors.

Using the Threshold Command

You sometimes will need to convert images to 1-bit color using just black and white. For example, if you have letterhead or a form for outgoing faxes, you might need to use a black-and-white version of your Web site logo. If you do not carefully reduce the color, the final image can appear too dark or too light, as shown in Figure 2-20.

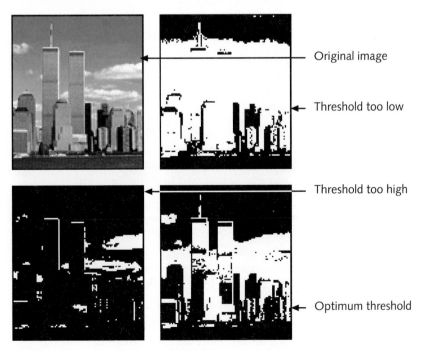

Original image

Threshold too low

Threshold too high

Optimum threshold

Figure 2-20   A 1-bit image reduced from a higher bit-depth

When you reduce colors to 1-bit color depth using the Indexed Color dialog box, Photoshop uses a **threshold** of 50%. This converts every pixel that is lighter than middle-gray to white, and every pixel that is darker than middle-gray to black.

A 50% threshold works well for most bitmap color images, but you might find that it produces images that are too dark or light, such as those produced by photocopiers or fax machines. In Photoshop, you can control the threshold using the Threshold command.

To use the Threshold command in Photoshop:

1. Click **Image** on the menu bar.

2. Point to **Adjust**.

3. Click **Threshold**. The Threshold dialog box appears, as shown in Figure 2-21.

 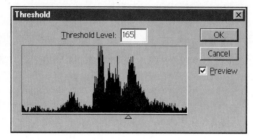

Figure 2-21   The Threshold dialog box

The Threshold dialog box shows a graph of all the color information in the image, with pure black at the left, pure white at the right, and middle-gray controlled by the slider bar in the middle. Each vertical line in the graph represents a shade of gray. Dark images have histograms with more lines on the left, and light images have more lines on the right.

4. Make sure the **Preview** box is checked.

5. To set the threshold at which grayscale pixels are converted to black or white ones, adjust the middle-gray slider. Drag the **slider** to the left to produce a lighter image, or drag it to the right to produce a darker one. Watch the image as it changes, and stop when you find the best setting.

Instead of dragging the slider, you also can enter a value in the Threshold Level text box to change the threshold.

6. Click **OK**.

7. Convert the mode to **Indexed Color** and use any of the conversion methods. Because the image already contains only black and white, the image should not change.

Different types of images require different color depths. Once you determine the needs of an image, you can set the depth, and select an appropriate file format.

WORKING WITH FILE FORMATS

2

Every computer file uses a particular kind of file format. Microsoft Word documents are saved in a .doc format, and Web pages are saved as .html files. Similarly, you can save graphics as .pict, .tif, or any of the many of existing graphics formats. Each format has different capabilities regarding color depth, transparency, animation, and other qualities. Most formats can be easily converted from one to the other.

Although you can save an image in Photoshop in a variety of formats, only a few formats can be used for images that will appear in a Web page. Web browsers on their own can display only three formats: GIF (.gif), JPG (.jpg or .jpeg), and PNG (.png). GIF and JPEG are standard formats and can be viewed in any browser. PNG is a newer format and is supported only by newer browsers. Although most users can see PNG images with their browsers, a small percentage cannot. Avoid using the PNG format unless you are confident that all users who visit your Web pages have the latest browsers.

Browsers can display formats other than GIF, JPEG, and PNG, but require additional special programs to do so. Some of these programs are helper applications, which open the images in a new window. Yet another type of program is called a **plug-in**, and is incorporated into the user's browser.

Using Plug-ins

Recall from the Introduction to Web Graphics chapter, that Web browsers cannot rasterize vector images, so they need additional software to convert vector images to bitmap images. The software that rasterizes vector images within a Web browser is one type of plug-in; you use a different plug-in for each vector format. You can even find plug-ins for nonWeb bitmap formats such as TIFF. One common plug-in is used for Flash, and allows browsers to display vector animations. You also can use a plug-in to view text documents, such as Microsoft Excel or Adobe Acrobat files, in a browser. The drawback to using plug-ins is that only some versions of browsers include certain plug-ins. This means you can never be sure whether your audience has the proper plug-in. If they don't, they won't see your image or animation.

When selecting a graphic file format, choose GIF or JPEG. They are the only format that do not require users to have a particular plug-in.

Using GIF Images

The **Graphics Interchange Format** (**GIF**) supports 8-bit color, but not 24-bit color. It is an appropriate format for images that can tolerate optimization through color-reduction. GIF supports transparency and even animation. Because of this, GIF is the most useful Web graphics format, and the one you probably will use most often for Web graphics.

GIF's strengths make it a good file format for small, fast-loading images, animations, and images that have irregular shapes. But it is not a good format to use for high-color images such as photographs.

You might occasionally see GIF referred to as gif87 or gif89. The version of the GIF format released in 1987 (gif87) does not support animation, but the version released in 1989 (gif89) does. Current image-editing programs save GIF files with the newer gif89 version.

 Before you save a GIF image, convert it to Indexed Color mode. If you are trying to save an image as GIF in Photoshop, but notice that GIF is not listed as an option in the Save as type list, change the image to Indexed Color, and then save the file.

CompuServe and GIF

When you save an image in the GIF format in Photoshop, the format in the Save as type text box is CompuServe GIF. This is because CompuServe owns the patent to the compression algorithm (known as LZW compression) used in the GIF format (and in the TIFF format). CompuServe charges licensing fees to companies such as Adobe so that they can use the LZW formula to open and save files in the GIF format. A few years ago CompuServe stated they will charge up to $5,000 for any site that uses GIF images created with software made by companies that have not paid the licensing fee. You, therefore, should be concerned about the source of your GIF images. If you use products like Photoshop, where Adobe pays the licensing fee to CompuServe, you won't be charged an extra fee. Exercise caution in using a freeware or shareware image editor. If the developers of those tools haven't paid the licensing fee, you are technically breaking the law by creating GIF files with them. The patent on LZW compression expires in 2002.

Using JPEG Images

The **Joint Photographic Experts Group** (**JPEG**) format supports 24-bit color, but not 8-bit color. The JPEG format is supported by all browsers and is an appropriate format for photographs and other high-color images. JPEG does not use color-reduction to optimize image files. It uses another type of optimization called **compression**. Compression is a mathematical manipulation of the file itself, and selectively eliminates areas of detail in the image to reduce the size of the file. This sort of compression results in lost image data and is called **lossy compression**. GIF images also use compression to reduce file size, but this compression does not discard image data and is called **lossless compression**.

You can adjust the amount of compression used in a JPEG image. A higher compression creates a smaller file, but also produces blocks of banded color called **artifacts**. These artifacts are more noticeable in images with areas of solid color, and appear near areas of high contrast, such as around text or where dark lines occur against a light background. For this reason, avoid using JPEG compression for images containing text.

Figure 2-22 shows an image with different compression settings. The image on the top is compressed at the minimum quality setting. The file is only 3 KB, but the image contains artifacts. The image on the bottom uses less compression. The file size is nearly 5 KB, but the image contains fewer artifacts.

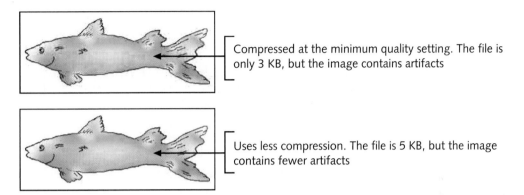

Compressed at the minimum quality setting. The file is only 3 KB, but the image contains artifacts

Uses less compression. The file is 5 KB, but the image contains fewer artifacts

Figure 2-22   An image with different degrees of compression

Each time you save a JPEG image with compression, new artifacts are generated. When you edit a JPEG file, use an original version that has not been compressed, if possible.

The JPEG format does not support transparency or animation. If you save an image that contains transparency as a JPEG, all transparent areas are filled in with the matte color.

Using PNG Images

A new, free format has emerged in the past few years, and is called **PNG** (pronounced "ping"). Although the acronym officially stands for **Portable Network Graphic**, the unofficial name is PNG Not GIF, as it is intended to replace the GIF format.

PNG has some advantages over GIF images. One is that PNG images can be 24-bit or 8-bit color, so PNGs can have small color palettes like GIFs or large color palettes like JPEGs. Another advantage is that PNGs support 8-bit transparency, while GIF supports only 1-bit transparency. This means the edge of a PNG fades smoothly into the background of a Web page, while GIFs tend to have ragged edges.

Another advantage of PNG is that the format is completely open-source, meaning anyone can develop software to work with PNG files without paying a license fee. Because some companies do not pay for the compression needed to open and save GIF files, many tools, especially freeware and shareware ones, cannot manipulate GIF images. However, these tools do support the open-source PNG format, suggesting that more programs will offer PNG-editing capability, while fewer will continue to support GIF.

One drawback to the PNG format is that only Netscape version 4 and higher and Internet Explorer version 4 and higher (commonly referred to as the 4+ browsers) display PNG images. Although most browsers currently used to visit Web sites are versions 4+, people using older browsers cannot see PNG images. Another drawback is that PNG does not support animation.

PNG also does not compress as well as JPEG. Even though you can store high-color images such as photographs in PNG, you cannot reduce their file size as you can with JPEG.

Table 2-4 shows the differences between the GIF, JPEG, and PNG formats.

Table 2-4   Comparison of the three Web graphics formats

	GIF	JPEG	PNG
Color	Indexed (8-bit)	RGB (24-bit)	Either indexed or RGB
Compression	Lossless or lossy	Lossy (strong)	Lossless (weak)
Animation	Yes	No	No
Transparency	1-bit	No	Full 8-bit alpha channel
Browser support	Full	Full	Partial

In general, because it supports transparency and animation, GIF is the most versatile image format and the best format to use for most Web graphics. The only reason not to use GIF is when you have a high-color image such as a photograph, in which case JPEG is the better format. As the Web develops, however, PNG might be used more often.

Emerging Formats

As the Web evolves, new file formats are developed for Web graphics. These emerging formats include SVG, JPEG2000, MNG, and XBMP. Each of these new formats is discussed in the following sections.

Scalable Vector Graphics

A relatively new image format allows designers to include vector images in their Web pages without requiring that users have a particular plug-in. The **scalable vector graphics (SVG)** format is similar to the common Flash format. While Flash is a proprietary format owned by Macromedia, SVG is a public, open format that can be created by a variety of programs. Like Flash, SVG creates vector graphics with small file sizes, and creates image displays that scale well and print clearly. Unfortunately, current browsers do not support this format without a plug-in. New versions might support this format.

JPEG2000

The developers of the JPEG format are updating the JPEG format to allow better compression. The new format, which uses the suffix **.jp2**, produces extremely small file sizes without any noticeable loss of image quality. There is no native browser support yet, although you can view JPEG2000 (JP2) images with a plug-in.

MPEG and MNG

JPEG has an associated animation format called **MPEG** that uses the same algorithms as JPEG, but requires a helper application to be viewed on the Web. Similarly, PNG has a related animation format called **MNG**. The standard is still being developed, so it will be a few years before you can create MNG animations of your own.

XBMP

Increasing numbers of Web sites offer wireless versions of their pages. These pages have less formatting so that they can fit on the screen of a hand-held device such as a Palm Pilot or Web-enabled cell phone.

Some of these devices display images, but only ones with very low color depths. Specifically, they display a 1-bit format called **X-Bitmap**, or **XBMP**. This format allows only black and white pixels. Most commercial software does not yet support this format, but free software is available that converts a GIF image to an XBMP image.

SAVING FILES AS WEB GRAPHICS

In Photoshop, you select a file format for an image when you save the file. To save an image as a Web graphic, first determine which color depth is appropriate for the image. For 8-bit depth or lower, save the image as CompuServe GIF. For 24-bit depth, save the image as JPEG. However, if the image has been converted to Indexed Color mode, the JPEG format does not appear as a format option in the Save As dialog box. Convert the image back to RGB mode to save it as a JPEG.

Saving Images in the GIF Format

If the image you want to save as GIF is in RGB mode, you can select the color reduction and dithering methods when you save the file. After you do this, or if the image has already been converted to Indexed Color, you can select the row order of the image, either Normal or Interlaced.

Normally, Web graphics take a few seconds to download from the Web server, and only when the complete file has been loaded does it appear in the Web page. When a GIF is saved with interlaced rows, an incomplete version of the image appears before the complete image has loaded. The rest of the image appears when the download is completed. Using interlaced GIFs is useful because it confirms to the user that an image is loading.

To save an image file as a GIF in Photoshop:

1. Open file **2-1.psd** from the Data Disk.

2. Click **File** on the menu bar, and then click **Save As**.

3. In the Save As dialog box, enter **2-1GIF** as the filename, and select the **Chapter 2** folder on your hard drive as the location for the file.

4. Click the **Format** list arrow, and then click **CompuServe GIF (*.GIF)**.

5. Click the **Save** button.

6. In the Indexed Color dialog box, click the **Palette** list arrow, and then click **Local (Selective)**.

7. In the Colors text box, type **32** (5-bit).

8. Make sure the Forced text box shows Black and White, the Transparency box is checked, the Matte text box shows None, and the Dither text box shows Diffusion.

9. In the Amount text box, type **50**.

10. Click the **Preserve Exact Colors** box to check it.

11. Click **OK**.

12. In the GIF Options dialog box, make sure the Normal option button is selected, and then click **OK**. This saves the image as a GIF with transparency and optimization through color reduction.

Saving Images in the JPEG format

Recall that you can save RGB mode images as JPEGs, although JPEG images cannot include transparency. If the image contains any transparent areas, you can set a matte color during the save process. Any transparent pixels are converted to the color you specify.

When you save an image as JPEG, you also can select a compression setting for the image. Compression settings run from the quality values 0 to 12. Zero is the maximum compression and creates a very small file at the expense of image quality. A quality value of 12 specifies minimal compression and creates a large file with little or no degradation of the image.

You can preview the effects of compression on an image as you adjust the compression settings. You also can preview the size of the final image file and view the estimated download time for a given modem speed. The default modem speed is 28.8 Kbps (kilobits per second, not kilobytes per second), which is slower than average for most users, but is a good benchmark to use. Use a compression setting that keeps the download time as short as possible without compromising the quality of the image.

You also can set the following format options for an image:

- *Baseline* ("Standard"): The default, this option produces JPEG images that appear in all browsers, but results in slightly larger files.

- *Baseline Optimized*: This option enhances the compression of the image, and creates even smaller file sizes. Very old browsers do not support images saved with this sort of optimization, so avoid using it unless you are confident that your audience is using newer browsers.

- *Progressive:* This option is similar to the interlacing of GIF images. Instead of the image appearing only after it has completely loaded, progressive JPEGs initially appear as a low-resolution version of the image. The resolution improves as the remainder of the image loads. Using the Progressive option sometimes increases file size, but actually reduces it for some images. It is not supported by some older browsers.

To save an image file as a JPEG in Photoshop:

1. Open file **2-1.psd** from the Data Disk.

2. Click **File** on the menu bar, and then click **Save As**.

3. In the Save As dialog box, enter **2-1JPEG** as the filename, and select the **Chapter 2** folder on your hard drive as the location for the file.

4. Click the **Format** list arrow, and then click **JPEG (*.JPG, *.JPE)**.

5. Click the **Save** button.

6. In the JPEG Options dialog box, click the **Matte** list arrow, and then click **None**, if necessary. This converts transparent pixels to white.

7. Make sure the Quality text box shows 5. If it does not, drag the **slider** until it does, or click the **Quality** list arrow, and then click **Medium**.

8. Under Format Options, click **Baseline ("Standard")**, if necessary.

9. Make sure the Preview box is checked and then note the file size and download time at 28.8 Kbps. The file should be about 6.3 K and download in 2.19 seconds on a 28.8 Kbps modem.

10. Click **OK**. This saves the image as a JPEG optimization through compression.

Just as you optimize 8-bit GIF images by reducing the colors in the Indexed Color dialog box, you optimize 24-bit JPEG images by applying a compression setting in the JPEG Options dialog box. Both of these methods are convenient, but Photoshop and ImageReady include additional features for optimizing images.

OPTIMIZING IMAGES WITH PHOTOSHOP AND IMAGEREADY

The most recent versions of Photoshop include a feature called Save for Web that opens a dialog box, allowing you to optimize an image in any format, while previewing the effects on the image. ImageReady takes this one step further, and has a special Optimize palette that allows you to control optimization settings at any time.

With Photoshop you optimize images after you finish editing. If you reduce color or compress a file and then make further edits, the quality of the image suffers. With ImageReady, however, you can set optimization settings that do not take effect until you save the image. This lets you see the effects of editing and optimization at the same time.

In ImageReady, you use three windows to optimize images: the main Image window (also called the document window), the Optimize palette, and occasionally the Color Table palette. These windows are shown in Figure 2-23.

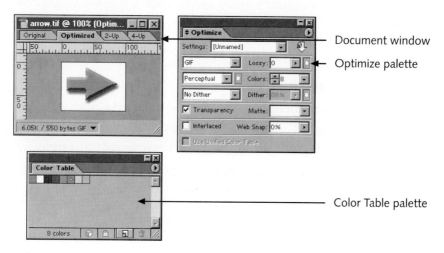

Figure 2-23   Three tools for optimizing an image in ImageReady

In Photoshop, these three windows are combined in the Save for Web dialog box, shown in Figure 2-24, along with a few tools from the toolbox.

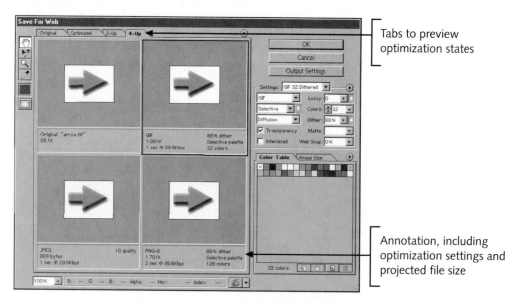

Figure 2-24   The Save for Web dialog box in Photoshop

To optimize an image in Photoshop, select Save for Web from the File menu. To optimize an image in ImageReady, use the Optimize palette. Make the palette visible by selecting Show Optimize from the Window menu.

Previewing Optimized Images

In ImageReady, the Image window always has four tabs along the top. Selecting these tabs allows you to preview different optimization states of the image. In Photoshop, you must select Save for Web to see these tabs. Each tab is described below.

- *Original:* This tab displays the original 24-bit image, without any optimization.

- *Optimized:* This tab displays the image with the currently selected optimization settings. This is a preview of how the image will appear after it is saved.

- *2-Up:* This tab displays two image preview panels next to each other. You can view the original image next to an optimized version, or compare two different optimization settings.

- *4-Up:* This displays four image preview panels in a 2 × 2 table. You can compare different optimization settings this way.

When you select the 2-Up or 4-Up tab, you see annotation about each optimized version at the bottom of every window. The annotation includes the optimization settings for the image and the projected file size of the image when you save it with those settings. As you experiment with different settings, look at the image previews to see how the settings affect the quality of the image. You can hide the annotations to make room for the image previews. You can do this in ImageReady by selecting Hide Optimization Info from the View menu.

If you do not show the annotations, look at the numbers at the bottom of the window to see how the settings affect file size. In ImageReady, at the bottom of the document window are additional choices for how to display information about the image. You can preview the size of the original file, how long it takes the optimized file to download at different connection speeds, or how much file space is saved by using a given optimization setting.

You have only limited editing capability when you preview an image in any panel other than the original, unoptimized view. To make changes to the image, first select the Original panel.

Using Predefined Optimization Settings

Although you can customize image optimization, you might find it easier to use one of the 12 predefined optimization settings in ImageReady. These contain seven color reduction settings for the GIF format, and use different color depths and dither options. The predefined optimization settings also contain three JPEG settings with different compression options, and two settings for PNG images.

To use a predefined optimization setting in ImageReady:

1. In ImageReady, open file **2-1.psd** from the Data Disk.

2. Save the file as **2-1Optimized.psd** in the **Chapter 2** folder on your hard drive.

3. In the Image window, click the **2-Up tab**.

4. Click the **right panel** to select the optimized version of the image.

5. In the Optimize palette, click the **Settings** list arrow, and then click the first preset optimization setting, **GIF 128 Dithered**. This reduces color to 7-bit using the Selective color reduction method, and activates 88% diffusion dithering for the image.

6. Look at the image previews and compare the quality of the images. Look at the annotation for each panel and compare the file sizes.

7. Select the other presets to find the setting that creates the smallest file without reducing the quality of the image.

8. Save the image with its current name (2-1Optimized.psd) in the Chapter 2 folder of your hard drive.

Once you find a preset that generates good results, you can fine-tune the settings by selecting other options in the Optimize palette. If you change the settings, the option in the Settings text box changes to [Unnamed]. This means that you are customizing the settings.

If you create an optimization setting that you want to save and use later for other images, click the right triangle on the Optimize palette to open the palette menu, and then click Save Settings. In the Save Optimization Settings dialog box, enter a descriptive name for the new setting, and then click the Save button. The new setting now appears in the Settings menu.

Optimizing GIF Images

When you select GIF as an image format or select one of the GIF presets in the Optimize palette in ImageReady or in the optimization settings area of the Save for Web dialog box in Photoshop, the options change to resemble the Indexed Color dialog box. In ImageReady, make sure to select Show Options from the Optimize palette menu. This expands the palette to display additional options, including transparency.

You then can select options for number of colors, color reduction method, dithering, and so forth. You also can add JPEG-style lossy compression and force the color table to use Web-safe colors. These two options are explained in the following sections.

Using Lossy Compression

By adding lossy compression, you can sometimes purposely reduce detail and quality of GIF images to reduce file size. Lossy compression is available only for GIF images that are not Interlaced and do not use the Noise or Pattern dither options.

In ImageReady, the Optimize palette includes the Lossy text box. To change the lossy compression, either enter a number from 0 to 100, or click the Lossy list arrow and then use the slider bar to change the value. A value of 0 means no lossy compression is applied. A value of 100 means the maximum amount of compression is applied. At a certain lossy compression setting, you will see artifacts begin to appear in the image. The exact setting depends on the amount of detail in the image. For most images, you should be able to apply up to 5% lossy compression without noticing a difference in image quality. However, this small change saves file size. Increasing the amount of lossy compression increases the amount of image data sacrificed for file size. You can generally apply up to 40% or 50% compression to an image before you significantly degrade the image.

Using lossy compression with GIF images produces artifacts, just as it does with JPEG images. Sometimes these artifacts actually improve the quality of an image by masking any banding between color areas.

Using Web Snap

Another option for optimizing GIF images is setting a percentage value for Web Snap. This setting controls how to reduce the color table. A Web Snap value of 0% indicates that you want to reduce the color table using the current color reduction method. A value of 100% indicates that you want to reduce the color table using only colors in the Web-safe color table. Recall that Web-safe colors are guaranteed to not dither in any browser in any monitor.

Using an intermediate value for Web Snap helps reduce the number of colors in the table, and helps reduce file size. However, higher values lead to banded color that cannot be remedied, even with full dithering settings.

Working with the Color Table

As you choose different optimization settings for the GIF format, you can see the colors in the color table change. In ImageReady, make the Color Table palette visible by selecting Show Color Table from the Window menu. From the Color Table palette menu, select Sort by Popularity to sort the colors in the color table from most used to least used. As you decrease the value in the Colors text box in the Optimize palette, the least popular colors are removed from the color table.

Sometimes a particular color is important, even if it is not often used in an image. You can lock specific colors in the color table so that they are not removed by any of the color reduction methods. In the Color Table palette, select a color that you do not want removed, then click the lock icon at the bottom of the palette. Now even when you reduce colors, the locked colors remain.

Optimizing JPEG Images

Optimizing JPEGs with the Optimize palette is similar to using the JPEG Options dialog box. The key to JPEG compression is the Quality setting in the Optimize palette. Higher quality means lower compression and larger file size. Lower quality means higher compression and smaller file size. Instead of the values ranging from 0 to 12, however, in the Optimize palette they range from 0% to 100%.

The Optimize palette also lets you set the Blur option. Because JPEG compression creates artifacts in an image, you can minimize their appearance by blurring the entire image. In the Blur text box, you can enter any value between 0 and 2, including decimal fractions, to control the pixel radius of the blurring. A high value eliminates most artifacts, but likely makes the image too blurry to use.

Optimizing by File Size

Often Web pages are designed with a fixed total page weight. For example, to make sure a Web page downloads in less than a few seconds, you might decide that all the elements of the page must have a combined file size of less than 60 KB. If the HTML file itself has a size of 30 KB, that leaves another 30 KB for all the graphics on the page. It is then convenient to optimize an image based on a fixed file size, rather than to find the maximum optimization that does not compromise image quality.

To optimize by file size:

1. In ImageReady, click the **right triangle** in the Optimize palette to open the palette menu, and then click **Optimize to File Size**.

   In Photoshop, click **File** on the menu bar, click **Save for Web**, click the **right triangle** next to the Settings text box, and then click **Optimize to File Size**.

   You will see the Optimize To File Size dialog box, shown in Figure 2-25. Use this dialog box to set parameters, and then let the software find the best optimization settings for you.

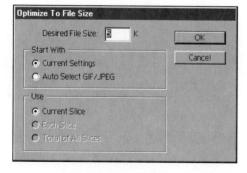

Figure 2-25   The Optimize To File Size dialog box

2. In the Desired File Size text box, enter a target file size for the optimized image.

You will have a good idea of what a reasonable size is after you have optimized several images of different sizes. The target size depends on the dimensions of the image and the number of colors it has. A small image of 50 × 50 pixels with a few colors can be optimized to less than 1 KB. A 200 × 200 pixel photograph, however, might require at least 20 KB. Start with a low number, such as 2, and see how the optimization affects the image. If the image quality deteriorates too much, try a larger target size.

3. To try only optimization settings for the file format currently selected in the Optimize palette, select the **Current Settings** option button. To choose an appropriate format based on the number of colors used in the image, select the **Auto Select GIF/JPEG** option button.

Generally, the Auto Select option produces the best results. However, if the image is an animation, or contains transparency, you must use the GIF format. Set the format to **GIF** in the Settings text box in the Optimize palette, and select **Current Settings** in the Optimize To File Size dialog box to find only optimal GIF optimization settings.

(The other options in the dialog box are for slices, which are covered in a later chapter.)

4. Click **OK** to optimize the image to the file size you specified.

Saving Optimized Images

After you set the optimization options in Photoshop, click OK in the Save for Web dialog box to save an optimized image. In ImageReady, choose Save Optimized As from the File menu. Both these actions open the Save Optimize As dialog box, where you can choose a location and name for the file. You can overwrite the original image, if you want, but it's a good practice to save optimized images with different names and preserve the original images in case you want to optimize them in the future.

 When optimizing, do not choose Save As in ImageReady; this saves the original image without any of the optimization settings.

You can also choose to save an HTML file along with the image. This is useful only if you are saving advanced types of Web graphics, such as image maps or image slices. For most optimized images, you can save the images only. To do so, in the Save Optimized As dialog box, click the Save as type list arrow, and then click Images Only.

CHAPTER SUMMARY

- The file size of an image is based on the dimensions of the image and the number of colors used in the image.

- Optimizing graphics means reducing the file size of an image as much as possible without sacrificing image quality. Whether you are creating image maps or animated rollovers, you must optimize all Web graphics.

- You can optimize images by reducing the number of colors used in the image.

- Color reduction can result in banding; a remedy for banding is to use dithering.

- Web pages can use three bitmap image formats: GIF, JPEG, and PNG. GIF and PNG images are optimized primarily through color reduction, while JPEG images are optimized through lossy compression.

- The JPEG format is best for photographs and other high-color images. GIF is best for most others.

- GIF is the only format that allows animation without requiring a plug-in.

- Compression can result in artifacts. The remedy for artifacts is to use less compression.

REVIEW QUESTIONS

1. How much bigger is one kilobyte than one kilobit?

    a. Same size

    b. Eight times bigger

    c. 24 times bigger

    d. 1000 times bigger

2. How long does it take to transfer a 5 KB image file over a 40 KB connection?

    a. Roughly one second

    b. Roughly four seconds

    c. Roughly five seconds

    d. Roughly eight seconds

3. If you have a 100 Kbps connection, what is the biggest image you could transfer in one second?

    a. 8 KB

    b. 12 KB

    c. 120 KB

    d. 800 KB

4. How many colors are in the palette of an image with a color depth of 7–bit?

   a. 24

   b. 64

   c. 128

   d. 256

5. How many color channels are there in a 24–bit image?

   a. 1

   b. 2

   c. 3

   d. 4

6. What is the maximum number of colors in a Color Look-Up Table?

   a. 8

   b. 256

   c. 512

   d. 65,536

7. What color depth should you use for your images while you edit them?

   a. 1–bit

   b. 8–bit

   c. 24–bit

   d. 32–bit

8. What is a good color depth for most photographs?

   a. 5–bit

   b. 8–bit

   c. 24–bit

   d. 32–bit

9. What is not a commonly used color reduction method?

   a. Adaptive

   b. Perceptual

   c. Selective

   d. Uniform

10. Why would you dither an image?

   a. To blur the image

   b. To enable transparency

   c. To minimize banding

   d. To reduce file size

11. Which format(s) can be viewed in any browser without a plug-in?

    a. GIF

    b. JPEG

    c. PNG-8

    d. PNG-24

12. Which of the following formats support transparency?

    a. GIF

    b. JPEG

    c. PNG-8

    d. PNG-24

13. Which of the following formats support animation?

    a. GIF

    b. JPEG

    c. PNG-8

    d. PNG-24

14. Which of the following formats support high-color images such as photographs?

    a. GIF

    b. JPEG

    c. PNG-8

    d. PNG-24

15. Which of the following formats can be optimized through color reduction?

    a. GIF

    b. JPEG

    c. PNG-8

    d. PNG-24

16. When would you use the Threshold command?

    a. When reducing color to 8-bit

    b. When reducing color to 1-bit

    c. When increasing color to 8-bit

    d. When increasing color to 2-bit

17. What does a Quality setting of High do to an image?

    a. Uses maximum lossless compression

    b. Uses maximum lossy compression

    c. Uses minimal lossless compression

    d. Uses minimal lossy compression

18. What is the maximum possible value for the Blur setting when optimizing JPEGs?

    a. 1

    b. 2

    c. 8

    d. 12

19. What does the Web Snap setting do?

    a. Allows the image to appear on the Web

    b. Allows interlacing rows

    c. Forces colors in the color table to shift to Web-safe colors

    d. Toggles between transparency and matte

20. Which JPEG options are sure to make the image visible in all browsers?

    a. Both Progressive and Optimized selected

    b. Progressive unselected and Optimized selected

    c. Progressive selected and Optimized unselected

    d. Progressive unselected and Optimized selected

HANDS-ON PROJECTS

Project 1: Using Interpolation When Resizing an Image

You need to resize an image that already has been optimized, but you see that the resulting image has jagged edges. Increase the color depth to improve the results.

1. In Photoshop, open the image file **2-1.tif** from the Data Disk.

2. Use the Image Size dialog box to increase the height to **100 pixels**, but constraining proportions.

3. The resulting image has jagged edges because there are not enough colors in the color table to resample and interpolate accurately. Undo the image resize.

4. Open the Color Table dialog box. Note the number of colors this image uses— only seven colors, plus one color for transparency. Close this dialog box.

5. Change the mode to **RGB**. This gives the image 16.7 million colors for interpolation.

6. Resize the image again. This time the pixels should be interpolated correctly.

7. The process of interpolation adds colors to the color table. Reduce the color depth back to its original level. Use the Indexed Color dialog box to reduce the number of colors to **8**.

8. Save the image as **2-1.gif** in the Chapter 2 folder on your hard drive.

Project 2: Copying Image Data Between Images with Different Color Tables

You have two images with indexed color modes. Each has a different clut. Copying image data from one image to the other produces undesirable results. Change the color depth to fix the problem.

1. In Photoshop, open the image files **2-1.tif** and **2-2.tif** from the Data Disk.

2. Select file **2-1.tif**, then select all the image data by clicking the Select menu, and then clicking All.

3. Copy the selected area, then select file **2-2.tif** and paste the selection into the image.

4. The selection adopts the clut of the new image and the colors change. Undo the Paste command.

5. Change the mode of the destination image to 24-bit so that the color table effectively has all colors.

6. Paste again (you do not need to recopy the selection). The selection maintains its original colors. When you are asked if you want to flatten layers, click **Yes**.

7. Use the Indexed Color dialog box to reduce the colors again. When Photoshop prompts you to save layers, click **OK**. For the color reduction method, select **Exact**.

8. Save the image as **2-2.gif** in the Chapter 2 folder on your hard drive.

Project 3: Creating a 1-bit Image

Your team is preparing a wireless version of your Web site for hand-held devices. They need a smaller, 1-bit version of the logo to appear on these devices.

1. Open the image file **2-3.tif** from the Data Disk.

2. Open the Threshold dialog box.

3. The slider at the bottom of the graph and the number box at the top let you control the dividing value between white and black. Make sure the preview box is selected, and adjust the levels until the image looks as clear as possible, while maintaining the general outline of the logo. When you are finished, click **OK**.

4. Select the **Zoom tool** and zoom in by clicking the image once or twice. You may notice some stray black pixels.

5. Set the background color to white by clicking the **Default Foreground and Background Colors button** near the bottom of the toolbar. This sets the foreground to black and the background to white.

6. Select the **Eraser tool**.

7. In the Options palette, make sure the brush shape is set to block.

8. Erase the stray pixels by clicking them with the eraser. If you need more control, zoom in further with the Magnifying Glass tool.

9. Change the color depth to **3** colors and save the image as **2-3.gif** in the Chapter 2 folder on your hard drive.

Project 4: Optimizing a Photograph

You need to optimize a photograph. Choose an appropriate format and optimization method.

1. In ImageReady, open the image file **2-4.tif** from the Data Disk.

2. Click the **4-Up tab** to compare multiple optimization settings.

3. Select the image preview in the upper-right panel, and select the **GIF 32 Dithered preset** in the Optimize palette.

4. Select the image preview in the lower-right panel, and select the **JPEG Low preset** in the Optimize palette.

5. Compare the two optimized versions with each other and with the original image in the upper-left panel. Both optimized versions look roughly the same.

6. Use the **Zoom** tool to magnify the image previews. You can see artifacts in the JPEG-optimized image. Increase the Quality to **20**.

7. Both optimized images have minimal banding, but the JPEG-optimized image is less than half the size of the GIF-optimized one. Save the optimized image as **2-4.jpg** in the Chapter 2 folder on your hard drive.

Project 5: Optimizing a Low-Color Graph

Diagrams and charts often use very few colors because they are generated from vector programs and have no gradient color. Optimize a low-color graph.

1. In ImageReady, open the image file **2-5.tif** from the Data Disk.

2. Select the **4-Up tab** to position the original image on the left of the screen, and a test optimized version on the right.

3. Set the image preview in the upper-right panel to the **GIF 32 Dithered preset**.

4. Set the image preview in the lower-left panel to **JPEG Low**.

5. Compare the two optimized versions. The JPEG version has a larger file size and several artifacts around the black lines in the image.

6. Reduce the colors in the GIF version to **5** colors, and record the file size.

7. Reduce the colors to **4**, and record the file size. Reducing colors in this instance has actually increased the file size by forcing the colors to dither.

8. Disable dithering. This reduces the file size further, but the red color is lost. Increase colors to **5** again.

9. This is a reasonable optimization. Save the optimized image file as **2-5.gif** in the Chapter 2 folder on your hard drive.

Project 6: Optimizing a Textured Image

Visual texture conceals banding, dithering, and JPEG artifacts. Images with a lot of visual texture usually can be optimized more than images without much visual texture. Optimize this drawing.

1. In ImageReady, open the image file **2-6.tif** from the Data Disk.
2. Use the **4-Up** view.
3. Set the upper-right panel to **GIF 32 Dithered,** and the lower-left panel to **JPEG Low**.
4. The JPEG version shows little degradation. Reduce the Quality to **0**, the maximum compression. The image still shows no obvious artifacts.
5. The file size is about 7.6 KB. Try optimizing through color reduction to reduce the file size.
6. Reduce the colors of the GIF optimization to **4** colors. The file size is smaller, but the black color of the tree trunk is missing.
7. Increase the colors to **16**, and find the dark green or black color in the Color Table palette. Select the color and lock it.
8. Reduce colors to **4** again. The file size is reduced, and the dark color is retained.
9. Save the optimized image as **2-6.gif** in the Chapter 2 folder on your hard drive.

Project 7: Fine-Tuning an Optimization

Often you can save a few extra kilobytes by tweaking the optimization settings. Optimize another drawing.

1. In ImageReady, open the image file **2-7.tif** from the Data Disk.
2. Use the **4-Up** view.
3. Set one of the panels to a GIF optimization preset, and set another to a JPEG preset.
4. Compare the two optimized previews with each other and with the original image. The image has dark lines, so the JPEG optimization produces noticeable artifacts. The image also has color gradations, so the GIF optimization produces noticeable banding.
5. Zoom in to one of the previews. Notice that all previews are magnified. Find the lowest Quality setting for the JPEG compression that produces no artifacts.
6. Choose **No Dithering** for the GIF preview, and find the fewest colors that do not produce obvious banding. The GIF optimization should have a slightly smaller file size than the JPEG optimization.
7. Try different color reduction methods and different lossy compression settings for the GIF preview to find the one that produces the smallest file size.
8. Save the optimized image as **2-7.gif** in the Chapter 2 folder on your hard drive.

Project 8: Optimizing to a Specific File Size

The target page weight for a Web page is 80 KB. The HTML file is 50 KB, and you already have 25 KB worth of other graphics on the page. Reduce the image in this project to 5 KB, sacrificing image quality as little as possible.

1. In ImageReady, open the image file **2-8.tif** from the Data Disk.

2. Use the **2-Up** view.

3. Open the Optimize To File Size dialog box, set the Desired File Size to **5** K, and then select **Auto Select GIF/JPEG**.

4. Click **OK**. ImageReady automatically optimizes the image using JPEG compression so that the file size is under 5 KB.

5. Save the image as **2-8.jpg** in the Chapter 2 folder on your hard drive.

CASE PROJECT

All of the images that will appear in your online portfolio need to be optimized. Take all the images of past work you have gathered for your portfolio, and optimize them as GIF or JPEG images, depending on what is appropriate for each image.

Think about how you will lay out the images in different pages of your portfolio. Determine a target size for each page, and make sure that the total file size of all the images on each page does not exceed the target size.

3

DISPLAYING WEB GRAPHICS

Controlling the Appearance of Graphics in Web Pages

In this chapter, you will:

♦ Prepare images for display on different hardware, browsers, and operating systems

♦ Learn how colors are represented on the Web

♦ Control the appearance of Web graphics with HTML

♦ Avoid common mistakes when using images in HTML

When creating any media, you need to understand the environment in which your work will be seen. Users will view your work on different operating systems, including Windows and Macintosh. They will use different browsers, and even different versions of Internet Explorer and Netscape Navigator. The size of their monitors also will vary. These different elements make up the user environment.

You cannot create graphics that will appear exactly the same way in all environments, so you need to design for the majority, yet include as many other environments as possible. On the Web, most people use Microsoft Windows and Internet Explorer. As you create Web graphics, you need to make sure that those users see the images as you intend, and still ensure that Mac and Netscape users are not left behind. This chapter explains how to prepare images for the widest range of hardware, browsers, and operating systems.

One way that environments differ is in the way browsers represent colors. An important part of designing graphics and pages for all browsers is having an understanding of how color is defined in HTML. Web colors are always defined in terms of RGB color, but you use special syntax to do so. This chapter also explains how colors are represented on the Web.

To create Web pages that display your graphics, you can code the HTML in a text file or use an editor such as Dreamweaver. Most designers prefer to use an HTML editor because the interface simplifies the process of producing

Web pages. However, HTML editors usually do not lay out pages with the accuracy you need. You should know at least some HTML so you can fix the code generated by the editors. This chapter discusses how you can control the appearance of Web graphics with HTML, and avoid the common mistakes in using images in HTML.

PREPARING CROSS-PLATFORM IMAGES

Web users have different kinds of hardware for viewing Web pages, and they use different browsers running on different operating systems. Ideally, you will create cross-platform pages and images, meaning they look similar, regardless of the hardware, browsers, or operating systems used. Creating cross-platform images often is impossible because environments differ dramatically. Someone using Netscape 3 on a Macintosh with a 21" screen sees pages and graphics differently from someone using Internet Explorer 5 on a Windows computer with a 13" monitor. Your goal is to develop images that look the way you want on the majority of systems, and look close enough on most others.

Considering Hardware

The hardware that most affects how others view your images is the standard desktop monitor. This is the tool most people use to surf the Web and view Web graphics. However, many people print pages before reading them, so you also need to be aware of how your graphics appear when printed. Although WebTV® is still in its infancy, television and the Internet are expected to be integrated in the future, making the television another display device to consider.

Computer screens, printers, and televisions all have different color **gamuts**. The gamut of display hardware is the range of colors that the hardware produces. In general, printers have larger gamuts than monitors and televisions. They can produce a broader range of saturated colors using ink on paper than the other hardware can using light on a screen. Televisions have the smallest gamuts. The colors that they can display are a subset of the colors that computer monitors can display.

The following sections discuss considerations for designing Web graphics for a variety of monitors, televisions, and printers.

Considering Monitors

A standard desktop monitor uses cathode-ray tubes (CRTs) to project light against the back of the glass screen; these monitors are called CRT monitors and work by emitting light through the screen. The other type of monitor uses a liquid crystal display (LCD) similar to that used in calculators. LCD screens can be much thinner than CRT monitors and work by selectively blocking light. They do not emit as much light as CRT monitors and are more difficult to view from an angle. Monitors differ from each other in size, resolution, and color depth. The images you create can have a certain size and color palette on one monitor and a different size and colors on another.

Designing for Monitor Size The size of a desktop monitor is measured diagonally on the glass part of the screen. Some manufacturers embellish the size of their monitors by measuring from corner to corner of the monitor, including the plastic case. You can find the true size by measuring the visible area of the screen with a ruler or tape measure. Sizes can range from 9 to 21" or more, but most people have 13-, 15-, or 17" screens. The size of your users' monitors affects your decisions about page layout more than it affects your decisions about graphics production. As a Web developer and producer, you need to make sure your pages fit within the viewing screen by limiting the width of Web pages. Some users set their browsers to fill the screen, and others use the default width, which covers only about half of the screen area. If the Web pages you create are no wider than about 600 pixels, they will fit on most browsers on most monitors.

Graphic artists also need to work within parameters. If you have a very large monitor, such as 21" or more, you might be accustomed to making very large images. An image that is 850 pixels wide may look good on your 21" monitor, but will not even fit on many 13" monitors, which usually can accommodate only 640 or 800 pixels, depending on resolution. When your images are placed on a Web page, you should preview the page in a mid-size monitor (13–17") to see how the average user will see it.

Designing for Monitor Resolution Most monitors have resolutions of 72 pixels per inch (ppi), and an image that is 144 pixels high appears 2" high. Some monitors, especially those that are sold with high-end graphics workstations, have resolutions of 96 ppi. On these monitors, the same 144-pixel-high image appears only 1½" high. The majority of users have 72 ppi monitors, so if you design on a standard monitor, you can be confident that most users see images the same size that you do.

Designing for Monitor Color The color displayed by a monitor is not determined entirely by the monitor, but also by the graphics card and the RAM in the computer itself. Depending on the card and the amount of memory, a monitor might display only 8-bit color (256 colors), 16-bit color (thousands of colors), or 24-bit color (millions of colors). The average user has a 16-bit monitor. Because of the difference in monitor color, an image can have smooth gradients when viewed on a 24-bit color monitor, but show slight banding or dithering when viewed on a 16-bit monitor. If you design on a 24-bit monitor, users with 16-bit monitors might see color artifacts that are invisible to you. You should preview your graphics on 16-bit and 8-bit monitors to see how they appear to users with those monitors.

The difference between monitor color depths is the same as between 8-bit and 24-bit images in an image editor. Lower color depth means banding or dithering in the image. The difference between 16-bit and 24-bit is usually not noticeable except for high-color images with smooth color gradients. Figure 3-1 shows a simulation of how a high-color image appears on monitors with three different color depths.

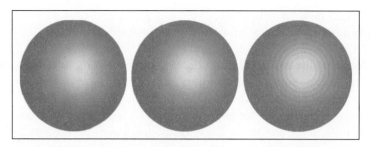

Figure 3-1   A high-color image displayed at different color depths

As a designer, you also might be accustomed to using high-color monitors and never see what your images look like on a 16-bit system. If you work on a 24-bit monitor, occasionally set your monitor to a lower color depth to see how your images appear to other users.

Both CRT and LCD monitors display colors that are less rich than in real life. This is especially true for bright shades of green. Limitations in the phosphors in computer monitors means they cannot re-create the green of objects such as the leaves of a healthy plant. To compensate for this, many graphics use a darker shade of most colors. Although a dark shade actually has less color, it appears richer to our eyes.

The colors at the top of Figure 3-2 are fully saturated. The colors on the bottom actually have less saturated color but appear to have more.

Designing for LCD Monitors LCD screens are used in devices such as cell phones and handheld computers, where their thinness is an advantage. These devices often display fewer colors because of memory limitations. Some can display up to 8-bit (256) color, but most can display only 1-bit color in black and white. LCD screens also are used for laptops and in more expensive, flat-panel desktop monitors. LCD panels typically have crisper lines than CRT monitors and less glare.

Most users will view your graphics on CRT or LCD screens, at a resolution and color depth equal to or less than what you use. Design your Web graphics to suit your users' monitors, which probably have smaller screen size and lower color depth than what you use.

3

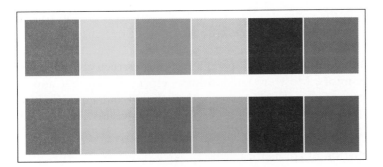

Figure 3-2 Compensating for weak saturation with darker colors

Designing for a TV Screen

WebTV® from WebTV Networks Inc. is a commercial product that allows you to surf the Web using a television instead of a computer monitor. Even though televisions also use CRTs to display images, they display images differently from monitors, primarily in their resolution and use of color.

Design for television output only if you are certain you need to cater to WebTV users. Currently, only users of WebTV use television as a display device for Web pages and graphics. You can find out how many WebTV users you have by analyzing your Web server log file. Every Web site has a server log, which records who visits the site and what browser and system they are using. You cannot use the logs to tell what people do with your Web pages, only what software they use to access and view them. For most sites, well under 1% of visits are from WebTV users. This percentage might increase as high-definition digital TV becomes more popular, and the Internet and television become more integrated.

When you design Web pages you know will be viewed on a TV monitor, consider the lower resolution, reduced color, and type of output standards the TV uses. For most pages, however, you can safely ignore these restrictions.

Designing for Television Resolution The resolution of a conventional television is much lower than that of a computer monitor. If you display a high-resolution image on a television, you see a shimmering effect, which is the result of **aliasing**: outputting high-frequency information through a lower-frequency device. Aliasing can happen in any medium when high-resolution data is output at a lower resolution. You've heard aliasing if you've ever listened to digital audio played back at the wrong rate. You've seen aliasing on TV if you've ever noticed a newscaster's striped shirt creating vibrant patterns on the screen. The stripes on the shirt have a higher resolution (lines per inch) than the lines on the TV. The TV tries, and fails, to reproduce the lines; the result is the shimmering effect.

The solution for this is to anti-alias any fine lines—lines thinner than two or three pixels. Anti-aliasing here simply means blurring. To anti-alias graphics that appear on a TV screen, use the Photoshop Gaussian Blur filter to blur the whole image at 0.5 pixels. The image looks fuzzy on the computer screen, but looks just right on TV. You can practice using the Gaussian Blur filter in Project 3-1 at the end of this chapter.

Designing for Television Color Colors on a television screen are much less saturated than colors on monitors. Most saturated colors—especially red, but also yellow and green—are too intense for a television screen. They distort and appear to bleed, causing unwanted effects. To reduce the saturation of colors for television screens, use the NTSC Colors filter in Photoshop.

To reduce the saturation of colors for television screens:

1. In Photoshop, open the **image** you want to modify.
2. Click **Filters** on the menu bar.
3. Point to **Video**, and then click **NTSC Colors**.

   The colors seem muddy when you view the image on your computer screen, but they will look fine on a TV.

Designing for NTSC Standards In the United States, parameters for output on a television must meet National Television Standards Committee (NTSC) standards. NTSC is also known as the American system. Most other countries use the Phase Alternation Line (PAL) system or the Sequential Coleur Avec Memoir (SECAM) system. NTSC standards were instituted in the 1950s. NTSC uses 60 fields per second and 525 lines per field. The other two systems are improvements on the NTSC system and were standardized in the 1960s. Because of the different electric current used overseas, PAL and SECAM use only 50 fields per second, but 625 lines per field. Therefore, European and Asian video has more resolution on every video frame than American video.

High-definition televisions (HDTV) systems offer even more resolution. Each system has a different resolution and color palette. The NTSC system is the oldest and most restrictive, so images that are edited for NTSC usually look good on the other systems as well.

Designing for Printers

Although no one uses a printer to surf the Web, many users print Web pages that contain a lot of text. On a printed Web page, the quality of elements such as navigation bars is not important. However, figures that accompany the text do need to be clear, as do logos and any advertisements. The main difference between an image displayed on a monitor and one that has been printed is the color system used. While monitors use RGB color, printers break primary colors into CMYK color space and use separate inks for cyan, magenta, yellow, and black. Because printers use different primary colors, and because printer inks have different limitations than the phosphors in a monitor, Web graphics often look different after being printed.

To preview what an image will look like when printed:

1. In Photoshop, open the **image** you want to preview.

2. Click **View** on the menu bar.

3. Point to **Proof Setup**, and then click **CMYK**.

   The image appears as it will when printed on a color printer. Most colors appear darker, especially blues and greens. Reds appear more orange, and magentas and cyans can appear washed out.

The CMYK preview simulates printer output, but does not exactly match what you see when you print the image. Monitors can display only 24-bit color, which means about 16.7 million available colors. Printers use four primaries and are capable of 32-bit color, which is equal to 4,294,967,296 (over four billion) possible colors.

Printers also can dither images regardless of how you optimized them. What was an area of pale color might show up on paper as a few stray pixels. To solve this problem, avoid using very pale colors on important images such as site logos.

Figure 3-3 shows a Web graphic as it appears on screen and on paper with different, dithered colors.

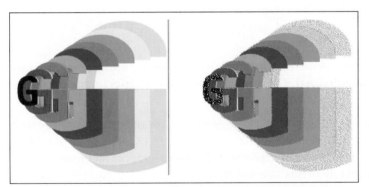

An image as seen on a computer screen

The same image, when printed, shows dithering and uses different colors

Figure 3-3   A Web graphic as it appears on screen and on paper

Considering Operating Systems

Most Web surfers use some version of Windows, such as Windows 95, 98, or 2000. According to WebSideStory's *Statmarket.com*, in June 2000, 93.6% of Internet users worldwide used a version of Microsoft Windows. Less than 5% use Macintosh, and an even smaller number use another type of operating system such as Linux or BeOS. Based on these findings, you should always design with a Windows audience in mind. This can be difficult, because if you're like most designers and graphic artists, you probably use Macintosh computers. Regardless of which system you use, be sure to preview your work in multiple environments.

The main difference between how Windows and Macintosh computers display graphics is that colors appear darker on Windows. The Windows operating system uses a lower **gamma** than Macintosh to display colors. Gamma refers to the point of middle-gray in a color system. This makes primary colors (reds, greens, and blues) appear richer on Windows than on Macintosh, and makes secondary colors (cyans, magentas, and yellows) appear richer on Macintosh than on Windows.

To see the difference in how Macintosh and Windows computers display colors:

1. In Photoshop, open an **image** file.

2. Click **View** on the menu bar.

3. Point to **Proof Setup**, and then click either **Macintosh RGB** or **Windows RGB** to see how the image appears on the different systems.

The other key difference in systems is how Macintosh and Windows PCs display text size. Macs display text about a third smaller than PCs. Mac text that appears about .5" tall appears about .75" tall on Windows.

As shown in Figure 3-4, text on a Windows computer (top) appears large and the primary colors are emphasized. On a Mac (bottom), primaries and secondaries are given equal weight and text is small.

As a designer, you might spend weeks preparing pages on your Mac, only to be shocked when you see how different they look on a Windows PC. The text differences are more of a concern to developers and producers than to graphic designers, though graphic labels and other text elements also are affected.

In general, design for Windows users, because they account for about 90% of your users.

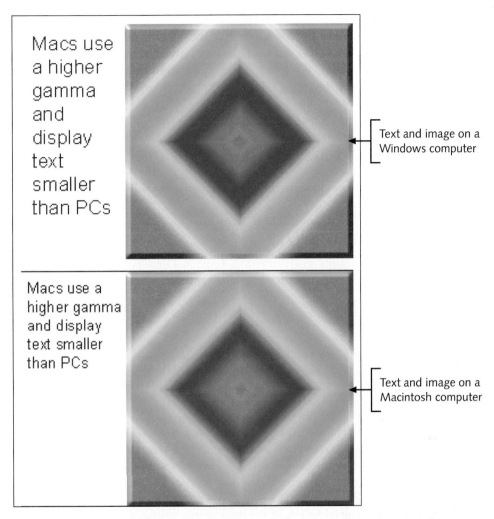

Figure 3-4   Text and colors as they appear on Windows and Macintosh systems

Considering Browsers

Just as the Microsoft operating system dominates the platform market, its Web client, Internet Explorer, also dominates the browser market. According to WebSideStory's *Statmarket.com*, in June 2000, 86.1% of Internet users worldwide used a version of Microsoft Internet Explorer. Its closest competitor is Netscape Navigator, which once was used by a majority of Web users, but now is used by less than 20%. Other brands of Web browsers represent an insignificant percentage of users.

The two main browsers display Web pages differently, but these differences all involve interpreting and rendering HyperText Markup Language (HTML). There is no significant difference in how they display graphics. However, the one difference you need to be aware of is how they display HTML colors. Almost any color you define in HTML might appear slightly darker in one browser than in another. In fact, of all 16+ million colors possible in the 24-bit RGB color space, only 216 are guaranteed to appear the same in both browsers. These colors make up the Web-safe color palette and are the subject of the next section. In truth, these 216 colors are not absolutely certain to appear the same in both Netscape and Explorer. Even different versions of Explorer can display these colors with slight differences. In general, however, if you use colors from the Web-safe color palette, your images will look the same regardless of the browser used.

Defining Color on the Web

Web graphics are simply grids of colored pixels. They have no actual edges or textures, and the appearance of images is controlled entirely by varying the colors in the pixels. To create and use Web graphics, then, requires a thorough understanding of how people see color as well as how it is created and used on the Web.

Every color is a mixture of different amounts of red, green, and blue. For Web graphics, colors are defined in a special syntax called hexadecimal notation. In this section you will learn basic color theory and how to define colors on the Web.

Understanding Color Theory

You probably have worked with primary colors before. With paint, the primary colors are red, yellow, and blue. From these three paint primaries, you can create nearly any color. Initially it's easiest to create the three secondary colors: red and yellow make orange, yellow and blue make green, and red and blue make purple. You can then make more subtle shades by adjusting the amounts of the component colors. This is how colors are created on computer screens as well, although the primaries used are not the same as they are with paint.

There are a few differences between painting on canvas and defining colors on a computer screen. These differences are discussed in the following sections.

Using Additive Versus Subtractive Colors

With paint, you apply a color directly to a white canvas or piece of paper. Each color you add darkens the color value. The orange you create by mixing red and yellow is darker than either component color, as shown in Figure 3-5. If you mix all the colors, you create a color that is nearly black. This method of color mixing is known as **subtractive color** because each additional color lessens the lightness of the final color.

3

 When mixing all colors, you don't create true black because the pigments in paint are not true colors. Instead, paint pigments rely on chemicals and metals that only approximate what our eyes see as pure colors.

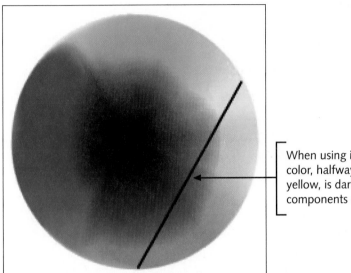

When using inks or paint, the orange color, halfway between pure red and pure yellow, is darker than either of the components colors

Figure 3-5   Paint uses subtractive color

With paint, you create new colors by mixing primary colors together. As more colors are added, the resulting color becomes darker. Computers also create new colors by mixing primary colors. However, as more primary colors are added in a computer graphic, the resulting color becomes lighter. Unlike paints, which generate colors through pigments, computer screens create color with light. A computer monitor shines a color on the screen, and each addition of color brightens the value of the overall color. This is known as **additive color**. Adding no color leaves a dark screen, and adding all colors makes the screen white. On a computer screen, the secondary colors are twice as bright as the primary colors, while with paints the secondary colors are half as bright, as shown in Figure 3-6.

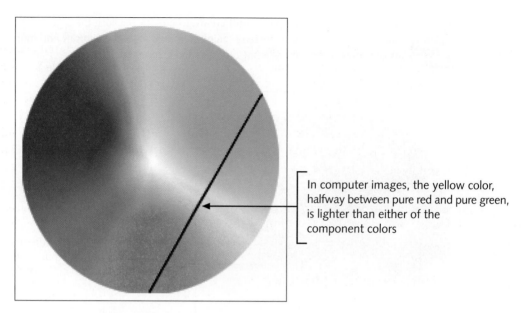

In computer images, the yellow color, halfway between pure red and pure green, is lighter than either of the component colors

Figure 3-6   Computer images use additive color

Using Different Primary Colors

The methods of mixing colors for paint and pixels are different, and so are the primaries they use. For paint, the primaries are red, yellow, and blue, while for pixels they are red, green, and blue. Theoretically, almost any three colors can be used as primaries, as long as they are spaced evenly around the color wheel. As mentioned earlier, most printers use the CMYK color system, which has cyan, magenta, yellow, and black as primaries. However, cyan, magenta, and yellow are usually regarded as secondary colors in computer graphics.

Just as red and blue make magenta on your monitor, cyan and magenta also can make blue on a printer. In both cases, mixing two colors generates a third color which appears between them on the color wheel. Green can be used as a primary in paints, but if you mix it with red, trying to make yellow, you create a very dark shade of yellow. The yellow is only half as bright as the green and the red used to make it. Paints rely on red, yellow, and blue because of the subtractive nature of mixing colors with paint. Because the color darkens with every addition of color, you need to start with the brightest colors you can. Yellow is the brightest color our eyes can see so it makes sense to use that as a primary when using paint. However, yellow is not inherently brighter than other colors. It is only because of the sensitivities of our eyes and brains that yellow appears so bright. The way people see colors affects how color is used in graphics.

Understanding the Human Eye

A computer screen's primary colors more closely approximate the natural primaries that our eyes use. In the backs of our eyes, the retina senses light. The retina is a membrane composed of several layers, including one layer that contains rods and cones. The long, thin rods are sensitive to white light. The cones are sensitive to three colors: red, green, and blue. Our eyes work like a computer monitor: when there is no light, we see black. When we see combinations of colored light, different cones are stimulated and we see the combined color. For example, when we see yellow light (either emitted from a light source, or reflected from a yellow surface) the red-sensitive cones and the green-sensitive cones are stimulated together, telling our brain that we are seeing yellow.

Design often seems arbitrary. Beauty is said to be in the eye of the beholder. In fact, much of what looks good or bad is based on the physical structures of our eyes and brains.

Using Complementary Colors

Retina cones work in pairs. Some cones detect either red or green. This is why there is no reddish-green or greenish-red, and also why red and green are **complementary** colors. Complementary colors are opposite each other on the color wheel, stimulate completely different parts of the retina, and have high contrast when seen together. The complementary color for blue is yellow, which results when the retina's red- and green-sensitive areas are stimulated. Blue text against a yellow background is much easier to read than blue text against a purple background, for example.

Blue and purple are **analogous** colors. Analogous colors are near each other on the color wheel, stimulate similar areas of the retina, and have low contrast when seen together. Orange, red, and pink also are analogous colors. Recall that mixing two primaries creates secondary colors. Mixing primaries and secondaries creates **tertiary** colors. Tertiary colors are analogous to the adjacent primary and secondary colors. Figure 3-7 shows complementary and analogous colors.

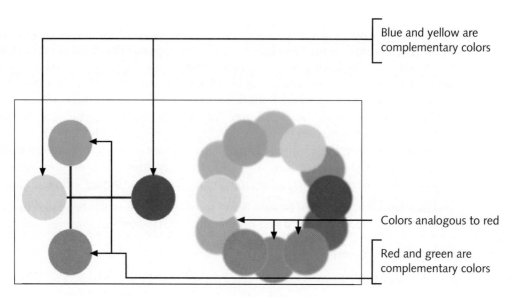

Figure 3-7   Complementary and analogous colors

The red and green retina cones are more sensitive than the blue cones, so blue is usually seen as a darker color. Even if the amount of blue light is the same as other colors, we see it darker because our eyes are less sensitive to blue than to red or green. This also explains why secondary colors appear brighter than primary colors in computer images. Yellow, for example, stimulates both red and green in the retina: In fact, it stimulates them twice as much as red or green alone. Because we are more sensitive to red and green than to blue, the mixture of red and green (yellow) appears brighter than the mixture of red and blue (magenta) or the mixture of green and blue (cyan).

When you design and position graphics in Web pages, be aware of whether the colors are analogous and have low contrast with each other, or whether they are complementary and appear bright. If you want colors to stand out, use them with a background that has complementary colors.

Understanding RGB Color

In a computer's RGB color system, each primary color has a channel, and each channel can take a value. Combining the channels determines the color. For example, 0% Red, 0% Green, and 0% Blue creates black, while 100% Red, 100% Green, and 100% Blue creates white.

Imagine that each of the three color channels could only be 0% or 100%; that is, only on or off. Then each color has two possible states, or only one bit of information is associated with each color. Because a computer has three color channels, with one bit per channel, it creates a 3-bit color system ($2^3 = 8$), providing eight possible colors.

Table 3-1 Colors created by combining the three primary colors

Possible colors	Red channel	Green channel	Blue channel
Black	0% – off	0% – off	0% – off
Red	100% – on	0% – off	0% – off
Yellow	100% – on	100% – on	0% – off
Green	0% – off	100% – on	0% – off
Cyan	0% – off	100% – on	100% – on
Blue	0% – off	0% – off	100% – on
Magenta	100% – on	0% – off	100% – on
White	100% – on	100% – on	100% – on

If a computer allotted four bits of color information per pixel, you would have 2^4, or 16 possible colors. In fact, the standard Windows palette is a 4-bit color system.

Eight bits per pixel provides 8-bit color, or 256 colors, and 24-bit color provides eight bits per color channel. Three channels provides 16,777,216 possible colors (2^8 Red, 2^8 Green, and 2^8 Blue gives 2^{8*3}, which equals 2^{24}).

Understanding the Color Cube

You can visualize any color system as a cube. Each of the eight corners is made up of a primary color, a secondary color, black, or white, as shown in Figure 3-8.

Figure 3-8   An 8-color cube

Now suppose that instead of just on and off, you could indicate different levels of color for each of your three primaries. Instead of just 0% or 100%, you could allow each color to have gradations of value in 20% increments. If each color were 0%, 20%, 40%, 60%,

80%, or 100%, then you would have six possible states for each channel. Three channels each with six possible states can combine into 216 colors. Just as two states for three colors gives $2^3 = 8$ colors, six states for three colors gives $6^3 = 216$ colors. These colors are known as the Web-safe color palette.

In this system, you can combine different values of colors. For example, 100% (or full) red, 0% green, and 0% blue yields pure red, and 100% red, 100% green, and 0% blue yields pure yellow. To create orange, which is between red and yellow, you need to lower the amount of green. For example, 100% red, 60% green, and 0% blue yields a yellowish orange; reducing green further allows red to dominate the color.

Figure 3-9 shows how full red with no green or blue results in pure red. Full red with full green and no blue results in pure yellow, and full red with 60% green and no blue results in a yellowish orange.

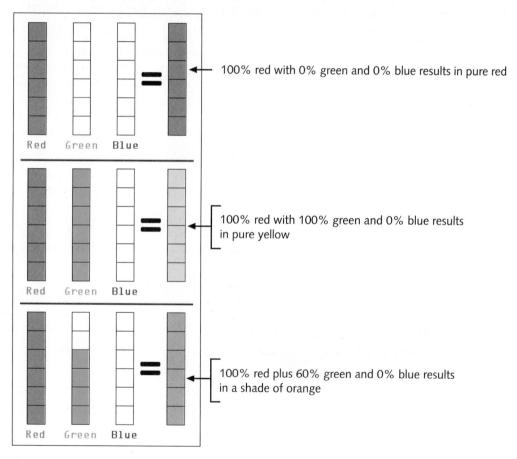

Red   Green   Blue

100% red with 0% green and 0% blue results in pure red

Red   Green   Blue

100% red with 100% green and 0% blue results in pure yellow

Red   Green   Blue

100% red plus 60% green and 0% blue results in a shade of orange

Figure 3-9   Mixing primaries to create different colors

Using Hexadecimal Notation

Often you do not know the percentage of color per channel, but you do know the value compared to 255. There are 256 colors per channel, but for HTML colors, the counting starts at zero, so the entire scale is from 0–255. A value of 0 for each channel yields black, while a value of 255 for each channel yields white.

Some software describes the relative amounts of the three primaries as percentages, as described in the previous Using the Color Cube section. On the Web, however, you need to use hexadecimal notation because a percent system cannot represent all the colors when each channel has 256 possible values.

To specify colors in HTML, you use a special syntax known as hexadecimal notation. Colors defined this way always have six characters and look like random series of numbers and letters, such as #0c48fb or # e62a15. However, hexadecimal notation is a system of highly ordered regular numbers that are easy to understand and use once you are familiar with their structure.

To understand a hexadecimal color, first break it down into three pairs. Each pair of numbers defines one RGB color channel. For example, in the number #048cfb, "04" defines the red value of the color and is equivalent to a value of 4 out of 256 when looking at the Color Picker dialog box in Photoshop. The hexadecimal value "8c" defines the green value and is equal to a value of 140 out of the 256 colors in the green color channel. The value "fb" defines the blue value and is equal to 251.

Counting systems each have a base number at which the counting repeats. The simplest base is base 1, where you use tick marks to indicate numbers. Base 2 is used in computer memory, where each unit has one of two values, 0 or 1. Hexadecimal means that the counting system is base 16.

Bases less than 10 simply eliminate certain digits from counting. In octal notation, which uses eight as the base, once the counting passes seven, you start counting again. Bases larger than 10, however, present counting problems, because there are not enough digits to express numbers such as 11, 12, and so on, in these bases. Bases larger than 10 use letters to express values greater than 10. Because the digits 1 and 0 (10) equal the value 16 in base 16, you need another character for the value of 10; hexadecimal notation uses the character A. For 11, it uses B, for 12 it uses C, and so on until 16. At that point the digits move to 16 and the counting starts again at 10, which is equivalent to 16 in decimal notation.

In base 10, the ones column repeats every 10 numbers. In base 16, the ones column repeats every 16 numbers. Table 3-2 shows equivalent values for three different counting systems: octal, decimal, and hexadecimal.

Table 3-2   Equivalent values for different counting systems

Base 8 — octal	Base 10 — decimal	Base 16 — hexadecimal
0	0	0
1	1	1
2	2	2
3	3	3
4	4	4
5	5	5
6	6	6
7	7	7
10	8	8
11	9	9
12	10	A
13	11	B
14	12	C
15	13	D
16	14	E
17	15	F
20	16	10
21	17	11
22	18	12
23	19	13
24	20	14
25	21	15
26	22	16
27	23	17
30	24	18
31	25	19
32	26	1A
33	27	1B
34	28	1C
35	29	1D
36	30	1E
37	31	1F
40	32	20
41	33	21
42	34	22

To use hexadecimal notation to describe the 255 Web colors, you need to know the relative values of red, green, and blue, and convert the values to hexadecimal.

Figure 3-10 shows a color that is 20% red, 80% green, and 60% blue. In hexadecimal, this is expressed as #33CC99. (Interpreting this number is explained below.) The number #33CC99 represents a Web-safe color because all values are in 20% increments, such as 0%, 20%, 40%, 60%, 80%, or 100%. In hexadecimal notation, these values translate to: 00, 33, 66, 99, CC, and FF, respectively. The case does not matter; cc is the same as CC.

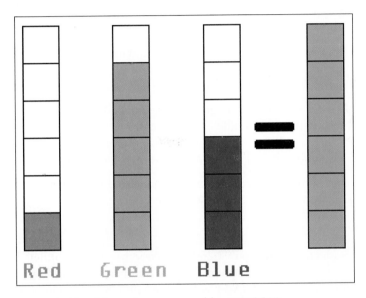

Figure 3-10   The color expressed by #33CC99

A good way to practice adding colors together is with the Color Picker dialog box in Photoshop. You can combine different values for red, green, and blue to generate different hexadecimal colors.

Each primary color has six Web-safe values that can be represented as percentages, fractions of 255, or as hexadecimal numbers. Table 3-3 shows the equivalent color values for the three common units: percentages, decimals between 0 and 255, and hexadecimals between 0 and FF.

Table 3-3   Equivalent Web-safe color values for different units

Percentages	Out of 255	Hexadecimal
0%	0	00
20%	51	33
40%	102	66
60%	153	99
80%	204	CC
100%	255	FF

To interpret a hexadecimal color value such as #1f6d9c, start with the first value. In this example, 1f is the red value, which is 31 in decimal, and under 20% of 255, which is 51. That means the red value for this color is low.

The middle two digits—6d—represent the green value. This value is higher than 66 (hex) or 102 (decimal), which is 40% of 255. The color therefore is 40% green. The blue value, 9C, is higher than 99 (hex) or 153 (decimal), which is 60% of 255. You can then determine that the color has almost no red, 40% green, and 60% blue—a gray-greenish blue.

 The pound sign (#) often precedes hexadecimal numbers. The pound sign is an optional notation indicating a numerical value.

Interpret another hexadecimal value: #F93C60. The easiest way to decipher the color is to round each number pair to its nearest hexadecimal number. Break it down into pairs: F9 - 3C - 60, and round to the nearest Web-safe values: FF - 33 - 66. The values are the same as 100% red, 20% green, and 40% blue, or red with a shot of hot pink. These color additions are shown in Figure 3-11. Remember that color mixing on the Web is additive, so by taking full red and adding a little green and blue, the result is a lighter color than the full red alone.

3

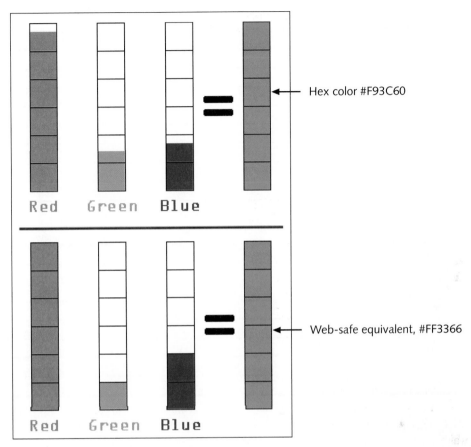

Hex color #F93C60

Web-safe equivalent, #FF3366

Figure 3-11 Hexadecimal color #F93C60 and its nearest Web-safe equivalent, #FF3366

The complete chart of all Web-safe colors and their hexadecimal codes is in the Appendix.

Using Color Names

Many people have trouble thinking of colors in terms of numbers, and prefer to use color names as much as possible. You can use names to identify colors in a browser, but not all will work. Netscape understands more names than Internet Explorer, including names such as papayawhip and darkgoldenrod (both are shades of yellow). However, Internet Explorer interprets the individual letters in names as hexadecimal characters, and produces colors other than what you intend. If you do use names, use the names of colors that both browsers understand. Only the 16 most common color names are understood by all browsers. These color names and their associated hexadecimal values are shown in Tables 3-4 and 3-5.

Table 3-4   The eight Web-safe color names

Color Name	Hexadecimal Value
Black	000000
Red	FF0000
Yellow	FFFF00
Lime	00FF00
Cyan, aqua	00FFFF
Blue	0000FF
Magenta, fuschia	FF00FF
White	FFFFFF

Table 3-5   The eight non-Web-safe color names

Gray	808080
Maroon	800000
Olive	808000
Green	008000
Teal	008080
Navy	000080
Purple	800080
Silver	C0C0C0

Using Web-Safe Colors

While #1F6D9C and #F93C60 are not Web-safe colors, they still appear properly in most environments. With blocks of solid color, such as backgrounds, the browser displays the closest approximation for the color. This approximation is different in different browsers, however. If you use a color with an intermediate value such as 80, one browser might round down to 66, and another might round up to 99. With images, the browser might also dither the non–Web-safe colors to approximate the colors.

Photoshop allows you to save images with the Web-safe color palette. This shifts all colors in the existing palette to the nearest Web-safe equivalent. However, you do not have to save images with the Web palette to have them appear in a browser. In fact, if you do, the image will probably become heavily banded. As with any color-reduction method, high-color images with color gradients tend to look distorted when reduced to the Web-safe palette.

The best time to use Web-safe colors is when you want to display an image on a colored background. The background color of the page and the background color of the image must both be the same Web-safe color, or the boundary between image background and page background might be visible. When you use Web-safe colors, the colored background of an image matches the background color of the page. Figure 3-12 shows an image displayed on a colored background. Both background colors are set to the same non–Web-safe color. The browser displays the two colors differently, and the seam between them becomes visible.

Figure 3-12   An image on a colored background using non-Web-safe colors

CONTROLLING WEB GRAPHICS WITH HTML

As a graphic artist, you can accomplish most of your HTML coding with a **what you see is what you get (WYSIWYG)** editor. To really understand page layout, however, and appreciate what the editor does for you, you need to understand the HTML code itself. You can use a number of markup languages to create Web pages. The most common is HTML, but you also need to be aware of CSS (Cascading Style Sheets), CSS-P (Cascading Style Sheets-Positioning), and XML (Extensible Markup Language).

As a graphics professional, you probably only need to know HTML. An HTML tag can have up to four types of elements. The basic structure of a tag is:

<TAG ATTRIBUTE="value"></TAG>

- The **tag** itself is surrounded by angle brackets and tells the browser to place something on the page. The image tag is written as <IMG>.

- Most text formatting tags require closing tags to indicate what text is being affected. The IMG tag, however, does not require a closing tag.

- The **attributes** are placed within the angle brackets after the tag name. You can have many attributes in one tag, and the order of attributes does not matter. Some of the attributes of the IMG tag are SRC, WIDTH, and BORDER.

- Most attributes have **values**, surrounded by quotation marks. For example, in the HTML code <IMG SRC="myImage.jpg">, SRC is the attribute and myImage.jpg is the value. Browsers usually treat the quotation marks as optional, meaning they understand the HTML whether or not you include them. However, future browsers are expected to require them, so it is good practice to always include quotation marks around values.

- The case of HTML tags does not matter. The tags and attributes can be written in uppercase or lowercase. (In these examples, tags and attributes are written in uppercase to aid readability). Filenames, however, are an exception. Some servers require the image filename and the value of the SRC attribute to match exactly, or they will not display the image.

Choosing HTML Editors

You have a few options for generating the HTML you need to make pages and display your images on the Web. Most Web production teams include a producer who is responsible for page layout, but graphic designers also often create Web pages. A popular tool you will likely use to create Web pages is a WYSIWYG editor such as Dreamweaver.

Using WYSIWYG HTML Editors

WYSIWYG refers to software with an interface that resembles the final output. A word-processing program is essentially a WYSIWYG text editor, because what you see on the screen is similar to what you get when the document is printed. Bold text appears in boldface on the screen, and different fonts and sizes appear on screen as they appear on paper. Plain HTML typically works differently. Text that appears in bold in a browser appears as plain text surrounded by bold tags in an HTML document. You can insert these tags by typing them in a text editor, or you can use software that lets you lay out pages without having to learn HTML. Although it is sometimes easier to learn to use a WYSIWYG editor than to learn all the HTML tags, the editors do not allow the same control as hand-coding HTML.

Most Web graphic artists and designers use the Macintosh as their OS, Netscape as their browser, and Dreamweaver as their HTML editor. The disadvantage to this setup is that these designers rarely see their work in the same way that most of their audience does. The majority of their audience uses a different operating system and browser. The advantage to this conflict is that it usually results in better cross-platform products. Web graphic artists and designers could primarily use Microsoft Windows as the OS, Internet Explorer as the browser, and FrontPage as the HTML editor. Because Microsoft tools work together in ways that tools from disparate companies cannot, Web pages developed with this approach are not as compatible in non-Microsoft environments. The major criticism of FrontPage is that it sometimes creates pages that work when viewed on Windows with Internet Explorer but don't lay out properly on other systems.

Using Straight Text Editors

Web purists claim that only hand-edited HTML code is good enough for creating Web pages, and for complex layouts they are correct. Even the best WYSIWYG editors cannot create code as clean or layout as pixel-perfect as you can with a text editor. A text editor is a program that edits only **ASCII text**. ASCII text is the list of 256 basic characters used in computer files. ASCII text includes all uppercase and lowercase letters, digits, punctuation marks, and various European letters. It does not include information about font or size.

You can use text editors to write programs in C or Java, and to write code in JavaScript, Cascading Style Sheets, XML, HTML, or just about any other computer language. Unlike word processors, which add hidden characters that format the text, text editors require you to explicitly state formatting code, usually in the form of tags. Most developers who code HTML by hand use Windows Notepad. The most popular commercial text editor for Mac users is BBEdit.

Using an HTML Converter Application

An HTML converter is a program that allows you to format text and add graphics in one application, and then converts the entire document to a Web page. Microsoft Word is the most common HTML converter; it allows you to save any Word document as HTML.

Converters often add unnecessary tags and characters to Web pages, resulting in pages that take longer to load than necessary. Converted pages also usually have poor layouts, with gaps between images and misplaced elements. Until converter applications overcome these weaknesses, use HTML converters only as a last resort, when no other tool is available.

Whether you use an HTML editor or code by hand, you need to be familiar with the HTML tags, including IMG and TABLE, used to display images in Web pages. These tags and their common attributes are discussed in the following sections.

Using the IMG Tag

The HTML tag used most often to add graphics to Web pages is the image tag: <IMG>. Though most HTML tags require a closing tag, <IMG> does not. This tag controls how images appear by using a variety of attributes, which are discussed in the following sections. Images can stand alone or be used as links. To use an image as a link, place an anchor tag, <A> and /<A>, around the image tag, as in the following code:

```
<A HREF="page2.html"><IMG SRC="myImage.jpg"></A>
```

This displays the image myImage.jpg and links it to page2.html.

Once a browser loads an image, it does not need to load the image again. Every file requested by the browser (whether HTML code, images, java, and so on) is stored in the browser's **cache** directory. The cache is a folder of previously viewed files that can be reused without retrieving them again from the server.

The advantage to caching is evident when you use the same image more than once. The first time the image is used, it is downloaded from the server, but each successive time it is accessed from the browser's cache, significantly reducing the time it takes to display the image.

For example, if you have a logo in the upper-left of every page, the logo image is loaded from the server only the first time the user visits a page. As the user visits additional pages, only the new images are loaded from the server.

The effect produced by the IMG tag is controlled by the following attributes: SRC, LOWSRC, WIDTH, HEIGHT, HSPACE, VSPACE, ALIGN, ALT, and BORDER. These attributes are described in the following sections.

Defining an Image with the SRC Attribute

The source attribute SRC tells the browser where to retrieve the image file. This is the only attribute required by the <IMG> tag. The value of the SRC tag includes the file path and the filename. The file path is the list of folders leading to the filename. A file path can be **relative** to the HTML file that contains the reference, or it can be **absolute**, meaning it is relative only to the root directory of the Web server. For example, <IMG SRC="images/new/myImage.jpg"> tells the browser to find a folder called images in the same folder as the HTML file. The browser finds a folder called new in the images folder, and then finds the file named myImage.jpg. The file path images/new/myImage.jpg is relative to the HTML file that contains the tag.

 The word directory is interchangeable with the word folder.

An example of an absolute file path is: <IMG SRC="/httpd/images/new/myImage.jpg">. In this case, the forward slash (/) at the beginning of the path indicates that the path is absolute, or relative only to the root directory. The reference is the same as in the other example, except the path begins at the root rather than at the HTML file's location.

For a path that travels up the directory tree, rather than down, use the following notation: ../(period, period, slash). This tells the browser to look in the parent directory of the current location. For example, <IMG SRC="../httpd/images/new/myImage.jpg"> tells the browser to look up one directory, then back down to httpd, then to the images directory, to the new directory, and then find the file.

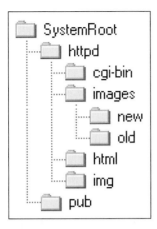

Figure 3-13   A sample directory structure

You also can indicate an absolute file path. This means the path is relative to the server root. The server root is the point from which all Web file paths originate. In the structure in Figure 3-13, the server root is the directory called httpd. Anything in the pub directory will not show up on a Web browser. The server root is different from the system root, which is the bottom-level directory on the server that contains all other directories.

Defining an Alternate Image with the LOWSRC Attribute

A Web page with large images might appear slowly as the browser waits for the images to load from the server. To solve this problem, you can use the low-source attribute LOWSRC. You can use LOWSRC to load a smaller version of an image first; that image is then replaced with the normal version. If you have an image of 120K, for example, you might not want the browser to wait. You can create a low-quality 2K version and set the LOWSRC attribute to show that version, as in the following code.

```
<IMG SRC="high-color.jpg" LOWSRC="low-color.gif">
```

The low-quality image loads first, then the rest of the page, and finally the high-quality version. You can use any image for the LOWSRC image.

Controlling Image Dimensions with the WIDTH and HEIGHT Attributes

You can specify the size of the image display with the WIDTH and HEIGHT attributes. If you want a 10 × 10 pixel image to appear as 36 × 72, you would use the following code:

```
<IMG SRC="myImage.jpg" WIDTH="36" HEIGHT="72">
```

However, browsers do not interpolate pixels the way image editors do. Using the code above, you end up with a blocky, pixelated version of the original. Figure 3-14 shows how using HTML to stretch an image results in jagged edges.

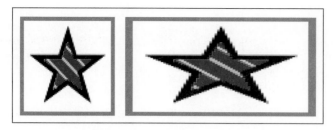

Figure 3-14   Stretching an image with HTML

You also can use percentages as widths. Setting the width to 100% stretches the image to the right of the browser window.

In general, you should always include the height and width attributes and set them to the actual size of the image. The browser displays the page more quickly if it already knows the dimensions of the images.

Creating Thumbnail Images Using WIDTH and HEIGHT Attributes   You also can force the image to appear smaller than its actual size by using smaller values for the height and width. If the original image is 640 × 480, for example, you can show a **thumbnail** version of the image. Thumbnails are small versions of a larger image, and usually are used as links to the full-size image. Thumbnails are discussed in detail in the Creating Thumbnail Galleries chapter.

One way to use thumbnails is to create small duplicates of every file, and then use those duplicates as links to the larger images. The other way is to use the large images themselves as the links, but scale them down with the height and width attributes.

To use duplicated thumbnails as links, you must create additional graphics for each thumbnail. When you use scaled thumbnails as links, all of the full-size images have to load completely even though you are using them only as buttons. However, once the images are loaded, they do not have to load again and they appear immediately when requested.

To illustrate the difference, imagine you have a gallery of 20 images, each one around 125K. If you make a 5K thumbnail version of each image, your gallery page has 100K (20 images at 5K) worth of graphics and loads in a few seconds on most modems. As each full-size image is requested, it is loaded from the server.

If your thumbnails are not small images, but are scaled-down versions of the actual images, the thumbnail page has 2,500K (125K × 20 images) worth of graphics to download. This takes a significant amount of time, even on fast connections. However, once all the thumbnails are loaded, the full-size images do not need to be loaded again because they are really the same images.

In general, small duplicates of images used as thumbnails provide quicker user access than pages with scaled down images.

Adjusting Image Margins with the HSPACE and VSPACE Attributes

You control the margins around images with the HSPACE (horizontal space) and VSPACE (vertical space) attributes. The values for these attributes are numbers which tell the browser how many pixels to pad around the image. Following is a line of HTML code using the HSPACE and VSPACE attributes:

```
<IMG SRC="myImage.jpg" HSPACE="5" VSPACE="0">
```

In this example, the browser pads 5 pixels on both sides of the image, and does not pad the top or bottom.

Positioning Images with the ALIGN Attribute

You use the ALIGN attribute to control where the image is positioned relative to the other elements. By default, an image appears with its bottom aligned to the baseline of adjacent text. You also can set this attribute to several different values:

- *Top*: Sets the top of the image to the top of the adjacent text
- *Bottom*: Sets the bottom of the image to the baseline of the adjacent text
- *Center or Middle*: Centers the image (Netscape and IE display centered images differently.)
- *Right and Left*: Positions the image on the right or left side of the browser window and allows adjacent text to wrap around the image

In Figure 3-15 the top image is not aligned and has a margin of 0 pixels, set by the HSPACE and VSPACE attributes. The middle image is left-aligned and has a margin of 5 pixels. The bottom image is right-aligned and has a margin of 10 pixels.

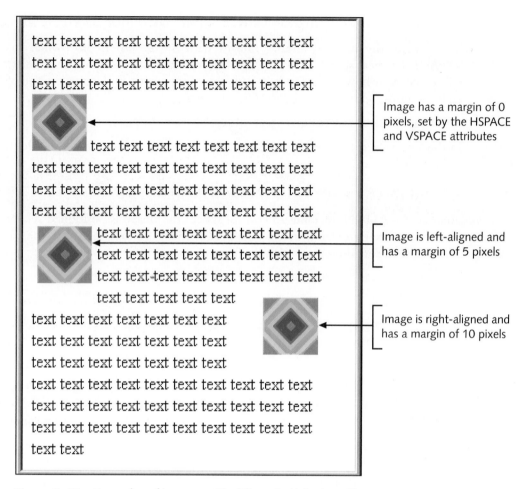

Figure 3-15   Examples of images with different attribute settings

Defining Alternate Text with the ALT Attribute

The value of the ALT attribute is that text appears when the image does not. Even after the image loads, the ALT text appears when the user points to the image. It is good practice to always include alternate text attributes in image tags.

ALT attributes can contain spaces and punctuation marks, as in the following example:

```
<IMG SRC="myImage.jpg" ALT="Drawing number 1">
```

The users who benefit from ALT attributes are:

- People who use text-only browsers such as Lynx
- People who have turned off image loading in their browsers to speed page loads

- People with slow connections and browsers that time out before all images are loaded

- Visually impaired users who use text-to-speech software to read Web pages

Another benefit of ALT attributes is that some search engines read them when deciding whether and how to index the page. Using the ALT attribute improves your site's ranking.

Setting the Image Border with the BORDER Attribute

Use the BORDER attribute to set a border for images you use as links. The default surrounds the image with a colored border equal to the LINK attribute set in the BODY tag (usually blue). You can turn off the default border by setting the BORDER attribute to 0, as in the following example:

```
<IMG SRC="myImage.jpg" BORDER="0">
```

Using the TABLE Tag for Layout

The table tag was originally intended only for the display of tabular data. Having no other method, developers began using tables to lay out Web pages as well. The version of Cascading Style Sheets called Cascading Style Sheets-Positioning (CSS-P, also referred to as layers) was the intended structure for layout, but even the newest browsers still do not support layers and positioning.

The TABLE tag encloses rows, defined by TR tags. Table rows enclose table delimiters (called table cells), defined by TD tags. All three tags can use the BGCOLOR attribute, which takes a hexadecimal color to define the background color, as in the following example:

```
<TABLE> <TR> <TD BACKGROUND="FF0000">top</TD> </TR> <TR>
<TD>bottom</TD> </TR> </TABLE>
```

This HTML code defines a table with two rows and one cell in each row. The top row has a red background.

The TABLE tag can take a number of other attributes. The following three attributes affect the spacing of elements:

- The value of the BORDER attribute sets the width of the bevel on the ridge that surrounds the table and separates the table cells. Setting the value to 0 removes the bevel.

- The value of the CELLSPACING attribute sets the width of the border between cells.

- The value of the CELLPADDING attribute sets the width between the border and the contents in the table cells.

Figure 3-16 shows two tables with two rows of two cells each. The table on the left uses the default values for BORDER, CELLSPACING, and CELLPADDING. This results in gaps between the images. The table on the right has all three attributes set to 0. This positions the images next to each other without margins.

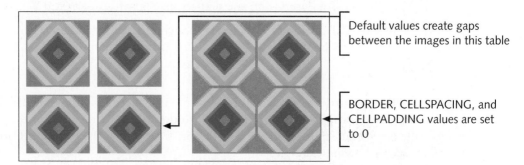

Figure 3-16   Images positioned in tables with and without margins

Using tables to lay out graphics is covered in the "Creating Splash Screens" chapter. For more information on table layout, see Joel Sklar's *Principles of Web Design.*[1]

AVOIDING COMMON MISTAKES

It's easy to include images in a Web page, but sometimes the images don't appear. The problem is that not all Web servers and browsers display images the same way; what looks good on your system might not load at all on another. The trick is to use HTML and filename conventions that are common to all systems and browsers. The following sections cover the solutions to the most common errors beginners make when using graphics in their Web pages.

Avoiding Unrecognized Characters in a Filename

When you save an image in an image editor such as Adobe Photoshop, avoid using unrecognized characters, including spaces, slashes, and apostrophes, so the Web server interprets the complete filename correctly. Most other punctuation marks also cause problems. In general, it's safest to use only uppercase and lowercase letters, numbers, and underscores.

Avoiding Spaces

It's often convenient to use a long, descriptive name such as My favorite picture.jpg, but the Web server stops reading the filename at the space. It then looks for a file called My. The solution for this problem is to use underscores (_) instead of spaces, as in My_favorite_picture.jpg.

---

[1] Sklar, Joel. 2000. *Principles of Web Design.* Boston, MA: Course Technology.

Avoiding Slashes

People often include dates in their filenames, such as WebCamPix-6/19/99.jpg. In this case, the Web server interprets the slashes as directory indicators. It looks for a file called 99.jpg in a directory called 19, which is itself inside a directory called WebCamPix-6. The solution here is to use a different syntax for dates. A better way to express dates on the Web is to indicate the year, month, and date in that order without punctuation. For example, the filename indicated above would be written as WebCamPix-19990619.jpg.

Avoiding Apostrophes

Another common mistake is to use apostrophes in filenames, as in My_dog's_portrait.jpg. In this case, the Web server interprets the apostrophe as a quotation mark and looks for a file called My_dog. Never use apostrophes or quotation marks in a filename.

Solving Format Problems

Web browsers can display images in only one of three computer graphic formats: GIF, JPEG, or PNG. If you have an image in the PICT format, for example, you cannot convert the image to the GIF format by simply changing the suffix to .gif. You must open the image in an image editor and save it in one of the three Web graphics formats. The basic steps for doing so in Photoshop are listed below. For more details see the "Optimizing Graphics for the Web" chapter.

To convert an image to a Web graphic format in Photoshop:

1. Open the **image** in Photoshop.

2. Click **File** on the menu bar, and then click **Save As**.

3. In the Save As dialog box, click the **Format** list arrow.

4. Click **CompuServe GIF (*.GIF)**, **JPEG (*.JPG, .JPE)**, or **PNG (*.PNG)**.

Solving File Suffix Errors

Web browsers rely on the image filename to define the image type. Specifically, they look at the suffix—the characters after the last period—to indicate the file format. If a filename doesn't include a suffix, the browser doesn't know the file type and ignores it. If a filename includes multiple periods, the browser looks only at the last suffix. For example, a file named my_image.gif.old appears to the browser as being of a format called OLD, and does not display it. If a file is named image.gif, the browser tries to display a gif image using the data in the file. If the file really is in the GIF format, it should appear. If it is actually in another format, such as JPEG, the browser tries to display the JPEG file as a GIF, and fails. Always include the proper format suffix when naming image files.

Avoiding Improper Capitalization

HTML tags do not need to be capitalized; <IMG SRC="... is the same as <img src="... which is the same as <ImG sRc=".... Web browsers ignore the capitalization of tags. However, it's common practice to capitalize all HTML tags to make them stand out from the rest of the text. Web server names can also be uppercase or lowercase. For example, <A HREF="HTTP://WWW.GIF.COM/... is the same as <A HREF="http://www.gif.com....

On UNIX servers case does matter for filenames. If you save an image as MyPicture.JPEG, you must refer to the image using that capitalization in the HTML code. If you use <IMG SRC="Mypicture.Jpeg">, for example, the UNIX server cannot find the file. Even if you work only on Macintosh or Windows servers, do not get into the habit of ignoring case in filenames.

Avoiding Incorrect Path References

The errors caused by incorrect path references usually are the result of an imperfect understanding of the concept of file paths. To reference a file in the same directory, set the attribute's value to the filename, as in the following example:

```
<IMG SRC="myFile.jpg">
```

If the HTML file and the image file are in different directories, you need to indicate the path. For example, if you have an HTML file in the directory called html and an image file called myImage.gif in the directory called images, the HTML code looks like the following:

```
<IMG SRC="images/myImage.gif">
```

As you learned earlier, this is called a relative file path because the directory structure is relative to the location of the HTML file. The drawback to using relative file paths is that if you move the HTML file, you might have to change the HTML code.

The benefit of absolute file paths is that they are not related to the location of the HTML file. If you move the HTML file, you do not need to change the HTML code that calls the image.

Be careful not to use paths that are local to your hard drive; they will not work when you upload them to the server.

CHAPTER SUMMARY

❑ People use a variety of monitor sizes, and it is better that your graphics appear at a reduced size than to be cut off by the edge of the browser. Design graphics assuming they will be seen on a 15" desktop monitor.

❑ WebTV is gaining popularity, but represents a small minority of users. Design within the limits of television display only if you are concerned with how those users see your graphics.

❑ Most designers use Macintosh computers, but most Internet users use Windows computers. Make sure to preview your images on a Windows computer.

❑ Most users use Internet Explorer as their Web browser, but many also use Netscape Navigator. Preview your work on both browsers.

❑ Color appears differently on different monitors, operating systems, and browsers. To guarantee that colors in images match colors in HTML, use the Web-safe color palette of 216 colors.

❑ Web color is defined in RGB color, where each primary has a value represented in hexadecimal notation.

❑ Hexadecimal color is a way of describing 24-bit RGB color, where the value of each channel is defined by a two-digit number from 0 to F, and where the letters A through F represent the numbers 10 through 15.

❑ Hexadecimal colors have three pairs of numbers, one for each channel; each pair represents 256 different values.

❑ Color names are easier to use than hexadecimal colors, but only 16 color names show a similar color on both popular browsers, and only eight are Web-safe.

❑ You do not have to save images with the Web-safe palette unless you are concerned with how their backgrounds will blend in with the background of the page.

❑ WYSIWYG stands for "what you see is what you get," and refers to software that displays your work the same way while editing as after output.

❑ WYSIWYG interfaces simplify the process of generating HTML but usually cannot lay out pages as accurately as hand-coded HTML.

❑ The basic structure of an HTML tag is <TAG ATTRIBUTE="value"></TAG>.

❑ You can use the IMG tag and its attributes to control how images appear in a Web page. The most common attributes for working with Web graphics are ALT, LOWSRC, ALIGN, HEIGHT, WIDTH, HSPACE, VSPACE, and BORDER.

❑ IMG tags should always include the HEIGHT, WIDTH, and ALT attributes.

❐ Using the TABLE tag is the primary way to control layout of Web pages. You use this tag to indicate background colors for tables, and especially to create effects without using images.

❐ Spaces, punctuation, and slashes in filenames cause problems with browsers and prevent images from appearing correctly.

❐ Image filenames must include the correct suffix.

❐ Windows and Macintosh computers ignore inconsistent capitalization of filenames, but most Web servers do not, and will prevent the display of images.

❐ Incorrect paths are one of the most common errors for new Web developers.

REVIEW QUESTIONS

1. What are the differences between Macintosh and Windows systems?

    a. Macintoshes have smaller text and lower gamma

    b. Macintoshes have larger text and lower gamma

    c. Windows systems have smaller text and lower gamma

    d. Windows systems have larger text and lower gamma

2. What is an average environment for most users?

    a. Netscape on Macintosh with a 19" monitor

    b. Internet Explorer on Windows with a 15" monitor

    c. Netscape on Windows with a 17" monitor

    d. Internet Explorer on Macintosh with a 13" monitor

3. What can you tell from analyzing your Web server log files?

    a. How many of your users print your pages

    b. How many of your users use Macs

    c. How many of your users have 15" monitors

    d. How many of your users view your pages in 16-bit color

4. What is the decimal equivalent of the hexadecimal value 10?

    a. 8

    b. 10

    c. 16

    d. A

5. What is the percentage of blue in the hexadecimal color #996633?

    a. 80%

    b. 60%

    c. 40%

    d. 20%

6. If the Photoshop Color Picker dialog box shows a red value of 204, a green value of 153, and a blue value of 0, what is the corresponding hexadecimal color?

    a. #CF9600

    b. #CC9900

    c. #966900

    d. #996600

7. What color is represented by the code #654321?

    a. Pale green

    b. Dark green

    c. Orange

    d. Dark red

8. What code below represents light blue?

    a. #012345

    b. #ABCDEF

    c. #AAFF33

    d. #FC9630

9. What happens when you use the word *green* to define a background color?

    a. Nothing, because *green* must be capitalized

    b. The background displays the hexadecimal color 008000, which is not a Web-safe color

    c. The background displays the hexadecimal color 00FF00, which is not a Web-safe color

    d. The background displays the hexadecimal color 00FF00, which is a Web-safe color

10. What tag is used primarily to lay out Web pages?

    a. IMG

    b. TABLE

    c. BODY

    d. DIV

11. Which parts of HTML must be capitalized?

    a. Tags

    b. Attributes

    c. Values of the attributes

    d. None of the above

12. Which attribute cannot be used with the IMG tag?

    a. ALIGN

    b. BORDER

    c. BACKGROUND

    d. HSPACE

13. Which tag uses the CELLSPACING attribute?

    a. IMG

    b. TABLE

    c. TR

    d. TD

14. What is the main use of Web-safe colors?

    a. In images so they appear on both Macs and PCs

    b. In HTML so pages appear on both Macs and PCs

    c. In images so they appear on both Netscape and Internet Explorer

    d. In HTML so pages appear on both Netscape and Internet Explorer

15. How do you use the LOWSRC tag?

    a. Set the value to the same image.

    b. Set the value to the same image, but use different HEIGHT and WIDTH attributes.

    c. Set the value to a different image.

    d. Don't set the value to anything; the LOWSRC attribute does not take a value.

16. Why would you set the value of the BORDER attribute in the IMG tag to 0?

    a. To allow text to wrap

    b. To remove horizontal margins

    c. To remove both horizontal and vertical margins

    d. To remove the colored outline

17. How do you make sure images can be reused in a page without forcing the browser to reload them from the server each time?

    a. Put them in the cache.

    b. Don't do anything special; the browser will put them in the cache.

    c. Make sure the user clicks the Reload or Refresh button.

    d. Duplicate the image each time you want to use it, and give it a different name.

18. You have two directories, one named httpd (containing your HTML files) and one named other (containing an image named logo.gif). Both directories are in the same parent directory. What is the file path needed to insert the logo into the HTML?

    a. `<IMG SRC="logo.gif">`

    b. `<IMG SRC="other/logo.gif">`

    c. `<IMG SRC="/other/logo.gif">`

    d. `<IMG SRC="../other/logo.gif">`

19. Which of the IMG tags successfully displays an image?

    a. `<IMG ALIGN ALT="Harold's birthday" SRC="Harold" HSPACE=0 BORDER=2>`

    b. `<IMG ALT="Harolds birthday" HSPACE=2 SRC="Harold.GIF" BORDER=0>`

    c. `<IMG SRC="Harold" ALT="Harolds birthday" HSPACE=0 BORDER=OFF>`

    d. `<SRC="Harold.GIF" ALT="Harold's birthday" HSPACE=2 BORDER= ON IMG>`

20. Which IMG tag below successfully displays an image?

    a. `<IMG SRC="Harolds_birthday_12-34-56">`

    b. `<IMG SRC="Harold's_birthday_12/34/56">`

    c. `<IMG SRC="Harolds birthday: 12-34-56">`

    d. `<IMG SRC="Harold's birthday: 12/34/56">`

HANDS-ON PROJECTS

Project 3-1 Prepare an Image for WebTV

Although less than 1% of your audience uses WebTV to view your site, your designer wants your site's logo to work on all platforms. Edit the image to look good when displayed on a television.

To edit an image for television in Photoshop:

    1. In Photoshop, open **3-1.tif** from the Data Disk.

2. Change the Mode to **RGB color**.

3. To fix the colors, apply the **NTSC Colors** filter. This darkens the bright colors so they don't distort when shown on a television.

4. Fix the fine lines. Blur the image with the **Gaussian Blur** filter and set the Radius to **0.3**. This blurs the entire image slightly, preventing the fine lines from aliasing on the television. You also can use one of the selection tools to select the area around the lines and blur only that area.

5. Optimize and save the image as **3-1.gif** in the Chapter 3 folder on your hard drive.

Project 3-2 Make a Simple Web Page and Align an Image

You can complete this and the following exercises with a WYSIWYG HTML editor, but you are strongly encouraged to use a simple text editor such as SimpleText or NotePad to learn how pages are constructed.

To align an image on a Web page:

1. In Photoshop, open **3-2.tif** from the Data Disk.

2. Select the **Canvas Size** tool and record the height and width of the image.

3. Optimize and save the image as **fish.gif** in a new directory on your desktop called **project_3-2**.

4. Open a simple text editor and create a new file called **fish.html**. Save it to the same directory as the image.

5. Add an IMG tag to the HTML file which indicates the source of the image and includes the necessary attributes (SRC, HEIGHT, WIDTH, and ALT). Note that you do not need to add the HTML and BODY tags and that the order of the attributes does not matter. It should look like this:

```
<IMG SRC="fish.gif" HEIGHT="120" WIDTH="300" ALT="Fish">
```

6. Save the HTML file and view it in a browser.

7. Add about 50 words of your own above the IMG tag.

8. Add another 50 words of your own below the IMG tag.

9. Within the IMG tag, add these attributes: ALIGN set equal to **right**, HSPACE set equal to **10**, VSPACE set equal to **5**. It should look like this:
<IMG SRC="fish.gif" HEIGHT="120" WIDTH="300" ALT="Fish" ALIGN="right" HSPACE="10" VSPACE="5">

10. Save the file and view it in a browser. The image should be aligned on the right, with a 10-pixel margin on the sides and a 5-pixel margin on the top and bottom.

Project 3-3 Use a Low-Source Image

The large fish image takes several seconds to load when using a slow modem. You want the rest of the page to load without having to wait for the image. Create a quickly loading version of the image, and include it using the LOWSRC attribute.

To use the LOWSRC attribute to quickly load a large image:

1. In Photoshop, open **fish.gif** from the Data Disk.

2. Set the Mode to **RGB Color**, and then set it to **Indexed Color**.

3. In the Indexed Color dialog box, set the palette to **4 colors**.

4. Save the image as **fish_lowsrc.gif**. in the directory called project_3-2.

5. In a text editor, open the **fish.html** file you created in Project 3-2, and add the LOWSRC attribute to the IMG tag to reference the new image. The HTML should look like this:
   <IMG SRC="fish.gif" HEIGHT="120" WIDTH="300" ALT="Fish" ALIGN="right" HSPACE="10" VSPACE="5" LOWSRC="fish_lowsrc.gif">

6. Save the file as **fish2.html** and view it in a browser. Unless you have a very fast computer, you should see the low-source image load and then be replaced by the final image.

Project 3-4 Use an Image as a Button

One common use for small images is to set them up as links to other pages, which effectively makes them buttons users can click to navigate a Web site.

To use an image as a button:

1. In Photoshop, open **3-2.tif** from the Data Disk.

2. Make sure the Mode is set to **RGB color** and reduce the size to **100 × 100** pixels.

3. Save the image as **fish_sm.gif** in the directory named project_3-2.

4. In a text editor, create a new HTML file, and save it as **index.html** in the project_3-2 folder.

5. Add an IMG tag to display the image.

6. Make the image a link to fish.html by adding an anchor tag. The final HTML should look like this:
   <A HREF="fish.html"><IMG SRC="fish_sm.gif"></A>

7. Save the HTML file and view it in a browser. The image will have a colored border around it.

8. To remove the colored border, add the **BORDER** attribute to the IMG tag and set the value to **0**.

9. Save the HTML file in the project_3-2 folder.

Project 3-5 Set File Paths to Display Images in Other Directories

A common mistake for new Web developers is to set file paths incorrectly. Practice using paths by referencing images in different directories.

To set a file path in HTML:

1. On your desktop, create a directory named **project_3-5**.

2. Within the directory, create two more directories. Name one **html** and name the other **images**.

3. Copy the files from Projects 3-1 through 3-4 to these new directories. Put **index.html** and **fish.html** into the html directory, and put **fish.gif** and **fish_sm.gif** into the images directory.

4. In a text editor, edit **index.html** to reference the image from the new directory. Set the SRC attribute in the IMG tag to **"../images/fish_sm.gif"**. The IMG tag should look like this:
   <A HREF="fish.html"><IMG SRC="../images/fish_sm.gif" BORDER=0></A>

5. Edit **fish.html** in the same way, changing the values of the SRC attribute.

6. View **index.html** in a browser, and click the **image** to open **fish.html**. The images should appear on both pages.

Project 3-6 Place an Image in a Page with a Colored Background

Many Web pages use colored backgrounds. To make the image fit in, it should not have a different background color. Create a page with a colored background, and include an image with the same background color.

To insert an image with a colored background on a Web page with a colored background:

1. In a text editor, create a new HTML file named **index.html** and save it in a new directory called **project_3-6**.

2. Give the page a pale turquoise background by using the BACKGROUND attribute of the BODY tag. Add this tag to the file: **<BODY BGCOLOR="#99FFCC">**.

3. A few lines below, add the closing tag: **</BODY>**.

4. Open file **3-6.tif** from the Data Disk and save it as **car.gif** in the project_3-6 directory. Leave the file open in Photoshop.

5. In the HTML file add an **IMG** tag between the BODY tags. Set the **SRC** attribute to **car.gif**.

6. Save the file and view it in a browser. You will see a white background around the image of the car.

7. Set the background color of the image to the same color as the page. In Photoshop, open the Color Picker dialog box for the foreground color and set the color to **99FFCC** in the hexadecimal box near the bottom. If you are using an older version which does not allow you to enter hexadecimal color, set red to **153**, green to **255**, and blue to **204**.

8. Select the **Paint Bucket** tool and look at the Options palette. Set the tolerance to **30** and make sure the **Anti-aliased** and **Contiguous** check boxes are selected. If you do not do this, you will leave a white halo around the car.

9. Fill in the white background with the pale green using the Paint Can tool.

10. Save the **image**, then reload the file in the browser by clicking the **Reload** or **Refresh** button. The background of the image should match the color of the page.

Project 3-7 Create a Transparent Image

You might not know the background color of the Web page that will contain your image, or the image might have to appear on pages with different background colors. In these circumstances, make the image background transparent so that the image can appear on any background color. Create an image with a transparent background and include it in an HTML table with a background color.

To create an image with a transparent background:

1. In Photoshop, open **3-7.tif** from the Data Disk.

2. Convert the background layer to a normal layer. (Double-click the **background layer** in the layers palette, and then click **ok**.

3. Select the **Magic Wand** tool. Set the tolerance to **32** and check the **Contiguous** box and the **Anti-aliased** box. Select the **white background** with the Magic Wand tool and then press the **Delete** key.

4. Change the Mode to **Indexed Color** and set the number of colors to **32**.

5. Make sure the Transparency box is selected and, for the Matte color, select the **pale turquoise** color. Set dither to none.

6. Click **OK** and save the image as **trans.gif** in a new directory named **project_3-7**.

7. In a text editor, create a new HTML file named **index.html** in the project folder (project_3-7).

8. Create a one-cell table with a pale turquoise background. The HTML should look like this:
   <TABLE><TR><TD BGCOLOR="#99FFCC>
   </TD></TR></TABLE>

9. Between the table delimiter tags, add the HTML code to reference the new image.

10. Save the **index.html** file to the directory called project_3-7 and view it in a browser. You should see a blue box containing the image, which now appears to have a pale turquoise background.

Project 3-8 Use Background Colors to Create a Smaller Image

Your designer has given you an image with large colored margins. You know that you can use background colors in HTML instead of creating large margins. The only trick is matching the HTML color to the image color. The image is a high-color JPEG image, and you cannot make the background transparent. Crop the image and place it in a table with the same color for the background.

To crop an image and include it in a table with a colored background:

1. In Photoshop, open **3-8.tif** from the Data Disk.

2. Use the **Eyedropper** tool to select the color of the background.

3. Look at the Foreground Color in the Color Picker dialog box to see its hexadecimal code. The color should be Web-safe so that the image matches the table color. HTML colors are three pairs of numbers; to be Web-safe, each pair must be 00, 33, 66, 99, CC, or FF. The color looks Web-safe at first glance, but it isn't. You can tell because the color cube icon appears near the top of the window. Click the **color cube** icon to make the color Web-safe. The color shifts to the nearest Web-safe color. Record the hexadecimal code.

4. Select the **Paint Bucket** tool, set the options to a tolerance of **30,** and select **Anti-aliasing**.

5. Replace the background color with the new Web-safe version.

6. Open the **Canvas Size** dialog box to see the image dimensions. Record the height and width.

7. Trim the image to remove all but a few pixels of the background color.

8. Optimize the image and save it as **3-8.jpg** in a new project directory named **project_3-8**. Use a high-quality setting.

9. In a text editor, create a new HTML file named **index.html,** and save it in the same directory.

10. Create a table of the same dimensions as the original image. Make the background color the same as the new Web-safe version of the image's background color. The HTML code should look like this:
    <TABLE HEIGHT="120" WIDTH="160" BGCOLOR="6699CC" BORDER="0"><TR><TD ALIGN="CENTER"> </TD></TR></TABLE>

11. Between the table delimiter tags, add an **image tag** to reference the new image.

12. Save the **file** and view it in a browser. What you see should look like the original image.

CASE PROJECT

By now, you should have collected several images to use in your online portfolio project, and optimized them for the Web. Your next step is to create Web pages to display the images. Using a WYSIWYG editor or a simple text editor, create a biography page that includes a picture of you. Create a gallery page that contains your images. The pages should link to each other. Preview the pages on at least two sizes of monitors, on both Netscape and IE, and both Macintosh and Windows. Notice the differences in how the pages appear. Edit the images and the Web pages to compensate for the differences.

3

4

ACQUIRING IMAGES

Collecting Graphics to Use on the Web

In this chapter, you will:

◆ Learn to use scanners and acquire analog images

◆ Fix problem scans

◆ Learn about using cameras and taking photographs

◆ Retouch photographs

◆ Acquire images from other sources

To produce a Web graphic, you must either create or acquire a bitmapped computer graphic. You can create an image by scanning an original drawing, using a paint program, or exporting an image from a vector-based program. Moreover, you can acquire photographs by scanning a photo, using a digital camera, or using stock photos from CD-ROMs.

After you acquire an image for a Web page, you should open the image in an image-editing program. As you examine the image, you might find problems such as artifacts—marks or other defects that are not part of the original image, but were introduced during acquisition. For example, film photographs can have scratches, and digital photographs can have artifacts created by digital compression. You correct problems such as these in an image-editing program where you can retouch photos to add or remove visual elements.

In addition to scanning images and taking photographs, you can find images in a variety of other sources. You can capture images from video, sketch them on a drawing tablet, or use images from stock photography CDs or other Web sites. This chapter explains how to acquire images and how to use Photoshop to correct any errors in the images.

USING SCANNERS

Image production for Web graphics is similar to audio production—no matter how sound or image originates, it is edited and delivered in a digital form. All recorded music is recorded with either analog equipment such as magnetic tape, or digital equipment such as digital tape or computer hardware and software. Nevertheless, music now is almost always edited in a digital environment, and is delivered in its final form as a digital file on a compact disc.

In the same way, Web graphics can originate in an analog form such as paper, or in a digital form such as an electronic file, but they are edited digitally and displayed as a digital image file on a Web page. This means you must convert analog images from photos or drawings into digital images. One way to do this is to import the images using scanners.

A scanner is an optical input device that uses light-sensing equipment to capture an image from paper or other media, such as photographic slides. The scanner converts the image into a digital file that you can open and edit with graphics software. Scanners are the most versatile input device for Web graphics because you can use them to make digital files of photographs, hand-drawn illustrations, and any other flat images. As demonstrated in Table 4-1, flatbed scanners are excellent for digitizing images on paper or other flat media.

Table 4-1   Acquiring original images with analog hardware and digitizing hardware

Image type	Medium	Digitizing method
Hand-drawn illustrations	Paper	Flatbed scanner
Photographs	Film print or slide	Flatbed or slide scanner
Vector image	Printout	Flatbed scanner
Video stills	Analog video signal	Video card or digitizing software

Flatbed scanners can import most types of analog images. If you can only have one device for inputting images, it should be a flatbed scanner.

Using Flatbed Scanners

Flatbed scanners work much the same way as photocopiers, with two main differences. The controls for the scanner are software-based and are manipulated on the computer, and the output of the scanner is a digital image file, not a paper copy.

The hardware, software, and digitizing techniques used with flatbed scanners are discussed in the following sections.

Flatbed Scanner Hardware

Flatbed scanners are affordable, most currently are available for a few hundred dollars, and many are available for under fifty dollars. Anyone seriously considering working with Web graphics should have a flatbed scanner. Although this was not true ten years ago, today even the least expensive scanners are adequate for most Web work. More expensive models have additional features that allow you to make color photocopies and send faxes.

To use a flatbed scanner to scan a drawing or photograph, generally from a book or paper document, you place the image on a glass surface. A scanning arm passes under the image, projects light through the glass and up against the image, and then registers the light that bounces back. The light then is captured as a digital image at a particular resolution.

Scanner resolution is based on pixels and measured in dpi (dots per inch) or ppi (pixels per inch). This measurement is linear, so a 300-dpi scanner scans at a density of 300 dots per inch horizontally across a page, and 300 dots per inch vertically down a page. A 300-dpi scanner actually generates 90,000 pixels per square inch. Scanning a full $8\frac{1}{2} \times 11"$ sheet of paper creates a rectangular bitmap image 2550 pixels wide and 3300 pixels long. Web graphics tend to be much smaller, usually less than a few hundred pixels wide. Because your final output is much smaller than the sizes produced by a scanner, a scanning resolution of 300 dpi is adequate for large source images.

At times, however, your source image is quite small. For example, if you are scanning a photograph from a driver's license, which is typically $1 \times 1\frac{1}{2}"$, you need a resolution higher than 300 dpi. At 300 dpi, the driver's license photo produces a 300×450 pixel image. Many photos develop scratches or wrinkles where they have been folded. Driver's license photos in particular tend to have many blemishes. To fix these blemishes, you need to scan at a higher resolution than you will use in the final Web graphic. You then can repair the scratches and reduce the image size. In general, you should scan images so that the image produced is at least twice the size you need. A 600 dpi scanner generates a 600×900 pixel image (the size of a $1 \times 1\frac{1}{2}"$ image), which is much larger than you need, but the image's higher resolution makes it easier to produce quality scans. Low-resolution scanners produce blurry images with less detail than high-resolution scanners. Currently, 600-dpi scanners also are inexpensive, and are the standard resolution for flatbed scanners. You need at least 600-dpi resolution to scan small source images. You also can find 1200-dpi scanners on the market, and the newest hardware scans at even higher resolutions. More resolution produces better scans. When purchasing a scanner, buy one with the highest resolution you can afford.

Using Scanning Software

Some scanners are set up to be used within image-editing applications such as Adobe Photoshop. In this case, you start Photoshop, click File on the menu bar, point to Import, and then click the name of the scanner. Other systems are set up so that you have to scan in one program, such as Ofoto, and then you save the image and open it in another program to edit.

Before software can send or receive data to and from devices such as printers or scanners, the computer needs a type of software called a driver. **Drivers** are software interfaces that let computers and external devices communicate with each other. Driver software is vendor- and device-specific, so you need a particular driver for a particular scanner. These drivers should come on a disk with the device, or they are available on the Web site of the device manufacturer.

Most major graphics hardware and software companies have agreed on a cross-platform standard for scanners known as TWAIN. (TWAIN does not stand for anything, although many say it is an acronym for Technology (or Toolkit) Without an Interesting Name.) Adobe is a member of the Twain Working Group, and Photoshop supports TWAIN-compliant scanners.

You often can find a default driver to use instead of the one intended for the particular hardware. However, using the right driver often produces better scans.

Using a Scanner to Create an Image File

Scanner operation depends on which scanner you use and how your computer is configured. However, because scanners and the software that drives them are similar, you can follow the steps below to scan a document with most scanner setups.

First check the scanner's user manual to see if you can import an image directly using Photoshop, or whether you have to use additional software. If you plan to edit the image with Photoshop, it is more convenient to scan using Photoshop. Otherwise you have to import the image in one program, save it, and then open it again in Photoshop.

To scan a document:

1. Turn on the scanner. If necessary, let it warm up.

2. Open the document cover lid on the scanner. Make sure the glass is clean and free of dust. To clean the glass, first check the owner's manual for the manufacturer's recommendations. Using certain chemicals or ordinary paper towels can leave marks on the glass.

3. Place the image face down on the glass. If you are scanning from a book or magazine, make the paper as flat as you can by pressing on the lid or weighing it down with a book. Do not put too much weight on the glass, however, as you could damage it.

4. Start the scanning software or an image-editing application such as **Photoshop**.

5. In Photoshop, click **File** on the menu bar, point to **Import**, and then select your scanning device.

   You can import scanned images directly from any scanner that has a Photoshop-compatible driver or that supports the TWAIN interface. See your scanner documentation for instructions on installing the scanner plug-in.

If your scanner does not have an Adobe Photoshop-compatible scanner driver, but supports the TWAIN interface, select **TWAIN Acquire** from the Import submenu.

If you can't import the scanned image using TWAIN, or you are not using Photoshop, use the scanner manufacturer's software to scan and save your images, and then open the files later in Photoshop or ImageReady.

6. Use the **Selection** tool to choose only the part of the document or image you want to scan. It wastes time and disk space to scan the whole document if you need only a portion of it.

7. Use as much resolution and color as possible without producing a file that is too large to manage. If you are scanning a black-and-white image, use 8-bit grayscale for the color depth. If you are scanning a color image, use 24-bit RGB color. You should see an estimated image file size that will be produced by the current settings. If you use maximum settings, you might produce an image file that is too large to edit easily. Adjust the selection area, color depth, and resolution so that the output image is a manageable size, such as 1 MB.

8. Press the appropriate button on your scanner or in the scanning dialog box; such as one labeled **Scan**, **Start**, or **Process**, to start the scan. As the scanner digitizes the document, leave the lid down and do not nudge the scanner. The scanning arm moves slowly. If the scanner is jostled during a pass, it can miss areas of the document and the resulting image might show wrinkles of missing information.

9. When the scan is completed, use the software to save the image file in a high-color, noncompressed format such as TIF or PSD. PSD is the proprietary format for Photoshop. Both formats support 24-bit color and do not create compression artifacts the way JPEG does.

   To save the image in Photoshop, click **File** on the menu bar, and then click **Save**. In the Save dialog box, click the **Format** list arrow, click **TIFF (*.TIF)** or **Photoshop (*.PSD, *.PDD)**, and then click **Save**.

The file produced by a scanner is a computer image. If the original document contains text, the text in the produced image is graphical and cannot be edited. You can use additional Optical Character Recognition (OCR) software to convert scanned text into text that you can edit. However, the accuracy of this software is less than 100%, and the text files that the software generates usually contain many errors.

Using Slide Scanners

Flatbed scanners are excellent for digitizing images on paper and other flat surfaces, such as transparency film, but they cannot scan slides. Photographic slides are attached to a cardboard or plastic frame so you cannot press the slide itself flat on the glass of a flatbed scanner. A slide scanned with a flatbed results in a dark, muddy image.

A different type of scanner, called a **slide scanner** or **film scanner**, does work with photographic slides and negatives. Instead of placing the slide on a sheet of glass, you insert the slide into the slide scanner. Unlike scanned paper documents, slides are a uniform size, so slide scanners position the scanning mechanism directly against the film. Slides usually have a higher resolution than printed photographs, so slide or film scanners also must provide better resolution than generally provided by flatbed scanners. Slide scanners also produce a more accurate image because they light the slide from behind, through the slide and into the sensors. Flatbed scanners project light against the image and the light bounces back into the sensors. Flatbed scanners have less accuracy sensing the light, and lower resolution than slide scanners.

Slide scanners are not as common as flatbed scanners, but are crucial for high-resolution images, such as an online archive of artwork or photographs. Slide scanners are simple boxes, with only a slot for inserting the slide. They are controlled by scanning software in the same way as flatbed scanners. Slide scanners are usually more expensive than flatbed scanners. High-quality slide scanners cost between $300 and $2000.

Using Drawing Tablets

To use a drawing as a Web graphic, you can either use a pointing device such as a mouse to draw the picture in a graphics program, such as Photoshop, or you can draw it on paper and then scan the drawn image. Both methods have drawbacks. Drawing with the mouse is clumsy because you don't have the same control as you do with a pen. Drawing on paper requires the additional step of scanning the drawing after it is created. An alternative is to use a drawing tablet, an input device that lets you use an inkless electronic stylus to draw directly on a sensitive panel. Moving the stylus over the panel produces a line similar to one created with a mouse or other pointing device. Drawing tablets eliminate the need for producing paper versions of illustrations. Instead of using the mouse, you draw with a stylus, which is similar to traditional drawing tools such as pencils or pens. This flexibility makes a drawing tablet a handy tool for creating and editing Web graphics.

A drawing tablet is particularly useful if you retouch a lot of photos. In Photoshop, a stylus provides you more precise control over retouching tools such as Dodge, Blur, and Airbrush than using a mouse. Not only is a stylus more comfortable and familiar in the hand than a mouse, but many allow you to adjust line weight based on how much pressure you apply.

FIXING PROBLEM SCANS

After you scan an image and open the image file in an image editing program, you might notice problems or flaws. Some might reflect defects in the source image, but most probably were created during the scanning process. Typical problems include low contrast, incorrect colors, stray marks or artifacts, and unexpected patterns of pixels. The following sections explain how to solve these common image problems.

Fixing Low Contrast

Scanned images often have low contrast. The white areas are not truly white and the black areas are not truly black. Figure 4-1 shows an image with low, normal, and high contrast.

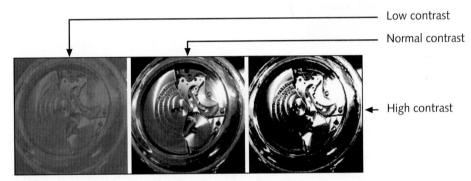

Figure 4-1   An image with different contrasts

You can solve the image contrast problem in Photoshop by using the Brightness/Contrast dialog box.

To adjust contrast using the Brightness/Contrast dialog box:

1. Click **Image** on the menu bar, point to **Adjust**, and then click **Brightness/Contrast**.

2. In the Brightness/Contrast dialog box, illustrated in Figure 4-2, make sure the Preview box is checked so you can see how changing the brightness and contrast affects the image.

3. Enter new values in the Brightness and Contrast text boxes. You also can drag the Brightness and Contrast sliders to change these values.

4. Click **OK** to close the dialog box and apply your changes to the image.

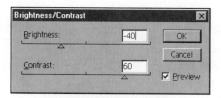

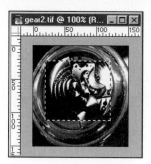

Figure 4-2 The Brightness/Contrast dialog box

Photoshop also has another, better tool that gives you more control over image contrast: the Levels dialog box. Use the Levels dialog box to adjust intensity levels of the shadows, midtones, and highlights in an image.

To adjust contrast using the Levels dialog box:

1. Click **Image** on the menu bar, point to **Adjust**, and then click **Levels**.

2. In the Levels dialog box, illustrated in Figure 4-3, make sure the Preview box is checked so you can see how changing the values affects the image.

3. To increase contrast, change the Input Levels by entering new values in the first and third Input Levels text boxes, or by dragging the first and third Input sliders.

4. To alter the lightness balance, adjust the gamma by entering a new value in the second Input Levels text box, or by dragging the second Input slider.

5. To decrease contrast, change the Output Levels by entering new values in the Output Levels text boxes or by dragging the Output sliders.

6. Click **OK** to close the dialog box and apply your changes to the image.

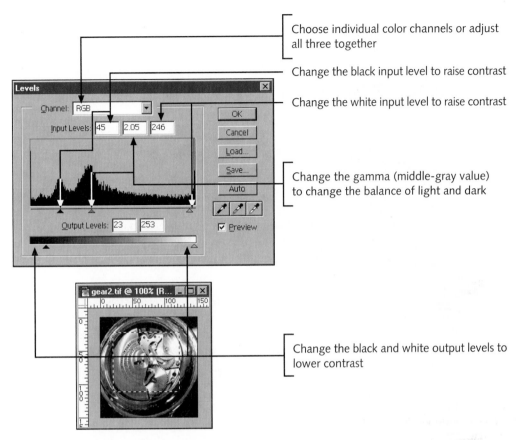

Choose individual color channels or adjust all three together

Change the black input level to raise contrast

Change the white input level to raise contrast

4

Change the gamma (middle-gray value) to change the balance of light and dark

Change the black and white output levels to lower contrast

Figure 4-3   The Levels dialog box

The Levels dialog box shows a graph called a histogram. The **histogram** is a visual representation of all the pixels in the image. The scale along the bottom represents brightness with pure black at the far left, white at the far right, and middle-gray or **gamma** in the middle. Look at the histogram, and you can see how the pixels in the image are dispersed across the brightness continuum. If part of the histogram is empty, the image has no pixels of that shade. If the empty pixels are at the far left or right of the histogram, the image has low contrast. Figure 4-4 shows histograms for the images shown in Figure 4-1. The first image has very low contrast, and the histogram shows no pixels at the far ends of the spectrum. The third image has very high contrast, and the histogram shows most of the image information concentrated at the ends. The second image has normal contrast, and the histogram shows evenly distributed image information.

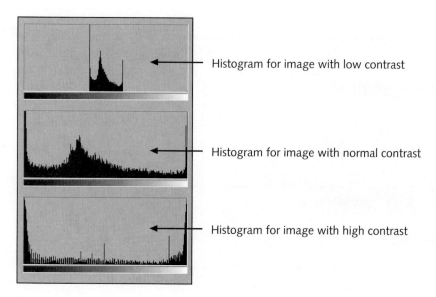

Histogram for image with low contrast

Histogram for image with normal contrast

Histogram for image with high contrast

Figure 4-4   Histograms for images with different contrasts

For images with low contrast, you should **normalize** the contrast. To do this, set the darkest colors of an image to pure black and the brightest colors to pure white. To normalize contrast, you remove the blank areas at the far ends of the histogram by dragging the slider arrows to reset the image's minimum and maximum levels.

In Photoshop, you also can use the **Auto Contrast** or **Auto Levels** tool to normalize contrast. Auto Contrast simply maps the lightest pixel in the image to pure white, and maps the darkest pixel to pure black. Auto Levels alters each color channel separately, normalizing the red, green, and blue channels independently. Use Auto Contrast for grayscale images and simple contrast normalization. Use Auto Levels for more precise normalization of color images. To use these features, click Image on the menu bar, point to Adjust, and then click Auto Contrast or Auto Levels. If the image seems too dark or light with optimized contrast, open the Levels dialog box as described earlier and adjust the gamma slider (the gray center slider arrow) in the Levels dialog box. If the contrast is too high, you can lower it by adjusting the Output Levels sliders at the bottom of the Levels dialog box.

Fixing Problem Colors

You might find that the colors in a scanned image are not as bright as in the source image. For example, the colors in the scanned image in Figure 4-5 look washed out.

Figure 4-5   A color scan with washed out colors

Washed out colors are a common problem when the source is printed on low-quality paper. In Photoshop, use the Hue/Saturation tool to solve muddy color problems.

To adjust color using the Hue/Saturation dialog box:

1. Click **Image** on the menu bar, point to **Adjust**, and then click **Hue/Saturation**.

2. In the Hue/Saturation dialog box, illustrated in Figure 4-6, click the **Edit** list arrow and then click the colors you want to adjust. For example, if only the reds are dim, click **Reds**. To change all the colors, click **Master**.

3. To make the selected colors more saturated, drag the **Saturation** slider to the right, or enter a positive value in the Saturation text box.

4. To dim the selected colors, drag the **Saturation** slider to the left, or enter a negative value in the Saturation text box.

5. Click **OK** to close the dialog box and apply your changes to the image.

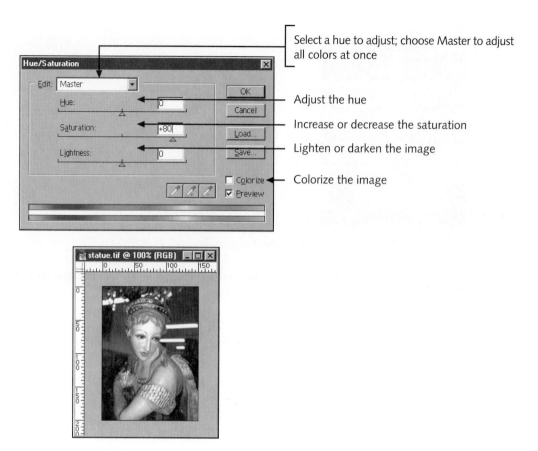

Select a hue to adjust; choose Master to adjust all colors at once

Adjust the hue

Increase or decrease the saturation

Lighten or darken the image

Colorize the image

Figure 4-6 The Hue/Saturation dialog box in Photoshop

Scanned images occasionally have a magenta or green blotch where the paper was not flat against the scanner bed during scanning. Use the Hue/Saturation dialog box to eliminate this problem.

To eliminate magenta or green scanning defects:

1. If the image already includes magenta or green, use a Marquee selection tool to select the area you want to adjust.

2. Open the **Hue/Saturation** dialog box, click **Image** on the menu bar, point to **Adjust**, and then click **Hue/Saturation**.

3. Click the **Edit** list arrow, and then click **Magentas** or **Greens**.

4. Set the lightness to 100% by dragging the **Lightness** slider to the right, or by entering **100** in the Lightness text box.

5. Click **OK** to close the dialog box and apply your changes to the image.

Adjusting HSV Color

A common way to describe color is **HSV: Hue**, **Saturation**, and **Value**. Photoshop often refers to value as brightness or lightness. Hue refers to the color itself and is measured from -180 to +180, where red is equal to 0. This numbering system comes from the color wheel convention, which has every hue placed in a circle. Each hue has a unique value equal to one of the 360° of the circle. Figure 4-7 shows the effects of changing the hue of an image.

4

Hue of -120

Hue of 0—original

Hue of +120

Figure 4-7   Changing the hue of an image

In Photoshop you adjust the hue with the Hue slider in the Hue/Saturation dialog box (see Figure 4-6). For this slider, and for many of Photoshop's color tools, Red is equal to 0, and the other colors continue up to 180 or down to -180, which are both equal to cyan. Table 4-2 shows the colors and their corresponding hue values.

Table 4-2   Hue values

Cyan	-180
Blue	-120
Magenta	-60
Red	0
Yellow	60
Green	120
Cyan	180

Saturation refers to how much of a color the image contains and is measured in percentages from –100% to 100%. If a color already is saturated, increasing the saturation has no effect. Setting saturation to –100% turns the color to an equivalent shade of gray. Figure 4-8 shows the effects of changing the saturation of an image.

Saturation of -100

Saturation of 0—original

Saturation of +100

Figure 4-8   Changing the saturation of an image

Lightness indicates how light a color appears and is measured in percentages from –100% to +100%. Lightness indicates how much black or white is in a color. A lightness of –100% is black, and a lightness of 100% is white. Figure 4-9 shows the effects of changing the lightness of an image.

Lightness of -50

Lightness of 0—original

Lightness of +50

Figure 4-9   Changing the lightness of an image

Removing Artifacts

Scanned images, such as drawings or printed figures, with white backgrounds often have small blemishes as a result of wrinkles or defects in the paper or dust on the scanner bed. These show up on the histogram as a peak in the far right of the graph, which indicates many pixels of light gray or off-white. To remove these blemishes, open the Levels dialog box and then move the white slider to the left of the peak. This sets all pixels lighter than the value in the rightmost Input Levels text box to 100% white. This method works only when the defects are lighter than the image itself. Figure 4-10 shows a scanned image with scanning defects and the histogram of the image.

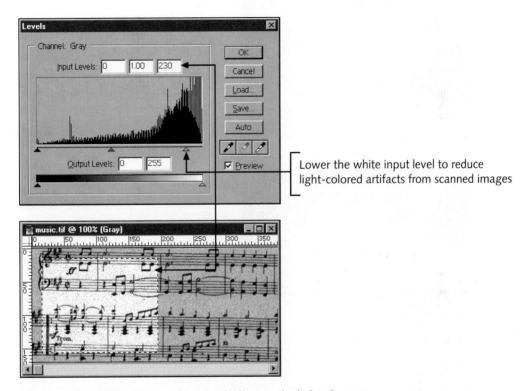

Lower the white input level to reduce light-colored artifacts from scanned images

Figure 4-10   Removing artifacts with the Levels dialog box

To correct blemishes that are as dark as the colors in the image, edit them with the Eraser tool.

Removing Patterns

When you scan a picture from a magazine or any other low-resolution print image, the dithered ink pattern is visible in the scanned image. In Figure 4-11, the original image has been scanned, producing a patterned image. These are called Moiré patterns and are caused by the scanning resolution interfering with the resolution of ink dots on the scanned image. The patterns appear as series of dots over the image.

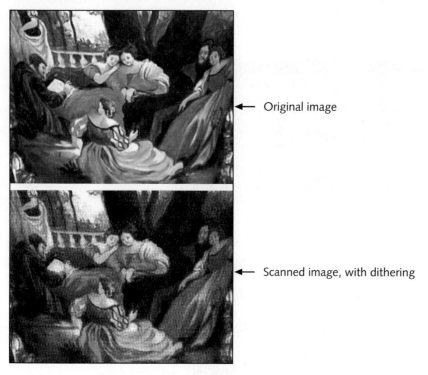

◀─── Original image

◀─── Scanned image, with dithering

Figure 4-11 A scanned image with visible Moiré patterns

To fix a Moiré, you blur the dots and soften the edges between the dots and the rest of the image. One method is to blur the entire image. Photoshop has several types of blur filters; the Gaussian Blur filter provides the most blur control. (To use this filter, click Filter on the menu bar, point to Blur, and then click Gaussian Blur.) With the Gaussian Blur filter, you can adjust the radius of the blur around each pixel. A higher radius means more blur. For most tasks you want a radius between 0.3 and 1. The drawback of using a blur filter to remove unwanted patterns is that you remove detail in the entire image, not just the unwanted pattern.

Besides blur filters, Photoshop also provides noise-reduction filters to add or remove **noise**, which Adobe defines as pixels with randomly distributed color levels. Noise filters remove defects such as dust and scratches from an image.

The Despeckle and Add Noise tools are two noise filters. You use the Despeckle tool to blur only the dots, and the pixels immediately around the dots. This removes patterns without affecting other detail in the image. Choose Despeckle (click Filter on the menu bar, point to Noise, and then click Despeckle) to find the edges in the image, and blur everything except the edges. The Gaussian Blur tool gives the most control for blurring images, but the Despeckle tool produces the best results when removing patterns from scanned images.

Another way to eliminate patterns is to actually add more noise using the Add Noise filter. Although adding noise to an image does not make it any clearer, it can reduce the appearance of regular patterns. The noise appears as a random pattern of dots over the image. The dots are of varying lightness and help mask existing patterns.

To eliminate patterns by using the Add Noise filter:

1. In Photoshop, click **Filter** on the menu bar, point to **Noise**, and then click **Add Noise**.

2. In the Add Noise dialog box illustrated in Figure 4-12, drag the **Amount** slider, or enter a value in the Amount text box to add noise to the image.

3. Click the **Uniform** option button to distribute noise in a uniform pattern across the image. Click the **Gaussian** option button to distribute noise in a speckled pattern, which produces a stronger effect.

4. Select the **Monochromatic** check box to show only black-and-white noise. Click the **check box** to clear it if you want the noise to be various shades of all colors.

5. Click **OK** to close the dialog box and apply your changes to the image.

Figure 4-12   Adding noise to an image

An image with highly visible Moiré patterns might not be salvageable. In this case, try scanning the image again at different resolutions to avoid patterns.

Solving Problems with Video Capture Stills

Besides print, the other type of analog media you might need to digitize is video. To capture video clips or stills, you need special hardware and/or software which digitizes an input connection from a TV or VCR. The newer Macintosh computers and many Windows computers have this hardware and software preinstalled. How to capture a still from a video input depends on the system you have and is beyond the scope of this book. The following sections include a few tips to improve video-capture stills.

Boosting Colors

Television screens cannot display colors as saturated as those on computer monitors, so a bright TV image appears dull as a captured still. Use the Auto Levels dialog box to normalize the contrast, as discussed earlier in Fixing Low Contrast. Additionally, use the Hue/Saturation dialog box to increase the saturation of the colors, as discussed earlier in Fixing Problem Colors.

Removing Lines

Video displays 30 **frames** per second; each frame is composed of two **fields**, each appearing at 1/60 of a second. One field contains the even-numbered lines of the image, and the other field contains the odd-numbered lines; each field contains only half the image. When you watch video on a television, the even and odd fields appear so quickly that they seem to be a complete interlaced image. However, a captured video still shows separated horizontal lines. The lines are actually two images 1/60 of a second apart, interlaced together. If the original video had movement in it, the difference between the fields is more significant and the interlacing is exaggerated. To remove this effect, use the Photoshop De-interlace filter. (Click Filter on the menu bar, click Video, and then click De-Interlace.) This filter removes one of the fields by removing either the even- or odd-numbered lines, and then fills in the gap with interpolated lines from the other field.

A standard video still is 640 pixels wide and 480 pixels high. By de-interlacing you remove half of the lines, so you should reduce the image dimensions to 320 × 240 to maintain a sharp image. (In Photoshop, you do this with the Image Size dialog box.) Figure 4-13 shows a video capture still before and after boosting colors and de-interlacing lines.

Digital video does not produce the interlacing effect. Instead of displaying 60 fields per second like analog video, digital video displays 30 frames per second. Each frame is a complete bitmap image that contains all necessary lines.

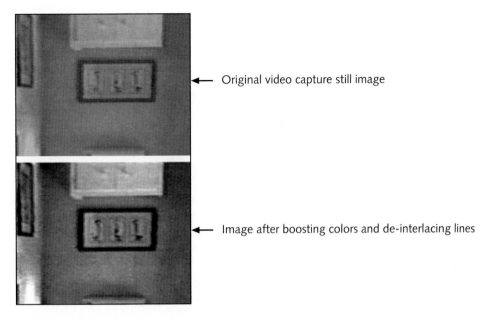

Original video capture still image

Image after boosting colors and de-interlacing lines

Figure 4-13   Fixing colors and lines in a video frame capture

Reducing the Effect of Motion

Just as you use the Blur or Despeckle filters to reduce patterns in scanned images, you use the Median filter to reduce the appearance of motion in photographs or video stills. The Median filter finds pixels of similar brightness and replaces the pixel between those pixels with an average of the surrounding pixels. To use the Median filter, click Filter on the menu bar, click Noise, and then click Median. This opens the Median dialog box, which shows a preview of your image and a slider for you to control the amount of motion reduction. This tool helps only when the appearance of motion is subtle. If an image has a lot of motion blurring, consider using a different image.

TAKING PHOTOGRAPHS

In the early years of the Web, including photographs on a Web page was a three-step process: use a camera to store an image on film, develop the film, and then scan the print. This technique is still pervasive and effective, but digital cameras provide a quicker option. With a digital camera, you capture the image directly as an image file, and don't have to record the image onto a file. Although the resolution of most digital cameras needs to catch up to the resolution of most film cameras, acquiring images is a one-step process with digital cameras.

The drawback of traditional film photography is that the image is locked into the medium—paper or slides. Prints can be retouched with airbrushing, but this post-production is time-consuming and can be performed only by experienced professionals.

The advent of the desktop computer and the desktop publishing revolution of the late 1980s, including the development of quality digital image editors such as Adobe Photoshop, changed photography again. Digital image editors let almost anyone manipulate photographs in ways previously reserved for experienced professionals.

As a Web graphic artist or designer, you might receive photographs as digital files, prints, or slides. You scan the photos or receive them in digital format, and then prepare them for the Web by editing them in an image-editing program such as Photoshop or ImageReady. If you work at a site, such as an online magazine, that handles lots of photographs, it's likely that someone else shoots the photographs. However, if you work at a small company, or one that doesn't have many photographs, you must be able to use a camera yourself to acquire images.

Using Film Cameras

Film cameras produce the highest resolution images possible. Although you display images on the Web at a low resolution, acquiring Web images with film cameras is valuable because these cameras are inexpensive and easy to use. You should familiarize yourself with the standard hardware, terminology, and developing techniques for working with film cameras.

Film Camera Hardware

Because image resolution on the Web is relatively low compared to print work, almost any point-and-shoot camera produces adequate images for Web work. However, when purchasing a camera and film, you should know the basic terminology defined in the following sections.

ISO   ISO refers to film speed, which is a measure of the light sensitivity of the film. ISO is an abbreviation for the International Organization for Standardization, which assigns universally accepted ratings for different types of photographic film. A low number such as 100 means the film is appropriate for the bright light of outdoors; a higher number such as 400 is more sensitive and appropriate for darker indoor shots. Choose a film with the appropriate ISO rating for what you plan to photograph.

F-Stop   F-Stop is a number that indicates the size of the camera's aperture, or opening that admits light. In bright light you close the aperture to create a sharper image. In low light you open the aperture to let in more light, though this lessens the detail.

Most consumer-quality cameras make aperture adjustments automatically. This makes it easy to create good photos in most lighting conditions. If you want more control over the lighting of your pictures, use a camera with manual f-stop adjustment.

Single-Lens Reflex Single-lens reflex (SLR) means the camera has only one lens for light to pass through. The light is sent to both the viewfinder and the film, so what you see is exactly what appears on the film. Inexpensive cameras have one lens to pass light to the film and a separate window for the viewfinder. What you see through the viewfinder of an inexpensive camera is not exactly what is recorded on the film. This difference is exaggerated at very close and very far distances. Single-lens reflex cameras use a series of mirrors to take some light from the lens and bounce it to the viewfinder. This lets you see exactly what will be registered on the film. SLR cameras produce superior results compared to non-SLR cameras. If you can afford the extra expense, and you plan to use a lot of high-quality photography on your site, consider buying an SLR camera.

Developing Film

After you take photographs with a film camera, you develop the film to produce slides, prints, or a photo CD. If you need high-quality Web images, such as product shots or other large detailed photos, develop slides, not prints. For other images, develop a print and scan it.

If you want slides, remember to use slide film to capture images on film and a slide scanner to import them into the computer. If you want prints, choose the highest quality paper available. High-color prints on quality paper create better scanned images than those on low-quality paper such as newsprint.

A relatively new option is to develop your film to a photo CD, where a film developer scans the negatives and produces high-quality digital images. This is an inexpensive and time-saving way to store many photographs in a digital format. The high storage capacity of a CD also makes it easy to archive photos. Having film photos developed onto a CD produces images of higher resolution than you can acquire from a digital camera or from scanning prints.

Scanning slides yields the highest resolution images; developing your prints as a photo CD creates the next highest resolution; and scanning prints produces the lowest resolution.

Using Digital Cameras

Professional photographers used to avoid digital cameras, which could not even approach the resolution of film. Now, however, you can create true print-quality images from the top-of-the-line digital cameras. Digital cameras save time when you are creating photographic images in a digital environment. Unlike film cameras, inexpensive digital cameras produce images with resolution too low for some Web graphic tasks. Choose a digital camera that produces at least 1-megapixel images, as discussed in the following section.

Before you purchase a digital camera, you should familiarize yourself with the hardware, terminology, and production techniques involved in working with digital cameras.

Film cameras record visual information on chemicals. This allows the resolution to be as fine as the individual molecules of silver nitrate on the film. Digital cameras have much coarser resolution based on pixels. When evaluating digital camera hardware, consider the highest resolution the cameras can produce, how they store images, the type of zoom they use, and whether they let you adjust virtual ISO.

Digital Camera Resolution

The resolution of digital cameras is often measured in **megapixels**; a megapixel is equal to one million pixels. The number of pixels is calculated by multiplying horizontal pixels by vertical pixels. For example, a digital camera that produces images which are 1280 pixels wide and 1024 pixels high can register 1,310,720 per image. Such a camera is described as a 1.3 megapixel camera.

When you select a digital camera to use to create source images for Web graphics, resolution should be your first concern. A camera that produces only 640 × 480-pixel images doesn't have enough resolution. Try to select a digital camera that produces at least 1-megapixel images. Even though these images are as large as an average computer screen, the detail in final Web graphics is sharper when you have larger source images.

Storing Images on a Digital Camera

Digital cameras save an image as a digital file to an internal disk or to a removable memory device called a **flash card**. Flash cards range in size from 2 MB to 40 MB. The smaller cards let you store only one or two high-resolution images.

To maximize the number of images saved on a disk or card, many digital cameras use lossy JPEG compression to reduce the size of the image files. However, this also reduces the quality of the images. Unless you have to take many photos at once, you should turn off the JPEG compression or at least set it to highest quality.

Because the flash card in a digital camera provides a finite amount of storage, most cameras let you store either several low-resolution images or a few high-resolution images.

Using Digital Zoom

Film and digital cameras both rely on lenses to focus light and use zoom lenses to magnify faraway subjects. Some digital cameras offer **digital zoom**, which doesn't require additional lenses and is an inexpensive alternative to standard **optical zoom**. Digital zoom crops the center of the image, expands the dimensions, and interpolates pixels. Images produced by digital zoom have much less detail than optical zoom images.

Setting Virtual ISO

Because digital cameras do not use film, lighting and film speed aren't major concerns, as they are with film cameras. However, many digital cameras still use ISO to indicate light sensitivity. You can adjust this virtual ISO to simulate ISO numbers as high as 1000, which lets you take pictures in very dim light.

PHOTOGRAPHIC TECHNIQUES

With analog photography, you must take great care when composing a shot. Once the image is locked into the medium of film, you can do little to change how it looks. With digital tools such as Adobe Photoshop, however, the composition of the shot is not as important because you can manipulate the image later on your computer.

However, you must follow the basic rules of image composition, because many aspects of photography cannot be repaired once the shutter snaps. For example, you cannot completely solve most poor lighting problems in post-production, so you must use proper lighting in the first place. In addition, you must carefully position the camera and subject when taking the photo, because you cannot change those factors afterward.

The following sections describe the basic rules of image composition.

Emphasizing the Subject

You take a picture because it has important visual features that you want others to see. Perhaps you're taking product shots for an online catalog, or collecting portraits for the staff bio page. Either way, you want to highlight the important and distinguishing features of your subject. You can emphasize these features by how you use angles and how you light the subject.

Using Angles

In general, shots you take from oblique angles are more informative than head-on shots. Most beginners simply shoot the front of the subject, disregarding anything on the sides. This can be effective in a photograph of a person, but does not create much interest or convey much information in other kinds of photographs. In Figure 4-14, the angle is straight-on and the sides and top are hidden from the viewer. With the camera at a 0° angle to the subject, only the front face is visible.

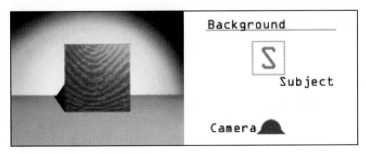

Figure 4-14   The camera at a 0° angle

By placing the subject at an angle to the camera, you make relative sizes visible. Additionally, the diagonal lines in such an image make the overall composition more dynamic. For most images, placing the subject at 30 degrees from the camera, as illustrated in Figure 4-15, is sufficient to create visual interest and communicate information. If you have a subject such as a car, where the sides are just as important as the front, a 45° angle is more effective because it lets you show as much of the car as possible. For a product such as a computer monitor, the front has most of the information and a 15° angle might be more appropriate. Rotating either the subject or the camera's perspective by about 30 degrees reveals more information.

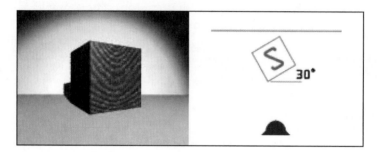

Figure 4-15   The camera at a 30° angle

For product shots, you can raise the camera 30 degrees above the subject to capture details from the top, as shown in Figure 4-16. By moving the camera this way, three sides become visible.

Figure 4-16   The camera at 30° to the side and 30° above

Lighting the Subject

Poor lighting is nearly impossible to fix in digital post-production, so it's important to light the subject effectively during the shoot. You can use a convention for lighting called 3-Point Lighting, which uses up to three lights. This lighting convention maximizes illumination and minimizes shadow.

The **key light** provides the most illumination of the subject. Direct the key light at the primary area of interest on the subject. Angle the key light about 45 degrees away from the camera to minimize glare and define the shape of the subject. If possible, use a diffuse light source to avoid harsh shadows. Figure 4-17 shows an object illuminated with a single key light. If you don't have access to professional lighting equipment, natural light from a window provides the most diffuse light and produces the best colors. If you have a choice, a slightly overcast day produces good light because clouds diffuse the light and eliminate harsh shadows. The more cloud cover, however, the less saturated the color, and the depth of focus will decrease. If you have to use indoor light, incandescent light (from light bulbs with filaments) produces warmer colors than fluorescent lights, which give subjects a bluish or greenish tinge.

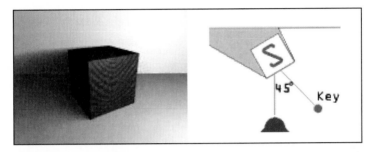

Figure 4-17   The key light

The key light usually produces strong shadows when used by itself, and might not illuminate the whole subject. You use a **fill light** for secondary illumination. Place a fill light on the opposite side of the camera from the key light to fill in or illuminate some of the shadows left by the key light, as illustrated in Figure 4-18. The fill light should not be as bright as the key light. Either use a weaker light source, or place it farther away from the subject than the fill light. If you are using light from a window for your key light, position the fill light on the opposite side of the subject to light the subject from both sides. If your indoor light is fixed, position the subject between the key and fill lights so that it is illuminated on both sides. A fill light reduces some of the shadows cast by the key light.

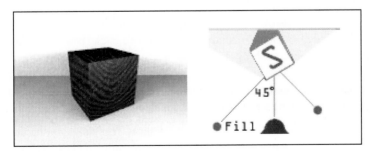

Figure 4-18   A fill light

You also can use additional lights called **back lights** or **point lights** to highlight specific areas of the subject. The fill light might not illuminate all the shadows cast by the key light, and might cast shadows of its own. Use point lights to illuminate shaded areas. Some modern photographers use fiber-optic cables to direct precise points of light. Point lights are most necessary when you take photos in a building with only overhead fluorescent lights. A small, directed incandescent light eliminates some shadows from overhead lights and creates warmer colors on the subject.

As stated, the fill light can create shadows of its own, and cannot fill in all the shadows left by the key light. Point lights illuminate specific areas. To fill in any remaining shadows, use a **background light** projected not on the subject, but on the background. Figure 4-19 shows how using back lights and background lights helps to reduce shadows and adds depth to an image.

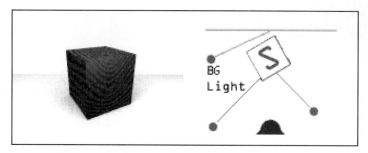

Figure 4-19   A background light

Deemphasizing the Background

As you probably know, the foreground is the subject of your photograph, while the background is whatever is behind the foreground. The background should not interfere with the foreground, but it can provide context for the subject or make the image more interesting. The ideal background has a different color and lightness from the subject, and has little texture to distract the viewer's attention.

To deemphasize outdoor backgrounds, you usually can adjust the focus and aperture on the camera so that the foreground is in sharp focus and the background is a little blurry. Make sure background objects; such as those that appear directly behind the subject, do not interfere with the subject. For example, a portrait with a telephone pole sticking out of a person's head looks silly. Position the subject so that only areas of color or texture (not objects with discrete edges) surround the subject.

You have more control over the background in indoor shots. You can use a background for context or interest's sake. For example, a plain white background makes the overall image seem dull, while subtly-colored or lightly textured fabric makes it more interesting. Use a background with low texture and colors that contrast with the subject to help the subject stand out. Avoid highly colored or intensely textured backgrounds, which draw attention away from the foreground. Also avoid backgrounds that have a color similar to the subject's.

In Figure 4-20, the background on the left side of the figure is blurry and darker than the foreground. This accentuates the subject and draws attention toward it. The background on the right side of the figurine has a lot of detail and bright colors. These compete with the foreground for attention and distract the viewer from the subject.

Figure 4-20   Background texture and color affect the appearance of the subject

Making the Image Interesting

Not only should the image provide visual information about the subject, it should be attractive or interesting enough so that people want to look at it. These terms are subjective, as there is no single standard for attractiveness. However, following a few fundamental rules can help make an image more interesting. Use margins, follow the rule of thirds, use diagonals, keep the image balanced, and maintain contrast to create visual interest.

Use Margins

When taking photos of people, many beginning photographers center the person's head in the image. This composition seems balanced in the viewfinder, but it leaves the upper half of the photo empty. Although you can crop a photo later in an image editor, you can compose a more appealing photo by shooting closer to the subject so that the top of the head is just below the top of the image. Be sure to leave plenty of headroom or you might crop off the top of the head. Include margins between the edges of the photo and the subject to frame the foreground. Your goal is to make the background spacing around the subject symmetrical, give the subject plenty of space in the composition, and include all of the visual information you need to communicate your message. A rule of thumb for margins is to leave left and right margins equal to about one-fifth the width of the subject, and leave a top and bottom margin equal to about one-fifth the height of the subject. If you know you'll have large margins, extra space near the bottom is more visually appealing than extra space near the top.

In Figure 4-21, the image on the left has too much room on the top and on the right, and not enough space at the bottom. The image on the right has enough room on all sides to center the subject and frame the area of interest. The left margin is larger than the others, but helps frame the primary area of interest, the face of the figure.

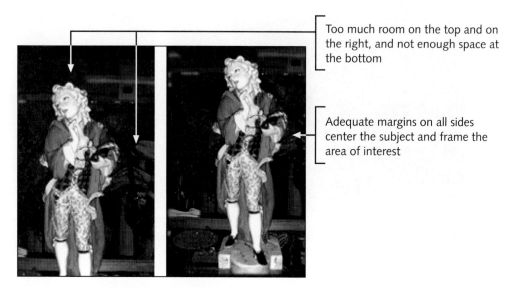

Too much room on the top and on the right, and not enough space at the bottom

Adequate margins on all sides center the subject and frame the area of interest

Figure 4-21   Contrasting use of margins

Follow the Rule of Thirds

Whether you are shooting outside and have a real horizon or are shooting objects on an indoor countertop, a horizontal line often intersects the image. By positioning the subject and the camera, you control where the horizon crosses the image. Position the camera so that the horizon line crosses one-third of the way down from the top, or one-third of the way up from the bottom. This is known as the **rule of thirds**. Follow this rule to add interest and balance to a picture and make it more dynamic. In Figure 4-22, the image on top has the horizon line at one-fifth below the top of the photograph. This creates the illusion that you are looking down on the object. The image at the bottom has the horizon line at the middle of the photograph, which results in a somewhat duller image. The image in the center has the horizon one-third from the top edge. This makes the image more interesting.

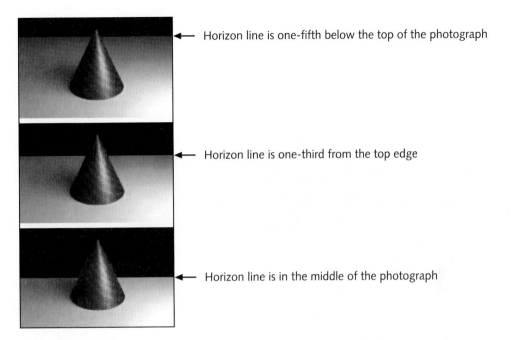

Horizon line is one-fifth below the top of the photograph

Horizon line is one-third from the top edge

Horizon line is in the middle of the photograph

4

Figure 4-22   The rule of thirds

Use Diagonals

Diagonal lines catch the eye more than vertical or horizontal ones. By angling the subject or the camera, the edges of the subject create diagonal lines on the image.

When we see, we tend to group visual elements together and connect imaginary lines between elements. If you position two objects in an image next to each other at the same height, or one directly above the other, the imaginary lines connecting them are simple horizontal or vertical lines. This composition is not as interesting as when you position the objects at different heights, creating imaginary diagonal lines between the objects. A diagonal composition is more dynamic. In Figure 4-23, the objects in the left image are aligned horizontally and vertically, which creates a dull composition. The objects in the center image are aligned along diagonals, which adds interest and directs the viewer's attention (in this case, to the object on the right). The composition of objects in the right image uses balance and spacing to distribute attention evenly throughout the image.

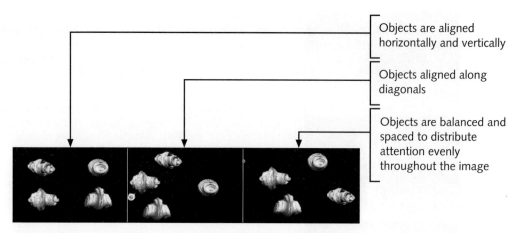

Figure 4-23 Objects with three different alignments

Labels pointing to the figure:
- Objects are aligned horizontally and vertically
- Objects aligned along diagonals
- Objects are balanced and spaced to distribute attention evenly throughout the image

Keep the Image Balanced

Balance means keeping the focus of an image near the center so that the viewer's attention does not drift away from the image, and so that it does not appear as though something is missing from the image. If you have one subject and a plain background, you normally would center the subject. If you have multiple subjects in the foreground, though, you want to make sure the picture is balanced. Think of the bottom of the image as a seesaw, and every distinct shape in the image as a weight; bigger elements, darker elements, and more textured elements are heavier. For a small child to balance a large child on a seesaw, the small child must be at the end and the large child must be near the fulcrum. If both children sit the same distance from the center, the large child causes an imbalance. In Figure 4-24, color, texture, and size all add visual weight to elements in an image. The image on the left seems unbalanced toward the right. Moving the heavier image toward the center and the lighter image to the left maintains the balance among the objects.

The image on the left appears unbalanced toward the right.
By moving the heavier image toward the center and the lighter
image toward the left, balance is maintained

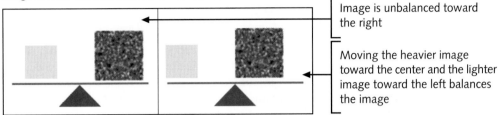

Image is unbalanced toward
the right

Moving the heavier image
toward the center and the lighter
image toward the left balances
the image

4

Figure 4-24   Balanced and unbalanced images

Maintain Contrast

One reason for setting up lights is to reduce glare and strong shadows. However, you don't want to completely eliminate these elements. They help give the subject a three-dimensional look and add interest to the image. Shadows create contrast, which makes an image visually interesting. You can use the following forms of contrast in your photographs:

- *Lightness contrast*: Light-colored objects show up better on dark backgrounds, and dark objects show up better on light backgrounds. If you can control the background, make sure it contrasts with the subject. If you can control the lighting, light the foreground and background so that the foreground stands out from the background. Lighter objects against a dark background stand out better than dark objects on a light background. Dark colors recede into an image, while light colors stand out.

- *Hue contrast*: In addition to lightness, the hue of the background can make the foreground stand out. A pink object against a red background creates lightness contrast, but no hue contrast. A better background would be dark green or blue. Choose hues that are opposite each other on the color wheel. In general, red and green are considered complementary opposites, as are blue and yellow. Because light colors against dark backgrounds stand out better than dark on light, use hues that support this idea. If you have a blue object against a yellow background, for example, the blue object recedes into the yellow, making the background the primary point of interest.

- *Saturation contrast*: Sometimes the foreground and background have similar hue and lightness, and the subject does not stand out. To resolve this, change the contrast between the saturation of the hues. If the blue and yellow in the image have the same saturation, for example, the yellow stands out. If you brighten the blue and lessen the saturation of the yellow, the blue stands out.

- *Texture contrast*: Use texture to draw focus to the subject and away from the background. Highly textured objects are noticed more easily than areas of flat color. Try to make your subjects more textured than the background. By adjusting the focus of the camera, you can make the background blurred, which reduces the visual texture. Figure 4-25 shows examples of high and low contrast of lightness, hue, saturation, and texture.

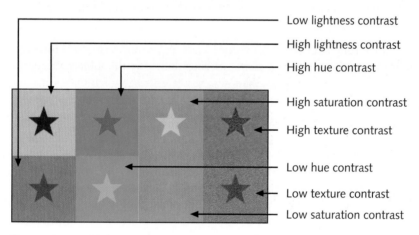

Figure 4-25   Lightness, hue, saturation, and texture contrast

RETOUCHING PHOTOGRAPHS

Photograph retouching used to involve airbrushing away unwanted elements, and using pens and sponges to reduce the appearance of scratches. Modern image-editing software gives you far more control than these traditional techniques. Instead of painting over areas of an image, you can adjust the color of individual pixels. The following sections discuss the tools and techniques you can use in Photoshop to retouch photographs.

Most digital photo-retouching tools are similar to the ones used to treat photo prints. Terms such as airbrush and sponge reflect the actual objects used for retouching film photography. Photoshop provides a variety of brushes to retouch photos, and provides selection tools to precisely select what you want to retouch.

Using the Photoshop Brushes

Most of the tools you use to retouch photos are either painting tools or editing tools, and all use brushes. You can adjust the size and softness of the mark left by the brush in the Options bar when you select one of the painting tools. Open an image you want to retouch, and then follow the steps below.

To adjust the size and softness of a Photoshop brush:

1. Click the **tool** you want to use. For example, click the **Paintbrush tool**.

2. Make sure the Options bar is open. To open the Options bar, click **Window** on the menu bar, and then click **Show Options**.

3. On the options bar, click the **Brush list arrow** to see the Brush menu, as illustrated in Figure 4-26.

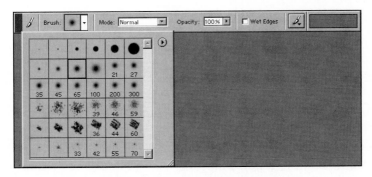

Figure 4-26   The Brush menu in the Options bar

4. Choose a **brush size** from the Brush menu.

5. Point to the open image—your pointer reflects the size and shape of the brush.

   Brushes usually are round, but can be any shape. The Spatter and Chalk brushes create artistic effects.

6. To load a new set of brushes or create new brushes, click the **right triangle button** on the Brush menu, and then click **New Brush** to open the New Brush dialog box, shown in Figure 4-27.

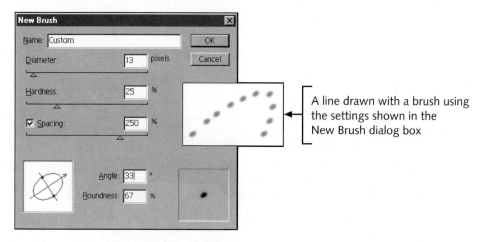

A line drawn with a brush using the settings shown in the New Brush dialog box

Figure 4-27   The New Brush dialog box

7. Change the settings described below, and then click **OK**. A new brush icon then appears in the Brush menu.

- The diameter of the brush stroke in pixels
- The hardness of the brush, where 0% is very soft and 100% is hard. A soft edge means the brush stroke fades to transparent.
- The spacing of the line. Anything over 100% creates a dotted line.
- The angle of the brush head, which matters only if the brush has a different roundness
- The roundness ranges from a normal 100% round brush, to an elliptical shape, to a 0% calligraphic brush.

8. To edit the settings for an existing brush, click the **brush icon** in the Options bar. This opens a menu with the same choices as the New Brush dialog box.

For photo retouching, you almost always want a round brush with a soft edge. Using a brush with a hard edge makes the edits more visible. The brush size depends on the accuracy you need for the particular task.

Using the Photoshop Selection Tools

You use the selection tools almost every time you use Photoshop. Before you can perform most tasks with a part of an open image, you first must select that part. When you select an area of the image, you see an animated dashed line, called a marquee, indicating the selected area. When you use a brush to edit the image, the changes occur only

4

within the selection. You can select an area in a particular shape or according to similarities among pixels. You can set most selection tools to be anti-aliased or not. (Recall that anti-aliasing means adding interpolated pixels to create a soft, feathered line.) Changes made to a selection that is not anti-aliased apply only to pixels within the selection. Changes made to an anti-aliased selection bleed through to the pixels directly adjacent to the selection.

The following sections discuss three popular Photoshop selection tools: the Marquee, Lasso, and Magic Wand tools.

Marquee Tools

Use the Marquee tools to select areas of images. Selection areas constrain the effects of filters and tools. Figure 4-28 shows selection areas defined with the Rectangular and Elliptical Marquee tools. To select a Marquee tool, click and hold the Rectangular Marquee tool in the toolbar, and then click the tool you want in the palette. Drag across the image to define the selection area.

Two tools you often use for photo retouching are the Rectangular Marquee tool and the Elliptical Marquee tool. Use the Rectangular Marquee to create rectangular selection areas. Use the Elliptical Marquee to create elliptical selection areas. For both of these tools, you can set the selection to maintain a fixed aspect ratio by holding down the Shift key as you drag. Doing so creates a perfect square or circle. If you already have selected an area, hold down the Shift key and then use a Marquee tool to select additional areas.

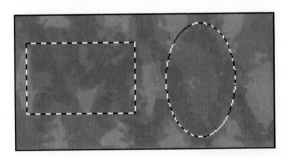

Figure 4-28   Using the Rectangular and Elliptical Marquee tools

Lasso Tools

The Lasso Tools in Photoshop let you draw a selection around specific pixels, as shown in Figure 4-29. While the Marquee tools define geometric selections, you use the Lasso tool to draw a selection line of any shape around an area. Use the Polygonal Lasso tool to create geometric selections with any number of lines and corners. Holding down the Shift key constrains the Polygonal Lasso Tool to 45° angles. Holding down the Ctrl key and clicking stops selecting. The Magnetic Lasso Tool is intelligent because as you select an area, it finds the nearest edge and sticks there.

Figure 4-29   Using the Lasso tool

Magic Wand Tool

The Magic Wand tool shown in Figure 4-30 also is intelligent. When you select a pixel with the Magic Wand Tool, it selects that pixel and every adjacent pixel of similar color. What counts as similar is determined by the Tolerance value in the Magic Wand Options dialog box. A setting of 0 means only pixels of the exact hue, saturation, and lightness are selected with the original pixel. A higher setting makes the tool select pixels which are similar in color. By default, the Magic Wand tool selects only adjacent pixels. You also can select nonadjacent pixels with the Magic Wand tool when the Contiguous box in the Options bar is unchecked.

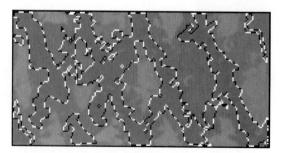

Figure 4-30   Using the Magic Wand tool

Using Other Photoshop Tools to Retouch Photographs

In general, you use Photoshop tools to adjust images in two ways: you use a filter to affect the whole image or a selected area of the image, or you use a brush tool to draw over the area you need to change. The following sections discuss both of these techniques, and also explain how to fix common problems such as red eye and poor lighting.

Using the Airbrush Tool

Use the Airbrush tool to fix minor blemishes in areas of fairly even color. In Figure 4-31, the Airbrush tool has been used to minimize the glare in the glass. The Airbrush tool is inappropriate for fixing textured surfaces such as the background cloth, however, where it leaves an obvious mark.

Figure 4-31   Using the Airbrush tool

The Airbrush tool paints a feathered line on an image. The Airbrush tool is similar to the Paintbrush tool, except the line created has a softer edge. Before applying the Airbrush to an image, pick the color you want to use. Use the Eyedropper Tool to select a color in the area you want to airbrush. If the area is textured, set the Eyedropper options in the Options bar to a 5 × 5 average sample size. Then the Eyedropper collects the 25 nearest pixels and averages their colors to set the foreground color.

After you select the color for the Airbrush, use a selection tool to select the area you want to airbrush; keep in mind that you want to affect only the problem area. In the Options bar, you can set the Airbrush options to low pressure, such as 10%. This creates a soft, mostly transparent line. A high pressure creates a heavier, more opaque line. If you want to make delicate edits, set the Airbrush tool to fade after a given number of steps. This prevents you from inadvertently painting too much on the image.

Start out with a small, soft brush. As you grow more comfortable with airbrushing, use higher pressure, turn off the fade, and use a larger brush.

Using the Dust & Scratches Filter

Photoshop has a filter explicitly designed to remove minor blemishes from photographs. Blemishes might result from dust on the camera lens or scanner bed, or from scratches in the original photo. This filter is called the Dust & Scratches filter and works by finding adjacent pixels that are of different colors, and blurring them.

To use the Dust & Scratches filter:

1. Select the **area** around the defect, or, if the image is full of blemishes, leave the image unselected.

2. To select the Dust & Scratches filter, click **Filter** on the menu bar, point to **Noise**, and then click **Dust & Scratches**. The Dust & Scratches dialog box opens, as shown in Figure 4-32.

3. Set the Radius value. Type a new value in the Radius text box, or drag the Radius slider to set the Radius value. A higher radius results in a blurrier image. Use the lowest value that eliminates the blemishes.

4. Set the Threshold value to define how different the pixels must be before they are blurred. Type a new value in the Threshold text box, or drag the Threshold slider to set the Threshold value. A low value produces a strong effect and a high value produces little or no effect. Experiment with both the Radius and Threshold sliders to find the values that remove the defects without affecting the rest of the image.

5. Click **OK** to close the dialog box.

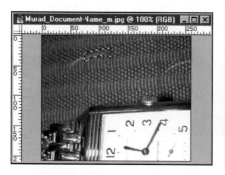

Figure 4-32   The Dust & Scratches dialog box

Using Selective Blurring

If you do not need to remove particular elements from an image, but want only to deemphasize the background, you can selectively blur that area of the image. Blurring reduces color contrast, lightness contrast, and texture contrast by blending adjacent pixels. In Figure 4-33, the left side of the background has not been blurred, and the right side has.

Figure 4-33 Selective blurring

Begin by selecting the problem area, and then pick a blur filter. Photoshop offers several, as discussed in the Removing Patterns section, but only the Gaussian Blur lets you preview the image as you adjust the parameters. You also can use the Blur tool, which works like other brush tools but instead of applying color, it blurs the pixels you brush.

After blurring the background, you can enhance the foreground by using one of the sharpen filters. Sharpening is the opposite of blurring. Instead of reducing contrast, sharpening increases contrast by finding the differences in color and lightness between adjacent pixels and exaggerating those differences. The **Unsharp Mask** filter gives you the most control over sharpening an image. For fine detail, use the Sharpen tool. Use the Smudge tool to smear adjacent pixels. Figure 4-34 shows the Photoshop Blur, Sharpen, and Smudge tools.

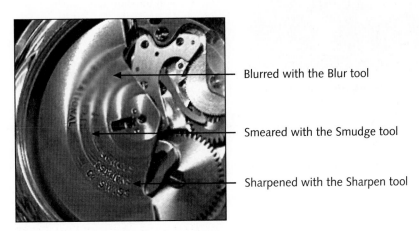

Blurred with the Blur tool

Smeared with the Smudge tool

Sharpened with the Sharpen tool

Figure 4-34 Using the Blur, Sharpen, and Smudge tools

Using Selective Saturation

In addition to blurring the background to deemphasize it, you can lower its color saturation. As discussed in the Maintain Contrast section, adjusting the color saturation of the background emphasizes the foreground and enhances the presentation of the subject.

To lower color saturation in Photoshop, open the Hue/Saturation dialog box (as instructed in the Fixing Problem Colors section), and slide the saturation slider to the left. As pixels become desaturated, they lose their hue. Reds and blues turn to black, yellows turn to white, and greens, cyans, and magentas turn to intermediate shades of gray.

For more control, use the Sponge tool. While using the Hue/Saturation dialog box is appropriate for affecting an entire image or selection area in an image, using the Sponge tool is more appropriate for making local changes to specific pixels. Select the Sponge tool from the toolbox. You use this tool to make pixels either more saturated or less saturated by selecting one of these options from the Mode menu in the Options bar.

You can apply lightness effects locally by using the Dodge and Burn tools. The Dodge tool makes pixels brighter, and the Burn tool makes them darker. All three saturation tools are illustrated in Figure 4-35.

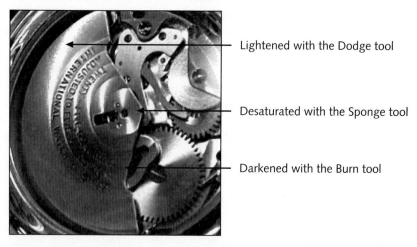

Lightened with the Dodge tool

Desaturated with the Sponge tool

Darkened with the Burn tool

Figure 4-35   Using the Dodge, Burn, and Sponge tools

Fixing Red Eye

Red eye occurs when the subject of a photograph looks directly into the camera and the light from the flash travels into the subject's eye, bounces against the back of the eye and travels back through the lens again. To reduce red eye, have the subject look away from the lens or don't use a flash. You can use Photoshop or another image editing tool to fix a photo with red eye. The quickest and easiest technique for reducing red eye is to zoom in to the red area and paint it with an appropriate color. Red eye occurs at the pupil, so replacing the red with black usually produces a realistic effect.

For more precise control, select the red area with one of the marquee selection tools, and then open the Hue/Saturation dialog box. Click the Edit list arrow, and then click Reds to specify that you want to affect only the red pixels in the eye. Then lower the Saturation and Lightness sliders to the left to remove the red pixels from the selected area.

Fixing Lighting Problems

Some lighting problems cannot be fixed in Photoshop. Some images have shadows so dark or highlights so bright that foreground detail is completely lost. For these photos, the best you can do is enhance the existing lights and shadows by selectively lightening and darkening the image. Your choices are to either lighten with the Dodge tool, or darken with the Burn tool.

These tools work like other brush tools, except that Burn and Dodge let you control the kind of pixels you want to change. You can set them to affect only Shadows, Midtones, or Highlights. If you want to lighten a dark area of an image, use the Dodge tool and set the Range to Shadows in the Options bar. If you want to darken middle-gray areas in an image, use the Burn Tool and set it to Midtones.

You also can select an area and use the Levels tool or Hue/Saturation tool, as discussed in the Fixing Low Contrast section, to increase or decrease the lightness.

Replacing Unwanted Elements

Replacing unwanted parts of a photo is one of the most fun aspects of editing images. As you explore the possibilities of the tools and techniques discussed in the following sections, you will realize that photographs can no longer be trusted to be true reproductions of reality. You can use the Smudge and Clone Stamp tools to change a photograph by copying and pasting.

The Smudge tool copies the area under the brush, and as you drag the cursor over the image, it pastes the copied area. It does this over and over again, giving the illusion that it is actually pushing the pixels. You adjust the distance between the copy and paste locations by changing the Pressure setting in the Options bar. The pressure setting is measured in percentages and the value is the percentage of the width of the brush you use. If you set the Pressure to 0%, the Smudge tool copies and pastes the selection in the same place. If you set the Pressure to 50% and the brush you use is 6 pixels in diameter, the Smudge tool pastes the selection 3 pixels away from where it was pasted. If you set the pressure to 100%, the tool pastes the original copied area 6 pixels away. Pressure settings below 50% are barely noticeable, and remove blemishes without affecting the rest of the image. Pressure settings above 50% provide interesting visual effects but are not useful for photo retouching.

In Figure 4-36, the image on the left has areas showing tarnish on the metal. The image on the right is the same image with the tarnish smeared away with the Smudge tool.

Tarnish is smeared away with the Smudge tool

Areas show tarnish on the metal

Figure 4-36   Using the Smudge tool

The Clone Stamp Tool (also called the Rubber Stamp tool) is similar to the Smudge Tool except that it allows you to control where to paste the copied selection. You set where to copy from by holding down the Option key on the Macintosh or Alt on a Windows computer, and then clicking. You can paste the copied area anywhere. As you drag the pointer over the image, it changes to a crosshair to show you the sample being pasted. If you select the Aligned option in the Options bar, the crosshair moves with the cursor, and is aligned to its position even when you stop dragging. If you do not select Aligned, the crosshair follows the cursor, but every time you stop dragging, the crosshair returns to its original location. When using the Clone Stamp tool, you achieve the best results by setting the brush to one of the Spatter brush heads. This leaves a random pattern, rather than a straight line. Using a normal brush often results in the edit being visible and obvious. The Clone Stamp tool, shown in Figure 4-37, lets you copy one part of an image onto another.

Area copied to

Area copied from

Figure 4-37   Using the Clone Stamp tool

Adding Lens Flare

Extensive photo retouching can reduce the realism of the original photograph and create an image that looks computer-generated, or too obviously retouched. The best way to minimize this artificiality is to be conservative when using the techniques described in the Using Other Photoshop Tools to Retouch Photographs section.

But you also can use a trick that makes these heavily edited images appear fresh again. Photoshop offers a filter under the Render submenu of the Filter menu called Lens Flare, which places artificial streaks of light in the image as though light was refracting in the camera lens. You can adjust the position and size of the flare as well as the type of lens you want to simulate. When positioning the flare, place it in the brightest area of the image. It doesn't look realistic if the lens flare is coming from a shadow; instead, place it over a light source in the image, such as a candle, window, or where light normally reflects, perhaps on glass or shiny metal.

In Figure 4-38, the image on the left has a lens flare coming from a shaded area. This looks artificial because there is nothing in the photo that could possibly cause such an effect. The image on the right has a lens flare placed where there already is a natural highlight.

Lens flare coming from a shaded area

Lens flare placed where there already is a natural highlight

Figure 4-38   Adding lens flare

Making Antique Photos

The Hue/Saturation dialog box contains the Colorize option. Selecting the Colorize check box preserves the brightness of the pixels in the image, but shifts the hue of each pixel to one particular value, creating a monochromatic version of the image. When colorizing an image, black stays black and white stays white, but every other color becomes a shade of the color set by the saturation slider.

By checking the Colorize option, you can create an antique effect in photographs. In the Hue/Saturation dialog box, select Colorize and then set the Hue to 30, which is orange—halfway between red and yellow. This gives the entire image the sepia color seen in old photos. Besides creating the visual effect, colorizing reduces file size by reducing colors. Figure 4-39 shows an image colorized this way.

Figure 4-39   Colorizing an image

ACQUIRING IMAGES FROM OTHER SOURCES

Using a scanner is a two-step process. First you have to find the image in an analog format, and then digitize it with a scanner. Using a digital camera is a one-step process. As soon as you click the shutter, you have a bitmap image that is ready to be used on the Web.

You can acquire images even more immediately by using images that already are in a digital form. You can take screen shots to capture images on your computer monitor, use images from stock photo CDs, or use images on other Web sites.

Taking Screen Shots

The image you see on your computer monitor is really one large bitmap image. You can see that by taking a screen shot and capturing the desktop image. To take a screen shot within the Macintosh operating system, press shift-command-3. This captures the screen image and saves it as a file in the .pict format called Picture 1 on your hard drive.

To take a screen shot using Windows as your operating system, press the Print Screen key (Prt Sc). This saves the screen image to the Windows Clipboard. Then you can paste the image into a file in an image-editing program such as Photoshop.

Using Stock Image CDs

When you need a photograph, but don't have time to take the picture, use stock photo CDs, which contain thousands of images. With most copyrighted images, you must give credit to the source and pay for the use of that image. With stock photos, you buy the disk and are free to use all the images. You also can buy stock photos on the Web where you can see low-resolution thumbnail versions of the images. When you find one you like, you can purchase the image, and then download a high-resolution version of the image.

Many companies also offer stock **clipart** CDs. Clipart refers to stock illustrations, images intended to be used by others. Originally these images were used in print media such as newsletters, so clipart traditionally meant images created in a vector drawing program and saved in a format such as PostScript.

In the past, to use these images on the Web, you had to first open them in a vector program and then rasterize them. Now, however, most companies that sell collections of clipart anticipate that the images will be used as Web graphics, so the images are saved in Web formats such as GIF or JPEG.

The quality of most clipart is rather low, and the style can be cartoonish, with black outlines filled in with solid colors. You probably will find clipart most useful when you need icons for a navigation bar, such as a simple mailbox to indicate an e-mail link.

Clipart collections are inexpensive to create, and you can find some for under $30 that contain tens of thousands of images.

Using Images from the Web

Another source of images is other Web pages. Some sites offer free online clipart and stock photo galleries. The quality of these images tends to be lower than those found on a commercial stock photo CD, but they are more accessible and are free.

To grab images from other Web sites, point to the image in a Web browser, and then click and hold the mouse button on a Macintosh, or right-click in Windows until a shortcut menu appears. The menu offers an option to save the image.

Almost every image you see on the Web has an implicit copyright, meaning someone owns permission even if it is not explicitly stated. You do not have the legal right to use images from other Web sites without explicit permission from the owners or operators of the site. Using any image violates the copyright on the image and is considered stealing.

Considering Copyrights

Many students are tempted to pirate software and use images from other Web sites without permission. But in the professional world, you have to be more careful. When a copyright violation has occurred, the practice is for the copyright holder to first contact the violator and ask that the image be removed. If the violator refuses or ignores the request, the copyright holder can sue.

Even one pirated image on a noncommercial site is illegal. If you use many pirated images, or if the site is commercial in nature, you jeopardize your entire company.

Unless explicitly stated, every image is copyrighted by the company on whose site the image appears. Even images which seem like they should be free, such as images of famous people, news photos, or images of paintings, are probably owned and need to be licensed to be used. Using a copyrighted image and editing it to make it different from the original does not protect you. Simply changing colors or resizing an image does not make it yours. You should always create your own images, or make sure that you have explicit permission to use images from other sources.

Watermarking Images

Some individuals, such as professional photographers and artists, put a lot of time and effort into creating their images and want to be able to track illegal usage. Often there is no way to prove that an image is yours, especially if you have not copyrighted the image. To prove that you are the creator of an image, you can add a watermark, which is a small amount of digital information that appears as noise on the image. The watermark endures image editing, and survives even if the image is printed and then scanned again.

Before embedding a watermark, you have to register with Digimarc Corporation at *www.digimarc.com*, which keeps a database of registrants. They provide you a unique ID that appears in the watermark information and affirms that you are the creator of the image.

Some images cannot hold watermarks. The image must have at least some variation of color and texture. Simple figures such as graphs with areas of flat color don't hold a watermark. Larger images also disguise a watermark better; an image should be at least 100 × 100 pixels, and larger if you plan to edit the image after the watermark has been embedded. Lossy JPEG compression and some filters can also degrade the watermark. So, for 24-bit images use a JPEG compression of at least 4, and run all filters before adding the watermark at the end.

CHAPTER SUMMARY

❏ You can acquire an image in a two-step analog process by drawing a figure and scanning the drawing, or in a one-step process by taking a picture with a digital camera. Or, you can gather existing images from stock photo CDs.

❏ A 600-dpi flatbed scanner is an inexpensive and versatile tool that you can use to digitize almost any flat source image.

❏ Fix scanning artifacts and Moiré patterns with the Despeckle and Blur filters.

❏ Fix poor color with the Levels and Hue/Saturation dialog boxes.

❏ Affordable digital cameras do not have the resolution of film cameras, but most can produce perfectly acceptable images to be used as Web graphics.

❏ When composing a photograph and editing the photo in Photoshop, use lighting, color, and texture to provide contrast between foreground and background. Utilize angles, balance, and contrast to compose an interesting and attractive image.

❏ Use the Blur, Dodge, Burn, and Sponge tools to apply local effects to an image.

❐ Use the Clone Stamp Tool to completely eliminate specific elements from an image.

❐ You can use stock photo and clipart images from commercial CDs, or use graphics from free image library Web sites.

❐ Although it is tempting to use existing images found on other Web sites, you cannot use them unless you have explicit permission to do so.

4

REVIEW QUESTIONS

1. If a scanner has a resolution of 600 dpi, how many pixels does it generate by scanning an area 4½" wide and 5½" high?

   a. 1,051,875

   b. 2,103,750

   c. 4,207,500

   d. 8,415,000

2. Which image will have the lowest resolution?

   a. A digital photograph taken with a 1-megapixel digital camera

   b. A film photograph developed to a photo CD

   c. A film photograph printed to slide and scanned with a slide scanner

   d. A film photograph scanned with a 600-dpi flatbed scanner

3. What is a driver?

   a. Hardware that controls hardware such as a scanner or printer

   b. Hardware that controls the scanning interface software

   c. Software that controls hardware such as a scanner or printer

   d. Software that controls the scanning interface software

4. What do you do when you change output levels with the Photoshop Levels tool?

   a. Increase brightness

   b. Reduce brightness

   c. Increase Contrast

   d. Reduce Contrast

5. Which Photoshop Blur filter allows you to control and preview the blurring?

   a. Blur

   b. Blur More

   c. Gaussian Blur

   d. Smart Blur

6. Which Photoshop Sharpen filter allows you to control and preview the sharpening?

    a. Sharpen

    b. Sharpen Edges

    c. Sharpen More

    d. Unsharp Mask

7. What tool, filter, or dialog box would you use to remove blemishes from scanning?

    a. Hue/Saturation

    b. Gaussian Blur

    c. Levels

    d. Clone Stamp tool

8. What is the best tool for removing patterns from images scanned from magazines?

    a. Gaussian Blur

    b. Add Noise

    c. Despeckle

    d. Median

9. What is a likely resolution of an image taken with a 2-megapixel camera?

    a. 1024 × 768

    b. 1280 × 1024

    c. 1600 × 1280

    d. 2000 × 1600

10. What does ISO refer to?

    a. Aperture opening

    b. Focal length

    c. Sensitivity to light

    d. Shutter speed

11. What is the fill light?

    a. The primary source of illumination of a subject

    b. The secondary source of illumination of a subject

    c. A tertiary source of illumination of a subject

    d. A source of illumination for the background

12. Which photographic technique is easiest to repair or simulate in Photoshop?

    a. Background

    b. Colors

    c. Composition

    d. Lighting

13. What Photoshop tool, filter, or dialog box would you use to repair washed-out colors?

    a. Clone Stamp tool

    b. Gaussian Blur

    c. Hue/Saturation

    d. Levels

14. In Photoshop, what are the differences between the Dodge, Burn, and Sponge tools?

    a. Burn lightens, Dodge darkens, and Sponge affects saturation

    b. Dodge lightens, Burn darkens, and Sponge affects saturation

    c. Dodge lightens, Sponge darkens, and Burn affects saturation

    d. Sponge lightens, Burn darkens, and Dodge affects saturation

15. What tool, filter, or dialog box would you use to remove unwanted areas of an image?

    a. Clone Stamp tool

    b. Gaussian Blur

    c. Hue/Saturation

    d. Levels

16. What tool, filter, or dialog box would you use to create antique-looking images?

    a. Clone Stamp tool

    b. Gaussian Blur

    c. Hue/Saturation

    d. Levels

17. To make an antique-looking photo, to what hue value should you colorize the image?

    a. –150

    b. –30

    c. 30

    d. 150

18. Which of the following is a method you would not use to deemphasize the background?

  a. Reduce the blurring of the background

  b. Reduce the hue saturation of the background

  c. Reduce the lightness of the background

  d. Reduce the texture of the background

19. Which of the following is a method you would not use to emphasize the subject?

  a. Blur the foreground

  b. Saturate the foreground

  c. Set the subject at an angle

  d. Sharpen the foreground

20. Which of the following retouching tasks would be difficult in Photoshop?

  a. Adding a light to illuminate the subject from the side

  b. Blurring the background

  c. Reducing red eye

  d. Removing a telephone pole from a photograph

HANDS-ON PROJECTS

All of the following projects use Photoshop and files provided for you in the Chapter04 folder of your Data Disk, or in the Student Data/Chapter04 folder of your hard drive.

Project 4-1: Fix a Low-Contrast Scan

Your department's graphic artist has given you a scan of a logo he drew. It's washed out and has a strong shadow. Boost the colors and remove the shadow.

1. Open the image file **4-1.tif** on the Data Disk.

2. Open the **Levels** dialog box and use **Auto Levels** to normalize the contrast.

3. Raise the Gamma to **2.00**.

4. Use the **Eraser** tool to eliminate any remaining shadows.

5. Use the **Crop** tool to remove excess margins around the image.

6. Reduce the dimensions to **150** pixels high, and save as an optimized GIF called **4-1.gif** in the Chapter 04 folder on your hard drive.

Project 4-2: Fix a Scan with Unwanted Colors

You scanned an image to try to improve the color. The scanner lid was not flat, however, and two corners of the image developed an unwanted tint of color. Remove the unwanted color while altering the original image as little as possible.

1. Open the image file **4-2.tif** from the Data Disk.
2. Use the **Rectangular Marquee** tool to select the corner of the image with the Magenta smear.
3. Open the **Hue/Saturation** dialog box.
4. Select **Magenta** as the color you want to remove.
5. Raise the Lightness slider to **100%** and click **OK**.
6. Some of the green area became desaturated in the process. Select the affected area with the **Rectangular Marquee** tool.
7. Open the **Hue/Saturation** dialog box again and select the **Colorize** check box.
8. Set the Hue to **120**, the Saturation to **35**, and the Lightness to **10**.
9. Use a similar procedure to eliminate the green area.
10. Reduce the dimensions to **150** pixels high and save as an optimized GIF called **4-2.gif** in the Chapter 04 folder on your hard drive.

Project 4-3: Retouch Lighting in a Photograph

An image was taken with light from a nearby window, creating harsh shadows and not illuminating the subject well. Enhance the existing lighting to emphasize the foreground more.

1. Open the image file **4-3.tif** on the Data Disk.
2. Use the Levels dialog box to normalize the contrast, and set the Gamma to **1.2**.
3. To deemphasize the background, select the **Burn** tool, set it to **Highlights** and set the Exposure to **50%**.
4. Select a brush around **50** pixels in diameter, and paint the bright areas in the background.
5. To emphasize the subject, select the **Dodge** tool, set it to **Shadows**, and set the Exposure to **30%**.
6. Use a smaller brush to daub the dark areas in the foreground.
7. Even out the lighting of the subject by using the **Burn** tool again. With the tool still set to Highlights, daub the bright areas in the foreground.
8. Normalize the levels again, optimize, and save as a JPEG called **4-3.jpg** in the Chapter 04 folder on your hard drive.

4

Project 4-4: Retouch Unwanted Areas of a Photograph

In addition to poor color, an image shows unsightly power lines. Retouch the image to remove these elements from the picture.

1. Open the image file **4-4.tif** on the Data Disk.

2. Normalize levels and set the Gamma to **1.6**.

3. This reveals some of the JPEG artifacts produced by the digital camera used to take the photo. To reduce the effect of these artifacts, add noise using the Add Noise filter. Set Amount to **5**, Distribution to **Uniform**, and deselect the **Monochromatic** check box, if it is selected.

4. Select the **Eyedropper** tool, and set the Sample Size in the Options bar to **5 by 5 Average**.

5. Select the **sky** near the utility lines with the Eyedropper Tool to set the Foreground Color to the bluish-white of the sky.

6. Select the **Airbrush** tool. Set the options to **Normal**, **50% Pressure**.

7. Use a 20- to 30-pixel brush, and paint over the power lines in the image.

8. Some power lines are near tree branches and cannot be painted without affecting the branches. Select the **Smudge** tool, and use a very fine brush (1 or 2 pixels). Smudge the power lines near the tree branches by pointing to the **branches**, and then dragging across the **power lines**. Zoom in with the **Magnifying Glass** tool to see what you are doing.

9. Optimize and save as a JPEG called **4-4.jpg** in the Chapter 04 folder on your hard drive.

Project 4-5: Replace Unwanted Areas of a Photograph

A picture has unwanted elements in front of a textured background that cannot be simply painted or smudged over. Brighten the image and remove the people crossing the bridge.

1. Open the image file **4-5.tif** on the Data Disk.

2. Normalize contrast and set gamma to **2.5**.

3. Mask the existing JPEG artifacts by adding noise. Select the **lower third** of the image where the artifacts are most apparent. With the **Add Noise** filter, set the Amount to **10**, Distribution to **Uniform**, and deselect the **Monochromatic** check box.

4. With the **Magnifying Glass** tool, zoom in about **400%** where the people are crossing the bridge.

5. Select the **Clone Stamp** tool, and make sure the Aligned check box in the Options bar is selected.

6. Move the pointer over an area of the railing near the people. Hold down the **Option** key on the Macintosh, or **Alt** in Windows to change the pointer to the Clone Stamp icon. Click to select the **area** as the origin.

7. Carefully daub over the people, replacing them with nearby pixels. This technique requires some practice to get it right. Look at the History Palette to see your recent actions. You can delete any of your past actions if you decide the effect was wrong.

8. Crop the **image** to remove the excess margins. Optimize and save as a JPEG called **4-5.jpg** in the Chapter 04 folder on your hard drive.

Project 4-6: Emphasize the Foreground of a Photograph

4

The background in a picture has several distracting elements. Deemphasize the background by reducing saturation, sharpness, and lightness.

1. Open the image file **4-6.tif** on the Data Disk.

2. Use the **Magnetic Lasso tool** to select the **violin** and the **case**. The tool is attracted to edges and follows the contours of the case.

3. The Magnetic Lasso does not create a perfect selection, so use the regular **Lasso** tool to add and subtract from the initial selection. Add by holding the **Shift** key, and subtract by holding the **Option** key on the Macintosh, or the **Alt** key in Windows.

4. When the selection is complete, inverse the selection by clicking **Select** on the menu bar, and then clicking **Inverse**.

5. Blur the background with the Gaussian Blur filter. Set the radius to **0.6**.

6. Some areas of the chair are particularly textured. Blur these further with the Blur tool.

7. Use the Levels dialog box to set the Gamma to **0.8**.

8. Reduce lightness and saturation with the Hue/Saturation dialog box. Set Saturation to **–30** and Lightness to **–10**.

9. Use the **Sponge** tool to desaturate the chair selectively. Set the option to **Desaturate** and use a 20-pixel brush.

10. Invert the selection again so that the violin and case are selected.

11. Use the **Unsharp Mask** filter to enhance the foreground. Set the Amount to **30%**, the Radius to **1** pixel, and leave the Threshold at **0** levels.

12. Sharpen the violin with the **Sharpen** tool. Set the Pressure to **50%** and use a 30-pixel brush.

13. Normalize levels, and boost saturation by **10**.

14. Click **Select** on the menu bar, point to **Modify**, then click **Border**. In the Border dialog box, enter a Width of **3** pixels. Apply a Gaussian Blur of **0.5** pixels.

15. Deselect to see the violin stand out in the image more than before.

16. Crop away excess margins, optimize, and save as a JPEG called **4-6.jpg** in the Chapter 04 folder on your hard drive.

Project 4-7: Give an Image a New Background

Remove the background from an image.

1. Open the image file **4–7a.tif** on the Data Disk.

2. Use the **Magic Wand** tool and the **Lasso** tool to select all of the area behind the guitar. Set the tolerance low, around **10**; and turn **off** the anti-aliasing option for the Selection tools.

3. Inverse and then copy the selection.

4. Open **4–7b.tif** on the Data Disk.

5. Make sure it is in RGB mode, and paste the selection onto the new background.

6. Click **Layer** on the menu bar, click **Flatten Image**, and then optimize and save as a JPEG called **4-7.jpg** in the Chapter 04 folder on your hard drive

Project 2-8: Compose the Layout of Several Elements in a Photograph

You have been given a photo of five products that will appear in an online product review. The photographer shot them in two rows, but the style of the page demands a more interesting layout. Group these objects together in one image that is 250 pixels wide and 200 pixels high.

1. Open the image file **4-8.tif** on the Data Disk.

2. Make sure the Background Color is set to **white**, and enlarge the canvas size to **500** pixels wide and **400** pixels high.

3. Select one of the objects with the Rectangular Marquee tool.

4. Select the **Move** tool and move the selected object to a new area.

5. Move all of the objects. Keep in mind the composition principles outlined in this chapter: create diagonals between objects, maintain horizontal balance, maintain vertical balance, and use margins that are about one-fifth the width of the entire image. Align your composition to the upper-left of the image.

6. When you are satisfied, select the **Crop** tool.

7. In the Options bar, select **Fixed Target Size**.

8. Set the Width to **250** pixels, and the Height to **200** pixels.

9. Drag the **Crop** tool over the image. You see that it maintains the aspect ratio of the dimensions specified in the Options bar. If the crop does not work with your layout, cancel the crop and reposition the objects. When you crop, the area will automatically scale down to 250 by 200 pixels.

10. Optimize and save as a GIF called **4-8.gif** in the Chapter 04 folder on your hard drive.

CASE PROJECT

For your portfolio, take your photograph and gallery pieces and clean them as described in this chapter. You should have at least one photograph of yourself and several scans or digital photos of visual work you've completed.

4

5

CREATING AND USING BACKGROUND IMAGES

Preparing Web Page Backgrounds

In this chapter, you will:

- ◆ Use painting tools
- ◆ Work with layers
- ◆ Use filters in Photoshop and ImageReady
- ◆ Design background images
- ◆ Use background images with HTML and CSS

One of the quickest ways to add interest to a Web page is to use a colored background. Although Hypertext Markup Language (HTML) makes it easy to color a background, it limits you to using backgrounds of one solid color. Fortunately, browsers also support the use of images in backgrounds. Many Web designers use background images because they are easy to use and have an immediate visual impact. As with most design elements, however, background images can be overused, creating Web pages that are difficult to read.

Creating a background image gives you an opportunity to be creative. You can use any Web graphic, edit existing images, and generate new ones. To work with background images, you need to be comfortable with image-editing software features, including painting tools, image filters, and layers. This chapter focuses on using Adobe Photoshop to create background images.

After developing a background graphic, you must use HTML or Cascading Style Sheets (CSS) to insert it into a Web page. This chapter defines backgrounds and explains how to use them in tables with both HTML and CSS.

USING PAINTING TOOLS

The Photoshop paint tools include the Eraser, Pencil, Airbrush, Paintbrush, Clone Stamp, Pattern Stamp, Smudge, Blur, Sharpen, Dodge, Burn, and Sponge. You apply each of these tools with a brush that varies in size and shape and leaves a mark when you drag it across an image. If you have already used a painting program, such as MacPaint or Windows Paint, most of the icons and conventions in the Photoshop paint tools will be familiar to you. In addition to these common features, Photoshop and ImageReady let you precisely control how these tools work.

To use a painting tool, you select it from the toolbox and then change its options to suit your task. You change options for the painting tools in the Options bar, shown in Figure 5-1.

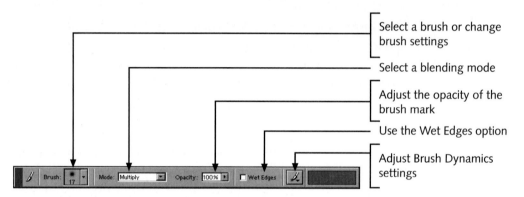

Figure 5-1   The Options bar with the Paintbrush tool selected

Using the Editing Brushes

The Brush palette contains many predefined brushes of different sizes and shapes. Some are round and others have spatter patterns. To select a brush, first click the inverted triangle next to the brush sample to open the Brush palette, and then click the brush you want. You also can create and edit your own brushes. To do so, open the Brush palette menu, and then click New Brush. In the New Brush dialog box, set the brush options.

If you want more control over the brush you selected, or want to edit the settings, click the icon in the Brush box in the Options bar. The Brush Options dialog box opens, as illustrated in Figure 5-2, where you can change the settings. The changes you make affect only the selected brush.

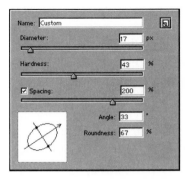

Figure 5-2   The Brush Options dialog box

Each option in the Brush Options dialog box is explained in the following list:

- **Diameter** is the width of the brush head measured in pixels.

- **Hardness** determines the softness of the brush mark. A setting of 100% means that the brush mark has a hard, unfeathered edge. A setting of 0% makes the mark very soft, fading from opaque at the center to transparent at the edge.

- **Spacing** controls whether the brush mark is a solid or dotted line. The spacing value refers to the size of the space between dots. A value of 25% produces a normal, solid line, while a value of 100% produces a dotted line, with the dots and the distance between them evenly spaced. A value of 1% produces an extra-thick feathered line.

- **Roundness** of the brush can vary from 100% (perfectly round) to 0% (a flat line). A flat brush is useful for producing calligraphic effects.

- The **Angle** setting applies only if you change the Roundness of the brush head. If the brush head is an ellipse, the angle determines the brush head's orientation, such as horizontal or vertical.

Use the options in the Brush Options dialog box to create elliptical brush heads. Brushes can be any shape, however, including a random shape such as the spatter brush, or a custom shape based on part of an image. You can use an image-based brush to apply the image anywhere you click the brush. In the following steps, you create such a custom shape.

To create a custom shape based on part of an image:

1. Select the **Rectangular Marquee** tool. In the Options bar, make sure the Feather value is set to **0**.

2. Select an area of an image with the Rectangular Marquee tool.

3. Click **Edit** on the menu bar, and then click **Define Brush**. Photoshop adds a new brush to the palette, based on the selection area. The new brush contains no color information; the color of its mark is determined by the current foreground color.

Using Blending Modes

In the Options bar you can select a mode for blending the effect of the Paintbrush tool with the existing image. The Blending mode controls how the painting tool affects the pixels it paints. The **base color** in the image combines with the foreground color, or **blend color**, and produces the **result color**. The default is the **Normal** mode, which replaces the base color with the blend color. For special effects, you can use one of the other 17 modes that lighten or darken the image in various ways.

Each setting in the Options palette is explained in the lists following the next four figures. Figure 5-3 shows a graphic with Dissolve, Multiply, Screen, and Overlay effects. Figure 5-4 shows the same graphic with Soft Light, Hard Light, Color Dodge, and Color Burn effects. The Darken, Lighten, Difference, and Exclusion modes are illustrated in Figure 5-5. The Hue, Color, Saturation, and Luminosity modes are illustrated in Figure 5-6. To better illustrate the results of using these modes, the figures show an entire image with the different modes applied.

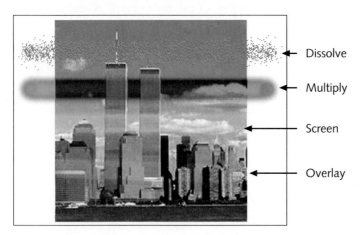

Figure 5-3   The Dissolve, Multiply, Screen, and Overlay effects

- The **Dissolve** mode displays opacity as a spatter pattern. The effect is most obvious with a layer of opacity around 50%.

- The **Behind** mode paints only on the transparent part of a layer. This mode has no effect on images that already contain white or colored pixels, and is not shown in the figure.

- The **Multiply** mode combines the base color and the blend color. If either color is black, the resulting color is also black; mixing with white does not change it. This mode usually produces a darker color than the blend color.

- The **Screen** mode is the same as the Multiply mode, but it inverts the blend and base colors, producing a lighter color. To invert means to use the opposite hue on the color wheel. For example, invert to use cyan for red or yellow for blue.

- The **Overlay** mode is similar to Normal mode with an opacity of 50%, but does not affect white and black pixels.

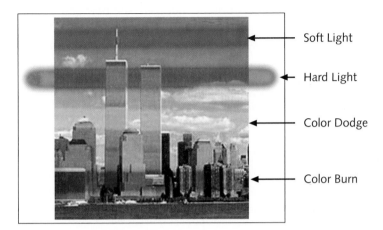

Figure 5-4   The Soft Light, Hard Light, Color Dodge, and Color Burn effects

- The **Soft Light** and **Hard Light** modes boost contrast, by lightening light colors and darkening dark ones. The Hard Light mode has a stronger effect.

- The **Color Dodge** mode lightens the base colors toward the blend color, ignoring black pixels.

- The **Color Burn** mode darkens the base colors toward the blend color, ignoring white pixels.

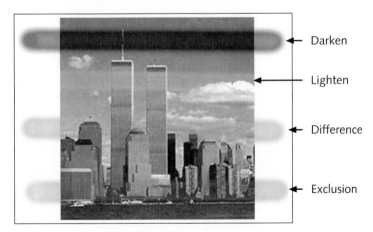

Figure 5-5   The Darken, Lighten, Difference, and Exclusion effects

- The **Darken** mode compares the base and blend colors, and then applies the darker of the two.

- The **Lighten** mode compares the base and blend colors, and then applies the lighter of the two.

- The **Difference** and **Exclusion** modes compare the base and blend colors and subtract the darker from the lighter. This is not the same as inverting the colors, but it looks similar. The Difference mode produces slightly higher contrast.

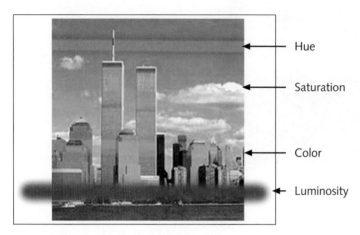

Figure 5-6   The Hue, Color, Saturation, and Luminosity effects

- The **Hue** and **Color** modes produce an effect similar to using the Colorize feature in the Hue/Saturation dialog box, except that the blend color determines the hue.

- The **Saturation** mode produces the same effect as using the Saturation slider in the Hue/Saturation dialog box. Both make the saturation of the image more like the saturation of the blend color.

- The **Luminosity** mode preserves the hue and saturation of the original colors, but changes the brightness to that of the blend color.

Changing Brush Mark Opacity

Opacity refers to the transparency of the brush mark. A setting of 100% opacity is fully opaque; 0% opacity is fully transparent. Fully opaque brushes produce simple brush marks. More transparent ones produce brush marks like those created by watercolors.

Using Wet Edges

When the Paintbrush tool is set to the Normal mode, the Wet Edges check box is available in the Options bar. Selecting the Wet Edges box lets you create a watercolor effect, so the edges of the brush mark are darker than the interior. Figure 5-7 shows marks made by the Paintbrush tool with and without Wet Edges selected.

In Figure 5-7, the two brush marks on the left have opacity set to 100%. The two on the right have opacity set to 50%.

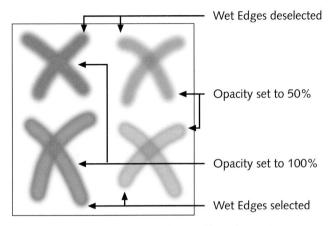

Wet Edges deselected

Opacity set to 50%

Opacity set to 100%

Wet Edges selected

Figure 5-7 Changing opacity and using Wet Edges

Changing Brush Dynamics

Photoshop and ImageReady let you create dynamic effects—those that change over time—with brush marks. To change brush dynamics, click the brush list arrow in the far right of the Options bar, and then click an effect. For example, click Fade and set the brush size to fade over 10 steps, which means that the brush mark shrinks from full-size to nothing over 10 steps. Each step equals the size of one brush head. Depending on the brush tool you select, you also can set dynamic effects for color and opacity. The results of these different settings are shown in Figure 5-8.

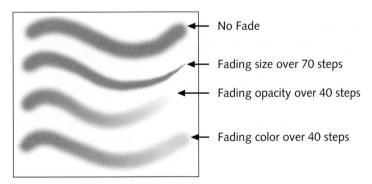

No Fade

Fading size over 70 steps

Fading opacity over 40 steps

Fading color over 40 steps

Figure 5-8 Different brush dynamics

If you are using a tablet to draw in Photoshop, you can set the stylus to control brush dynamics. To do so, click the Brush Dynamics button in the options bar to open the Brush Dynamics dialog box. Then set size, opacity, or color to stylus.

Changing the Cursor

You can edit preferences in Photoshop to control the shape of the pointer used with the Paintbrush tools.

To edit preferences:

1. Click **Edit** on the menu bar, point to **Preferences**, and then click **Display & Cursors** to open the Preference dialog box, illustrated in Figure 5-9.

2. Select a pointer style. Choose **Standard** to use the Paintbrush icon as the pointer. Choose **Precise** to use a crosshair pointer. Choose **Brush Size** to use the selected brush icon as the pointer.

   Only the Brush Size pointer visually indicates the size and shape of the brush mark. You also can toggle between the Precise and Brush Size pointer by pressing the Caps Lock key.

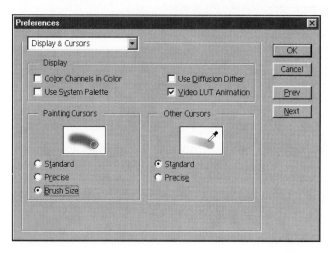

Figure 5-9   Selecting a pointer style in the Preferences dialog box

WORKING WITH LAYERS

Adobe added the layers feature to Photoshop (version 4) to meet the needs of graphic artists and designers. Layers are so useful in image editing that they have their own palette window and menu. Think of a layer as a sheet of clear plastic. You can paint it, and the area not covered by paint stays transparent. You can have many layers stacked on top of each other, with a different graphical element on each layer. Having distinct layers lets you rotate, color, and manipulate each element separately, without affecting the others. For example, if your complete graphic includes images of a mountain, sun, and hawk, you can store each image on a separate layer, and then change only one image, such as the hawk, without affecting the mountain or sun.

Creating Layers

Create a layer when you want to store an image on it. Every image has a default background layer. The easiest way to add a new layer is to copy an area in the image and then paste it. Instead of incorporating the pasted graphic into the existing image, Photoshop creates a layer on top of the default layer or background layer. You also can create an empty layer: click the right triangle in the Layers palette, and then click New Layer. (You also can click Layer on the menu bar, point to New, and then click Layer, or click the Create New Layer icon at the bottom of the Layers palette.) After you create a layer, you can set the layer options, which are illustrated in Figure 5-10.

5

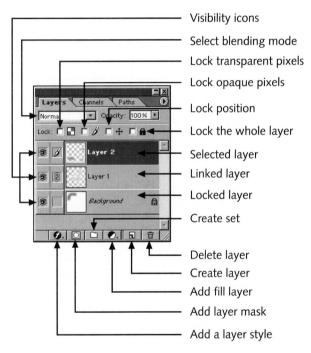

Visibility icons
Select blending mode
Lock transparent pixels
Lock opaque pixels
Lock position
Lock the whole layer
Selected layer
Linked layer
Locked layer
Create set

Delete layer
Create layer
Add fill layer
Add layer mask
Add a layer style

Figure 5-10   The Layers palette

Setting Layer Opacity

Use the Opacity text box in the Layers palette to control the transparency of a layer. A setting of 0% opacity means that the layer is fully transparent and the colored pixels in the layer are invisible. A setting of 100% opacity means that the layer is fully opaque and the elements in the layer completely obscure the layers behind it. However, even a fully opaque layer can contain transparent areas that make lower layers visible.

Using Modes

The mode of a layer determines how it blends with the layers below it. The modes for layers are the same as those for the Painting tools (see Using Blending Modes earlier in this chapter). Layer modes differ in how they affect the layer's appearance. You change a layer's blending mode only when you want to create complex effects; Normal mode is adequate for most projects. Still, you should experiment with the different modes to see their effects. Note that you cannot adjust the opacity or mode of the base background layer.

Locking Layers

Near the top of the Layers palette are check boxes for locking the transparent pixels, image pixels or position of a layer, or to lock the entire layer itself. You check a box to prevent the particular layer part from being edited, as described in the following list:

- Locking transparent pixels means that only colored pixels change when you use a tool or filter. This is the same action as selecting all nontransparent pixels with the Magic Wand tool.

- Locking image pixels has the reverse effect of locking transparent pixels—only transparent pixels are affected by tools or filters.

- Locking position prevents the layer from being moved with the Move tool.

- Locking all prevents any edits to the layer, although you still can move the layer in the stacking order of the Layers palette.

Setting Visibility

On the far left of each layer row in the Layers palette is a check box for visibility, indicated with an icon of an eye. Use the Visibility check box to toggle a layer between 0% opacity and the value set in the Opacity window. Click the eye icon in a layer's row of the Layers palette to show or hide the layer. Hiding one layer lets you see how other layers look without the selected layer blocking the view.

Linking Layers

The selected layer is indicated by a paintbrush icon next to the image preview in the Layers palette. Clicking the second box in an unselected layer's row adds a chain icon to the box, indicating that the two layers are linked. Linked layers accept modifications you make to other layers in the same chain. If you rotate or apply a filter to one of the linked layers, for example, all the other linked layers change as well.

Adding Other Layer Options

You can add layer effects to any layer other than the background layer. Other layer options are described in the following list:

- Click the Add Layer Style button at the bottom of the Layers palette to add styles such as Drop Shadow, Bevel, and Emboss. (Layer styles are covered in detail in the "Creating and Using Buttons" chapter.)

- Click the Add Mask button at the bottom of the Layers palette to create a new mask. This creates a new channel, visible in the Channels palette, that selectively hides areas of layers behind it.

- Click the New Set button to create a new layer set. Layer sets are similar to folders containing layers. If you have many layers in an image, it is convenient to organize them in separate sets.

- Click the New Fill or Adjustment Layer button to add special layers you use for experimenting with color. Fill layers allow you to quickly fill an entire layer with a solid color, gradient, or pattern. Adjustment layers allow you to add controls such as level adjustment to a separate layer. When visible, these layers affect all layers below them in the stacking order.

Merging Layers

The GIF and JPEG formats cannot contain layer information, so before you save an image in a Web format, you must merge all the layers. Merging layers means combining two or more layers into one. By using the **Merge Linked** command from the Layers palette menu, you control which layers merge. If you want to merge all the layers into one, you use the **Flatten Image** command. The **Merge Down** command merges all layers behind the selected layer. The **Merge Visible** command combines all visible layers.

To save an image file with layers, you must do so in the proprietary PSD format of Photoshop. You must also flatten the layers using the Flatten Image command before you can save an image in a Web format.

Arranging Layers

You can change the stacking order of your layers to see how the image looks with different parts in front of or behind other parts of the image. To change the stacking order, drag the layer row to the desired position in the Layers palette. You also can click Layer on the menu bar and then select options from the Arrange submenu. You can bring a layer forward one position or all the way to the front, send it back one position or to the very back. Nothing can be placed behind the background layer, so a layer sent to the back is positioned directly above the background layer.

Transforming Layers

The transformation options in the Edit menu apply to the selected area of a layer. If no area is selected, the options apply to the entire layer. Click Edit on the menu bar and then point to Transform to open the Transform submenu. From there you can select one of several options:

- *Scale*: Increase or decrease the size of the selection by changing the scale. As you drag to scale the image, hold the Shift key to maintain the proportions of height and width.

- *Rotate*: Rotate the selection around a central anchor point by dragging the side or corner tabs. You also can drag the central anchor point to a new position to change the center of rotation.
  Figure 5-11 shows a selection being rotated.

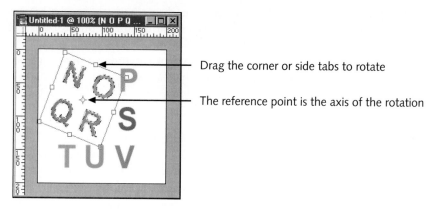

Drag the corner or side tabs to rotate

The reference point is the axis of the rotation

Figure 5-11   Rotating around a central anchor point

- *Skew*: Change the angle of the selection by skewing the sides. Skew maintains parallel edges of the selection.

- *Distort*: Completely change the shape of the selection by dragging any side or corner tab. Distort does not maintain parallel edges of the selection.

- *Perspective*: Simulate 3-D perspective by dragging the corner tabs. The selection then appears to recede into the distance. Figure 5-12 shows a selection being transformed with skew, distort, and perspective

- *Rotate by degree*: Rotate the selection in fixed amounts, either 90 degrees clockwise or counterclockwise, or 180 degrees.

- *Flip*: A horizontal flip switches the left and right sides of the selection, creating a mirror image of the original selection. A vertical flip switches the top and bottom of the selection. Figure 5-13 shows the results of rotating and flipping a selection.

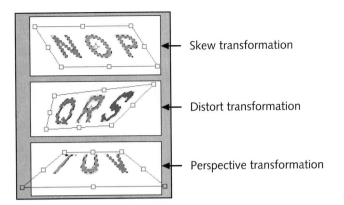

Skew transformation

Distort transformation

Perspective transformation

5

Figure 5-12   Skewing, distorting, and adding perspective to a selection

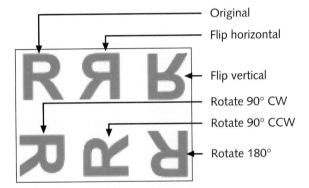

Original

Flip horizontal

Flip vertical

Rotate 90° CW

Rotate 90° CCW

Rotate 180°

Figure 5-13   Rotating and flipping a selection

You also can set your own transformation to produce special effects.

To set your own transformation:

1. Select the **layer** you want to transform.

2. Click **Edit** on the menu bar, and then click **Free Transform**. You see a transformation box around the selection. The box has tabs in the corners and in the centers of each side and a reference point in the middle.

3. Drag the **tabs** to translate, scale, skew, or rotate the layer. When you finish the transformation, double-click within the selected area to set the changes.

When transforming a layer, the Options bar displays text fields for entering numeric values for the transformation, as shown in Figure 5-14. It often is easier to control transformations using numeric values than by dragging the selection tabs.

Figure 5-14 Transformation options

The transformation options are explained in the following list:

- *X and Y*: Use these text boxes to set the position of the selection. By default the values are absolute, measured from the upper-left corner of the image. Click the triangle icon between the X and Y fields to use relative positioning for moving the reference point. This measures the position of the selection relative to its initial position.

- *W and H*: Use these text boxes to set the scale of the selection as a percentage of the original. Adjust the width by changing the W value, and adjust the height by changing the H value. A value of 200% doubles the scale, and a value of 50% halves it. Click the chain icon to maintain the aspect ratio of height and width. This constrains the proportions of height and width so that changing one value changes the other by the same amount.

- *Angle icon*: Use this icon to control the angle of rotation in degrees.

  H and V: Use these text boxes to control the horizontal and vertical skew in degrees.

- *Ok and Cancel buttons*: Click the check mark button to set the transformation. Click the X button to cancel the transformation.

The Options bar does not include special fields for distort or perspective.

USING FILTERS IN PHOTOSHOP

A filter often is called a **plug-in**. Just as Web browsers use plug-in programs to render images, Photoshop uses plug-ins to add visual effects to an edited image. Most filter plug-ins work by scanning an image, pixel by pixel, performing a mathematical transformation as they go. The Blur filter, for example, interpolates the values for every pair of adjacent pixels. This reduces the contrast of edges, and makes an image appear softer. Filters in Photoshop work only when images are in RGB color or grayscale.

The benefit of using plug-in filters is that third-party development companies and individual developers can create their own filters and share their work with other users who can plug them into Photoshop. Many filters that are now standard in Photoshop were originally written by users. Several additional third-party plug-ins also are available on the Adobe Web site and elsewhere on the Web.

Filter Categories

Photoshop includes too many filters to cover individually in this book. Most have settings you can adjust, allowing you to create many different effects. The best way to see what individual filters do is to experiment with them on an original image. You already have covered some filters, such as Sharpen and NTSC Colors, to solve problems in images; other filters produce artistic effects. Photoshop groups filters into nine categories, which you access from the Filter menu.

5

- **Artistic** filters imitate other media by making the source image appear to have been created with traditional techniques like watercolors or colored pencils. For example, the **Plastic Wrap** filter can help you create fire and smoke effects.

- **Brush Stroke** filters also imitate other media with techniques such as crosshatching or paint spattering.

- **Distort** filters do not change the values of pixels as much as translate them across and around the image, creating the appearance of ripples and bumps.

- **Pixelate** filters group similarly colored, adjacent pixels into clusters to create mosaic and pointillist effects.

- **Render** filters are more sophisticated and don't easily fall into the other categories. The **Clouds** filter generates a cloud pattern using the existing Foreground and Background colors. The **Difference Clouds** filter is similar, but combines a cloud pattern with the existing image.

- **Sketch** filters are similar to the Artistic and Brush Strokes filters, and imitate traditional media by adding texture to the original image. The **Bas Relief** filter produces particularly striking and interesting effects.

- **Stylize** filters add artificial depth by exaggerating the edges in an image. The **Emboss** filter is one of the most popular, and simulates a 3-D engraving of the original image.

- **Texture** filters are combinations of the Pixelate and Sketch filters. They group similar pixels into clusters to create texture effects.

■ The **Other** filter category includes the **Custom** filter, which lets you create your own filter, and the **Offset** filter, which lets you preview the edges of tiled background images. The effect of the Offset filter is shown in Figure 5-15. The remaining filters are advanced and beyond the scope of this book. They include Dither Box (to create and apply custom dither patterns), High Pass (to exaggerate edges), Maximum (to enhance the light areas of an image), and Minimum (to enhance the dark areas of an image).

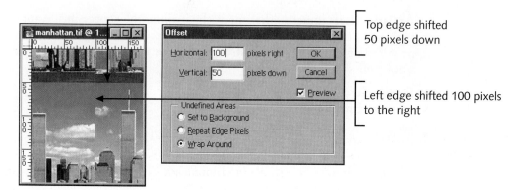

Figure 5-15 The Offset filter

Each filter in the previous list works in one of three ways:

■ Most filters must be applied to an existing image. Running the Glass filter, for example, on a white or colored background produces no noticeable effect. You can, however, run the Noise filter or draw random lines on a blank image to give the filters some image data with which to work.

■ Some filters, however, produce an effect even when applied to a blank image. The Patchwork and Conte Crayon filters, which add texture to images and solid colors, are two examples of such filters.

■ A few filters completely overwrite any image to which they are applied. For example, the Clouds filter replaces the existing image with a new randomized cloud pattern.

Using the Tile Maker Filter

ImageReady includes one filter in the Other category that Photoshop does not. The Tile Maker filter allows you to create seamless background images. When used as a background image in a Web page, most images create unattractive seams as they tile across and down the page, as illustrated in Figure 5-16.

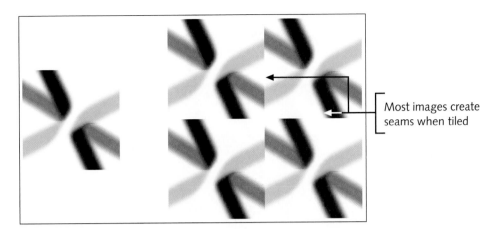

Most images create seams when tiled

Figure 5-16   Tiled image with visible seams

In Photoshop, you can eliminate the appearance of these seams by blending opposite edges or by creating a **kaleidoscopic** image. This method makes the image tile seamlessly, as shown in figure 5-17. A kaleidoscope is an image that is flipped horizontally and vertically so that each edge is a mirror reflection of the opposite edge, as illustrated in Figure 5-18. The figure shows how turning the image into a kaleidoscope also reduces the appearance of tiling seams.

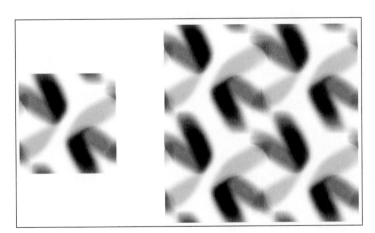

Figure 5-17   Blending opposite edges

Figure 5-18   Making the image kaleidoscopic

The Tile Maker filter in ImageReady automates both of these techniques. To open the Tile Maker dialog box shown in Figure 5-19, click the Filter menu in ImageReady, point to Other, and click Tile Maker. When you select **Blend Edges**, the filter copies the outer edge of the image to the opposite side, fading it into the existing image. When you select **Kaleidoscope**, the filter copies the image, flips it horizontally and vertically, and blends these copies with the original to create a symmetric design.

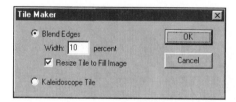

Figure 5-19   The Tile Maker filter in ImageReady

DESIGNING BACKGROUND IMAGES

Most Web pages include a background image to add visual interest to the page. To create a solid color background, set the background color in HTML. You should use images when you want a textured background or a layout that requires large curves, which you cannot easily create using HTML tables.

You can use animated GIFs as background images, but many users find them annoying. The background should support the overall design, which means keeping it understated.

When designing your background image, consider the page as a whole and how the background fits with the other page elements. To achieve the best effects, you should reduce contrast, use repetition and tessellation, and find the appropriate dimensions for the image.

Reducing Contrast

To read text in a Web page, there must be contrast between the foreground and background. To achieve this, you must use a low-contrast background image. A high-contrast background makes the foreground text illegible because the text can't be distinguished from the background, as shown in Figure 5-20. Use a low-contrast background to create plenty of contrast between the background and the text. Most sites use black text, so light, faded backgrounds make text easier to read. Bright, textured background images often obscure text.

Figure 5-20   Background images with high and low contrast

An easy way to reduce contrast is with the Brightness/Contrast dialog box, illustrated in Figure 5-21. This dialog box appears when you click Image on the menu bar, point to Adjust, and then click Brightness/Contrast. Drag the sliders to lower the contrast and raise the brightness. This produces a light, faded image that does not compete with the dark text above it. Another way to reduce contrast is to first open the Levels dialog box by clicking the Image menu, pointing to Adjust, and clicking Levels. Then raise the value of the black Output Level.

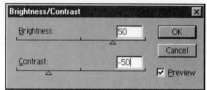

Figure 5-21   Reducing contrast

Color contrast also helps readability. For example, if you have a dark blue background, light yellow text shows up much better than light blue text. The light blue text has lightness contrast with the dark blue background, but the yellow has both lightness and hue contrast.

Using Repetition

Background images, by default, repeat across the page from left to right and top to bottom. The right edge of one image copy butts up to the left edge of the copy next to it, and the bottom and top edges also touch. This effect usually is called **wallpapering** or **tiling**. Tiling sometimes creates odd or unattractive patterns that aren't obvious when viewing the single untiled image. Tiling is obvious when adjacent edges of the tiled image do not match, producing visible seams. The easiest way to avoid this problem is to have blank space around the objects in the image. You then avoid having hard lines where the tiles touch. Most of the artistry in creating background images is in having them repeat without seeming to repeat, and having the repetition be seamless.

Understanding Tessellation

Tessellation is a pattern that fits together tightly like a jigsaw puzzle, with no blank space left over. To create a tessellated image, like the one shown in Figure 5-22, you need to edit the edges of the image, the places where it bumps up against itself, using tools such as the Tilemaker or offset filters. The image needs to seem continuous when it tiles across the screen, which means the top and bottom edges have to match, and the left and right edges have to match. A tessellated image appears to be one large, continuous image when tiled.

> The master of tessellated images is M.C. Escher, a Dutch artist who created his most famous works using woodcuts—carving a pattern in a flat piece of wood, then rolling ink onto the wood and pressing paper against it.

5

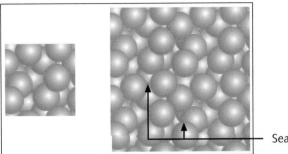

Seams are invisible

Figure 5-22   A tessellated image

Finding the Appropriate Dimensions

When using a large background image, you should avoid tiling altogether. Imagine that your design contains a large curved line that extends from the upper-right of the screen to the lower-left, like the one shown in Figure 5-23. The image doesn't repeat, so you cannot create the curved effect with a tiled background. In fact, if your background image does tile, your whole design might fail. Users with extra-wide monitors might see the left edge of the second tile of your background image. So you want to make the background image large enough to spread across the whole monitor, even when the monitor is set at full-screen.

The average monitor size increases every year. To fill the largest screens, a full-page background image should now be at least 1280 pixels across. Only someone with an even larger monitor would see a full-page background tile to the side. As for height, you control page length by how much content you put in. Most pages are longer than they are wide, so generally it is easier to use a background that tiles vertically. The drawback to using large images is that they also tend to have large file sizes. Although the user's browser caches the image, you still don't want to force the user to download large images on the first page. If you use highly patterned or faded images in the background, you can heavily optimize the image with no noticeable degradation of image quality.

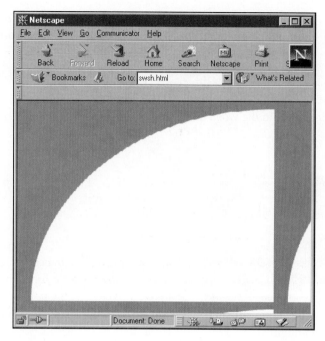

Figure 5-23   Background image that tiles unattractively

If you have a small tiling area, such as a two-color, 8 × 8 pixel checkerboard like the one shown in Figure 5-24, you might think that the ideal image would be a two-color, 8 × 8 pixel image. The drawback to using such small images is that the browser actually takes longer to render them on the screen. An 8 × 8 pixel image on an 800 × 600-pixel window would have to tile over 7000 times. Even a browser on a fast computer would take a few seconds to display this tiling. A few seconds is too long. A better choice is to stick to background images that are at least 30 × 30 pixels. You might have duplicated information, and the load time will be a little longer, but the render time will be much faster. In Figure 5-24, the image on the left loads slightly faster, but renders much more slowly than the image on the right.

Figure 5-24   Different sizes of a tiled image

USING BACKGROUND IMAGES IN WEB PAGES

After you create a background image, you need to incorporate it into a Web page. You can either use HTML or CSS.

Defining Backgrounds with HTML

The simplest type of HTML background is shown below:

```
<body BGCOLOR="yellow">
```

This coding sets the BGCOLOR attribute of the BODY tag to yellow. The next easiest background is to add an image to the body. You can use any image you want, but remember, it has to be in a Web format such as GIF, JPEG, or PNG.

```
<body BACKGROUND="my_background.jpg">
```

This code uses a different attribute, the BACKGROUND attribute. You can use both the BGCOLOR and BACKGROUND attributes. If the image failed to load for some reason, the background color would appear; otherwise, the image would cover the color altogether. If the background image were a GIF image with transparency, the background color would show through the image.

 HTML tags often are written in uppercase to make them more distinguishable from the rest of the text. However, the new standard for HTML, known as XHTML, requires that all tags be written in lowercase.

Using Table Backgrounds with HTML

All browsers support using backgrounds in the body tag. Modern browsers also support the BACKGROUND attribute in table delimiter (TD) tags.

You use the background attribute in TD tags the same way you do in the BODY tag. In the following example, the background image is in a directory called images and appears in the left cell of a two-column table. The resulting image is shown in Figure 5-25.

```
<table WIDTH="200">
    <tr>
        <td BACKGROUND="/images/myBackground.gif">
            some text
        </td>
        <td>
            some other text
        </td>
    </tr>
</table>
```

Figure 5-25   A background image in a table

Using more than one background image per page usually is considered excessive. Background images tend to draw attention away from the actual content of a Web page, and multiple background images may distract the reader. If you have a patterned background in the body, you probably should not use backgrounds in your tables. If you have a solid-color background and want to use a background in a table cell, make it small and create the background image with reduced contrast.

Although all browsers support background images in the body of a Web page, only Netscape and Internet Explorer versions 4 (or later) browsers support table backgrounds. Therefore, if users with Netscape version 3 visited your page, the background images would not be visible.

The preceding example is why you should use both the BACKGROUND and BGCOLOR attributes of the BODY and TD tags; users with older browsers will get the color, and users with newer browsers will get the image.

Using Background Images with CSS

CSS (**Cascading Style Sheets**) is a way to define how HTML displays Web pages. You use CSS by writing a style sheet inside an HTML document. The style sheet acts as a library of instructions for that page. CSS can accomplish all the effects that HTML can, plus many more.

Using style sheets to add backgrounds to Web pages has two advantages: You can control how the tiling repeats, and you can add backgrounds to additional block elements. The basic style sheet to assign a background image to the BODY tag looks like this:

```
<style TYPE="text\css">
<!—
body {
     background-image: url(images/my_image.jpg)
     }
//—>
</style>
```

This code can appear anywhere in the HTML document but is placed conventionally between the HEAD tags. The style sheet sets the background-image attribute of the BODY tag to the file named my_image.jpg, inside the directory named images. The url in the code tells the browser to expect a filename, as opposed to a numeric value. Once the style sheet is in place, you don't have to declare anything special with the BODY tag.

Using Background Images in Tables with CSS

If you want to add a background image to a table cell after adding one to the body, you might be tempted to create a style sheet declaration for the TD tag that looks just like the one for the BODY tag. The problem with this method is that every table cell on the page will then have the same background image. In most cases you won't want to use this approach.

Every Web page has exactly one BODY tag, so you can directly declare the attributes of the element. With tags such as TD, however, you're better off declaring a class in the style sheet that you then refer to explicitly in the TD tag. The **class** contains a definition for how a tag should appear, but is not associated with any particular tag in the style sheet. Only when a tag calls the class does it follow the class definition.

Here's an example:

```
<style TYPE="text\css">
<!—
body {background-image: url(images/my_image.jpg)}
.bgimage {background-image: url(images/my_image2.jpg)}
//—>
</style>
```

The class in the above example has the arbitrary name of .bgimage. The browser knows it's a class because a period occurs before the name. This class is set to another image in the images directory named my_image2.jpg. To use this class, you simply add the CLASS attribute to the appropriate TD tags:

```
<table WIDTH="200">
    <tr>
        <td CLASS="bgimage">
            some text
        </td>
        <td>
            some other text
        </td>
    </tr>
</table>
```

This code creates a table with two cells, the left one with a background image. Note that when the class name is used as a value, the period is dropped from the name. Now that you have this class, you can assign it to any block element, including paragraphs (P), headers (H1, H2, and so on), and block quotes. You don't need to change the style sheet; just add the class attribute to the appropriate tag.

Controlling Repetition with Style Sheets

In addition to assigning backgrounds to other block elements, style sheets allow you to determine how a background image repeats in a Web page. Recall that by default, all background images tile across the screen from left to right and top to bottom. You can use CSS to force the background to repeat only horizontally or vertically.

The following style sheet uses the background-repeat attribute to control how the background image tiles:

```
<style TYPE="text/css">
<!–
body {
background-image: url(my_image.jpg);
    background-repeat: repeat-y;
}
//–>
</style>
```

In the preceding example, the background-repeat attribute is set to the value of repeat-y, which tells the browser to tile the image only along the y-axis (up and down, but not across). To create a page with a white background and a patterned column on the left, you could create a two-color image that is 1280 pixels wide and just a few pixels high. The image would repeat down the page, creating the colored column on the left.

The drawback to this method is that you have to use a large image, even though all but the strip on the left is solid white. Modern browsers allow a better solution. Using style sheets, you can create columns without all the extra white area on the side. Just create the image for the patterned column, create a style sheet that uses the background-repeat attribute of the body element, and set the value to repeat-y. The result of this technique is shown in Figure 5-26.

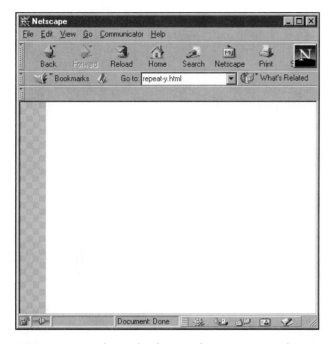

Figure 5-26   Tiling a background image in one direction

Although background is an attribute of the BODY tag, and background-image is an attribute of the body element, you cannot switch them around. For example, you could not use:

```
<body BACKGROUND="my_image.jpg" background-repeat:
repeat-y>
```

Also note how the style sheets use colons (:) instead of equals signs (=) to set values.

CHAPTER SUMMARY

- ❐ Every image-editing program offers painting tools to apply color or lines to an image. Photoshop adds options such as opacity and different blending modes to its painting tools.

- ❐ You can save any selected area as a brush, and then use the brush to create repeated patterns.

- ❐ Layers are like sheets of virtual film with adjustable opacity. Each layer can contain different elements of an image.

- ❐ An image file with layers must be saved in the PSD format. You must flatten the layers before you can save the image in a Web format.

❐ Photoshop has dozens of creative filters that can be used alone or in combination to create thousands of different effects.

❐ The Tile Maker filter in ImageReady automates the construction of blended and kaleidoscopic images.

❐ Your background image should be interesting, but should be low contrast and not interfere with the legibility of the text above it.

❐ A tiled image may appear to have seams where the edges meet. Eliminate the seam to make the image look professional.

❐ Using straight HTML, you can add background images to the body and tables of Web pages.

❐ With style sheets you can add background images to any block element and control how the image tiles.

REVIEW QUESTIONS

1. Using the Saturation mode with the Paintbrush tool, and black as the foreground color is the same as using which tool?

   a. Airbrush

   b. Burn

   c. Dodge

   d. Sponge

2. Which mode can you use to create a spatter effect?

   a. Brush Strokes

   b. Dissolve

   c. Multiply

   d. Screen

3. Which modes all produce darker images?

   a. Color Burn, Darken, and Multiply

   b. Darken, Multiply, and Screen

   c. Darken, Color Burn, and Overlay

   d. Darken, Overlay, and Screen

4. Which of the following brush spacing values produces a dotted line in which the spaces are twice the size of the brush marks?

   a. 33%

   b. 50%

   c. 100%

   d. 200%

5. Which of the following formats allows you to save layers with the image?

   a. GIF

   b. PSD

   c. Both GIF and PSD

   d. Neither GIF nor PSD

6. Which of the following commands can you use to merge all layers together?

   a. Flatten Layers

   b. Merge Visible

   c. Merge Down

   d. All of the above

7. How can you reposition a layer?

   a. With the Free Transform command

   b. With the Translate command in the Transform submenu

   c. With the Move tool

   d. All of the above

8. Which of the following filters allows you to preview the seams produced by a tiling image?

   a. Tile Maker

   b. Offset

   c. Custom

   d. Find Edges

9. What could you do if none of the Photoshop filters fit your needs?

   a. Search for third-party filters

   b. Use the Custom filter

   c. Combine multiple filters

   d. Any of the above

10. What happens if you run the Clouds filter over a completely red image?

   a. You see a red cloud pattern.

   b. You see white clouds over a blue background.

   c. You see white clouds over a black background.

   d. You see a cloud pattern based on the current foreground and background colors.

11. Many background images don't need a large color palette. Therefore, what image format is usually better for background images?

   a. GIF

   b. JPEG

   c. PNG

   d. Either GIF or JPEG

12. What is the easiest way to create a solid orange background?

   a. Set the body's background attribute to orange.

   b. Use a 1 × 1 pixel orange graphic in the background.

   c. Use a 1280 × 1024 orange graphic in the background.

   d. Any of the above

13. If you want to use yellow text on your page, what would be a good background image?

   a. One that is mostly light colors

   b. One that is mostly dark colors

   c. You should never use light-colored text, because it is too hard to read.

   d. One that is mostly yellow

14. How do you remove the seams in a tiled image?

   a. By blending opposite edges

   b. By turning the image into a kaleidoscopic image

   c. Either *a* or *b*

   d. You can never completely remove tile seams.

15. What is one of the last steps in creating a background image?

   a. Removing the seams

   b. Selecting the color

   c. Creating the pattern

   d. Reducing the contrast

16. Which technique would be inappropriate for removing the seams from a photographic background?

   a. Using the Blend Edges feature of the Tile Maker filter in ImageReady

   b. Using the Kaleidoscope feature of the Tile Maker filter in ImageReady

   c. Using the Offset filter and removing the seams with the Smudge tool

   d. Using the Offset filter and removing the seams with the Blur tool

17. What is a drawback of using style sheets to assign background images?

    a. No existing browser can display images this way.

    b. Only users with older browsers can see the images.

    c. Only users with newer browsers can see the images.

    d. You don't know who can or cannot view the images.

18. Where can you use a background image without using style sheets?

    a. Only in the body background

    b. Only in table backgrounds

    c. In the background of any block element

    d. Only in body and table cell backgrounds

19. Is background an HTML tag or an attribute?

    a. Tag

    b. Attribute

    c. Either *a* or *b*, depending on how you use it

    d. Neither

20. How would you make a background image tile vertically but not horizontally in Netscape version 3?

    a. By setting the background attribute in HTML

    b. By setting the background-repeat attribute in CSS

    c. With either method in *a* and *b*

    d. Netscape version 3 cannot tile background images this way.

HANDS-ON PROJECTS

All of the following projects use Photoshop and files provided for you in the Chapter05 folder of your Data Disk, or in the Student Data/Chapter05 folder of your hard drive. You can write the HTML or CSS in any HTML or text editor.

Project 5-1: Create a Striped Background and Put in a Web Page

You have been using solid-color backgrounds in HTML because your manager does not want extra image files to slow the loading of pages. You convince him that a simple striped background image will make the pages much more attractive, but will also load quickly.

Complete these steps:

    1. Create a 30 × 30 pixel image file called **stripeBackground.gif**.

2. Choose your colors. Click the **foreground color box** to open the Color Picker dialog box. In the Web color window next to the pound sign (#), type **009999** and click **OK** to produce a teal color. If you're using an older version of Photoshop, type **0** in the R box, **153** in the G box, and **153** in the blue box to produce the same teal color. Use **white** as the background color.

3. Select the upper-half of the image with the **Rectangular Marquee** tool. Use the rulers to see how much you've selected.

4. Color the upper-half of the image. Select the **Paint Bucket** tool. Fill the selected area with your foreground color.

5. Optimize the image. In the Indexed Color dialog box, set the Palette to **Exact**.

6. Save the image as **stripeBackground.gif** in a new directory on your desktop named |**project_5-1**. This image should be small and therefore load quickly, even with a slow modem.

7. In your text editor, open a new file and type the following code:

```
<html>
<body BACKGROUND="stripeBackground.gif">
some text
</body>
</html>
```

8. Save this file as **bg-test.html** in the project_5-1 folder.

9. Open your browser and open the new HTML file, **bg-test.html**. You'll see the stripes repeating across and down, covering the entire window.

10. The text is difficult to read. Add a table with a white background to contain the text. Your HTML file should look like this:

```
<html>
<body BACKGROUND="stripeBackground.gif">
<table BGCOLOR="#ffffff"><tr><td>
<some text
</td></tr></table>
</body>
</html>
```

11. Save **bg-test.html** and refresh your browser.

Project 5-2: Create a Tessellated Kaleidoscope

The striped background image you created in Project 5-1 is only a little more interesting than a solid color. Create a pattern that tiles seamlessly across the page.

Complete these steps:

1. Create a **100 × 100 pixel** image in Photoshop.

2. Select a **blue** foreground color, and scribble over the image with the **Paintbrush** tool, making sure to go over the edge.

3. Click **Filter** on the menu bar, point to **Texture**, and then click **Craquelure**. Use the default settings or adjust them to create an effect you like.

4. Save this image as **kaleidoscope.jpg** in a new folder named **project_5-2**.

5. Copy **bg-test.html** to the new folder, and edit it to make this new image the background image. View the HTML file in your browser. You can see that the edges are visible where they meet. You can remove the seams by using mirror images of the original.

6. Select the entire **image** and copy it.

7. Increase the Canvas Size to **200 × 200**, keeping the original image anchored in the upper-left corner.

8. Paste the clipboard selection three times. You see three new layers in the Layers palette.

9. Select **Layer 1** in the Layers palette, and move it to the upper-right corner of the canvas area.

10. Click **Edit** on the menu bar, point to **Transform**, and then click **Flip Horizontal**.

11. Select **Layer 2** in the Layers palette, and move it to the lower-left corner of the canvas area.

12. Click **Edit** on the menu bar, point to **Transform**, and then click **Flip Vertical**.

13. Select **Layer 3** in the Layers palette, and move it to the lower-right corner of the canvas area.

14. Click **Edit** on the menu bar, click **Transform**, and then click **Rotate 180**. Now all the layers reflect each other vertically and horizontally.

15. Click **Layer** on the menu bar, and then click **Flatten Image**.

16. Save the image as **kaleidoscope.jpg** and refresh your browser. The image should tile seamlessly.

Project 5-3: Create a Seamless Photo Tile

You have been given a photograph to use as a background. You realize you cannot use the kaleidoscope technique, because it would create backward and upside-down images. Remove the seams by blurring the edges.

Complete these steps:

1. Open **5-3.tif** from the Data Disk.

2. Click **Filter** on the menu bar, point to **Other**, and then click **Offset**.

3. Set the **Horizontal** offset to roughly half the width of the image (in this case, **50**).

4. Set the **Vertical** offset to roughly half the height of the image (in this case, **50**).

5. Under **Undefined Areas**, select **Wrap Around**. You see the seamed edges as they would appear in a tiled background image.

6. Use the **Blur** tool to blur the seams.

7. Use the **Smudge** tool to smear the edges near the seams, obscuring them. Do not smudge outside the canvas area.

8. Use the Levels dialog box to lighten the output levels.

9. Optimize the image, and save it as **photo.jpg** in a new folder named **project_5-3**.

10. Copy **bg-test.html** to the new folder, and edit it to make this new image the background image. View the HTML file in your browser.

Project 5-4: Create a Tiled Photo with ImageReady

ImageReady can automate the creation of tiled background images. It does not allow the same control as the process in the previous project, but it makes the process easier.

Complete these steps:

1. In ImageReady, open **5-3.tif** from the Data Disk.

2. Click **Filter** on the menu bar, point to **Other**, and then click **Tile Maker**.

3. In the dialog box that appears, select **Blend Edges** and set the **Width** to **10%**, and check the **Resize Tile to Fill Image** checkbox.

4. Click **OK**. Note that the outer 10% of the image has been removed and added to the opposite edge, and that the image has been resized accordingly.

5. Trim away the margin of transparent pixels.

6. Optimize and save this image as **photo2.jpg** in a new folder named **project_5-4**.

7. Copy **bg-test.html** to the new folder, and edit it to make this new image the background image. View the HTML file in your browser.

Project 5-5: Create a Large Background Image

Your client wants a large curved line over the top of the Web page. Style sheets will not help with this. You need to use a very large background image that will not tile.

Complete these steps:

1. Create a **1280 × 1024-pixel** image in Photoshop. This image is large enough to not tile on most monitors.

2. Select the **Elliptical Marquee** tool.

3. Move the pointer to the **100 × 100-pixel** mark, then drag down and to the right until you reach the lower-right corner of the canvas area.

4. Use the **Rectangular Marquee** tool to square off the upper-right corner, the lower-right corner, and the lower-left corner of the selection area.

5. Click **Select** on the menu bar, and then click **Inverse**.

6. Use the **Add Noise** filter to add some texture to the selection.

7. Click **Filter** on the menu bar, point to **Sketch**, and then click **Bas Relief**. Use the default settings, or adjust them as you like.

8. Use the Hue/Saturation dialog box to make the selection **green**.

9. This is a large image, but it needs to have a small file size. Optimize it to around **30K** and save it as **arc.jpg** in a new folder named **project_5-5**.

10. Insert the image as the background image in bg-test.html, and preview the page in a browser.

Project 5-6: Create a Patterned Tile

You need a background that looks like snowflakes. Although you have some snowflake images to work with, you do not want to smudge or blur them as the other techniques require. You need to create a brush for each type of footprint and paint these seamlessly over a background image.

Complete these steps:

1. Create a **100 × 100 pixel** image and give it a **light yellow** background.

2. Select a **dark blue** as the Foreground color.

3. Select the **Paintbrush** tool. From the Options bar, open the **Brush palette**.

4. Open the **Brush palette menu**, select **Assorted Brushes**, and then click **OK**.

5. From the Brush palette, select the **Snowflake** brush icon.

6. Click the **Snowflake** brush in the Brushes palette, and type **250** for the Spacing in the dialog box that appears.

7. Drag the pointer across the image from the bottom to the top of the image. You should see a line of snowflakes moving up the page. Repeat this step to create another line of prints. Try not to go over the edge of the image.

8. Set the Background color to the **yellow** in the image, and erase any snowflake that is cut off by the edge of the canvas area.

9. Click **Filter** on the menu bar, point to **Other**, and then click **Offset**. In the dialog box that appears, enter the same values as you did for Project 5-3.

10. Fill in the gaps with more snowflakes, making sure not to paint outside the canvas area.

11. Optimize and save this image as **wallpaper.gif** in a folder named **project_5-6**.

12. Insert the image as the background image in bg-test.html, and preview the page in a browser.

Project 5-7: Use a Background in a Table Using CSS

You can use style sheets to place backgrounds in table cells, but don't use the same method as you do for the body. If you do, every table cell will have the same background image. To control which cells display the background, you need to use a class.

Complete these steps:

1. In your text editor, create another HTML file and save it as **bg-test2.html** in the project_5-6 folder.

2. Type this code into your file:

```
<html
<head>
<style TYPE="text/css">
<!—
.bg2 {
background-image: url(wallpaper.gif);
background-repeat: repeat-x
}
//—>
</style>
</head>
<body>
<table HEIGHT="100%" WIDTH="100%" BORDER="1">
    <tr>
        <td WIDTH="200" BGCOLOR="#FFFFFF">
            some text
        </td>
        <td WIDTH="250" CLASS="bg2">
            some more text
        </td>
    </tr>
</table>
</body>
</html>
```

3. Save the file and view it in your browser. The cell on the right calls the bg2 class you defined in the style sheet and should display the background image, tiled horizontally.

Project 5-8: Create a Complex Background with Multiple Filters

Each filter lets you create many different effects. When you combine different filters you can create thousands of effects. Combine two filters to create a fire and smoke background.

Complete these steps:

1. In Photoshop, create a **200 × 200 pixel** image.

2. Set the Background color to **black** and the Foreground color to **red**.

3. Click **Filter** on the menu bar, point to **Render**, and then click **Clouds**. You should see a black background with red clouds. Run the filter a few more times to try different random patterns.

4. Use the Offset filter to preview the seams of the image.

5. Select the **Smudge** tool, select one of the specialty spatter brushes, and gently smudge away the seams. Use the **Blur** tool to further reduce the appearance of edges.

6. Click **Filter** on the menu bar, point to **Artistic**, and then click **Plastic Wrap**. Set the Highlight Strength to **10**, the Detail to **10**, and the Smoothness to **5**.

7. Click **OK**. You should see a fiery red and black background with wispy white smoke.

8. Reduce the contrast, optimize and save the image as **weird.jpg** in a new folder named **project_5-8**.

9. Copy bg-test.html to the folder, edit it to use this new image, and preview it in a browser.

CASE PROJECT

Add background images and colors to the pages you've completed so far for your portfolio. On at least one page, use a background image in the body of the page, setting the style sheet so that the image tiles vertically, but not across. On another page, use a background image in a table. Both background images should have reduced contrast so that text that appears over the image can be easily read.

6

CREATING AND USING ICONS

Designing and Making Bullets, Symbols, Icons, and Logos

In this chapter, you will learn:

- How to work with small images
- About creating bullets and symbols
- How to implement icons in Web pages
- About designing logos
- How to create and implement favorites icons

Different types of Web graphics accomplish different objectives. Photographs usually provide informative content along with text, while background images decorate Web pages and can make them appealing and attractive. A third type of Web graphic, an icon, does both. Icons provide the user information in a decorative way.

Icons include bullets, symbols, logos, favorites icons, and buttons. Buttons deserve special attention and are covered in detail in the "Creating and Using Buttons" chapter. This chapter focuses on all other types of icons.

The first step in designing icons is to understand their function relative to the other elements of a Web page. All icons share the purpose of qualifying and identifying accompanying text. A logo identifies a page or site, a bullet indicates that nearby text is important, and a button reinforces a text link by helping to identify its destination.

Because their role is to complement the content of a page, icons typically are small and have reduced color palettes. Trying to convey meaning in a small space is a challenge. To meet this challenge, you can use symbols, which usually represent larger concepts. When created properly, a good icon can replace several lines of text.

WORKING WITH SMALL IMAGES

The biggest challenge in creating an icon is working within a small area. Instead of using the bold strokes of a paintbrush, you often need to precisely manipulate individual pixels. You can create small graphics by drawing them in an image editor, using text, or by reducing the dimensions of a larger image.

Setting the Environment

Before you create an icon, you must set up your work environment so you can easily see what you are doing. The following techniques use Photoshop, but you can use other image-editing applications.

Increasing Magnification

In general, you should work at a magnification near 1000%, then return to 100% to preview the icon as it will appear in the Web page. The easiest way to zoom in and out is with the Magnifying Glass tool, also called the Zoom tool. To zoom in, click the Zoom tool and then click the image; to zoom out, hold down the Alt key (Windows) or Option key (Macintosh) and click the image. You also can drag the Zoom tool across the image to zoom in to the selected area, as shown in Figure 6-1.

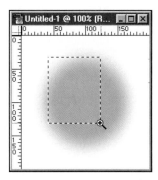

Figure 6-1   Dragging the Zoom tool across an image

You can change magnification in other ways. You can click View on the menu bar, and then click Fit on Screen to zoom in to the image until the outer edges of the canvas area fill the visible Photoshop window. To return the magnification to 100%, click View on the menu bar, and then click Actual Pixels; you also can double-click the Zoom tool to change magnification.

Another way you can control magnification is in the Navigator palette, shown in Figure 6-2. The Navigator palette usually is found with the Info palette in the upper-right corner of the workspace. If you do not see it, select Show Navigator from the Window menu. Drag the slider to the left to reduce magnification, and to the right to magnify the image.

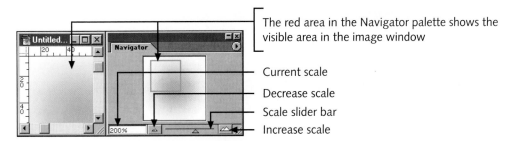

The red area in the Navigator palette shows the visible area in the image window

Current scale

Decrease scale

Scale slider bar

Increase scale

Figure 6-2   Using the Navigator palette for zooming

Using Grids

6

After you magnify an image, it is difficult to distinguish one pixel from another within a solid color. In Photoshop, you can place a grid over images to show the position of every pixel, as shown in Figure 6-3. In the figure, every pixel that composes the letter R is clearly delineated.

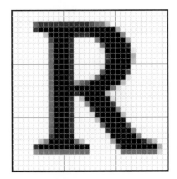

Figure 6-3   Using a grid to clearly distinguish pixels

After you display the grid, you can set its spacing.

To display the grid and set spacing:

1. Click **View** on the menu bar, point to **Show**, and then click **Grid**. You see a grid similar to the one shown in Figure 6-3.

2. To set the spacing of the grid, click **Edit** on the menu bar, point to **Preferences**, and then click **Guides & Grid**.

3. In the Preferences dialog box, shown in Figure 6-4, change the values in the Gridline and Subdivisions text boxes. Set the Gridline to appear every **10** pixels, and set the Subdivisions to **10**; the grid displays a gray line between every pixel, with a thicker black line every 10 pixels.

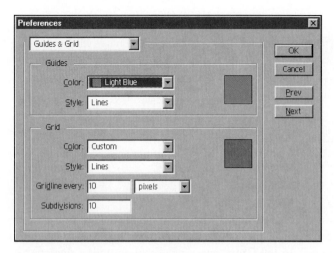

Figure 6-4 Adjust grid settings in the Photoshop Preferences dialog box

Using a Transparent Background

To indicate transparency, Photoshop uses a different grid which you also can use as a guide when creating small images. You see this grid when you create an image. At that time, Photoshop presents three options for filling the background. Select white to give the new image a white background. Select Background Color to fill the background layer with the color you select as the background color. Select Transparent not to fill the image, but to display a white and gray checkerboard pattern that disappears as you add colors to the image. Figure 6-5 shows an image with a transparent background. The checkerboard pattern appears only in Photoshop or ImageReady. In a Web page, the transparent pixels are not visible.

Figure 6-5 An image with a transparent background

You can adjust the size and colors of the transparency grid. In the Preferences dialog box, click the top list arrow and then click Transparency & Gamut. The options shown in Figure 6-6 appear. The transparent background grid does not always correspond one-to-one with each pixel in the image, but it helps you keep your place as you draw or move layers.

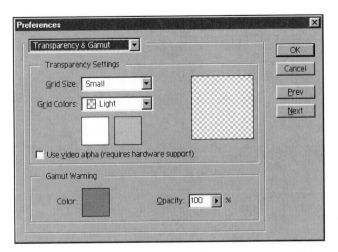

Figure 6-6   Adjust transparency grid settings in the Photoshop Preferences dialog box

Using Other Tools to Work with Small Images

You can use any tool to create or edit an icon, but the most useful ones, such as the Pencil and Line tools, offer fine control. If you need to add simple shapes or special characters for use in your icons, use the Type tool or the Custom Shape tool. Each of these tools is in the main toolbar of Photoshop, as shown in Figure 6-7.

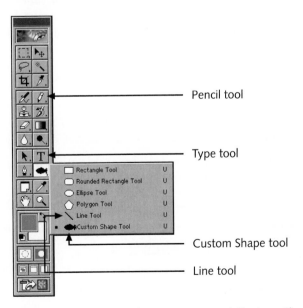

Figure 6-7   The Pencil, Type, Line, and Custom Shape tools

Using the Pencil Tool

The Pencil tool is essentially the same as the Paintbrush tool, except that the drawn line has a sharp, jagged edge. The Paintbrush tool draws lines with fuzzy edges, where the nearby pixels take on some of the color of the lines. The Pencil tool, however, draws only the pixels indicated by the brush head. Figure 6-8 shows a mark made with the Pencil tool and one made with the Paintbrush tool. On the right side of the figure is a close-up view of the two marks. Note how the jagged Pencil mark is composed of only black pixels, while the smooth Paintbrush mark is composed of many intermediary shades of gray. While the smooth lines usually look better, you have less control with the Paintbrush tool than with the Pencil tool. The crisp line of the Pencil tool gives you pixel-perfect control when you work on images that might be as small as 20 pixels wide.

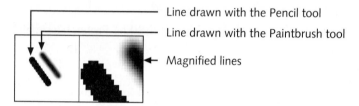

Figure 6-8   Marks created with the Paintbrush and Pencil tools

You can use any brush tool, including the Pencil tool, to draw straight lines. To do so, you click the pixel where you want the straight line to start, and then you hold down the Shift key and click another part of the image. Photoshop automatically fills in the pixels between the two points and creates a straight line.

Using the Line Tool

You also can use the Line tool to draw straight lines. The Line tool is grouped with the Shape tools in the Photoshop toolbox. Like the other Shape tools (covered in the "Creating and Using Buttons" chapter), the Line tool can create vector outlines as well as color pixels.

When you select the Line tool, the Options bar displays three options for the type of line to create. Figure 6-9 shows the Options bar when the Line tool is selected.

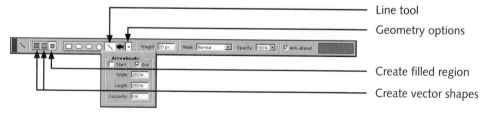

Figure 6-9   Line tool options

The three buttons on the far left of the Options bar determine whether the Line tool creates a vector shape or a normal line. Select the third button, named Create Filled Region, to create nonvector lines of colored pixels. In the Weight text field, enter the width of the line in pixels. You also can select the blending mode, opacity, and whether the line is anti-aliased.

Making Arrows

You use the Line tool to create arrows by adding an arrowhead to a line.

To create an arrow in Photoshop:

1. Click the **Line** tool in the toolbox.

2. Click the **Geometry** list arrow in the Options palette to display the Arrowheads palette.

3. Select whether you want an arrowhead at the start, end, or both ends of the line.

4. Define the size and shape of the arrowhead. Adjust the width and length of the arrowhead as a percentage of the line width. For example, if the line is 4 pixels wide, set the arrowhead width to **600%** and the height to **300%** to create an arrowhead that is 24 pixels long and 12 pixels high.

You also can adjust the concavity of the arrowhead from –50% to 50%; the concavity affects the angle of the back of the arrowhead. Figure 6-10 shows the possible arrowhead shapes.

Three possible shapes for arrowheads

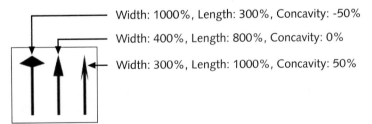

Width: 1000%, Length: 300%, Concavity: -50%

Width: 400%, Length: 800%, Concavity: 0%

Width: 300%, Length: 1000%, Concavity: 50%

Figure 6-10   Possible arrowhead shapes

Using the Custom Shape Tool

Like the Line tool, the Custom Shape tool creates both vector and bitmap shapes. The vector options also are described in the "Creating and Using Buttons" chapter. When you select the Custom Shape tool, the Options bar provides settings for size and shape, as shown in Figure 6-11.

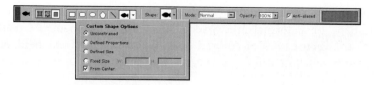

Figure 6-11 Custom Shape Options

Click the Shape list arrow to select a custom shape. These custom shapes are like custom brush heads, but you can size them. If you want more custom shapes, click the palette options button in the Custom Shapes palette, then click Custom Shapes.csh. You can either replace the current list of shapes, or append it. To use a shape, click the Create Filled Region button in the Options bar, and drag the pointer across the image as you would when using a Marquee tool. You can create shapes with fixed or unconstrained sizes.

Click the Geometry list arrow in the Options bar to display the Custom Shape Options palette. Then select the size of the custom shape as described below:

- *Unconstrained:* This lets you create the shape with any size or proportion.

- *Defined Proportions:* This forces the shape to maintain the default proportion.

- *Defined Size:* This forces the shape to maintain the default size.

- *Fixed Size:* This allows you to enter a height and width for the shape.

- *From Center:* This creates the shape so that the center remains where you first click the mouse. If you do not select this, the shape is drawn from one of the corners.

Using Text to Create Symbols

You can draw icons with the Pencil tool, but often it is easier to use a shape from a symbol font. Most computers have several symbol fonts such as Wingdings or Dingbats, which can include over 200 symbols instead of the standard letters, digits, and punctuation marks in most fonts. You can download many additional font libraries for free from the Web.

Both Windows and Macintosh operating systems include font preview utilities that let you see exactly which symbols and characters are available in each font. The utility is called Unicode Character Map in Windows and Key Caps in Macintosh.

In Windows, click the Start button in the taskbar, point to Programs, click Accessories, and then click Character Map. This displays the Unicode Character Map, shown in Figure 6-12.

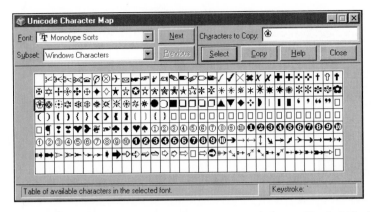

Figure 6-12   The Unicode Character Map dialog utility in Windows

6

In Macintosh, click the Apple menu, and then click Key Caps. This displays the dialog box shown in Figure 6-13. Select a font from the Key Caps menu.

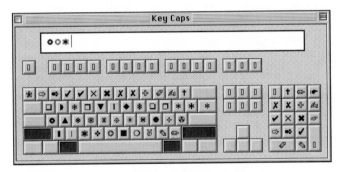

Figure 6-13   The Key Caps utility in MacOS

You can choose any character in any font, copy it, and paste it in Photoshop.

Reducing Larger Images

If the symbols in your font libraries are inadequate, you might want to find a larger source image and reduce its dimensions to create an icon. You also can reduce your own icons as you create multiple versions for different areas on the site. However, smaller images have less detail than larger ones, and need additional contrast to be seen clearly.

Boosting Contrast

Subtle differences in shading that create smooth text and lines for large images make the same text and lines difficult to read in small images. Increase the contrast of reduced images to make the image's detail more visible, as shown in Figure 6-14. Click Image on the menu bar, point to Adjust, and then click Levels to open the

Levels dialog box. Use the Levels dialog box to normalize contrast before and after changing the image size. You also might want to erase the pixels that create soft lines at the edges of the image.

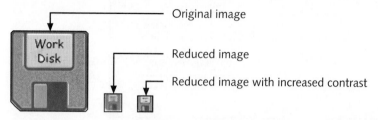

Figure 6-14   Reduced image with increased contrast

Reducing Colors

You also can increase contrast by decreasing the number of colors used in an image. Color reduction removes the less frequently used colors, which are usually the soft-edge pixels. Switch to Indexed Color mode to minimize the number of colors in the palette. Click Image on the menu bar, point to Mode, and then click Indexed Color to open the Indexed Color dialog box.

In the ImageReady Optimize palette, indicate the number of colors you want to use.

Working with Transparency

You can save GIF and PNG format images with transparency. A transparent image includes pixels that are clear, and have no color value. When transparent images appear in a Web page, background color or images show through the transparent pixels.

Transparency is useful for images that appear on patterned backgrounds. Without transparency, these images require solid color squares around them to avoid mismatched patterns. Transparency also is useful if you use the same icon on different color backgrounds. Transparent backgrounds let you use the same icon on any page, regardless of background color, then you don't have to create different icons for every color background used in your site. Figure 6-15 shows the awkward results when graphics without transparency are used over patterned backgrounds.

To make pixels transparent, select the pixels, and then press the Backspace or Delete key. Use the Magic Wand tool to select pixels of similar color. You get the best results by setting the Magic Wand tool options in the Options bar to a Tolerance of 0, and deselecting Anti-aliased and Contiguous. Then only pixels of identical color are selected.

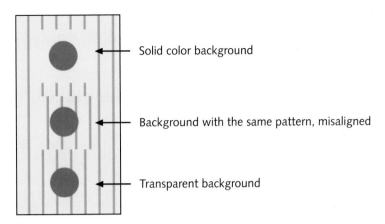

Solid color background

Background with the same pattern, misaligned

Transparent background

Figure 6-15   Web page images, with and without transparency

Using the Background Layer

When working with an image with a white or colored background, erasing pixels does not make them transparent, rather, it reveals the background color. In this type of image, the background layer is indicated in the Layers palette by the word *Background* in italics next to a lock icon. This background layer preserves the color you choose when you create the file. If you want to show transparent pixels when you erase parts of the foreground, you first must convert the background layer to a normal layer.

To convert the background layer to a normal layer:

1. In the Layers palette, double-click the **background layer** to open the Layer Options dialog box. You also can open the Layer Options dialog box by selecting Layer Options from the Layer menu or from the Layers palette menu.

2. Click **OK**. Photoshop converts the background layer to a normal layer. Now when you erase pixels on this layer, it shows transparent pixels.

Avoiding Aliasing

Some Web graphics have an unattractive halo, as in Figure 6-16. The image at the top of the figure has an anti-aliased white edge and is on a white background, so no halo is visible. The image at the bottom of the figure has the same blurred edge, but is set against a gray background, so the halo is visible.

The halo is caused by pixels that are neither transparent, nor part of the foreground image. When an image has an anti-aliased edge, the border between foreground and background blurs and develops a gradient between the foreground and background colors. When the background color is made transparent, the blurred edge remains and results in the halo effect. To avoid these halos, you must either create your image using the same background color as the one that will be used in the Web page, or edit the edge pixels to remove any pixels of the wrong color.

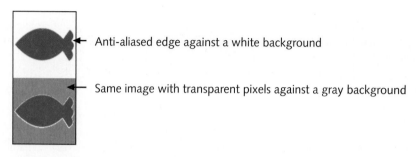

Anti-aliased edge against a white background

Same image with transparent pixels against a gray background

Figure 6-16   A transparent image with a halo of unwanted color

Choosing the Right Background Color

The easiest way to eliminate halos is to use an image background color similar to the color used behind the image in the Web page. The colors and patterns do not have to match exactly. The blurred edge caused by anti-aliasing is a gradient between foreground and background colors. If your image has the right background color in the first place, the blurred edge blends smoothly with the background in the Web page.

The Optimize palette in ImageReady and the Indexed Color dialog box in Photoshop include a Matte option and Transparency check box. Click the Matte list arrow to select a color to use as the background color. If the Transparency box is not checked, the matte color is applied to all transparent pixels. If the Transparency box is checked, only the edge pixels are converted to the matte color.

Editing Edge Pixels

You can minimize the appearance of a halo by zooming into the edge between the colored and transparent pixels, and then deleting the edge pixels.

To edit the color of the halo pixels in ImageReady:

1. Show the **Optimize** palette and the **Color Table** palette.

2. In the Optimize palette, make sure that the Transparency check box is checked and the format is set to GIF or PNG-8.

3. The Color Table palette shows all the available colors, including transparent ones. Use the Eyedropper tool to select an **edge pixel** in the image. The selected color swatch is outlined in the Color Table palette.

4. Click the **trash can** icon in the Color Table palette to delete the color.

   You also can double-click the color swatch to open the Color Picker dialog box. Then choose a new color that produces a less-noticeable effect. Deleting or editing a color affects all pixels of that color in the image.

Using the Alpha Channel with PNG Images

One advantage of the PNG format over the GIF format is that PNG images can use up to 256 values of transparency. Just as each primary color in an RGB image has a separate color channel, the transparent pixels in an image are collectively called the **alpha channel**. In GIF images the alpha channel is a 1-bit channel, so a pixel has only two possible transparency values: on or off.

Having only two transparency values, means GIF images often have jagged edges—there are not enough transparency values to create soft edges. PNG graphics use an 8-bit alpha channel, so each pixel has up to 256 possible transparency values ranging from fully opaque to fully transparent. Figure 6-17 shows a GIF image on the left with 1-bit transparency and a PNG-8 image on the right with 8-bit transparency. With the option of 256 transparency values, you can blend the edge of any PNG image from opaque to transparent, rather than from one color to another.

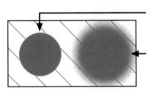

Two values for transparency in GIF images results in hard edges

256 values for transparency in PNG images results in soft edges

Figure 6-17   *Differences between 1-bit GIF transparency and 8-bit PNG transparency*

Now that you are familiar with the tools at your disposal, you can learn how to create icons for the Web.

CREATING BULLETS AND SYMBOLS

Bullets and other small icons guide the reader's attention toward important information on the page. They should not overwhelm the text itself, and should be only as large as necessary to convey information. To express an idea in a small space, you need to rely on abstraction and symbolism.

Understanding Types of Bullets and Symbols

Logos are used to identify or qualify an entire Web page. Bullets and other icons identify or qualify elements such as links or blocks of text within the page. Bullets simply point to adjacent text, while other types of icons convey information.

Using Ratings Symbols

One common type of icon is the symbol used in ratings scales. These icons are usually decorative and add interest to a Web page. Their main function, however, is to provide site or product information to the reader at a glance. Ratings symbols illustrate numeric information that is already on a page. For example, a movie review site that rates movies on a scale of one-to-five might use an icon with a thumbs-up image to represent the rating. Five thumbs-up images represent a high rating, while one represents a low rating.

To make a ratings symbol or any other icon stand out from the rest of the page, choose appropriate shapes and colors for the symbols. Ratings symbols also must be large enough to see, but should not crowd out other information on the page. Finally, the symbols must accurately reflect the numeric values they represent.

To indicate fractional values, such as a rating of 2.5, designers often use a combination of whole and half symbols. Make sure any shape you use for a rating symbol is easy to interpret when it is halved. A half-star is clearly different from a whole star, but half a house might look like a narrow house instead of a fraction. Also, fractions smaller than one-half are difficult to distinguish, so if you need to use them, consider using a different scale or a simple bar to indicate percentage values.

To use rating symbols effectively, you must show how the parts relate to the whole. For example, if a software review gets a four-star rating, is this four stars out of four, or ten? Without an indication of relative amounts, the rating is meaningless. The rating box can include text that defines the highest possible value, but a visual cue is easier and faster for readers to understand.

You should include blank or empty ratings symbols to show a rating relative to the highest possible rating. For example, if you are using yellow stars on a blue background, you could use gray stars to indicate the remainder of the rating scale, as shown in Figure 6-18. Include remainder symbols to the right of the actual ratings symbols.

Figure 6-18   Relative ratings symbols

Using Review Symbols

Another popular type of icon is the review symbol, which provides quick impressions of movies, books, and other products. These icons usually appear in a tabular list, such as on a search results page, a download page, or a comparative review page. Review symbols can be simple check mark graphics or more descriptive ones to indicate an editor's choice, popular choices, free selections, and new or popular selections.

Unlike ratings symbols, review symbols must be distinctive and convey a particular meaning. For example, the reader must know if an icon signifies new selections or signifies popular selections. In Figure 6-19 the two columns on the left signify something good, the dark blue skulls represent something dangerous, and the dollar signs signify money.

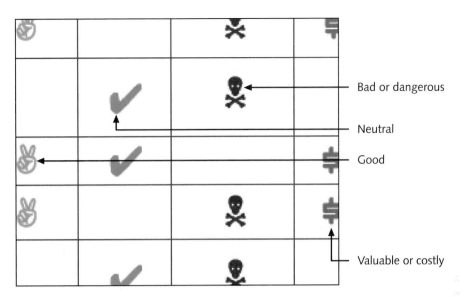

Figure 6-19   Possible review symbols

Using Bullets

You can use HTML to include text bullets in a Web page, but you often will want to create graphical bullets to add decoration to a page. Bullets, like other icons, are small and are used with accompanying text. However, icons and symbols contain information, but bullets do not. Bullets are used only to guide a reader's attention toward specific text. Using bullets is similar to using indentation, boldface, underlining, or other formatting features to emphasize words or sentences. Unlike symbols, bullets should not call attention to themselves, and should only be visible enough to point a reader to adjacent text.

Bullets always are used with text, as in a bulleted list, but other icons can stand alone.

Using Symbolic Icons

Symbolic icons are similar to bullets because they direct a viewer's attention to text, but they also provide additional information about the text. A bullet indicates only that a line of text is particularly important, but symbolic icons also can qualify the text and indicate just why it is important.

One common symbolic icon is the New icon, which points to content that did not exist during the user's previous visit. Another general icon is the Look or Hot icon, which indicates information that is new or popular. One of the most popular symbolic icons is the Under Construction icon. It appears beside a link to a page that is not ready to be viewed, or on the unfinished page itself. (Programmers and designers debate the merits of using Under Construction icons; some argue that a page under construction should not be linked in the first place.)

Designing Bullets and Symbols

You should follow a few simple rules when designing icons. In general, you should consider the most appropriate shape, size, and color for the particular icon. These rules are not written in stone, but usually they help you create conventionally attractive icons.

Figure 6-20 shows some sample bullets and icons. The bullets use soft colors and shapes to blend into the page and indicate that the adjacent text is important. The symbolic icon uses bright colors and angles to demand reader attention. The New icon not only announces that the text is important, but also explains why—it's new.

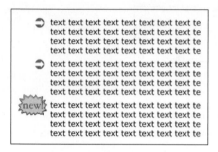

Figure 6-20   Bullet and icon designs

Selecting a Shape

The shape of a symbol must capture the attention of the reader. The following guidelines help you choose an eye-catching shape for ratings symbols:

- Angled lines are more eye-catching than curved lines.
- Diagonal lines are more noticeable than horizontal or vertical lines.

Ratings symbols often use a five-sided star, which observes both of these rules. A lightning bolt or even a simple X also follows the rules and attracts the eye. A square or a circle, on the other hand, might not be noticed at all.

In some ways, bullets and ratings symbols have opposite purposes—a ratings symbol draws the reader's attention to itself, while a bullet points to the accompanying text. Therefore, the rules for selecting symbol shapes are reversed for bullets. Instead of using angles and diagonal lines, bullets should use curves, horizontal lines, and vertical lines. Common shapes for bullets are simple circles, squares, and horizontal lines.

Selecting a Color

Shape is not the only element of an icon that makes it stand out; bright colors that contrast with the background also are necessary. If you use a color-neutral symbol such as a dollar sign, you can choose a color to contrast with the background (for example, red on white). If you use a symbol such as a gold star or stop sign, the color is integral so you must change the background color to make the symbol stand out. A yellow star on a white background is not as noticeable as a yellow star on a dark blue background. You do not need to alter the entire background of the page—you can merely add a colored bar behind a symbol. For example, a dark blue or black background bar makes yellow symbols more noticeable.

Although you normally want the colors of Web graphics to share a common color palette, icons should stand apart from the rest of the page. Therefore, it is acceptable for icons to have different colors from the other graphics on the site.

Bullets also need to contrast with the background to be noticeable, but should not be so bright that they divert attention from the text. If you choose a very low-contrast color for a bullet, the reader sees nothing. A better choice is to make the bullet fit the text by imitating the text color, or by using a lower-contrast version of the text color. For example, if the text is black on a white background, a black or gray bullet would be your best choice.

Selecting a Size

Icon size can vary, but in general icons should be only as large as necessary to convey information. An average size is 30 × 30 pixels. However, if you use an icon as a button, use a larger size to make it easier to click (about 50 × 50 pixels).

Ratings symbols also should follow these guidelines. Web programmers usually fit ratings symbols in rows that are 150 pixels wide. The size of each symbol is the total width divided by the number of rankings in the scale. A five-star scale, for example, requires that each star be 30 pixels wide, and a ten-star scale requires that stars be 15 pixels wide. However, these widths also must include margins. A rule of thumb is to allow margins that are 25% as wide as the symbol itself. For example, a five-star scale should have stars that are 20 pixels wide, with five pixels on either side.

Bullets should only be large enough to be visible, and should be proportional to the size of the text. A bullet that is one pixel wide is too small; a bullet that is 30 pixels wide overwhelms the nearby text. A rule of thumb is to make bullets no smaller than a lowercase "o" and no larger than two uppercase "W"s. Bullets, therefore, should be about 15 pixels high and 20 pixels wide, depending on the size of the text.

Using Symbolism

A graphical symbol is an object or other visual element that represents a more complex idea. An effective icon uses symbolic colors and shapes that are universally recognized. A standard American mailbox is not standard elsewhere in the world, so people in other countries might not understand that it symbolizes mail. An image of an envelope with a stamp is more universal, however, and is more likely to be understood.

As you create icons, consider how people interpret different colors and shapes.

Using Symbolic Colors

Color symbolism is important not only in designing icons, but in entire Web sites. When you design icons, keep in mind the color scheme of the page and the meanings attached to colors.

Many Web icons take their color schemes from road signs and traffic lights. Because most people are familiar with these conventions, designers know that green icons might mean go, and red might mean stop, for example.

Color also can have more literal meanings. For example, gold often refers to wealth, and green often refers to plants and the natural world. Many literal meanings are culturally based, however. Americans associate a certain shade of green with money because all U.S. paper currency uses that color. In countries that use different colors on their money, the significance can be lost.

Other colors are associated with attitudes or values. Dark blue often indicates conservative values and is used prominently in financial Web sites. Black and other dark colors sometimes indicate "alternative" values and are used in music sites and other sites targeted at young adults. Bright, primary colors usually indicate children, and pastels can indicate romance or baby-related themes.

Using Symbolic Shapes

The shapes you use in your icons are your primary means for communicating through images. Some shapes, such as an exclamation point to indicate an alert, have universal meaning. Other shapes are relative to their subject. Many symbols are already standard on the Web, so the best way to start choosing symbols for your icons is to imitate the ones you now see on Web pages. A few symbol conventions include the following:

- Keys and locks represent online security
- Envelopes and mailboxes represent e-mail and communication
- A building with columns represents a government Web site
- A trash can represents the act of deleting

These symbols have literal meanings because they relate directly to known objects in the real world. Literal symbols are straightforward. A tree can represent a forest and a gavel can represent an online auction. Other symbols are less literal and require **abstraction** or reducing an idea to its essential qualities. You use abstraction to convey concepts that have no visual representation. To represent the idea of newness, for example, consider the qualities that distinguish new objects from old ones. New objects are often shiny, so you could indicate newness by simulating light beams reflecting off the surface of the icon. You also could achieve this effect by making several lines radiate from the icon.

Another example of abstraction is an icon that expresses the idea of working together. There is no obvious physical representation of this, so you should use visual metaphors. The image of a handshake or multiple lines converging could suggest the idea of collaboration.

The shape, angle, and thickness of the lines you use also suggest meaning in subtle ways. Thick horizontal and vertical lines indicate sturdiness, while thin curved lines suggest grace. Children's themes often are suggested by a wavering line, representing a child's handwriting. Web sites for children sometimes use 45-degree angles in icons, suggesting action and movement. Skewed lines at uncommon angles and lines with varying thickness are often used in alternative images. Figure 6-21 shows line weights, angles, colors, and shapes that create different impressions.

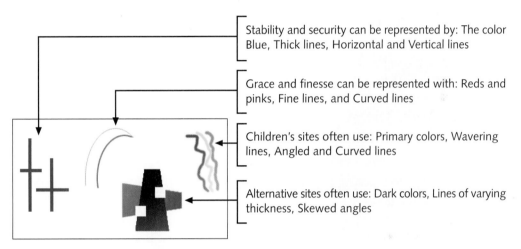

Figure 6-21   Creating impressions through symbolism

IMPLEMENTING ICONS IN WEB PAGES

You can use most icons in a Web page with a simple IMG tag in HTML. However, some types of icons require additional coding.

Implementing Ratings Symbols in a Web Page

When creating icons to be used as ratings symbols, create one version of the icon, and perhaps a halved version depending on the scale you use. When you implement the icons in a Web page, you must repeat the creation process several times, using several IMG tags. Having two versions of the icon is an advantage, since you must create only one or two graphics that load only once before being cached in the browser. However, when it comes time to change the rating, you must edit several lines of HTML.

Often, it's easier to create a separate graphic for every possible value in the ratings system. In a four-star ratings system, for example, you create a file called 0.gif that contains no stars, a file called 1.gif that contains one star, and so on. You have to create additional image files, but editing the HTML files is much simpler. When a rating changes from 3 to 4, for example, you change the HTML to call 4.gif instead of 3.gif. Another advantage of creating a separate file for each value is that it's easier to control the spacing between icons. Figure 6-22 shows how breaking up the symbols requires using only a few graphics, while keeping the symbols as single units requires using many more image files.

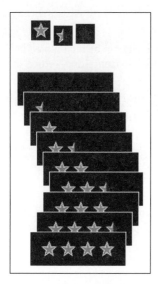

Figure 6-22   Implementing rating symbols

Using Bullets in a Web Page

To use bullets in a Web page, you can place them to the left of the text. However, this often creates extra line spacing above the bullet because text incorrectly wraps around the bullet. You can solve this problem with extra HTML code or by using style sheets.

Implementing Bullets with HTML

Bullets in HTML are created with the UL, OL, and LI tags. These bullets are either alphanumeric characters, discs, circles, or squares. You cannot use graphics in HTML bulleted lists. If you place bullet graphics in a Web page, lines break unexpectedly as the text wraps around the graphic. You can, however, use the ALIGN attribute of the IMG tag to control how the text wraps. Set the ALIGN attribute to the left to force the text to wrap without adding extra lines.

You also can use the HSPACE and VSPACE attributes to control the margin around the bullet. For example, this tag would lead to incorrect spacing in the wrapped text:

```
<img src="bullet.gif">
```

This tag would not:

```
<img align="left" src="bullet.gif">
```

And this tag would force a seven-pixel margin between the bullet and the text:

```
<img align="left" src="bullet.gif" hspace="7">
```

Implementing Bullets with CSS

The HTML solution does not allow you to indent text following a bullet the way text indents when you use HTML bullets. Style sheets, on the other hand, let you replace the standard discs used for HTML bullets with your own icons. Netscape Navigator version 4 does not support this option, but version 6 does. Internet Explorer version 5 and later versions support this option.

In your style sheet, add this definition:

```
ul { list-style-image: url(image) }
```

Where "image" is replaced by the path and filename of your bullet. Every time you use the LI tag in an unordered list, your icon will appear as the bullet.

Figure 6-23 shows graphical bullets implemented with HTML at the top of the figure and with style sheets at the bottom.

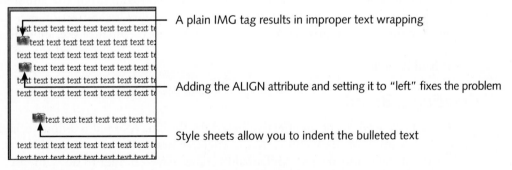

A plain IMG tag results in improper text wrapping

Adding the ALIGN attribute and setting it to "left" fixes the problem

Style sheets allow you to indent the bulleted text

Figure 6-23   Displaying graphical bullets with HTML or CSS

Designing Logos

The best way to learn how to design logos is by examining logos on the Web. Try to gain an understanding of what makes them succeed or fail. Then start sketching ideas on paper and ask people to review and comment on your sketches.

Logos must communicate as concisely as possible, using metaphors and symbolism. Site logos also should make people remember the Web site, build site identity, and help sell the site.

Abstracting the Subject of the Site

If a logo represents an entire Web site or organization, it must communicate the essence of the site. To create such a logo, you must consider all aspects of the site, and then include only the most important ones. This process requires the same abstraction you use to create symbolic icons.

A caricature is an abstraction of a human face, and includes only the essential elements. Similarly, a logo is a sort of caricature of a Web site. To begin designing a logo, consider how you can represent an entire Web site with a small picture. Start by making a list of keywords associated with the site, such as those in the following list:

- The name of the site or organization

- General adjectives that describe the site (modern, high-tech, old-fashioned, American, global)

- What the site does (commerce, content, community)

- The subject of the site (books, sports, women, kids)

For example, for a site about children's games, list keywords such as children, fun, and games; for a site about online financial advice, list keywords such as money, stocks, and wealth.

For each word in the list, think of a visual element that represents the word. The elements can be letters or numbers, shapes, colors, or textures. For the children's games site, appropriate visual elements might be primary colors, an abstraction of a child playing, and simple game pieces such as dice or jacks. For the finance site, appropriate visual elements might be a dollar sign, an abstraction of a stock chart, and the color known as banker's blue.

Creating a Brand

A site logo needs to be an effective brand for the site. A brand is a unique, easily identifiable symbol for the Web site. Many effective brands do not relate in any way to the nature of the company. The McDonald's arches have nothing to do with fast food, and the NBC peacock has nothing to do with television. However, these symbols are so frequently associated with their companies that you know the name of the company because you recognize its logo.

To create an effective brand, use a simple logo. Think in terms of basic lines and shapes, as if you were creating an extra letter of the alphabet. The logo should unambiguously represent the site.

A brand need not always apply only to a company. Some Web developers create an **author stamp**, which they include at the bottom of pages they've designed. The author stamp should link to the developer's own page, but even if users do not follow the link, they still see the stamp and associate the quality of the site with it.

Including the Name

Big corporations often use just a symbol for their logo, one that does not tie in to the product or name. For example, McDonald's and Disney have logos that are identifiable by themselves, and need no text description.

Most sites, however, need a logo that identifies the site and includes its name and address. Not only do people need to remember your logo, they need to remember your URL. You can incorporate the URL of the site in small type at the bottom of the logo, or use the URL itself as the logo, dressing it with colors and special type.

Incorporating the Logo into the Page

Logos almost always are placed in the upper-left corner of Web pages, and are the first thing a reader sees as the page loads. In addition to position, you need to incorporate the logo into the design of the site. Often a logo is designed along with the site's page layout. Ideally, the layout and logo share a design, and use a color palette (usually two to five colors) and other common elements, such as textures, fonts, and line weights. The logo should look like it's part of the site.

Making Multiple Versions

Logos should have only a few lines, shapes, and colors. Simple logos are easier for readers to recognize and remember, and are easier for you to scale.

Your logo will appear not only on your Web pages. Other sites might link to your site using a smaller version of the logo. You might also want to print the logo on business cards and stationery, often in black and white. The logo should not require color or a large size to be recognizable.

As you design your logos, start by creating small, black-and-white versions. When you are satisfied with the general shape, create larger versions and add color.

CREATING AND IMPLEMENTING FAVORITES ICONS

Internet Explorer version 5 (or later) displays a special type of icon called a **favorites icon**, also known as a **favicon**. The favicon appears on the left side of the address bar and in the Favorites menu of the Internet Explorer Web browser, shown in Figure 6-24. Although Internet Explorer is the only browser capable of displaying favicons, it is the browser of choice for a majority of Web users. Adding a favicon is an easy way to give a professional touch to a Web site.

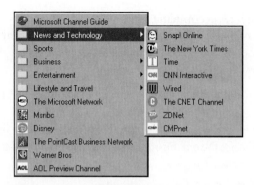

Figure 6-24 Favicons of several popular sites

Viewing Favicons

Usually you view favicons from the browser's address bar, but you also can use options in the Favorites menu, which lists favicons for several corporate Web sites. Drag a URL to the desktop to create a larger version of the favicon on the desktop. The desktop favicon is a shortcut to its associated Web site. Double-click the desktop favicon to open a browser window and jump to the site. The larger desktop version is not necessarily a stretched copy of the icon that appears in the address bar. The favicon file is not one bitmap image like a GIF or JPEG file. Favicon files are created in the .ico format, which is a special type of directory. An .ico file is actually a collection of a few different icons, which have different dimensions and color depths. The particular image shown depends on which software displays the favicon. When a browser calls the favicon to appear in the address bar, it uses a version that is 16 × 16 pixels large and has 16 colors. When the operating system calls the favicon to appear on the desktop, it uses a version that is 32 × 32 pixels large and has 256 colors. If a favicon includes only one size, it is stretched to create the other size.

Creating Favicons

As of this writing, no major graphics software, including Photoshop, lets you create favicon files directly. Several freeware and shareware tools do, however. The easiest tool to use is a Java applet-based tool available at *www.favicon.com*. This tool allows you to draw a 16 × 16 graphic in 16 colors, and then e-mails you the favicon.ico file free of charge.

Using Existing Favicons

Although you cannot create favicons in Photoshop, you can use Photoshop to reduce existing logos. In general, only the 16-color, 16 × 16-pixel version is shown, so you don't need to make the 256-color, 32 × 32-pixel version.

When you reduce logos to fit in a small space, eliminate all but the most necessary aspects of the logo. Examine the favicons on other sites, and note which ones are shrunken versions of their logos, and which ones were altered for clarity.

Using Favicons in a Web Page

When you browse the Web with Internet Explorer, the browser automatically scans the root directory of every site you visit, looking for a file named favicon.ico. If it finds the file, the favicon appears in the address bar. Otherwise, the browser displays the default Internet Explorer logo. The browser uses either the icon or the default logo when displaying any page from any directory in the site.

You can use different favicons for different sections of a site by including a line of HTML in the head of the HTML file.

```
<link rel="SHORTCUT ICON" href="/filepath/myLogo.ico">
```

The name of the favicon must end in .ico and you must use the same name in the HTML code.

Sometimes Internet Explorer does not automatically find the favicon in subdirectories. You could place a favicon in every directory to be found by the browser, but it is simpler to add the HTML tag to every file in the site.

CHAPTER SUMMARY

- ❑ When working with icons and other small images, use grids and increased magnification to clearly see what you are doing.
- ❑ You can create icons by drawing with the Pencil tool, by using text, or by reducing a larger image.
- ❑ Symbolic icons must stand out from the rest of the page and convey information in a small space.
- ❑ Icons convey meaning not just with symbols, but with colors, line weight, and texture.
- ❑ Bullets should blend in with the text, calling attention to the text rather than to themselves.
- ❑ You can implement bullets in a Web page with HTML or with CSS.
- ❑ Your logo represents your Web site. It might not indicate the exact content of the site, but it does suggest a personality.
- ❑ Begin designing your logo by sketching it on paper, starting with a simple black-and-white version.

❐ Favorites icons (favicons) are tiny graphics that appear in the address bar of Internet Explorer version 5 and later.

❐ The standard favicon uses 16 colors and is 16 × 16 pixels large.

REVIEW QUESTIONS

1. What is the best way to display lines over an image to help you see where each pixel is located?
   a. Show Guides option
   b. Show Grid option
   c. Transparent background
   d. Any of the above

2. Which Photoshop tool do you use to draw arrows?
   a. Pencil tool
   b. Pen tool
   c. Paintbrush tool
   d. Line tool

3. How many levels of transparency can you save in a PNG image?
   a. 0
   b. 1
   c. 16
   d. 256

4. Which file formats allow transparent areas in an image?
   a. GIF and JPEG
   b. GIF and PNG
   c. PNG and JPEG
   d. GIF, JPEG, and PNG

5. How do you set the magnification to 100%?
   a. Double-click the magnifying glass.
   b. Use the Zoom slider in the Navigator palette.
   c. Click View on the menu bar, and then click Actual Pixels.
   d. Any of the above

6. What is the main difference between bullets and symbols?

   a. Bullets are smaller than symbols.

   b. Symbols are smaller than bullets.

   c. Bullets convey more information than symbols.

   d. Symbols convey more information than bullets.

7. What shape(s) are best for a ranking scale that includes 20 possible ranks?

   a. 20 stars, 5 pixels wide each

   b. 20 circles, 5 pixels wide each

   c. 5 stars, each with ¼, ½, and ¾ divisions

   d. 1 bar

8. What color bullet is most appropriate to use with white text on a dark red background?

   a. Red

   b. Black

   c. White

   d. Green

9. Which is not an example of a visual metaphor?

   a. A small graph to represent financial data

   b. An @ sign to represent an e-mail link

   c. A lock and key icon to represent online security

   d. A logo of a credit card

10. How big is an average-sized symbolic icon?

    a. 15 × 15 pixels

    b. 30 × 30 pixels

    c. 60 × 60 pixels

    d. 72 × 72 pixels

11. Which HTML tag stretches an image to 20 pixels high and 35 pixels wide?

    a. `<img src="bar.gif" width="35" height="20">`

    b. `<img src="bar.gif" wide="35" high="20">`

    c. `<img src="bar.gif" horizontal="35" vertical="20">`

    d. `<img src="bar.gif" w="35" h="20">`

12. Which browsers support using graphics as bullets with CSS?

    a. Internet Explorer and Netscape versions 4 or greater

    b. Internet Explorer version 5 or greater

    c. Netscape version 4 or greater

    d. No browser supports this feature yet.

13. Which style sheet definition uses a file named ball.gif as a bullet in an unordered list?

    a. `UL { list-style: "/ball.gif" }`

    b. `OL { list-style: image(/ball.gif) }`

    c. `OL { list-style-image: "/ball.gif" }`

    d. `UL { list-style-image: url(/ball.gif) }`

14. How should you design multiple versions of a logo?

    a. Start with a large, high-color version.

    b. Start with a large, low-color version.

    c. Start with a small, low-color version.

    d. Start with a small, high-color version.

15. Should Web site logos include the site's URL?

    a. Usually, yes

    b. No

    c. Only if the URL is very short

    d. Only if the URL is very long

16. Where are site logos usually positioned in a Web page?

    a. Upper-left

    b. Top center

    c. Upper-right

    d. Center left

17. What are the dimensions of favorites icons that appear in the URL address window?

    a. 8 × 8 pixels

    b. 16 × 16 pixels

    c. 32 × 32 pixels

    d. 64 × 64 pixels

18. How many colors can you use in a favicon that appears in the URL address window?

    a. 8

    b. 16

    c. 32

    d. 64

19. What browsers can display favicons?

    a. Internet Explorer versions 4 and 5

    b. Netscape version 4 or later

    c. Internet Explorer and Netscape versions 4 or later

    d. Internet Explorer version 5 or later

20. What is an .ico file?

    a. a bitmap image

    b. a type of GIF image

    c. a vector image

    d. a collection of bitmap images

HANDS-ON PROJECTS

Before beginning these projects, set the grid preferences as described in this chapter, and turn on the grid.

Project 6-1: Create a Graphical Bullet

You use HTML bullets in several places in your site, but one page needs more graphical treatment to make it interesting. You decide to create a simple bullet.

Complete these steps:

1. In Photoshop, create an image that is **20** pixels wide and **15** pixels high, with a **transparent** background.

2. Set the foreground color to **black** and select the **Line** tool.

3. In the Options bar, click the **Create filled region** button. Set a weight of **3**, and deselect the **anti-aliased** option.

4. Set the Geometry options to place arrowheads at the end of the line.

5. Adjust the shape of the arrowhead to **300%** Width, **300%** Length, and **10%** Concavity.

6. Zoom in to at least **500%** magnification. Draw a line across the middle of the image while holding down the **Shift** key, to keep the line perfectly horizontal. You should see a very short arrow. If the arrowhead is not symmetrical, erase and redraw the line, or use the **Pencil** tool to touch it up.

7. Click **Image** on the menu bar, point to **Mode**, click **Indexed Color**, and accept the default settings. Make sure the Transparency check box is selected and Matte is set to None.

8. Click **OK** and save the file as **arrow_bul.gif** in a new directory named **project_6-1**.

Project 6-2: Create an Icon

Your site has some new links that you want to emphasize with an icon.

Complete these steps:

1. Create an **image** that is **60** pixels wide and **40** pixels high, with a **transparent** background and **RGB** color.

2. Set the foreground color to a shade of **red** and select the **Type** tool.

3. In the Options bar, select any font and set the size to **14** points. Type **new!** in the text area in the bottom half of the window.

4. Center the text with the **Move** tool.

5. Select the **Custom Shape** tool. From the Shape menu in the Options bar, select the **10 Point Star**.

6. Set the options to **Create filled region**. Create a new layer behind the text layer.

7. Set the foreground color to **yellow**.

8. Drag the **Custom Shape** pointer over the rear layer to create a **yellow star** behind the text.

9. Set the foreground color to **green**. Select the **background layer**, click **Edit** on the menu bar, and then click **Stroke**.

10. In the dialog box that appears, set the Width to **1** pixel, set the Location to **Outside**, and leave the other settings at their default values. Click **OK**. You should see a one-pixel wide, jagged loop outlining the star.

11. Trim the extra transparent background pixels.

12. Reduce colors by setting the image to **Indexed Color** mode. Preserve transparency.

13. Save the image as **new.gif** in a new folder named **project_6-2**.

Project 6-3: Create Ratings Symbols

You are creating a site that reviews romance novels. The books are rated on a scale of one to four, with half rankings allowed. You decide to represent the ratings with heart-shaped icons. Naturally, you choose red for the color. It will stand out on the page's white background.

Complete these steps:

1. Create a 26 × 26-pixel RGB image.

2. Set the foreground to a rose color by entering **204** for Red, **51** for Green, and **102** for Blue (**#CC3366** in hexadecimal).

3. Select the **Custom Shape** tool and select the **Heart** from the Shape menu. Make sure the Anti-aliased check box is selected.

4. Drag the **Custom Shape** pointer to add the shape to the image.

5. Trim the extra background pixels.

6. Optimize the image and save it as **heart.gif** in a new folder named **project_6-3**.

7. Select the right half of the heart with the **Rectangular Marquee** tool.

8. Use the Hue/Saturation dialog box to desaturate the right half of the image.

9. Save the new image as **heart_half.gif** in the project_6-3 folder.

10. Desaturate the left side of the image in the same way and save this image as **heart_gray.gif**.

11. Create a new HTML file and save it as **index.html** in the project_6-3 folder.

12. Add the following HTML code:

```
<img src="heart.gif"><img src="heart.gif">
<img src="heart.gif">

<img src="heart_half.gif"><img src="heart_gray.gif">
```

13. Save the HTML file as **index.html** and preview it in a browser. You should see three and one-half hearts out of five.

Project 6-4: Create a Warning Symbol

Your site includes a page of links to other sites, some of which contain adult language. You want to warn your readers, but text alone does not have enough impact. You decide to create a warning icon to alert readers and guide them toward explanatory text. You choose to imitate the shape and color of a yellow road sign, and to use an exclamation point.

Complete these steps:

1. In ImageReady, create a **50- × 50-pixel RGB image** with a **transparent** background.

2. Set the foreground color to **black** and select the **Line** tool. In the Options bar, set the type to **Create filled region**. Set the weight to **2** pixels and deselect the **Anti-aliased** option.

3. Create a **straight line** across the bottom of the image.

4. Click the lower-left corner of the image and create a **60-degree line**. Look at the Info palette and watch the A value to note the angle of the line.

5. Click the lower-right corner of the image and create a **120-degree line** that connects the two existing lines. Use the **Eraser** tool to eliminate any leftover line segments.

6. Use the **Type** tool to add an exclamation point to the image. Make the size **35 points** or any size that nearly fits the triangle.

7. Set the foreground color to **pure yellow**. In the Optimize palette, set the Matte tool to the foreground color.

8. Save the optimized image as **alert.gif** in a new folder named **project_6-4**.

9. Create an HTML file with the following HTML code:

```
<body bgcolor="ffff00">
<img src="alert.gif">
</body>
```

10. Save the HTML file as **index.html** in the project_6-4 folder.

11. Preview the HTML file in a browser; you should see a yellow page with the transparent alert icon. Because the matte color is set to yellow, there is no halo around the icon.

Project 6-5: Create a Chat Room Icon

Your site has a new chat room feature, and you want to link to it from your home page with an icon. You cannot easily represent a chat room, so you decide to use the metaphor of a speech balloon used in comics.

Complete these steps:

1. In ImageReady, create a **30 × 30-pixel RGB image** with a **white** background.

2. Select the **Elliptical Marquee** tool. Set the Feather to **0** and select **Anti-aliased**. Create an ellipse in the upper two-thirds of the image.

3. Click **Edit** on the menu bar, and then click **Stroke**. In the dialog box that appears, set the Width to **1** pixel, set the Location to **Inside**, and leave the Blending at **100%.** Set the Contents to **Use Black**. Click **OK**.

4. Set the foreground color to **black**. Select the **Paintbrush** tool. Use a one-pixel brush with anti-aliasing. Draw a **tail** below the ellipse. Erase any extra pixels.

5. Set the foreground color to **dark gray**. Set the **Line** tool to a width of **1** pixel and draw **four dark lines** across the balloon, separated by three or four pixels each. The lines should not quite meet the edges of the balloon.

6. The icon appears over a teal background. In the Optimize palette, set the Matte color to **#336699**.

7. Double-click the **background layer** in the Layers palette. In the Layer Options dialog box, click **OK** without changing any of the values.

8. Select the **Magic Wand** tool. Set the Tolerance to **0**, and then select **Anti-aliased** and **Contiguous**. Click anywhere in the white background surrounding the balloon image.

9. Click the **Optimized** tab in the document window. Press the **Backspace** or **Delete** key. You should see the white background disappear, and a teal halo appear around the image.

10. Give the icon a color that will help it stand out from the teal. Set the foreground to **#CC6600** and draw **four more lines**, each directly below one of the black lines.

11. Optimize the image and save it as **chat.gif.** in a new folder named **project_6-5**.

12. Copy the **HTML file** from project 6-4. Replace the background color with the **teal** color used in this project, and replace the image with **chat.gif**. Save the HTML file as **index.html** in the project_6-5 folder.

13. Preview the **HTML fil**e in a browser.

Project 6-6: Design a Logo

For this project, you have to make many of the decisions. There might be more than one correct answer. However, some solutions are more appropriate than others. Follow the guidelines mentioned in this chapter, and ask your instructor for help if necessary.

You have been asked to create a logo for a site called matchstick.com, which brings together students from different countries by setting up pen pals.

Complete these steps:

1. Write 10 words that describe the site. Consider the name, matchstick, and that the site deals with international correspondence.

2. Think of one visual representation for each word on your list. In addition to symbols that represent physical objects, consider symbols that represent actions.

3. With pencil and paper, begin sketching the symbols. Select the two symbols that look most attractive together.

4. Consider which colors, line weights, angles, and textures represent the words on your list.

5. Sketch the two symbols again, considering your answers in step 4.

6. Begin executing your design in an image editor such as Photoshop. Place each visual element on a different layer so you can rotate, scale, and change the colors of each element separately.

7. Your final logo should contain the name of the site, be no wider than 180 pixels and no higher than 120 pixels, and use no more than 16 colors in the color palette.

8. Save the logo as **logo.gif** or **logo.jpg**, as appropriate, in a new folder named **project_6-6**.

Project 6-7: Design an Author Stamp

You have created several Web sites for your friends and you want to use the pages to advertise your Web design skills. You create an author stamp for yourself and place it at the bottom of these pages. Like Project 6-6, this project has no singular correct answer, but some solutions follow the guidelines of this chapter better than others.

Complete these steps:

1. Determine the size of your stamp. Since it is essentially an advertisement, you do not want it to overwhelm the actual content of the page. Also, you do not want the stamp to hinder loading of the page. Keep the stamp as small and as highly optimized as possible.

2. Select one symbol to use in the stamp. You could use your initials, a silhouette of an animal, or a geometric shape.

3. Choose colors, textures, and line treatments that reflect your design style.

4. Execute your design in Photoshop.

5. Save your stamp as **stamp.gif** or **stamp.jpg**, as appropriate, in a new folder named **project_6-7**.

Project 6-8: Create a favicon.ico File

To give your site professional polish, you decide to create a favicon.

Complete these steps:

1. Open **6-8.tif** from the Data Disk.

2. You must use space wisely. Crop the image to trim the two outer rectangles.

3. Use the Canvas Size dialog box to crop and pad the image with black to make it square.

4. Normalize the contrast, and reduce the dimensions to **16 × 16** pixels.

5. Use the **Pencil** tool to darken the obscured **2** in the upper-right part of the image.

6. Start your browser and visit *www.favicon.com*.

7. Either use the Java applet or download the free software to your desktop.

8. If you are using the applet, follow the instructions and copy your image into the 16 x 16 grid in the Favicon Generator tool. When you finish, click **File** on the menu bar of the Generator tool, click **Save**, and enter your e-mail address. The completed favicon.ico file will be mailed to you.

   If you use the downloaded software, follow the directions and save the finished file as **favicon.ico** to a new folder named **project_6-8**.

9. View the file in Internet Explorer version 5 or higher.

CASE PROJECT

Design and create a logo for your site. Study logos used on other sites for ideas about size, shapes, and color schemes. Think about what you want to express with the logo. If someone links to your site, they might use your logo as a link. The logo needs to clearly identify your Web site even when it stands alone.

Modify the logo to use as a favicon. Use the applet available at *www.favicon.com* or some other software, such as Icon Forge, that generates favicon files.

6

7

CREATING AND USING BUTTONS

Using Three-Dimensional Effects

In this chapter, you will:

♦ Design buttons
♦ Work with text in Web graphics
♦ Create shapes and paths
♦ Create 3-D effects
♦ Implement buttons in Web pages

Unlike other icons, buttons add functionality to Web pages. Imagine a Web page in terms of an electronic device: Web icons are like stickers on the device, such as those identifying the manufacturer, or those that warn against using the product near water. Web buttons are like physical buttons, such as the on/off switch. Standard icons provide some information to the user, but a button also must encourage an action, such as following a link or submitting a form.

You must design buttons that encourage clicking. The most clickable buttons imitate the qualities, such as size and shape, of buttons on physical appliances. Buttons also should appear to be three-dimensional (3-D). You achieve this effect by adding highlights, texture, and shadows, and by rounding the edges of the buttons.

The purpose of a button is often more difficult to express symbolically than the purpose of an icon. When symbols are unclear, use text to inform users about button functions. This chapter covers the design, creation, and use of 3-D buttons.

DESIGNING BUTTONS

When designing a button, use a style that matches its importance. Emphasize buttons that perform important functions, and de-emphasize others. The best way to de-emphasize a button is to not use a graphic with it, and leave it as a simple text link. The best way to emphasize a button is to imitate those on actual appliances by rounding corners and simulating 3-D effects.

Understanding Different Types of Buttons

All buttons prompt the user to perform an action. Usually the action is to follow a hyperlink to another page, but a button click also can close a window, submit a form, or send a message. You can separate buttons into several thematic categories, including site content, site information, and account information. Buttons that are part of the same theme should look similar and must be easily distinguished from buttons with different themes. For example, imagine a page with the following links: Sign up for FREE E-Mail, E-MAIL US, and E-Mail this Page to a Friend. You can represent each link with an image of an envelope, as shown in Figure 7-1, but that makes the relative meanings unclear. Although additional text in the buttons would explain their functions, the envelope icon is ambiguous and is what makes the additional text necessary.

Figure 7-1   Similar, ambiguous buttons

Meaningful symbols for these buttons would exploit the differences among them, as shown in Figure 7-2. Instead of using the image of an envelope for each button, focus on the unique tasks of each function. The first button could use a graphic of a pencil filling in a form to suggest the concept of signing up, and the third button could use an image of a face to suggest the idea of a friend.

Figure 7-2   Unique, unambiguous buttons

Imagine also that the page contained these additional links: Edit Your Account and Print this Page. You could group all five buttons by theme, using similar designs, as shown in Figure 7-3. The FREE E-Mail and Edit links both relate to a user account and should share a design. Similarly, the E-Mail to a Friend and Print links both relate to manipulating the page content, and also should share a design.

Figure 7-3   Buttons with shared themes and designs

Some examples of different types of links are:

- *Site Information*: Links that lead the user to information about the site, such as advertising, event calendars, contacts, and privacy policies

- *Navigation*: Links that lead the user to the content of the site, such as auctions, chat rooms, downloads, news, reviews, and tutorials

- *Account*: Links relating to the user's account on the site, such as editing account information, registration, making the page a home page, and personalizing the site

- *Page Content*: Links that reformat the page or lead to another version of the same page, such as Mail this Page to a Friend, Print this Article, Bookmark this Page, and Save this Page

- *Directional*: Links that lead to pages related to the current page, such as Home, Next, Previous, and Top

- *Media Player*: Links that control audio or video players in the page, such as Listen, Play, Stop, Reverse, and Fast Forward

- *Functional*: Links that manipulate the browser window, such as E-MAIL US, Fit Browser to Screen, and Close this Window

Figure 7-4 shows a conventional Web page layout, often called a C-clamp because the navigation and advertisements form the shape of the letter *C* around the actual content in the center of the page. The figure has a black line representing the page fold. In a newspaper, the fold is in the center of the paper, where it is folded in half. Important news is placed above the fold so that it is seen even when the newspaper is folded. In a Web page, the fold is at the bottom of the browser window, where the bottom of the page is cut off and the user must scroll to see more. The position of the fold is different for every size of monitor, but typically it is about 800 pixels from the top of the page.

Important information, such as the logo and navigation symbols, must be positioned above the fold, so that users see it without having to scroll. Important information is more likely to be represented by graphical buttons instead of text links. Less crucial information, such as links within content, or obligatory links such as copyright information, tends to be placed below the fold and probably is represented as text links rather than as graphical buttons.

Links surrounding the text (the *C* part of a C-clamp layout) probably are represented as graphical buttons, while the links in the text (the material enclosed by the *C*) probably are left as text links. This design is very conventional. The challenge for all Web designers is to discover ways of laying out pages that are as clear and navigable as the C-clamp design, but are also innovative and interesting.

As shown in Figure 7-4, links along the top and left of a page usually are buttons, while links within the content itself and site information links at the bottom normally are text links.

There are no conventions about how different types of buttons should look, as long as they stay consistent within their types.

Imitating Physical Buttons

Users must be able to immediately distinguish between static icons that merely provide information and dynamic buttons that perform an action. When Web page text is blue and underlined, you immediately know that it is a link. Users should have the same reaction to the buttons you design—they should know that buttons are links and that icons are for information only.

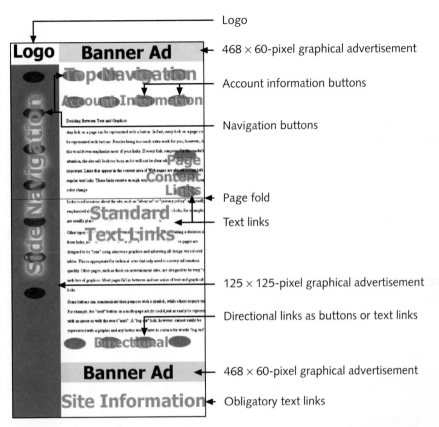

Figure 7-4   Positioning of different types of buttons in a conventional page layout

If it is ambiguous whether a graphic is a standard icon or a button, users waste time clicking icons that lead nowhere, or they hunt for a button that is in plain sight but does not appear to be clickable. You need to use a convention such as the blue underline to cue the reader that a button is a link. The most common convention to make buttons look clickable is to simulate 3-D effects on the buttons. Figure 7-5 shows two buttons that prompt the user to submit a form. The button on the left is flat, and a user may not understand that it should be clicked. The button on the right uses several 3-D cues so the reader knows the image is a button, and that clicking it causes an action.

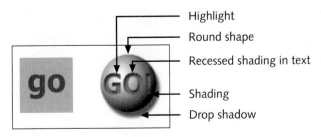

Figure 7-5   A flat button and a 3-D button

In the case of buttons, three-dimensionality is a cue both on the Web and in everyday life. This is especially true for media player software buttons, whose actual functions mimic those on devices such as CD players. Make the Play button in a Web-based music application resemble the Play button on an actual CD player, as in Figure 7-6, and the reader knows immediately what the button does.

Figure 7-6   Media buttons

Designing a Tabbed Interface

A common problem for site architects is fitting all of a site's links in one navigation bar. The simplest solution is to put them together in a list, as in Figure 7-7. To do so, you place the navigation bar on the side, because the top of the page cannot accommodate more than five or six buttons, and most sites have dozens of links in the navigation area. However, a side navigation bar overwhelms the reader with choices, and many links get lost below the fold and are not visible until the reader scrolls down.

Figure 7-7   Side navigation bar

If you use a **hierarchical**, or nested, menu in the navigation bar, as shown in Figure 7-8, you avoid presenting too many choices. The menu in Figure 7-8 includes only four or five categories, which expand into more topics when you select a category. The drawback to this approach is that it usually requires lots of extra HTML or special coding in Java or JavaScript.

Figure 7-8   Hierarchical menu on the side

In a **tabbed interface**, as the user clicks each tab, submenu links appear below the tab, as shown in Figure 7-9. The tabbed interface is a relatively new convention for site navigation, but it is already used on most major Web sites. It allows designers to move navigation bars from the left side of the page to the top, and frees up more page width for content. You also can create a tabbed interface entirely with HTML, without additional client-side programming. The tabbed interface also is a type of hierarchical menu system.

Figure 7-9   Hierarchical menu on the top

Each tab serves as a button, and often does not use 3-D effects, because its purpose is clear without the additional cues. The design of the navigation tabs is simple; rounded corners reinforce the association with actual file folders.

Tabbed interfaces require at least two versions for each tab: one for the tab when it links to the current page, and one when it links to another page. Incidentally, using two versions also is popular for buttons on side navigation bars. All buttons appear in their default state, but when you click a button, a new page appears with the button in a different state.

To emphasize the selected tab, draw it to create the illusion that it overlaps the adjacent tabs, as shown in Figure 7-10. Use a brighter color than the other tabs to reinforce the impression that the tab is in the foreground.

Figure 7-10   Tabbed interface

Rollover Effects

Readers need cues to know that clicking a button causes an action. In addition to 3-D shading, rounded corners, and simple text instructions, many designers use **rollover effects**, which call attention to a button and signify it as a link. Your Data Disk includes an example of a button with rollover effects.

To view a button with rollover effects:

1. In a Web browser, open the file named **rollover.html**.

2. Move the pointer over the **image** to see one type of rollover effect.

3. Click the **image** to see another type of rollover effect.

Although often overused as a design element, rollovers can add interest to a page and make it feel more interactive. You can create rollover effects with JavaScript or style sheets, and most WYSIWYG HTML editors generate the code for you. This book dedicates an entire chapter to rollover effects.

Deciding Between Text and Graphics for Buttons

You can use a button to represent any link on a page. In fact, you could use buttons to represent *every* link on a page, but it would be time-consuming and ineffective because most of your links would be overemphasized. If every link competes for the reader's attention, the site looks too busy, and it's unclear which links are most important. Links that appear in the content area of Web pages almost always are left as regular text links. These links receive enough emphasis with standard underlining and color differences.

Good candidates for text links are links to obligatory information and links that cannot be represented by graphics. Links to information about the site, such as About Us or Privacy Policy, usually are de-emphasized. These links connect to information the site must provide, and usually appear at the bottom of pages as simple text links. Some concepts, such as logging off a network, are difficult to represent with a graphic, and therefore need text to make their purpose clear. If a link requires text for clarity, you save bandwidth by not using a button.

You can represent other types of links as either text or buttons. For example, you could represent the Next button on a multipage article with an arrow or with the word Next. Before you make decisions about these links, you must determine the overall page design. You will design some pages to be lean, and use colored tables coded in HTML instead of graphics. A lean design is appropriate for technical sites that simply convey information quickly. You will design other pages, such as those on entertainment sites, to be very rich, with lots of graphics. Most pages fall between these two extremes and use a mix of text and graphical links.

You can display text in Web pages only with fonts that are installed on the user's computer. When using fonts in a graphic, however, you can select from the fonts on your own computer. If you want to use a nonstandard font in a Web page, placing text in graphics is sometimes the only way to guarantee that your chosen font will appear.

Graphical buttons with clear, well-designed images provide meaning and create visual interest on a Web page. They also work well with international audiences. Most users correctly interpret a button with an arrow to be a link to the next page. However, they might not be able to interpret the words "Next Page" in a text link. Links that need emphasis also can attract more attention if you represent them as buttons. In general, use buttons as links when it suits the overall design of the site, to add visual interest and emphasis, and to provide universal meaning.

WORKING WITH TEXT

Most buttons use text to describe their function. You add text to graphics in Photoshop with the Type tool. In older versions of Photoshop you add the text in a separate window, but in newer versions you type directly over the image.

In Photoshop, click an image with the Type tool to open a new layer that appears in the Layers palette. A "T" appears in the Layer thumbnail area, as shown in Figure 7-11, and indicates that it is a type layer. A **type layer** contains active, unrendered text. You must **render**, or rasterize, the type layer before you can apply filters or other effects. Once you render the type layer, you can no longer edit the text. Until the type is rasterized, the text is treated as vector information, so you can modify it. You can add text to an image, and then apply different settings to the text to see how it looks with the rest of the image.

Figure 7-11 A type layer

To add text to an image:

1. In Photoshop, create an **image**.

2. Click the **Type** tool and set the options in the Options bar to **Create a text layer**. Set the foreground color to **black**.

3. Click the **image** and type the text you want, such as **Next Page**.

4. Click the **text** and change the **font**, **size**, and **color**.

5. When you finish editing, click **Layer** in the menu bar, click **Rasterize**, and then click **Type**.

The Options bar when the Type tool is selected is shown in Figure 7-12.

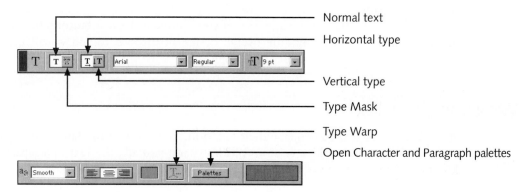

Figure 7-12   Type tool options

Setting Type Options

The type options in Photoshop are similar to those in any word-processing program. Photoshop 6 includes separate Character and Paragraph palettes, shown in Figure 7-13, to adjust kerning, leading, and other text settings. Most text options apply only to several lines of text, such as a paragraph. Most Web graphics use only individual words or phrases.

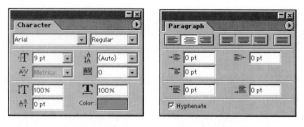

Figure 7-13   Character and Paragraph palettes

Some options in the Character palette are useful when you design buttons. **Kerning** and **tracking** refer to the distance between characters. Use these options to squeeze text into a small space or stretch it to fit a larger space. Similarly, **leading** controls the spacing between lines of text. You can adjust leading to fit multiple lines of text in a given space, although few buttons have more than one line of text. Examples of leading and tracking are shown in Figure 7-14.

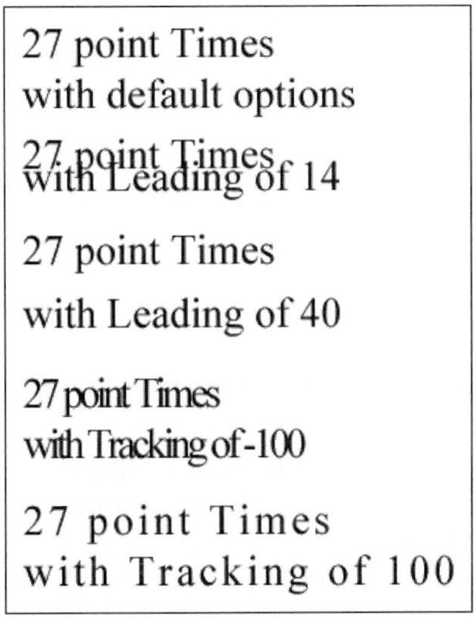

27 point Times
with default options

27 point Times
with Leading of 14

27 point Times

with Leading of 40

27 point Times
with Tracking of -100

27 point Times
with Tracking of 100

Figure 7-14   Type leading and tracking

You can set most fonts to regular, bold, italic (oblique), or bold italic. The following "Selecting a Font" section provides more information about text fonts on buttons.

The **Anti-Alias** option allows you to control the smoothness of the text. Selecting None gives the text a jagged edge, which can be useful if you are using transparency. Because the text in buttons almost always appears on a nontransparent background, you should use another anti-aliasing option, such as the Smooth option, which produces the best results.

Selecting a Font

Buttons usually are only as large as necessary. Therefore, you need to make button text as small as possible, yet still keep it legible. To do so, you choose between serif and sans serif fonts, select text attributes, and set the type size. **Serifs** are short lines or small additions to the ends of letters. Serifs help differentiate letters and font types. **Sans serif** fonts do not include serifs in their letters (*Sans* is French for without.) Some serif fonts are New York and Times Roman; some sans serif fonts are Arial and Helvetica. Serif and sans serif fonts are illustrated in Figure 7-15.

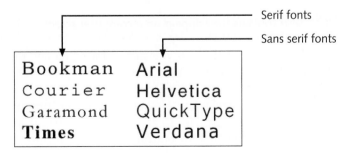

Figure 7-15   Examples of serif and sans serif fonts

To understand how serifs are useful, look at the words in Figure 7-16. Without serifs, the letters *cl* appear to be a *d* when the tracking is reduced. In the serif font the letters are easier to distinguish and the word is clearly legible.

Figure 7-16   Differences between serif and sans serif fonts with reduced tracking

Serifs work well in print, where the resolution of ink molecules on paper is effectively millions of dots per inch. On computer screens, however, the resolution is too low to make serifs enhance the readability of text. In fact serif text on a computer screen is often less readable than sans serif text. Therefore, most Web pages use fonts such as Arial and Helvetica for body text and other small text; for variety they use fonts such as Times for headlines and other large text. Most print media, in contrast, use sans serif type for headlines and serif type for body text.

Just as serif text is more difficult to read on computer screens, so is italicized text, especially at small sizes. See Figure 7-17 for an example. Buttons normally use small text, so select a font that is easy to read, nonitalic, and sans serif. Use italics only in buttons with larger text. The most legible text is lowercase with the first letter of each word capitalized. Avoid all-uppercase or all-lowercase words.

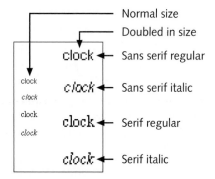

Figure 7-17   Serif and sans serif fonts as they appear on a computer screen

Bold formatting increases the width of letters, so you may want to reduce the kerning on boldface text to keep the overall width within an acceptable range. A new sans serif font, Verdana, was developed for the Web, and is especially easy to read because its letters are wider than those in Arial and Helvetica. However, using Verdana may require wider buttons than you want, or you might have to reduce the font size to fit the text in the button. In general, avoid using Verdana for buttons, or reduce kerning to help fit the text. Figure 7-18 shows four lines of text; although all have the same point size, they have quite different widths.

Figure 7-18   Varying widths of sans serif fonts

Setting the Type Size

By default, type size is measured in points. You must adjust Preferences to use pixels as the type size unit in Photoshop.

To set type size units in Photoshop:

1. Click **Edit** in the menu bar, point to **Preferences**, and then click **Units & Rulers**.

   The Units & Rulers Preferences dialog box opens.

2. Select **pixels** (or **millimeters**) for the type units.

Warping the Text

Another new feature in Photoshop 6 is the ability to warp text. Warped text is effective for use as distorted text. Text can be warped only before it has been rendered.

To warp text in Photoshop:

1. Create an **image** and add text using the Type tool. Select the **text**.

2. Click the **Create Warped Text** button in the Options bar, and select a style and direction.

3. Modify the effect with the other three slider bars.

4. Click **OK** to see the warped text.

5. Select the **text** with the Type tool and warp it again with a different setting. Text can be warped using only one setting.

Even after the text is distorted, you still can edit it. The warping feature works better in logos and larger types of Web graphics than in buttons. Buttons usually do not have room for distorted text, so use this option sparingly.

Using the Type Mask Tool

The left part of the Options bar includes buttons that set the Type tool to create either a text layer or a type mask. The **Type Mask** tool creates a selection area in the shape of text, rather than normal, colored text. This tool is used to create visual effects with the text outline when the background has a color or texture. For example, you can boost or reduce the contrast or run a filter, and make the changes occur only within the type mask.

Unlike regular type, you do not have to render the type mask before applying filters or other effects. The word "mask" is used often in Photoshop, and refers to the area outside a selection. A mask lets you protect areas where you apply effects such as filters. The area you do not select is masked, or protected from editing.

Photoshop also includes the Vertical Type tools, which work like the other type tools, except that the resulting text runs from the top to the bottom of the page or area, instead of from left to right.

To create a selection using the Type Mask tool:

1. Create a new **image**. Select the **Type** tool and click the **Create a mask or selection** button in the Options bar.

2. Click the **Vertically orient text** button to have the text read down rather than across.

3. Click the **image** and type the text you want. The image temporarily changes color as you add text.

4. When you finish, click the **Commit any current edits** (check mark) button in the Options bar to commit the edits, or select another tool from the toolbox. You should see a selection area in the shape of the text you added. You cannot edit this as you would normal text.

5. Select the **Paintbrush** tool and set the brush to one of the spatter brush heads. Use **black** as the foreground color and daub the pointer on each letter.

6. Deselect the selection area to see your text.

CREATING SHAPES AND PATHS

Traditionally, graphics software worked exclusively with either bitmap images or vector images, but not both. Recently, however, these programs are converging. Photoshop 6 and other new image-editing tools now include vector tools in addition to their bitmap tools. You no longer have to use programs such as Adobe Illustrator or FreeHand to create vector images; you can now do so directly in Photoshop.

The vector tools in Photoshop work with paths, which are vectors with a different name. **Paths** are made up of anchor points connected by straight or curved lines. Paths are used only to guide you in creating shapes and selection areas; they are not part of the finished image. When a path forms a complete loop, it is called a **shape**. Shapes are similar to selection areas, but are easier to edit and give you more precise control. Unlike selections, you can save paths and shapes with an image in most common formats, including GIF and JPEG. The path information can be understood even by some vector-based graphics software such as Adobe Illustrator.

Creating Shapes

To simulate physical-world buttons, you often want to create round buttons or rectangular buttons with rounded corners. Older versions of Photoshop had tools to create ellipses and rectangles, but did not let you directly create polygonal shapes or rectangles with rounded corners. To make complex shapes, you had to combine elliptical and rectangular selection areas. Photoshop 6 now includes separate tools to create these shapes. If you use an older version of Photoshop or another image editor, you need to use a different method to create rounded corners.

The most recent version of Photoshop includes a new tool called the Shape tool. This tool makes shapes much easier to create than they were in previous versions of Photoshop. You can create rectangles, circles, rounded rectangles, and polygons, as well as more complicated shapes. Just as you preview layers in the Layers palette and view the different channels and masks in the Channels palette, you can view paths and shapes in the Paths palette. Keep this palette open as you create and edit shapes and other paths. Figure 7-19 shows the Paths palette.

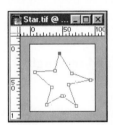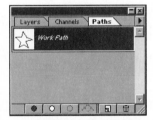

Figure 7-19   The Paths palette

When creating a path, you can choose whether to create a clipping path or a work path. A **work path** is a temporary path in an existing layer, and is discarded after use. A **clipping path** is created in a new layer of its own and is more appropriate for creating buttons. When you click the Create a New Shape Layer button in the Options bar, a Layer Style menu appears with many preset layer styles. This option lets you create clipping paths with several options for buttons.

Creating Squares and Circles

The Rectangle and Ellipse shape tools work like the Rectangular and Elliptical Marquee tools. Use the Marquee tools to create a rectangular or elliptical selection area around pixels.

Use the Shape tools to create a rectangular or elliptical path over the image. You convert the path to a selection by clicking the Loads path as a selection button at the bottom of the Paths palette. You also can convert a selection to a path by clicking the Makes work path from a Selection button. Combining shapes is the same as combining selection areas—each additional shape adds, subtracts, or intersects with the existing shapes, depending on which option you select from the Options bar. Unlike selections, you also can combine shapes to exclude only the intersection of the new and existing shapes.

While Marquee tools require using the Shift, Control, and Option (or Alt in Windows) keys to control parameters such as aspect ratio, you control Shape tool settings with menu selections in the Options bar. There you can force specific sizes or ratios, and determine whether to draw the shape from the center or from the upper-left corner.

Creating Rounded Rectangles

Photoshop 6 offers graphic artists an easy way to create rounded rectangles. Unlike the Rectangle tool, the Rounded Rectangle tool has a Radius option. This value indicates the amount of curvature in each corner of the shape. Think of a rounded rectangle as having four circles that define each corner of a rectangle. The radius of the curve in each corner is the same as the radius of each circle.

To create a rectangle with round corners in Photoshop:

1. Create an **image**.

2. Select the **Rounded Rectangle** tool. (This is different from the Rounded Rectangle Marquee tool in ImageReady.)

3. In the Options bar, set the Radius to **10** pixels.

4. Drag the pointer over the **image** to create a **rounded rectangle**.

5. Set the radius to **30** pixels.

6. Create another **rounded rectangle**. Note how the curvature of the corners in the second rectangle differs from the first.

Creating Polygons

You also can use the Shape tool to create **polygons**, which are shapes with many sides. You can use the Polygon option to create triangles, stars, octagons, and other shapes. You control the exact shape of the polygon by setting the following options:

- *Sides*: Set the number of sides. Five-point stars and pentagons both are considered to have five sides, although the star actually has 10.

- *Radius*: Set the distance from the center of a polygon to its outermost corners.

- *Snap to Pixels*: Force the shape around the gridwork of pixels. Paths normally ignore the pixels in an image and only snap to pixels when the path is converted to a selection.

- *Smooth Corners*: Round the points of the polygon.

- *Smooth Indents*: Round the interior corners of stars.

- *Indent Sides*: Draw the polygon as a star. The percentage value sets the size of each point; larger percentages create thinner, sharper points, while smaller percentages create thicker points.

Editing Shapes

Once you have created a shape, you can move or modify it. You can use the Move tool to move a selection and its contents, or use one of the Marquee tools to move just the selection. To move shapes, you can use the Path Component Selection tool in the tool-box, as shown in Figure 7-20. When the shape is a clipping path, the contents are moved with the path; when the shape is a work path, only the path itself is moved.

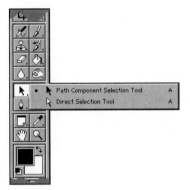

Figure 7-20   The Path Component Selection tool and Direct Selection tool

You use the Direct Selection tool to modify the positions of the anchor points that define the path and shape. With this tool, you can drag the anchor point to a new position. Normal anchor points are defined by their position, which indicate the vertex of the angle formed by two joined line segments, as shown in Figure 7-21.

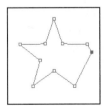

Figure 7-21   Anchor points in a vector path

The Pen tools also allow you to manipulate the anchors of a path. Using different variations, you can add and delete anchor points from a path to make it less or more smooth, and you can convert anchor points from curves to straight angles.

Combining Shapes

In Photoshop and ImageReady, you can combine selection areas and vector paths in different ways. Once you have created at least one shape, the Options bar displays buttons allowing you to add, subtract, intersect, or exclude overlapping areas. Figure 7-22 shows these buttons in the Options bar.

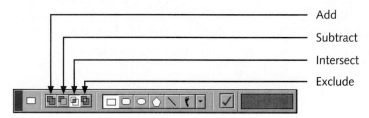

Figure 7-22 Controls for combining shapes

The buttons also determine how a new shape interacts with existing shapes. This is useful for creating complex shapes. Figure 7-23 shows the possible ways of combining shapes or selection areas; those ways are listed below:

- *Add*: Create a shape, or add one shape to another.
- *Subtract*: A new shape removes area from an existing shape.
- *Intersect*: The working area is the area overlapped by both shapes.
- *Exclude*: The working area is the area of the second shape not covered by the first shape.

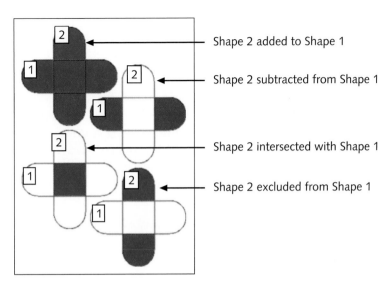

Shape 2 added to Shape 1

Shape 2 subtracted from Shape 1

Shape 2 intersected with Shape 1

Shape 2 excluded from Shape 1

Figure 7-23   Possible ways to combine shapes

Creating Custom Shapes

Just as you can create custom brushes, which are essentially customized selection areas, you can create custom shapes. Use the Pen tool or any of the Shape tools to create a shape and edit it by adjusting the anchor points. When you finish, select the path, click Edit on the menu bar, and then click Define Custom Shape. Next, you set options for the new shape:

- *Defined Size:* The shape is always drawn with an exact width and height.

- *Defined Proportions:* The width and height of the shape can vary, but the aspect ratio remains the same.

- *Unconstrained:* The default setting; the shape is drawn without a set width and height.

- *From Center:* Force drawing the shape from the center. Otherwise, the default is to start drawing the shape from the upper-left.

You then can select custom shapes by clicking the Custom Shape icon in the Options bar or the tool palette. Click the inverted arrow next to the shape and choose a shape from the palette that appears.

Working with Shapes

Once you have defined a shape, you can convert it to a selection area and use the selection to create the rest of your image. You also can use the shape itself to color pixels in the image and add styles and effects. You can quickly switch between selections and shapes by clicking the icons at the bottom of the Paths palette. Be careful when you have a selection area and a path selected at the same time; if you move or delete one of them, Photoshop might move or delete the other.

The two easiest uses for shapes are to fill or stroke an area, as you would with a selection area. Filling a shape uses the foreground color to **fill** the path. When you **stroke** a shape, the path is outlined with a one-pixel line. Figure 7-24 shows the difference between these options.

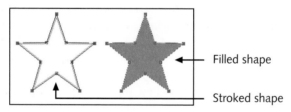

Filled shape

Stroked shape

Figure 7-24   Using Fill and Stroke

CREATING 3-D EFFECTS

Because Web pages and graphics always appear on two-dimensional surfaces, you obviously cannot create true three-dimensional objects. You can easily create the illusion of 3-D, however, by using the principle that light almost always illuminates from above. Therefore, light consistently produces highlights on the upper surfaces of objects and creates shadows below them.

You can imitate this natural effect. Place highlights at the tops of objects in an image, and they appear to extend away from the rest of the page. Place shadows at the bottoms of objects in an image, and they appear to recede. You can reverse the illusion by inverting the shadows and highlights. If you turn this book upside down, the images in Figure 7-25 seem to reverse direction.

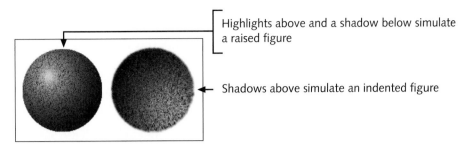

Figure 7-25   3-D effects

Using the Z-Axis

According to Cartesian coordinates, horizontal distances are measured along the x-axis, and vertical distances are measured along the y-axis. The height and width of images and their positions on Web pages often are measured in terms of x and y. This x-y coordinate system is the standard two-dimensional model used in all graphical interfaces.

Three-dimensional tools refer to another dimension that is perpendicular to the x- and y-axes. This third dimension is called the z-axis, and is used to measure the **virtual** distance between an image and the baseline surface of the rest of the field. In the left-handed coordinate system, a positive z value means the object is behind the screen, while a negative z value means the object is in front of the screen. In a right-handed system the reverse is true. Figure 7-26 shows the three main axes of the 3-D coordinate system.

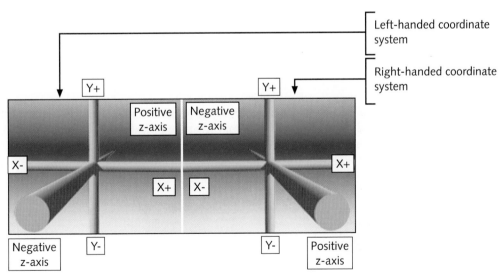

Figure 7-26   The 3-D coordinate system

Keeping the Light Consistent

Because light shines from above in the natural world, you see button highlights as pointing toward the virtual light source and shadows as pointing away. The highlights and shadows must be opposite each other to reinforce the illusion of light. When they do not match, as shown in Figure 7-27, the illusion is disturbed. Although the effect is probably not ruined altogether, mismatched shadows and highlights can distract the reader.

The convention is to use light not only from above, but also angled from the side. This technique adds more highlights and shadows on the sides of graphics, and increases the 3-D illusion. The angle can be from either side, but usually is from the upper-left, causing highlights on the upper-left side of the graphic and shadows on the lower-right.

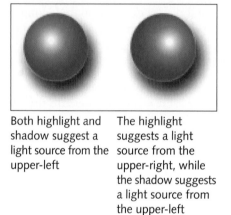

Both highlight and shadow suggest a light source from the upper-left

The highlight suggests a light source from the upper-right, while the shadow suggests a light source from the upper-left

Figure 7-27   Matched and mismatched lighting effects

Using Beveled Edges

The most common 3-D effect is the **beveled edge**, which is a slanted or inclined edge. This effect is used on most icons and windows in graphical interfaces, and in standard desktop operating systems. To create the illusion of beveled edges, you add a highlight to the upper edge and left side of the image, and add a shadow to the lower edge and right side. See Figure 7-28 for examples. You can use any of the painting tools to create this effect, or you can use the Burn tool for the shadows and the Dodge tool for the highlights.

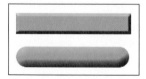

Figure 7-28   Hard and soft beveled edges

Using Gradients

Gradients are one of the more useful Web graphics effects, and they quickly add a professional polish. **Gradients** are smooth transitions from one color to another. The drawback of gradients is that they require a large color palette, which results in larger files.

In Photoshop, the gradient tools include the Linear Gradient tool, the Radial Gradient tool, the Angle Gradient tool, the Reflected Gradient tool, and the Diamond Gradient tool. Figure 7-29 illustrates these gradients, using white as the foreground color and black as the background color.

Each tool works in a similar way, creating a graduated color shift between two or more colors. The difference between the tools is in the shapes they create.

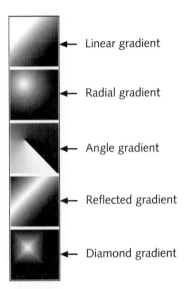

← Linear gradient

← Radial gradient

← Angle gradient

← Reflected gradient

← Diamond gradient

Figure 7-29   Five types of gradients

- *The Linear Gradient tool:* This tool creates a simple transition from one color to another in one direction.

- *The Radial Gradient tool:* This tool creates a point of one color that radiates in all directions as it shifts to other colors.

- *The Angle Gradient tool:* This tool creates a circular gradation from one color to another around a central point.

- *The Reflected Gradient tool:* This tool creates a linear gradation from one color to another, then back to the first color.

- *The Diamond Gradient tool:* This tool is similar to the Radial Gradient tool, but creates diamond shapes as it shifts from one color to another.

The gradient tools replace all selected pixels with the gradient, so make your selection carefully, or use the gradient tools in an empty layer. The tools share the same options in the Options palette. In addition to Mode and Opacity, you can control which colors are used in the gradation. The default selection of Foreground to Background causes the gradient to use the foreground and background colors as end points. The Foreground to Transparent gradient fades from the foreground color to completely transparent, which is useful for adding subtle shading to images. Photoshop includes several other preset gradients and allows you to create your own.

Using a Drop Shadow

A **drop shadow** creates the illusion that a button is hovering above the rest of the page. Notice in Figure 7-30 how a stronger drop shadow causes the boxes to seem to be lifted off the page.

Figure 7-30   Drop Shadows

Drop shadows are more convincing when they fade into the background, but faded edges make it more difficult to use transparent backgrounds. When using drop shadows, make sure to use the same background color for the button and the page. When used within a button, drop shadows create the illusion that the selection is carved out of the rest of the button.

You can create a drop shadow by painting with a dark color around the button. Another option is to copy the button to a new layer.

To create a drop shadow by copying a layer:

1. Duplicate the layer containing the button image.

2. Move the lower layer **five** to **10** pixels down and to the side.

3. Darken and blur the colors of the lower layer to simulate shading.

Photoshop and ImageReady automate this technique with the Drop Shadow effect, which is one of several automated layer styles.

To use styles to create a drop shadow effect:

1. Select the **layer** containing the button image.

2. Click the **Add a layer style** button at the bottom of the Layers palette and then click **Drop Shadow**. You also can click **Layer** on the menu bar, point to **Layer Style**, and then click **Drop Shadow**.

3. In the Layer Style dialog box, shown in Figure 7-31, adjust the various options or use the defaults.

4. Click **OK**. You should see a style icon in the affected layer. Any edits you make to this layer will adopt the same style.

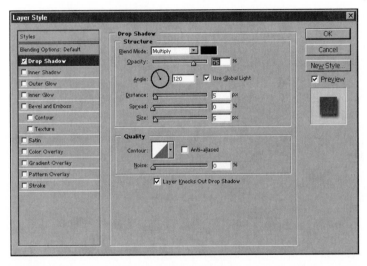

Figure 7-31   The Layer Style dialog box

The Drop Shadow effect offers several parameters to adjust the darkness and softness of the shadow, but the default settings are generally best. A similar effect is the Outer Glow, which uses a light color as a shadow. This effect is useful for buttons that appear over dark backgrounds.

Using Layer Styles

Layer Styles allow you to add several effects to any layer in your image. Unlike other filters, the effects are applied to the entire layer rather than to the selected area. You can use multiple effects at the same time, and you can turn the effects on and off as long as the layer is separate. The effects are permanently set when you flatten the layers; Photoshop finds the transparent areas in the layer and applies the effects to the edge between transparent and opaque areas. You can see the effects of using Layer Styles in Figure 7-32.

The effects that help you create 3-D buttons are the Drop Shadow, Inner Shadow, Inner and Outer Glow, and Bevel and Emboss. For each effect, you can adjust the Mode, the Opacity, the angle of the simulated light source, the distance along the z-axis, the blur, and the intensity.

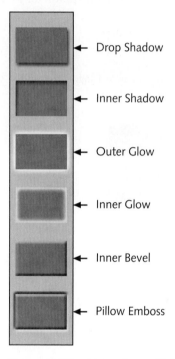

Drop Shadow

Inner Shadow

Outer Glow

Inner Glow

Inner Bevel

Pillow Emboss

Figure 7-32 Using Layer Styles

All layer effects use the **global angle**, which is a standard angle for simulated light. When you set the global angle, all effects use the same angle. In Photoshop, angles are measured counterclockwise starting from the rightmost point on a circle (3:00 on a clock face). The standard global angle is from the upper-left at 120 degrees. Using a different angle can cause reverse shading and highlighting. In particular, an angle of 120 degrees with the Inner Shadow effect causes the image area to appear to recede, while an angle of -50 degrees causes the styled (or affected) area to pop out of the image.

Using 3-D Software

Until the mid-1990s, creating quality 3-D graphics required expensive software on high-end computers such as Silicon Graphics workstations. Now many 3-D software packages are available for desktop computers. These programs tend to be more difficult to learn than other graphics software, and understanding them in depth requires an entire course or sequence of courses. These tools are more appropriate for video and animation projects, and provide an abundance of features to produce images for the Web. You can use basic Photoshop tools to produce all the 3-D effects you need for most Web graphics.

Using Distort Filters in Photoshop

Photoshop and most other image editors include various distortion filters that create 3-D effects by making images appear to move in and out of the z-axis. Most of these filters are not appropriate for creating buttons, but they still are useful for creating 3-D effects in other graphics. The Pinch filter pulls a point out of the image and pushes it in or pulls it out along the z-axis. The Spherize filter is similar, but creates a more rounded effect. The ZigZag filter is like the Spherize filter but creates ripples like those in water. You can see examples of these effects in Figure 7-33.

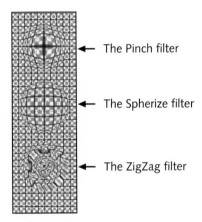

← The Pinch filter

← The Spherize filter

← The ZigZag filter

Figure 7-33   Three distort filters

IMPLEMENTING BUTTONS IN WEB PAGES

Just as buttons can be divided into several thematic categories, you also can divide them into four functional categories: simple links, form submission buttons, those that control media within a page, and those that open or close windows. While the thematic categories affect the design of the buttons, the functional categories affect how you place the buttons in Web pages.

Using a Graphic for a Link

Buttons themselves contain nothing that links to something else. The link is coded in the anchor tag that surrounds the button. For example, the following code creates a text link to a page called next.html, using the word continue as the link:

```
<a href="next.html">continue</a>
```

The following code, however, creates a button that links to next.html. Note that the anchor tag is identical in both examples, but the example below uses an image instead of the word continue:

```
<a href="next.html"><img src="continue.gif" alt="Continue"
width="103" height="28"></a>
```

The only modification you need to make to the IMG tag is in the BORDER attribute. By default, when an image is enclosed in an anchor tag, the browser displays the image with a border of the same color as the link color, usually blue. Notice in Figure 7-34 that the graphic appears with a blue line around it. Although the border is an effective cue that the image is a link, most designers choose to remove it. To remove the border, add the BORDER attribute to the IMG tag and set its value to 0:

```
<a href="next.html"><img src="continue.gif" alt="Continue"
border="0" width="103" height="28"></a>
```

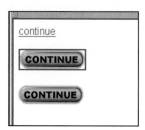

Figure 7-34 Text and button links

Using a Tabbed Interface

Tabs are usually implemented in a tabbed interface by the producer rather than the designer, but you are expected to slice the image into its component parts. A design example for a tabbed interface is shown in Figure 7-35. Each of the three rows must appear at the top of a different page. To make each tab have a different link, you could use an image map, which we cover in the "Creating Splash Screens" chapter, or chop the tabs into separate buttons.

Figure 7-35 A design for a tabbed interface

Slicing tabs for a navigation bar can be more difficult than it seems. If the tabs you designed overlap at all, you cannot slice the graphics between the tabs. If you try, the tabs will be mismatched. One solution is to design three or even four versions of each tab, and have each tab contain a bit of the neighboring tabs. Figure 7-36 shows the four versions of the Reviews button that would be necessary to avoid mismatched tabs.

Figure 7-36   Multiple versions of a tab button

You also can create just two versions of each tab, and create spacers to be placed between each tab. Figure 7-37 shows the two necessary versions for each tab, as well as the spacer images that go between the tabs.

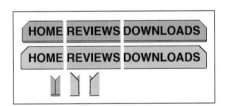

Figure 7-37   Two versions of each tab with spacers

When you place these graphics in a table, make sure that the TABLE tag has its sizing attributes set to 0. The following HTML code produces the layout in Figure 7-38:

```
<table>
<tr>
<td>
<img src="home1.gif">
</td>
<td>
<img src="btwn2.gif">
</td>
<td>
<img src="reviews2.gif">
</td>
<td>
<img src="btwn1.gif">
```

```
</td>
<td>
<img src="downloads1.gif">
</td>
</tr>
</table>
```

Figure 7-38   Tabbed interface with default table attributes

You must set the CELLSPACING, CELLPADDING, and BORDER attributes to 0. Additionally, you must remove all white space between the IMG tags and the surrounding TD tags. Many WYSIWYG HTML editors miss this step, so you may have to edit the white space by hand.

The following HTML produces the layout in Figure 7-39:

```
<table cellspacing="0" cell padding="0" borders "0"><tr>
<td><img src="home1.gif"></td>
<td><img src="btwn2.gif"></td>
<td><img src="reviews2.gif"></td>
<td><img src="btwn1.gif"></td>
<td><img src="downloads1.gif"></td>
</tr></table>
```

Figure 7-39   Tabbed interface with flush table cells

Using a Graphic for the Submit Button

All forms require a Submit button. Whether it is a simple log-on box or a complex survey, you must include a button that allows users to send the form data to a server. The default Submit button is gray, beveled, has rounded corners, and contains a word (usually Submit). You can use HTML to specify which word appears in this button, but you cannot control the shape, size, or color.

The following HTML code creates the form in Figure 7-40:

```
<form method="post" action="/cgi-bin/join.cgi">
<input type="text" name="E-mail_Address" value="my@e-mail"
size="10">
<br><br>
<input type="submit" value="Join Now!">
</form>
```

The INPUT tag is used to define most form elements. When you set the TYPE attribute to "submit," the browser displays a standard gray button. This button displays Submit or Submit Query unless you set the VALUE attribute to display specific text.

Figure 7-40   A basic form with default submit button

You can replace these gray Submit buttons with graphics that you create. This procedure does not require using style sheets and is supported by all modern browsers. To use a graphic as a Form Submit button, use an INPUT tag, but set the TYPE to "image" instead of "submit." The browser will replace the standard gray button with an image.

You must indicate which button to use with the SRC attribute, and just as with a normal IMG tag, you should set the HEIGHT and WIDTH attributes, and the BORDER attribute to 0.

The following HTML code creates the form in Figure 7-41:

```
<form method="post" action="/cgi-bin/join.cgi">
<input type="text" name="E-mail_Address" value="my@e-mail"
size="10">
<br><br>
<input type="image" src="join.gif" width="100" height="19"
border="0">
</form>
```

Figure 7-41   A basic form with graphical submit button

Using Buttons for Other Functions

You can use buttons to control audio and video players in Web pages, as well as open and close windows. The functionality of these buttons comes from client-side scripting such as JavaScript, not from the buttons themselves.

Regardless of its purpose, a button is displayed using an IMG tag, as you have seen in previous examples. The surrounding anchor tag contains the extra coding.

CHAPTER SUMMARY

❑ You can create several types of buttons, but you should design buttons of the same type within individual pages so that they look similar.

❑ Buttons must indicate that clicking them causes the browser to perform an action. The best way to achieve this effect is to make the buttons resemble physical, three-dimensional buttons.

❑ Links that need emphasis attract more attention if you represent them as buttons. Links that do not need emphasis should remain as text.

❑ Using text in an image editor is similar to using text in a word processor.

❑ Usually you create buttons as circles or rectangles with rounded corners. To do so in Photoshop, you use a variety of Shape tools.

❑ Shapes are made of paths and can be converted to or from selection areas.

❑ You create 3-D effects by simulating a light source above the button. Make the button appear to have highlights at the top and shadows below it.

❑ You can simulate light and shadow by beveling edges, using gradients, and by adding drop shadows.

❑ To make a button clickable, wrap the IMG tag with an anchor tag.

❑ Form submissions use a gray button by default. You can set a form to use your own graphics as submit buttons.

REVIEW QUESTIONS

1. What two types of links can you best represent as buttons?

   a. Site information

   b. Account information

   c. Media player

   d. Directional

2. Which pair of buttons should share a similar design?

   a. Contact Us and Mail This Page to a Friend

   b. Log In and Log Out

   c. Home and News

   d. Help and Next Page

3. Which of the following is not a cue to tell the reader that a button is clickable?

   a. 3-D effects

   b. Rollover effects

   c. Bright colors

   d. Rounded corners

4. Which links can you represent as buttons?

   a. Media player and site content links

   b. Navigation links

   c. Any link other than links within blocks of text

   d. You can use buttons for any link.

5. How would you create text that reads down instead of across?

   a. Use the Warp Text option.

   b. Rotate the layer 90 degrees.

   c. Use the vertical orientation option.

   d. You cannot do this in Photoshop.

6. Which of the following are standard for text used in buttons?

   a. Italic, bold, uppercase, Arial

   b. Nonitalic, nonbold, lowercase, Times

   c. Italic, nonbold, uppercase, Times

   d. Nonitalic, bold, lowercase, Arial

7. Which of the following is not a reason to use text links instead of buttons?

   a. Saving bandwidth

   b. De-emphasizing links

   c. Keeping the page uncluttered

   d. You are not sure if readers have the proper fonts installed to display the buttons correctly.

8. When do you have to rasterize text?

   a. When using the Type Mask tool

   b. When you want to edit a text layer

   c. When you want to use filters

   d. When you want to apply layer styles

7

9. What is the difference between the Rectangular Marquee tool and the Rectangle tool?

   a. The Rectangular Marquee tool creates vectors, and the Rectangle tool creates paths.

   b. The Rectangular Marquee tool creates selection areas, and the Rectangle tool creates shapes.

   c. The Rectangular Marquee tool creates shapes, and the Rectangle tool creates vectors.

   d. There is no difference between the two.

10. Which of the following formats can save path information?

    a. PSD only

    b. PSD, TIF, and PS

    c. Any image format

    d. Most image formats, including GIF and JPG

11. Which of the following tools quickly makes rectangles with rounded corners?

    a. Rectangular Marquee tool

    b. Elliptical Marquee tool

    c. Ellipse tool

    d. Rounded Rectangle tool

12. How would you create a triangle with rounded corners?

    a. Use the Rounded Rectangle tool, set the number of sides to 3, and select Smooth Indents.

    b. Use the Polygon tool, set the number of sides to 3, and select Smooth Corners.

    c. Use the Polygon tool, set the number of sides to 3, and select Smooth Indents.

    d. Use the Ellipse tool, set the number of sides to 3, and select Indent Sides.

13. Which gradient tool creates a spot of one color that fades to another color in circles around the initial point?

    a. Linear Gradient tool

    b. Radial Gradient tool

    c. Angle Gradient tool

    d. Reflected Gradient tool

14. What is the direction of a conventional light source?

    a. From the side

    b. From the upper-left

    c. From directly above

    d. From the upper-right

15. What is the z-axis?

    a. The width of a vector path

    b. The line around which 3-D objects are rotated

    c. The diagonal line between the x-axis and y-axis

    d. An imaginary line coming out of the screen

16. Which of the following tools can create a highlight that fades to a shadow?

    a. Burn tool

    b. Paint Can tool

    c. Gradient tool

    d. Dodge tool

17. How do you make a button link to another page?

    a. Add an SRC attribute to the IMG tag.

    b. Enclose the IMG tag with an anchor tag.

    c. It happens automatically.

    d. Place the button on both pages.

18. How do you make a button open a new window?

    a. The button itself is no different; just change the anchor tag.

    b. The shape's path needs to include JavaScript.

    c. You must create the button with a WYSIWYG HTML editor.

    d. Place the button on both pages to indicate to the browser which pages are linked.

19. What sort of menu usually requires client-side scripting?

    a. Tabbed interface

    b. Hierarchical menu

    c. Side navigation

    d. Top navigation

20. Which browsers support the use of graphics as form-submission buttons?

    a. Internet Explorer version 5 and later

    b. Internet Explorer version 4 and later

    c. Netscape Navigator and Internet Explorer, versions 4 and later

    d. All modern browsers

7

HANDS-ON PROJECTS

Project 1: Create a 3-D E-Mail Button

You have an e-mail link at the bottom of your Web page and you want to replace the text link with a stylized symbol.

Complete these steps:

1. Create an **image** that is **50** pixels wide and **50** pixels high.
2. Select the **Type** tool.
3. Set the Font to **Arial** and **Bold**. Set the font size to **36** points.
4. Click in the middle of the image and type the **@** symbol.
5. Center the character with the Move tool.
6. Click **Layer** on the menu bar, point to **Layer Style**, and then click **Drop Shadow**.
7. In the Effects dialog box, Set the Blend mode to **Multiply**, the opacity to **75%**, and the Angle to **12°**. Set the Distance to **5** pixels, the Spread to **10%**, and the Size to **5**. Use the default settings for the other options.
8. Select **Bevel and Emboss** from the menu in the Layer Style dialog box.
9. Set both Opacity values to **100%**, the Style to **Inner Bevel**, the Depth to **200%** pixels, the Size to **5** pixels, and the Soften to **3** pixels. Click **OK**.
10. Flatten all the layers.
11. Select the **Levels** tool, and use it to set the Gamma to **1.5** (the center Input Levels text box). Click **OK**.
12. With the **Hue/Saturation** tool, select **Colorize**, set the Hue to **240**, and then click **OK**.
13. Optimize the image and save it as **e-mail.gif** in a new folder named **project_7-1**.

Project 2: Create a Faded Next Button

You have complete navigational controls at the top of your Web page. The controls allow users to navigate between pages in a multipage article. You want to add a subtle reinforcing link at the bottom.

Complete these steps:

1. Create an **image** that is **200** pixels wide and **100** pixels high.
2. Create a second **layer**, and fill it with white.
3. Select the **Type** tool and click the **Create a mask or selection** button in the Options bar. Set the Font to **Arial**, **Bold** and **30** points.
4. Type **Next->** in the new layer. Commit the text by clicking the **Commit any current edits** (check mark) button in the Options bar or by selecting another tool from the toolbox.

5. Center the selection.

6. Click **Select** on the menu bar, and then click **Inverse**.

7. Select the **Airbrush** tool and select a **soft round brush** with a diameter around **65** pixels. Set the Pressure to **25%**. Set the foreground color to **black**. Use the normal mode.

8. Drag the pointer over the **text** to create a **gray outline** around the text.

9. Click **Layer** on the menu bar, point to **Layer Style**, and then click **Drop Shadow**. Adjust the settings or use the default settings. The text should appear to be cut out of the image.

10. Flatten the layers and trim the image.

11. Optimize the image and save it as **next.gif** in a new folder named **project_7-2**.

Project 3: Create a Beveled Next Button

You do not have to use advanced features of Photoshop or ImageReady to create 3-D effects. You can create highlights and shading with basic tools found in any graphics program.

Complete these steps:

1. Create an **image** that is **60** pixels wide and **40** pixels high.

2. Select the **Line** tool. In the options bar, select the Create filled region button, and set the Weight to **20** pixels. Deselect **Anti-aliased** if it is selected.

3. In the Geometry options list, insert a **check mark** in the End check box for arrowheads. Set the Width and Length to **150%**, and set the Concavity to **0%**.

4. Set the foreground color to a **medium green** (**#00cc00**) and draw an **arrow** from left to right across the image. Hold down the **Shift** key to keep the line horizontal.

5. Select the **Pencil** tool and use a brush that is **2** pixels in diameter.

6. Set the foreground color to a **lighter green** (**#99ff99**) and zoom in on the image.

7. Draw **straight lines** along the upper and left inner edges of the arrow.

8. Set the foreground color to a **darker green** (**#006600**) and draw **straight lines** along the lower and right inner edges of the arrow.

9. Blur the image with the Gaussian Blur filter, using a Radius of **0.7**.

10. Optimize the image and save it as **next2.gif** in a new folder named **project_7-3**.

Project 4: Create Two Buttons for a Web Jukebox

You have a JavaScript-based audio player and need buttons to use in the interface. You will start with just the Play and Stop buttons as prototypes and create the other buttons later. You want the buttons to resemble the buttons on CD players as much as possible.

Complete these steps:

1. Create an **image** that is **60** pixels wide and **40** pixels high.

2. Select the **Gradient** tool. In the options, choose **Reflected Gradient**. Set the Gradient to **Foreground to Background**.

3. Set the background color to **black** and the foreground color to a **grayish-blue** (**#666699**).

4. Move the pointer to the **center** of the image, hold down the **Shift** key, and drag the pointer to the **bottom** of the image.

5. Create a second **layer**.

6. Set the foreground color to **red** (**#ff0000**)

7. Select the **Rectangle** tool. In the Options bar, click **Create filled region**.

8. Create a **15 × 15** pixel **square centered** in the left half of the new layer.

9. Set the foreground color to **green** (**#00cc00**)

10. Select the **Polygon** tool. In the Options bar, set the Sides to **3**, click the **Geometry** options arrow, and set the Radius to **10**. If Anti-Aliased is selected, deselect it.

11. Create a **triangle** pointing toward the right and centered in the right half of the new layer.

12. Click **Layer** on the menu bar, point to **Layer Style**, and then click **Inner Shadow**. In the dialog box that appears, set the Distance to **7** pixels and the Choke to **0%**. Click **OK**.

13. Flatten the image and save it as **buttons.psd** in a new folder named **project_7-4**.

14. Select the **Canvas** tool and use it to crop the Stop button (square) at **30** pixels wide.

15. Optimize the image and save it as **stop.gif**.

16. Open **buttons.psd** again and crop the Play button (triangle) at **30** pixels wide.

17. Optimize the image and save it as **play.gif**.

Project 5: Create a Cartoon Button

You are creating buttons for your top navigation bar to link to the content areas of your site. You want a cartoon look for the buttons.

Complete these steps:

1. Create an **image** that is **60** pixels wide and **60** pixels high.

2. Select the **Rounded Rectangle** tool. In the Options bar, click **Create new shape layer**. Set the Radius to **10**. On the Style menu, click the style named **Color Target (Button)**. Open the Rounded Rectangle Options menu and select **Unconstrained**.

3. Drag the pointer over the **image** to create the button.

4. In the Layers palette, expand the **shape layer** and double-click the **style** icon next to the words Drop Shadow to open the Layer Style dialog box. In the dialog box, change the distance to **10** pixels.

5. Select the **Direct Selection** tool. Select each **corner anchor tab** to change the shape of the button.

6. Flatten the image. Use the Levels dialog box to raise the black output level to **75**.

7. Using **black**, type **Games!** in the image.

8. Click the **Warp Text** button in the Options bar to open the Warp Text dialog box. Set the style to **Inflate**. Set the Bend to **75%**.

9. Flatten the image, **optimize**, and save it as **games.jpg** in a new folder named **project_7-5**.

Project 6: Create a Button with Emphasized Text

Create a button in which the text appears to be lifted away from the textured background.

Complete these steps:

1. Create an **image** that is **120** pixels wide and **60** pixels high.

2. Set the background color to **blue** and the foreground color to **white**.

3. Run the **Clouds** filter.

4. Select the **Levels** tool and set the black Output Level to **127**.

5. Select the **Type** tool and add a **type mask** of the word **Reviews** in a **bold, 24-point**, **Verdana** font.

6. Click **Select** on the menu bar, and then click **Inverse**.

7. Normalize the contrast within the selected area.

8. Select the **Burn** tool and darken the area around the text.

9. Click **Select** on the menu bar, and then click **Inverse**.

10. Normalize the contrast within the type mask. Copy the **selection** and paste it in a new layer.

11. Add the **Outer Glow** style with the Layer Style dialog box. From the Contour menu, select the contour named **Ring**.

12. Flatten the image, normalize contrast, optimize, and save it as **reviews.jpg** in a new folder named **project_7-6**.

Project 7: Create a Vertical Button

Create a button that looks as though it is standing vertically on the page.

Complete these steps:

1. Create an **image** that is **120** pixels wide and **50** pixels high with a **transparent** background.
2. Select the **Type** tool and use it to add **Gallery** as a type mask in a new layer. Select a **bold sans serif font**, and select a size that fits within the shape.
3. Fill the text with the foreground color, blue (#0033CC).
4. Duplicate the **layer**. Select the **bottom layer**.
5. Click **Edit** on the menu bar, point to **Transform**, then click **Skew**. Reduce the height to about **80%**, move the selection down so that the bottom edge of the selection is aligned with the bottom edge of the text in the other layer. Skew the selection horizontally by about **[-30]** degrees.
6. Click **Image** on the menu bar, point to **Adjust**, and then click **Invert**.
7. Set the foreground color to **black**. Select the **Gradient** tool. In the Options bar set the gradient to **linear**, from **Foreground to Transparent**. Create a gradient from bottom to top of the selection. Make sure that transparency is locked.
8. Raise the Gamma to **2**.
9. Flatten the image, optimize, and save it as **gallery.gif** in a new folder named **project_7-7**.

Project 8: Create Another Standard Button

Create a standard button to use in a navigation bar.

Complete these steps:

1. Create an **image** that is **120** pixels wide and **35** pixels high with a **transparent** background.
2. Select the **Rounded Rectangle** tool. Set the **Radius** to **10**. Set the layer style to **none**.
3. Create a **white-filled region 100** pixels wide and **20** pixels high.
4. Add every possible layer style except Texture and Stroke. Use default settings or experiment with the various features.
5. Save the image as **button.psd** in a new folder named **project_7-8**.
6. Use this image as a basis for several navigation buttons. Use text of a complimentary color over the button to create buttons with the words: **Store**, **Reference**, and **Help**.

7. Adjust the color of the base button so that the hue is slightly different and the saturation is reduced. Use text of a complimentary color to create buttons with the words: **Books**, **Music**, **Glossary**, **FAQ**, **Phone #s**, and **Guide**.

8. Optimize and save all of these images in the **project_7-8** folder.

CASE PROJECT

Create a navigation bar for your site. This bar should be a vertical column of at least 10 buttons. Four or five of the buttons are category headings that contain subcategories. The category buttons should be distinct from the subcategory buttons. Create 3-D buttons for each link on the bar.

Create navigation buttons for your site that communicate their purpose without using words. The buttons should convey the concepts of Back, Next, and Home, among others. The buttons also should share a common design.

7

CREATING THUMBNAIL GALLERIES

Automating Tasks with Photoshop

In this chapter, you will:

- ◆ Use actions
- ◆ Process tasks in batches
- ◆ Save and share actions
- ◆ Create thumbnail galleries
- ◆ Use the other automate commands

Web sites often contain online image galleries, such as those that have examples of the designer's work, or photographs of the products sold through the site. The galleries usually use several small images that link to larger versions of the images. These small images are called **thumbnails**. When creating galleries of thumbnail images, a graphic designer is faced with the task of manipulating dozens, or perhaps hundreds of images.

Many image-editing tools let you create scripts that automate image editing, allowing the computer to make the necessary changes to your images. You can save these scripts and use them later for other images. Even if you are not creating a gallery, you will find it easier to eliminate repetitive tasks by combining them into single commands.

This chapter explains how to create Web galleries, and how to process multiple images at the same time.

USING ACTIONS

In Photoshop or ImageReady, an **action** is a sequence of commands, similar to a macro in other applications. An action can contain commands from almost any feature of Photoshop, including resizing, running filters, or making other edits. Consider an action as a kind of script that instructs Photoshop or ImageReady to perform, in order, the defined list of commands. You sequence the commands to create an action, and then play back an action to affect a single image file or a folder with many image files. For example, you can use an action to resize an image to 100 × 75 pixels, boost contrast, and save it as an optimized JPEG. Instead of having to select these commands individually, you can combine them into a single action that performs all of the commands when you play that action.

When you create a thumbnail gallery, you resize and optimize many images, usually so that they are all the same size and in the same format. Because actions let you process images in this way, actions are especially helpful when creating thumbnail galleries.

In Photoshop and ImageReady, actions are stored in the Actions palette. Figure 8-1 shows the first four actions in the action set named Default Actions.atn. The action named Sepia Toning (layer) is expanded, making visible the individual steps of the action. Some steps are actions themselves, and contain subsets of additional actions and steps. The Sepia Toning action is a parent action to the steps and actions contained within it. When you play the Sepia Toning action, Photoshop first makes a snapshot of the affected image, and then makes a new layer. The action merges the visible layers, desaturates the image, and makes a new layer with new settings.

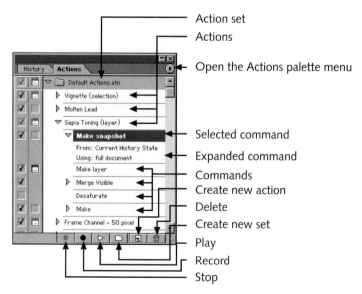

Figure 8-1   The Actions palette

While the History palette records recent commands applied to an image, the Actions palette saves groups of commands as actions. Use the Actions palette to create, edit, play, delete, and store actions.

To open the Actions palette, choose Show Actions from the Window menu. You can display actions in the Actions palette using **List view** or **Button view**. Select Button Mode from the Actions palette menu to view the available actions as color-coded buttons as shown in Figure 8-2. Deselect this option to display them as a list. The List view displays more information about each action than Button view does, while the Button view lets you see the actions with color-coding. You can set the color for an action only when in List view. Figure 8-1 shows available actions in List view. When you create an action, you select the commands from the Actions palette using either List view or Button view. See the Playing Actions section for other considerations when choosing between List and Button view.

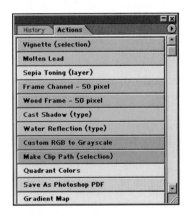

Figure 8-2   Button view

Just as you sequence commands to create an action, you can arrange actions into **sets**. In other words, you use sets to organize your actions.

Photoshop and ImageReady come with several preset actions which perform common tasks, such as resizing images to a fixed output size or adding various filter effects. The actions are specific to the software in which they were created. You cannot use Photoshop actions in ImageReady, and vice versa.

You can use the preset actions, record your own actions, edit actions, and manipulate the playback of actions. The following sections explain how to play, record, and edit actions.

Playing Actions

Playing an action applies the series of commands in the action to an opened image file. You can play an entire action (all the commands), one command in an action, or only a subset of the commands. When actions are listed in Button mode, you can only play entire actions.

To play an entire action, select the action name in the Actions palette and click the Play button or choose Play from the Actions palette menu. You also can use the keyboard shortcut assigned to the action.

To play part of an action, first expand the action in the Actions palette by clicking the triangle to the left of the action name. This displays the full sequence of edits in the action. Select from the sequence the first command you want to apply to the image. When you play the action, it starts with this command. If you select one command, playback runs from that command to the end of the sequence. If you select consecutive commands, playback runs through only that subset of commands.

To play a single command from an action, select the command, hold down the Macintosh Command key or the Ctrl key in Windows, and double-click the command or click the Play button.

Save your images before applying an action to them. The Undo command reverses only the last command in an action, not the whole action. To restore the image to its state before you played the action, use the Revert command.

To play an action:

1. Create a new image file of any size in Photoshop and save it as **action_test.tif** in your Chapter 8 folder.

2. Open the Actions palette and click the **triangle** next to Default Actions to expand the set of actions that comes installed with Photoshop.

3. Make sure the actions are displayed as a list rather than as buttons. If they are displayed as buttons, click the **right triangle** to open the Actions palette menu and click **Button Mode** to deselect it.

4. Scroll down the list of actions and find the one named Molten Lead. Click the **triangle** next to Molten Lead to expand the list of commands in the action. Then click the first **indented triangle** to expand the first substep for the Make Snapshot command. Figure 8-3 shows the expanded list of commands for the Molten Lead action.

5. See if the check box to the left of the Molten Lead action name contains a dialog box icon. If it does, click the **check box** to deselect the icon.

6. Click **Molten Lead** to select it, and then click the **Play** button on the Actions palette toolbox. (Refer back to Figure 8-1.)

7. You see each command highlighted in turn as the action plays through the sequence, and you see the History palette filling with states. You also see the changes taking effect in the image.

Figure 8-3   The expanded list of commands for the Molten Lead action

8. When completed, the blank image you created shows the Molten Lead effect, as illustrated in Figure 8-4.

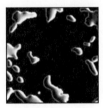

Figure 8-4   The Molten Lead effect

Modifying Playback

Sometimes you want to use an action on an image, but realize that not all of the commands are appropriate. Rather than create an entirely new action, you can modify an existing action by adding, excluding, deleting, or editing steps. You can modify the preset actions included in Photoshop or ImageReady, or modify an action you have created yourself. To exclude specific commands from an action, open the Actions palette in List mode. Click the check mark to the left of the command you want to exclude. This removes the check mark, indicating this command will not be performed—it is excluded or disabled. The check mark of the action turns red, as shown in Figure 8-5, indicating that one step in the action has been disabled. To include the command in the action, click the command. The action performs only checked commands and skips unchecked ones.

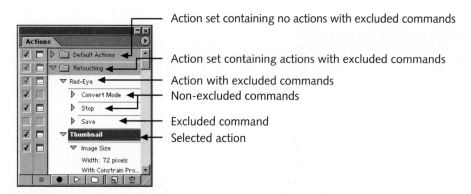

Action set containing no actions with excluded commands

Action set containing actions with excluded commands

Action with excluded commands
Non-excluded commands

Excluded command
Selected action

Figure 8-5   The Actions palette with some commands excluded

If you play the action named Red-Eye as shown in Figure 8-5, the first two commands would be performed, but the last step, saving the file, would be skipped.

If you want to permanently exclude a command, you can delete it in three ways. First select the unwanted command, and then use one of the methods listed below:

- Click the trash can icon in the Actions palette and click OK.

- Drag the action or command to the trash can icon.

- Choose Delete from the Actions palette menu.

Using Modal Controls

Most features in an action play without needing additional information from you. Other features require you to enter values or respond to messages during playback. For example, converting the mode from Indexed color to RGB color is a simple process needing no input from you. Changing the image size, however, requires that you enter values into the Image Size dialog box.

To pause the playback of an action so you can enter values in a dialog box, use a **modal control.** You can set modal controls only for actions that launch dialog boxes. If you do not set a modal control, dialog boxes do not appear when you play the action, and the commands use the values that were last used by the command. In the Actions palette, a modal control is indicated by a dialog box icon to the left of a command, action, or set. A red dialog box icon means one or more commands with a modal control are excluded, as shown in Figure 8-6.

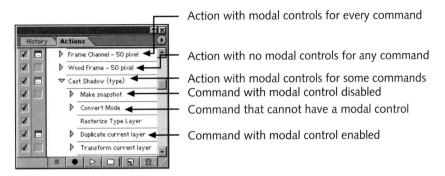

Action with modal controls for every command

Action with no modal controls for any command

Action with modal controls for some commands
Command with modal control disabled
Command that cannot have a modal control

Command with modal control enabled

Figure 8-6   The Actions palette with some modal controls disabled

In Photoshop you must be in List mode to set a modal control. You can add modal controls by clicking the dialog box icon to the left of the command in the Actions palette. When you play the action, it pauses at the command, and opens the appropriate dialog box so you can add values.

The Molten Lead action you worked with earlier in this section used modal controls to retrieve information from you while the action played. Complete the steps again, but this time deselect the dialog box icon to the left of the name of the action. When you play the action now, it will use default settings for all commands, and will run without needing input from you.

To enable modal controls when playing an action:

1. Create a new image file of any size in Photoshop and save it as **action_test2.tif** in your Chapter 8 folder.

2. Make sure the check box to the left of the Molten Lead action name contains a dialog box icon. If it does not, click the **check box** to enable modal controls.

3. Click **Molten Lead** to select it, and then click the **Play** button on the Actions palette toolbox.

4. Several dialog boxes appear asking for information from you. For each dialog box, click **OK** to accept the default values, or change the values in some way to alter the effects of the commands. When the action stops for the Plaster command, enter **3** for the Image Balance value.

5. You see each command highlighted in turn as the action plays through the sequence, and you see the History palette filling with states. You also see the changes taking effect in the image.

6. When completed, the blank image you created will show a variation of the Molten Lead effect, as illustrated in Figure 8-7.

Figure 8-7   A modified Molten Lead effect

Creating Actions

You have examined the Molten Lead action, a preset action Photoshop provides by default, and learned how to modify an action by disabling commands and setting modal controls. If none of the existing actions performs the task you want to automate, you can create an action. To do so, you perform the task while Photoshop or ImageReady records the commands you use. You can record most, but not all, Photoshop and ImageReady commands when creating actions. The following sections explain how to record actions in both Photoshop and ImageReady and how to set recording options in ImageReady only.

Recording Actions

Most, but not all, of the commands in Photoshop and ImageReady can be recorded and incorporated into actions. Actions can include **stops** and **modal controls**, which delay the playback of the action to allow you to perform tasks or enter values that are specific to the image being edited. You also can assign keyboard shortcuts for actions.

The record feature in Photoshop and ImageReady records nearly every command, including opening, closing, and saving images. The commands that cannot be recorded are those that involve using tools, such as the Paintbrush tool, as opposed to a dialog box, such as the Levels dialog box. Keep that in mind as you create actions. If you open the image after you begin recording, the action will include a command to open that image. Because you do not want the action to open the same image each time, have an image open before recording. Photoshop or ImageReady then performs the task on any open image. Before you begin recording, you might want to first perform the operations on an image to test the steps and make sure you are performing the task correctly.

Before creating an action, you should organize your actions into sets. This makes it easier to find a particular action later. For example, imagine you want to automate the creation of thumbnail images. Create a new set for all your image-resizing actions. Then create a new action containing specific commands to resize images into thumbnails. First create an action set called Resize, and then create an action called Reduce to Thumbnail within the Resize set.

To create an action set:

1. Click **New Set** from the Actions palette menu.

2. In the New Set dialog box, enter **Resize** as the name and click **OK**.

Names such as Set 1 will only confuse you later. Use descriptive names such as photo retouching or reduce and optimize. This will help you identify your sets and actions later.

3. Choose **New Action** from the Actions palette menu or click the **New Action** button on the Actions palette toolbox. The New Action dialog box opens, as shown in Figure 8-8.

Figure 8-8   The New Action dialog box

4. Type **Reduce to Thumbnail** for the action name and choose **Resize** as the set.

   If you think the action you are recording is one that you will use frequently, assign a keyboard shortcut. You can choose any combination of a function key (F1, F2, etc.), the Ctrl key (Windows) or Command key (Mac OS), and the Shift key (for example, Ctrl+Shift+F4). In Photoshop you also can select a color for the action, to help you organize it in the palette.

5. In the New Action dialog box, choose **F6** as the function key and select the **Shift check box**. This sets the keyboard shortcut as Shift+F6.

6. Select **Yellow** for the action color and click **Record**. The record button turns red, indicating that the software is recording the commands.

Unlike audio or video recording, recording commands is not time-sensitive. You can perform the steps as slowly as necessary to be accurate.

7. Open the Image Size dialog box and enter **72** for both the Height and Width. Click **OK**.

8. Stop the recording by either clicking the **Stop** button on the Actions palette toolbox, selecting **Stop Recording** from the palette menu, or pressing the **Escape** key. You can stop recording and start again by selecting the Start Recording command from the Actions palette menu.

Tips for Recording and Editing Actions

The results of some commands are affected by existing software and file settings, such as the foreground color or the mode of the image. If the software settings when you created the action do not match those when you play the action, you might see unexpected results.

When you record settings in dialog boxes, only those settings that you change are recorded. Even if a dialog box already contains the right values when you open it, you must type them again to make sure they are recorded.

Modal operations and tools use the units that are set in the ruler when the action is run. Make sure you always use the same units, or record the units you switch in the Preferences dialog box. In Photoshop you might want the ruler set to a percentage, rather than an absolute unit such as pixels or inches. This causes the actions to affect the same relative area, regardless of the actual size of the input file.

When you are finished adding commands, select Save a Copy from the File menu. Select the format and optimization options. Save to an existing folder. Do not create a new folder now, otherwise a new folder will be created for every file processed with this action. If you want the processed images to be saved to a new folder, create the folder before recording.

Click File on the menu bar, click Close to close the original image, and then click Don't Save. This ensures that the action will create new images while leaving the originals as backups. Make sure you do not accidentally create an action that overwrites existing files.

If you do not like the action you have created, you can rerecord the entire action. To do so, select the action name in the Actions palette, and choose Record Again from the Actions palette menu.

You can produce complex actions by recording an action in which you play other actions. This results in nested actions, where one action accesses another. This can be useful if you want to create modular actions. For example, you could have one action that saves an image as a 7-bit GIF image. This action can then be called by many other actions which each resize an image in a different way.

Recording Options in ImageReady

While Photoshop is a good all-purpose image-editing tool, ImageReady is designed specifically for creating Web images. In some cases you have more control over images in ImageReady than you have in Photoshop.

Resizing images is one of the most common procedures for actions, but a resize command in an action might not always work the way you expect. Your input images might not always be of the same original size or ratio, and this can produce unwanted results. For example, imagine you have several images that are all at least 400 pixels in height. You might record an action that reduces these images to 100 pixels in height. However, if you then apply that action to an image that is 50 pixels high and 300 pixels wide, the action doubles the height and width. This produces an image that has been stretched to 100 pixels by 600 pixels and is too large for most Web graphics.

In ImageReady, you have more control over how the images are resized. For example, you can constrain the sizing so that the images do not change beyond a set value. When recording an image size change in ImageReady, select Action Options from the bottom of the Image Size dialog box, as shown in Figure 8-9.

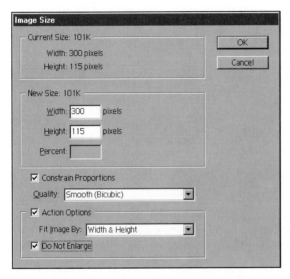

Figure 8-9 The Image Size Action Options in ImageReady

Change the options in this dialog box according to the guidelines below:

- Select Width to constrain proportions using the set width value.
- Select Height to constrain proportions using the set height value.
- Select Width & Height to constrain proportions using either the width value or the height value, depending on the dimensions of the image.
- Select Percent to constrain proportions using the percentage value.
- Select Do Not Enlarge to prevent images that are smaller than the set dimensions from being enlarged.

If you want all images to be saved with the exact same dimensions, you can then use the Canvas Size tool to pad the remaining space.

Editing Actions

Once an action is created, you can edit the action and the steps inside it. You can change or delete values, add new commands, rearrange existing ones, and add pauses to the action.

Sometimes you want two actions to perform similar functions. Rather than creating the second action from scratch, you can duplicate an existing action and use it as the basis for the new action. Duplicate the action by dragging it to a new location in the Actions palette while holding down the Option key for the Macintosh or the Alt key in Windows. You also can duplicate an action by selecting it in the palette and choosing Duplicate from the Actions palette menu, or dragging it to the New Action button at the bottom of the palette. In Photoshop you can duplicate entire sets as well as actions and commands.

The following sections explain how to change commands, insert new commands and stops, and troubleshoot an action.

Changing Commands

To edit a command in an action, double-click the command, enter the new value and click OK. If the command is a modal tool, change the effect by double-clicking the command, use the tool differently, and press the Return key (or Enter in Windows).

Inserting New Commands

When creating actions in ImageReady, you can drag commands from the History palette to an action in the Actions palette. Some commands in the History palette appear in italics, as in Figure 8-10. These commands are **nonactionable**, meaning they cannot be included in saved actions. These commands cannot be dragged into the Actions palette.

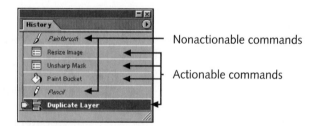

Figure 8-10 Nonactionable commands

Some commands cannot be recorded. These are called modal commands and include commands involving the **modal tools** such as painting tools, tool options, view commands, and window commands. However, you can insert some modal commands using the Insert Menu Item command. You can then select a command from a Photoshop menu and include it in an action. This does not record dialog box values, so is useful only for recording menu items that do not have variable settings. If the command does use a dialog box, the dialog box appears during playback, and the action pauses until you click OK or Cancel. When you use the Insert Menu Item command to insert a command that launches a dialog box, you cannot disable the modal control in the Actions palette.

You also can record new commands. Select a command to act as an insertion point in the action list and select Start Recording from the Actions palette menu, or click the

Record button. Select an action name to append the newly recorded command to the end of the command list. The new command appears after the insertion point. You can rearrange commands in an action and actions in a set by dragging the command or action to a new position.

Inserting Stops

When playing actions, you can include a **stop** to carry out a task that Photoshop can't record or to communicate with the user. You use a stop to perform a nonmodal task such as using a paint tool, or to add a message explaining the action. You also need to include a Continue button so you can restart the action after it reaches the stop command. The Record Stop dialog box is shown in Figure 8-11.

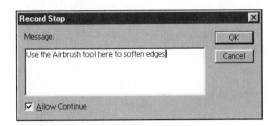

Figure 8-11   The Record Stop dialog box

You are unlikely to use nonmodal features such as painting when processing images in bulk, and you should avoid stopping to read instructions for every image. It is more likely that you will prepare an action to use for photo-retouching. You can preset the resizing and optimizing tasks in the action, but perform the red-eye reduction manually.

Troubleshooting

When creating actions, you might find they do not always work as you intended. You can troubleshoot the action to find the command that is producing unwanted results. Slow the playback of the action to make it easier to see the results of each action. You also can control whether to have audio annotations play in entirety before continuing with the other commands. Choose Playback Options from the Actions palette menu, and then select one of the following options:

- *Accelerated*: Play the action at normal speed
- *Step by Step*: Redraw the image after each command before continuing to the next command in the action
- *Pause for*: Enter an amount of time to delay each command
- *Pause for Audio Annotation*: Play the entire audio instruction before continuing. If this option is not selected, the commands will continue regardless of whether the audio has finished playing

PERFORMING BATCH PROCESSING TASKS

You can apply an action to an opened image by playing the action. To apply an action to multiple images, use the Batch command. Batch processing lets you perform many actions on many images without your intervention. When batch processing images, you should disable all stops and modal controls in the action. Otherwise, you will be prompted for every image; this defeats the purpose of batch processing. If you are saving the processed files to a new location, you can create a new folder for the processed files before starting the batch.

Batch processes can take a long time, perhaps hours, depending on the number of image files to process, the complexity of the action, and the processing speed of your computer. All commands are registered in the History palette, even commands that are executed as part of an action. You can speed the performance of batch processes by reducing the number of history states registered in the History palette. Every edit you perform on an image is recorded as a state in the History palette to allow you to undo changes. For better batch performance, open the General options in the Preferences dialog box, as shown in Figure 8-12. Reduce the number of History States. The default is 20; select a smaller number, such as 5.

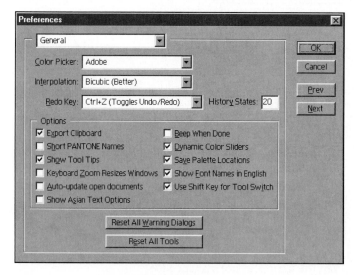

Figure 8-12   The History States option

Additionally, open the History Options in the History palette and deselect the Automatically Create First Snapshot option. The History Options dialog box is shown in Figure 8-13. Both of these methods help to reduce the amount of memory needed to play an action.

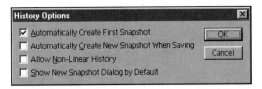

Figure 8-13   The History Options dialog box

Using the Batch Dialog Box

To apply an action to multiple images, click File on the menu bar, point to Automate, and then click Batch. The Batch dialog box opens, as shown in Figure 8-14. Choose Set and Action options from the drop-down lists. If you want to apply multiple actions, create a new action in which you record yourself playing the other actions.

8

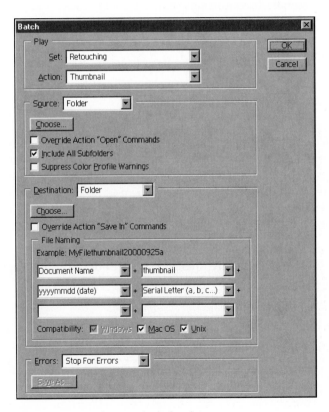

Figure 8-14   The Batch dialog box

Selecting Source Images

The Batch command lets you play an action on a folder of files and on subfolders. Although you could batch process a single image file, it is simpler to open the image and play the action directly.

In the Batch dialog box, select the source folder for the source to play the action on files stored in a folder on your computer. Before processing your images, make sure they are collected into one folder. If you want to batch process multiple folders, create aliases (shortcuts in Windows) for the other folders and place them in one folder. Click Choose in the Batch dialog box to locate and select the folder. When the source is a folder of images, you have three additional options:

- Select Override Action "Open" Commands if you want open commands in the action to refer to the processed files, instead of the files specified in the action. You can generally leave this unselected.

- Select Include All Subfolders to process files in subfolders. You should select this if your folder of images contains other folders with images you want to process.

- Select Suppress Color Profile Warnings to turn off the display of color policy messages. You can generally leave this unselected.

Rather than selecting a folder of images as the source, you can import files directly from a peripheral device. Select Import for the source to import and play the action on images from a digital camera or scanner. If you have a digital camera or a scanner with a document feeder, you might be able to import and process multiple images with a single action. The scanner or camera needs an acquire plug-in module that supports actions. Some acquire plug-ins do not support importing multiple documents, and do not work during batch processing.

Select Opened Files for the source to play the action on all open image files. This will apply the action to any image file currently opened within Photoshop or ImageReady.

Selecting a Destination

Once you have chosen the source of the images to be processed, you need to select where to save the newly processed files. You can leave all the files open, close and save the changes to the original files, or save modified versions of the files to a new location, leaving the originals unchanged. Choose the third option so that you don't lose images if the batch process is interrupted.

Also in the Batch dialog box, select None for the destination to leave the files open without saving changes. Choose this option if you want to continue working with all of the images after processing them. You should also select this option if the action contains commands or options specifying how to save the images.

Select Save and Close to save the files in their current location, overwriting the original files. You should select this option only if you made backup copies of your original files. It is very easy to accidentally overwrite all of your original files with improperly processed ones. You should get in the habit of always making backup copies of your images. After you process the images you can process again if there was a problem, or delete the originals once you are sure the processing was successful.

Toward the bottom of the Batch dialog box, select the folder for the destination to save the processed files to an existing folder. Click the Choose button and locate a folder where you want to save the processed images. Choose a folder other than the one where your originals are. Select Override Action "Save In" Commands if you want save as commands in the action to refer to the batch processed files, rather than the filenames and locations specified in the action. You can usually leave this box unselected.

Selecting a Naming Convention

If you chose Folder as the destination, you can specify a file naming convention and select file compatibility options for the processed files. Click a File Naming list arrow to select elements from the lists, or enter text into the fields to be combined into the default names for all files. Filenames can include up to six elements, each of which can be one of five options:

- *New word*: The new word can be any word or phrase you type, but should include no spaces or punctuation marks.

- *Original image name*: The original image name can be formatted as uppercase, lowercase, or title case (the first letter of each word is capitalized).

- *Serial number*: The serial numbers can be one, two, or three digits, and increment for each image processed. For example, selecting Document Name and 2 Digit Serial Number produces files with names such as MyImage01 or MyImage02.

- *Serial letter*: The serial letters can be uppercase or lowercase. You should always include a serial number or letter in the filenames so that they are all unique. If you do not do this, every file will save as the same name, replacing each other.

- *Current date*: The date can be formatted in many ways. The most common format for the Web is yyyymmdd, which indicates a four-digit year, followed by a two-digit month and a two-digit day of the month. For example, July 4, 1776, would be represented in yyyymmdd format as 17760704.

- *File extension*: The file extension can be uppercase or lowercase, and should always appear as the last element in the filename. You should always include the extension to any image you create. The extension is what tells the browser whether the image is a GIF, JPEG, or other format.

8

Saving files using the Batch command options always saves the files in the same format as the original files. If you want to create a batch process that saves files in a new format, record the Save As command followed by the Close command as part of your original action.

You also can select a Compatibility option for filenames. Macintosh and Windows operating systems both allow spaces in filenames and are not case sensitive (that is, they do not distinguish between uppercase and lowercase names). For example, a filename such as Red button.gif is allowed, and is not different from red BUTTON.Gif. UNIX systems are more strict about filenames and do not allow any spaces. They are also case sensitive. For example, the filename Red button.gif is not allowed, and filenames such as Blue.gif and blue.gif are treated as different files. Select the UNIX compatibility option to replace spaces with hyphens. You do not always know what type of operating system is running on the computer that serves the Web pages containing your graphics. Most Web servers run UNIX, however, so you should always make your filenames UNIX-compatible. Selecting Mac OS for the compatibility cuts off any characters past 32. Some versions of the Macintosh operating system do not allow filenames to have more than 32 characters.

Although filenames can have both uppercase and lowercase letters, most Web sites use the convention of always using lowercase filenames. When typing the HTML code that calls the images, you save a little time if you avoid pressing the Shift key to create uppercase letters. Also, because UNIX servers are strict about case, it is easier to be consistent and use all lowercase for filenames. In general, give your images names that are compatible for all operating systems.

Solving Handling Errors

Occasionally, batch processing a set of image files causes errors. You can either have the process stop and alert you of each problem, or continue processing the remaining files while saving the error messages to a log file. In the Batch dialog box, click the Errors list arrow and select what you want to do when the batch process finds an error. Selecting Stop for Errors suspends the batch process until you confirm the error message. Selecting Log Errors to File records each error message to a log file without stopping the process. In general, it's a good idea to stop for errors. Otherwise, you might have to re-create the image files after you examine the log file. However, if you are using an action that has worked successfully before and are confident that it should work again, you can log the errors and review the problems later. If you log errors, do not save the log file to the source image directory.

SAVING AND SHARING ACTIONS

While batch processing is convenient for some projects, you cannot use it during ongoing projects while you are still creating and acquiring images. For example, an online magazine might include a new photo on its home page every day. You cannot process in bulk because you receive a new image every day. In these circumstances you can use a droplet, a small application represented by an icon. Save an action as a droplet so you can process image files when necessary. To process an image file, drag it over the droplet icon.

The following sections explain how to save and load actions in Photoshop and ImageReady and how to use and create droplets.

Saving Actions

Each action you create is saved as part of an action set in a file with an .atn extension in the Photoshop Preferences folder. If you delete this file, any actions you created are lost. You can save your actions to a separate actions file so that you can recover them if necessary.

Saving Actions in Photoshop

In Photoshop all actions must reside in a set, and you can save only the entire contents of a set, not individual actions. This means you must selectively delete and rearrange your actions so that you end up with a set of appropriate actions, or only one action. Select the set, and select Save Actions from the Actions palette menu. You can then share the action with colleagues, or copy it to multiple computers. You also can save actions to a text file by holding down the Command and Option keys (Ctrl and Alt keys in Windows). The text file can be useful for reviewing the process of editing an image, but it cannot be reloaded into Photoshop.

Loading Actions

To load a set of actions, choose Load Actions from the Actions palette menu, and then locate and select the action set file. To load a preset action set, select an action set from the bottom section of the Actions palette menu, or select Load Actions from the Actions palette menu to open the Load dialog box, shown in Figure 8-15. Use the Load dialog box to locate an action set. To restore actions to the default set, choose Reset Actions from the Actions palette menu. Click OK to replace the current actions in the Actions palette with the default set, or click Append to add the set of default actions to the current actions in the Actions palette.

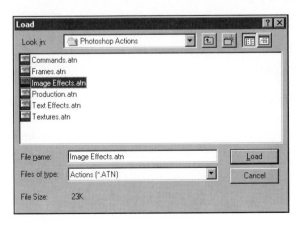

Figure 8-15 Loading a preset action set

Using Actions in ImageReady

In ImageReady, all actions you create are saved with the extension .isa in a folder named ImageReady Actions in the Photoshop Preferences folder. Any action used with ImageReady must be stored in this folder. ImageReady does not allow you to load actions through the software; to add actions, you must drag them directly into the Actions folder. You can archive action files by dragging them out of the Actions folder. You can also delete actions by deleting them from this folder. Whenever you add or remove files from the Actions palette, you have to instruct ImageReady to scan the Actions folder. Do this by selecting Rescan Actions Folder in the Actions palette menu.

Using Droplets

Actions are useful when you need to process many files in a particular way. For some projects, such as creating a thumbnail gallery, you must process all of the images at once. For these projects you create an action, apply it to your images, and either save it for later or delete it. However, if you need to add a few more images to the gallery months later, you need a convenient way of processing only a few images. You could open Photoshop, open the image, and then apply the action, or you could set up a batch process. However, it is easier to use a stand-alone application called a droplet. A **droplet** is a small application that applies an action to one or more images that you drag onto the droplet icon. You can save a droplet on your desktop or share it with colleagues. A droplet appears on your desktop as an icon, similar to the one shown in Figure 8-16.

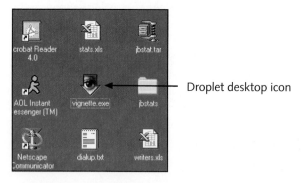 — Droplet desktop icon

Figure 8-16 A droplet on the desktop

Use a droplet when you need to process many images, but cannot process them at the same time. For example, imagine you are responsible for the graphics on the home page of an online news magazine. Every day you need a new image for the home page, but because they are news photographs, you never receive them until that morning. The final graphics need to be a specific size to fit the layout of the page, so you need a simple utility that will take any image and convert it to the size you need without having to actually manipulate actions every time. Droplets are the answer.

Droplets are stand-alone actions. First you create the action, and then you create the droplet. To use a droplet, drag an image file or a folder of image files onto the droplet icon. The droplet launches Photoshop or ImageReady, if it is not already running, and plays the action over the file or files. In ImageReady you can use control buttons to pause, resume, or stop the processing.

Creating a Droplet From an Action

Creating a droplet is almost identical to running a batch process. Click File on the menu bar, point to Automate, and then click Create Droplet. The Create Droplet dialog box opens, as shown in Figure 8-17.

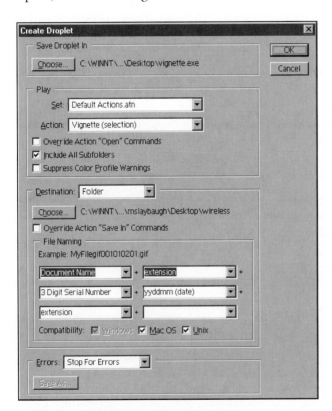

Figure 8-17   The Create Droplet dialog box

Click Choose in the Save Droplet In section, and select a name and location to save the droplet. You can use your droplets on both Macintosh and Windows systems. These two systems have different naming conventions, however. The Mac OS has no requirements for naming, but Windows requires that all applications end in the extension .exe to indicate that the application is an executable file. When creating droplets on a Mac, add the .exe extension to your droplet names to make them compatible with both systems. If you create a droplet in Windows that you also want to use on a Mac, copy the droplet to a Mac and drag the droplet icon onto the Photoshop icon. The droplet will then be updated to be used on Macs.

The rest of the options for creating the actions in a droplet are the same as when preparing a batch process.

Creating Droplets in ImageReady

ImageReady contains a few features and options not available in Photoshop. By default, ImageReady processes images using the optimization settings that were active when the droplet was created. You should add a Set Optimization command to the droplet to control how the processed images are optimized. To do so, adjust the settings in the Optimize palette, and then drag the droplet icon from the Optimize palette onto the Actions palette. To actually create the droplet in ImageReady, you can save the action as you would in Photoshop, or you can drag the action name from the Actions palette to the desktop.

Editing Droplets in ImageReady

In ImageReady, you can edit the commands in a droplet in the same ways you edit the commands in an action. You also can set batch options for a droplet before or after you create it. For example, you can set the droplet to operate in the background during execution so that you can work in other applications while ImageReady processes images.

To edit a droplet, double-click the droplet. This opens the ImageReady droplet window, which resembles the Actions palette. You can then rearrange, delete, or add commands by dragging states from the History palette into the droplet list.

Using Droplets to Automate Optimization Settings in ImageReady

In ImageReady, you also can create droplets from the Optimize palette. This lets you apply Optimize palette settings to individual images or folders of images. To create a droplet that automates Optimize palette settings, first open an image and select your optimization settings in the Optimize palette. Then drag the droplet icon from the Optimize palette to the desktop, or select Create Droplet from the palette menu. You can add droplets to an existing action by dragging the droplet icon in the Optimize palette to the Actions palette. This incorporates the optimization settings into the action.

Setting Batch Options for Droplets in ImageReady

Droplets are almost always used in ImageReady to batch process image files, so you can set batch options directly in the droplet. You can open the options of a droplet by selecting an action that you want to turn into a droplet, and then select Batch Options in the Actions palette menu. You also can open the options of an existing droplet by double-clicking the droplet and then double-clicking Batch Options in the droplet list.

The batch options shown in Figure 8-18 are similar to the options in the standard Batch dialog box.

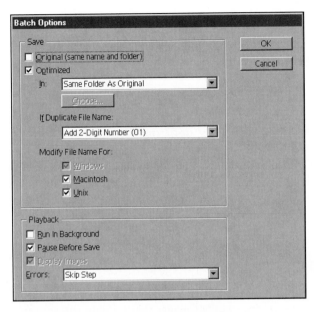

Figure 8-18   Batch Options for Droplets

You can select Original in the Save area of the Batch Options dialog box. This replaces your original images with the processed ones, meaning you can lose your original images if you make an error. Keep this option unchecked unless you already have backups of the images.

Select Optimized as a save option to optimize the processed image files, and then choose where you want to save the images. Generally, you should select Specific Folder and choose a folder that is different from the one where your originals are saved. If you choose to save the processed images in the same directory as the originals, you can set the If Duplicate File Name option. Here you can choose whether you want to overwrite the original or save a new file using the same name appended with a serial number or letter.

Under Modify File Name For, check all the boxes to make the filenames compatible with all other operating systems.

Setting Playback Options

ImageReady also includes options for how it runs when you play the droplet. In the Batch options dialog box, select Run In Background to have ImageReady process all of the images without displaying any information about them. This makes the process run more quickly and allows you to work with other programs during the processing.

However, all modal controls are disabled when the process runs in the background and you cannot add any user input. Additionally, when ImageReady is running in the background, it is not available for other image-editing tasks.

Select Pause Before Save to halt the processing of each image before saving it. Similarly, select Display Images to show the images as they are being processed. This allows you to confirm that the droplet is processing the images as you need them to be. This is a useful option when testing a new droplet, but it slows the process and is inconvenient if you want the droplet to run without needing feedback from you.

You also can choose how you want ImageReady to handle errors which occur during the process. Select Stop to suspend the process until you have confirmed the error. Select Skip Step to not process commands that cause errors. Select Skip File to not process images that result in errors. For new droplets, select Stop so that you can quit the process and adjust the commands in the droplet. When you are confident that the droplet works properly, select Skip File. If image files are skipped during the process because of errors, you can edit them individually later.

CREATING THUMBNAIL GALLERIES

Photoshop includes one other command that automates the process of creating a thumbnail gallery. It even generates the HTML pages that contain the thumbnail images and the links to the individual full-size images. This command, called the Create Web Photo Gallery command, is not appropriate for all Web galleries, but it can eliminate some repetitive tasks. In some cases, you can use the Create Web Photo Gallery command, edit the HTML pages, and re-edit the images. In other cases, you can create the HTML and edit the images yourself.

Creating Gallery Pages Manually

Web graphics usually support textual content in a Web page. Sometimes, however, the Web graphics are the content. Professional photographers showcase their work by placing digital versions of their portfolios on Web pages. The full-size versions of photographs are inconvenient to use in Web pages because their large dimensions prohibit viewing more than one or two at a time. Additionally, their large file sizes mean they load slowly. A solution to these problems is to use a thumbnail gallery, where every image is represented by a smaller version of itself. Because these images have smaller dimensions, many can be placed in a single page. The thumbnail images also have smaller file sizes, so a user does not have to invest much time before deciding which full-size images to load. Other types of Web pages also can show thumbnails of graphics. A news site often has snapshots of scenes that are too large to place with the text. To efficiently lay out the page, use a thumbnail in the text that links to the full-size version. You can use a text link to reference the full-size image, but the small thumbnail informs the reader what to expect from the larger image. You should use thumbnail images only when the information they convey is worth the additional download time caused by the additional files.

There are two ways to use thumbnail images. The first way is to create a copy of the full-size image and reduce the dimensions and color palette to make it load as quickly as possible. This involves creating two versions of every image and means the user has to download twice as many files. However, if you optimize the thumbnails well, each should be less than 1 KB. This means a gallery page with even 20 or more thumbnail images still loads quickly.

The second way to use thumbnail images is to use only one version of each image. You can display the image as a thumbnail by using reduced HEIGHT and WIDTH attributes in the IMG tag. The advantage to this is that you do not have to process the images. The disadvantage is that the user has to download the full-size version of every image, even though only a thumbnail is shown. If you have 20 images in a gallery page, and each image is 50 KB, the total download is about 1 MB. On a slow modem, this is frustratingly slow. However, once the thumbnails have loaded, clicking one opens the full-size version immediately, as it is already in the browser cache.

In general, you should use the first method of creating two copies of the images to generate thumbnails, especially if the full-size versions are large. The second method involving the IMG tag is useful if you are confident that readers will view all of the full-size versions. Only then can you justify the initial wait as the thumbnails download.

Regardless of which method you choose, consider using the LOWSRC attribute when displaying the thumbnails. While the SRC attribute references the thumbnail image, the LOWSRC attribute references another image first as a placeholder while the thumbnail loads. Typically, the images referenced by the LOWSRC attribute are highly reduced. Often the images are converted to 1-bit, black and white versions that load quickly. The advantage is that users with slow connections can view at least a low-quality version of each image. If you do not use the LOWSRC attribute, the user must wait for each thumbnail to load before knowing what the image looks like.

Just as you have two methods for creating thumbnails, you have two methods for linking to the full-size versions of the image. The easier way is to link to the image itself in the HTML code. Instead of linking to an HTML file in the anchor tag, you can link directly to the image file. This involves less work for you, but means the image appears with no navigation or accompanying text. It is quick and easy, but does not look professional.

The second method is to place each full-size version in its own HTML page. These pages can contain captions, ads, navigation, or any other standard Web page elements. Creating separate pages for every image in a gallery involves more work, but looks much more professional than simply linking to the image.

8

Using the Create Web Photo Gallery Command

A Web photo gallery is a Web site that features a home page with thumbnail images and gallery pages with full-size images. Each page contains links that allow visitors to navigate the site. For example, when a visitor clicks a thumbnail image on the home page, a gallery page with the associated full-size image loads. Use the Web Photo Gallery command in Photoshop to automatically generate a Web photo gallery from a set of images.

Although using the Web Photo Gallery command can reduce the amount of work necessary to create a thumbnail gallery, it has limitations. For example, the command only outputs JPEG format images. This is appropriate for photographic images but not for graphics such as line drawings, which should be saved as GIF images. Also, the generated HTML files do not contain LOWSRC attributes in the IMG tags. If you want to use reduced-size images this way, you have to process the thumbnails yourself and add the LOWSRC attributes manually.

Photoshop provides a variety of styles for the gallery; you can choose a style when you select the Web Photo Gallery command.

To create a Web photo gallery:

1. Click **File** on the menu bar, point to **Automate**, and click **Web Photo Gallery**. The Web Photo Gallery dialog box opens, as shown in Figure 8-19.

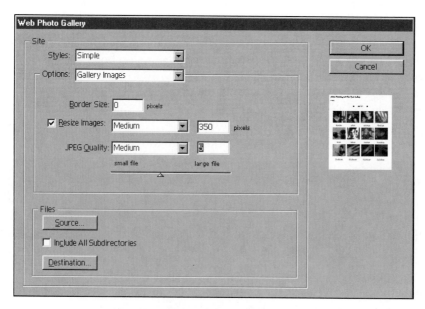

Figure 8-19   The Web Photo Gallery dialog box

2. Click the **Styles** list arrow to select one of four styles for the gallery. A preview of each style appears in the dialog box.

Choose the **Simple** style to create index pages with thumbnails in columns and rows. The number of rows and columns are set in the Gallery Thumbnails options.

Choose the **Table** style to create index pages in the Simple style, but with a border around the thumbnail images.

Choose the **Horizontal Frame** style to create an HTML frameset with a bottom frame containing a row of thumbnail images. Clicking one of the thumbnails causes the full-size version of the image to appear in the top frame.

Choose the **Vertical Frame** style to place the thumbnails in a column in a vertical frame to the left of the full-size frame.

Many Web developers prefer not to use framesets in their Web pages as it increases the number of files they need to manage. Also, because many search engines penalize sites that use frames, doing so may reduce the traffic your site gets from search engines. Still, thumbnail galleries that use frames are easier to navigate and you may choose to use them despite their disadvantages.

3. Click the **Options** list arrow to choose an option for creating the gallery.

Choose **Banner** to adjust the descriptive text in the generated gallery pages. Under this option, you can enter a title for the gallery under Site Name, an author under Photographer, and a date. You also can set the font and size of the text.

Choose **Gallery Images** to adjust options for the full-size images in the gallery.

Choose **Resize Images** if you want to resize the original images. You can then choose an image size for all images and an optimization setting.

Choose **Gallery Thumbnails** to adjust options for the main gallery page. Select Use Filename to display the filename of the image under each thumbnail. Select Use File Info Caption to display the caption text from the File Info dialog box under each thumbnail and on each gallery page. Using the File Info dialog box is described later in this section.

Choose **Custom Colors** to set the colors used in the HTML pages of the gallery. Each different element is listed with a swatch showing its color. Click a swatch to open the Color Picker dialog box and select new colors.

4. In the Files area, click the **Source** button to select the folder containing the images for the gallery. Check the **Include All Subdirectories** check box to include images in any subfolders of the selected folder.

5. Click the **Destination** button to select the destination folder that you want to contain the images and HTML pages for the gallery.

6. Click **OK** to start creating a thumbnail gallery of photo images.

8

Like all automated tasks in Photoshop, creating the gallery can take a few minutes or a few hours depending on the number of source images and the speed of your computer. During the process, three folders are created. One is named images and contains JPEG versions of all your source images. The second folder is named thumbnails and contains JPEG thumbnail versions of all your source images. The third folder is named pages and contains the HTML pages that hold the full-size images in the images folder. The process also generates HTML pages with names such as index.htm and index_2.htm. These pages hold the thumbnail images contained in the thumbnails folder.

For most projects, it is a good idea to edit the HTML files generated by Photoshop to adjust layout and add other elements.

You can add information to images in Photoshop and choose to show this information as captions under each thumbnail and on each gallery page. To do so, use the File Info dialog box as described in the following steps. Then open the Web Photo Gallery dialog box, click the Options list arrow, click Gallery Thumbnails, and select Use File Info Caption.

To add a caption to an image:

1. Open the file to which you want to add a caption.

2. Click **File** on the menu bar, and then click **File Info**. The File Info dialog box opens, as shown in Figure 8-20.

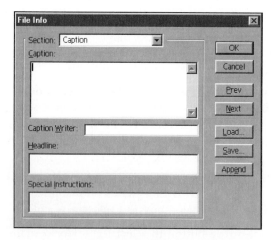

Figure 8-20   The File Info dialog box

Here you can add text, known as **metadata**, to images. Metadata is literally data about data, or in the case of images, image data that is contained within the image. The metadata available in an image's File Info can include information about copyright, authorship, and keywords. Not all image formats support this metadata. JPEG and PNG images can save the information, but

GIF images cannot. In most cases, your images will not contain any text information unless you have added it yourself. You also can add this text information to the HTML pages after you have created them.

3. If necessary, click the **Section** list arrow and then click **Caption**.

4. In the Caption text box, type descriptive text you want to appear as a caption when the image appears full-size or as a thumbnail.

5. Click **OK** to close the dialog box.

USING THE OTHER AUTOMATE COMMANDS

The Automate commands in Photoshop simplify complex procedures by combining them into one command. The Automate commands are found under the File menu in Photoshop. The Batch command and Create Droplet command are the two Automate commands you will probably use most often. Photoshop includes additional commands under the Automate submenu for more specific tasks. Photoshop also supports external automation using OLE (Object Linking and Embedding) Automation in Windows or using AppleScript in Mac OS. This book does not cover these topics in detail, but you can explore them on your own for complex procedures. One example of an externally automated task is a script that shuts down your computer when the process has completed. Another example is a script that processes your images, and then uploads them to your Web server.

Creating Contact Sheets

In traditional photography, a contact sheet is a single print that contains miniature versions of all the photos from a roll of film. The Contact Sheet command takes multiple images and creates one large image containing thumbnail versions. This is different from a thumbnail gallery, which is an HTML file containing many separate images. You would not use this command to create thumbnail galleries, but you might use it to share images with colleagues without having to deal with many separate files.

To create a contact sheet:

1. Make sure all of the images you want to use on the contact sheet are closed.

2. Click **File** on the menu bar, point to **Automate**, and then click **Contact Sheet II**. The Contact Sheet II dialog box opens, as shown in Figure 8-21.

3. Click the **Choose** button to select the folder containing the source images. Check the **Include All Subdirectories** box, if necessary, to specify that you want to include subfolders.

4. In the Document area, specify the dimensions, resolution, and color mode for the contact sheet.

8

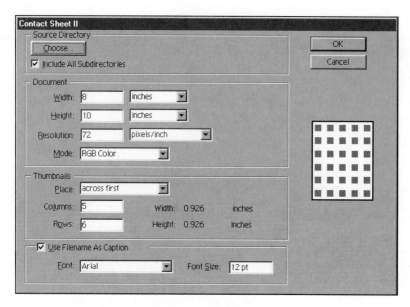

Figure 8-21   The Contact Sheet II dialog box

5. In the Thumbnails area, specify whether to place the thumbnail images in rows or columns, and specify the number of columns or rows per sheet.

6. To apply the name of each image file as a label under the image, check the **Use Filename As Caption** box, if necessary.

7. Click **OK** to close the dialog box.

A picture package is similar to a contact sheet, but includes multiple copies of an image in different sizes. The Picture Package command does not apply to creating Web images. You would use a contact sheet for sharing multiple images without having to create multiple files.

You also can use other preset automation commands to change color mode, fit images, or convert PDF documents to Photoshop image documents. Follow steps similar to those described earlier in the Creating Contact Sheets section to work with the Automate commands.

Using the Conditional Mode Change Command

The Conditional Mode Change command changes the color mode of an image. The dialog box for this command is shown in Figure 8-22.

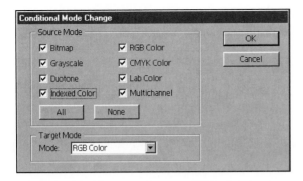

Figure 8-22   The Conditional Mode Change dialog box

Record this command as part of an action to guarantee that all source images have the same color depth. This prevents errors caused by using source images of differing color depths. If your original images have the same color depth, you can ignore this command. In most cases, you should select All for the Source Mode, and RGB Color for the Target Mode. The Conditional Mode Change command should be one of the first commands in an action.

Using the Fit Image Command

The Fit Image command scales source images to the height and width specified in the Fit Image dialog box, shown in Figure 8-23.

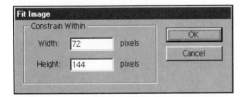

Figure 8-23   The Fit Image dialog box

Changing the Width and Height options in this dialog box does not change the aspect ratio of the images, it only enlarges or reduces the images until both dimensions are less than or equal to the set values. This command resamples the images, interpolating data between pixels if necessary. You can include this command in actions instead of using the Image Size command.

CHAPTER SUMMARY

◻ You can combine multiple commands into actions by recording the steps of editing an image.

❏ ImageReady contains special options for setting the height and width of images that are processed by actions.

❏ Actions can include stops, which pause the sequence of commands to let you enter values in a dialog box or use a modal tool such as the Paintbrush tool.

❏ The Batch command lets you apply an action to multiple files.

❏ You can save actions to use later, or to share with colleagues.

❏ You can save actions as droplets, which are stand-alone applications to process images one at a time.

❏ Actions and droplets created in Photoshop are not compatible with those created in ImageReady and vice versa.

❏ You can create thumbnail galleries by creating reduced versions of images. Use the LOWSRC attribute to improve the user experience.

❏ The Web Photo Gallery command automates the creation of thumbnail galleries.

❏ Photoshop has commands to generate contact sheets, and automate the processes of changing color depth and resizing images.

Review Questions

1. What is an action?

   a. A command inside a droplet

   b. A sequence of commands in Photoshop or ImageReady

   c. A stand-alone application that sits on the desktop

   d. A way to batch process images

2. How can you tell if a command is nonactionable?

   a. It appears in bold in the Optimization palette.

   b. It appears in italics in the History palette.

   c. It appears with a red check mark in the Actions palette.

   d. It appears with underlining in the droplet list.

3. How can you speed up the process of playing actions?

   a. Enable modal controls.

   b. Do not have the actions run in the background.

   c. Reduce the number of History States in the preferences.

   d. Set the Playback Options to Step by Step.

4. How do you convert an action created in ImageReady into an action that is usable in Photoshop?

   a. Actions created in ImageReady cannot be used in Photoshop.

   b. Add the .exe suffix.

   c. Export the list of commands as a text file, and then import the file into Photoshop.

   d. First convert it into a droplet, and then import it into Photoshop.

5. What happens if you use the Undo command after playing an action?

   a. Nothing happens.

   b. The action is deleted.

   c. The entire action is undone.

   d. The last command in the action is undone.

6. What is a reason to use a modal control?

   a. To manually set values in the Canvas Size dialog box

   b. To speed the playback of an action

   c. To use the Pencil tool

   d. All of the above

7. How do you include using the Dodge tool in an action?

   a. Add a Stop to the action with instructions to use the Dodge tool.

   b. Drag the command from the History palette to the Actions palette.

   c. Make sure the rulers are set to percentage units.

   d. Use the Insert Menu Item command.

8. How do you make an image filename compatible with UNIX systems?

   a. Make sure the filename contains a format suffix.

   b. Make sure the filename contains no spaces or punctuation.

   c. Make sure the filename contains no uppercase characters.

   d. Make sure the filename has fewer than 32 characters.

9. What could be a possible image filename if the Batch File Naming options were set to: 1 Digit Serial Number + Serial Letter (a,b,c...) + mmddyy (date) + extension?

   a. 3c091001.gif

   b. 04D20010910.JPEG

   c. 005f010910.GIF

   d. 06H100109.jpg

8

10. What should all batch filenames contain?

    a. A new word

    b. The original image name

    c. A serial number or letter

    d. The current date

11. How do you make a droplet created in Mac OS work in Windows?

    a. Add an .exe suffix.

    b. Drag it over the Photoshop icon in Windows.

    c. Remove all spaces from the droplet name.

    d. Remove the .exe extension.

12. When is it better to use a droplet instead of the Batch command?

    a. When you have to process images in different ways at different times

    b. When you have to process images in different ways at the same time

    c. When you have to process images in the same way at different times

    d. When you have to process images in the same way at the same time

13. How do you set a droplet to skip individual commands that cause errors in ImageReady?

    a. Select Log to File.

    b. Select Skip File.

    c. Select Skip Step.

    d. Select Stop.

14. What is the LOWSRC attribute used for?

    a. It is the same as the SRC attribute.

    b. To provide metadata for an image

    c. To reference a placeholder while another image is loading

    d. To reference a thumbnail image

15. What is not a way to display thumbnail images?

    a. Create a smaller version of the full-size image

    b. Use reduced values for HEIGHT and WIDTH attributes

    c. Use the Fit Image command

    d. Use the Web Photo Gallery command

16. What is not a possible style you can create with the Web Photo Gallery command?

    a. Thumbnails in a column, next to a frame containing a full-size image

    b. Thumbnails in a grid, linking directly to the full-size images

c. Thumbnails in a row, above a frame containing a full-size image

d. Thumbnails in a table, linking to separate pages containing the full-size images

17. If you have 20 images, where the full-size version of each is 100 KB, the thumbnail version of each is 10 KB, and the low-source version of each is 1 KB, how many kilobytes have to be downloaded to view the gallery page?

 a. 220 KB

 b. 2020 KB

 c. 2200 KB

 d. 2220 KB

18. If you have 20 images, each is 100 KB, you are not using low-source images, and you are using the full-size version reduced via HTML as the thumbnail versions, how many kilobytes have to be downloaded to view the gallery page?

 a. 2000 KB

 b. 2020 KB

 c. 2200 KB

 d. 4000 KB

19. What does the Conditional Mode Change command do?

 a. Automates the changing of color depth

 b. Automates the optimizing of images

 c. Automates the resizing of images

 d. None of the above

20. What does the Contact Sheet II command do?

 a. Creates one image containing small versions of multiple images

 b. Creates one image with multiple-sized versions of other images

 c. Creates thumbnail galleries

 d. None of the above

HANDS-ON PROJECTS

Project 1: Modifying an Existing Action

You want to use one of the preset actions that come installed with Photoshop, but it does not do exactly what you want it to do. Modify the playback of the action to suit your needs.

Complete these steps:

1. In Photoshop, open the **Actions palette** menu.

2. Expand the action set named **Default Actions**.

3. Select the action named **Quadrant Colors**.

4. Open image file **fish.tif** from the Data Disk.

5. Disable modal controls for the action, but enable modal controls for the Levels command. Play the action.

6. When the action stops to display the Levels dialog box, enter **0.5** for the gamma.

7. Save the resulting image as **fish.jpg** in a new folder named **project_8-1**.

8. Open image file **fish.tif** from the Data Disk again.

9. In the Actions palette, disable all modal controls for the **Quadrant Colors** action.

10. Exclude the **Desaturate** command.

11. Play the action again. You will not be prompted to enter values in dialog boxes.

12. Save the resulting image as **fish2.jpg** in the project_8-1 folder.

Project 2: Editing an Existing Action

You want to use one of the preset actions that come installed with Photoshop, but it does not do exactly what you want it to do. Edit the commands in the action to suit your needs.

Complete these steps:

1. In Photoshop, open the **Actions palette** menu.

2. Select **Frames.atn**. This restores one of the included sets to the Actions palette.

3. Expand the set, scroll down, and expand the action named **Wild Frame – 50 pixel**.

4. Open image file **fish.tif** from the Data Disk.

5. Open the **Actions palette** menu again and select **Playback Options**.

6. In the dialog box, select **Step by Step** and click **OK**.

7. In the Actions palette, expand the second **Fill** command to expose the details.

8. Double-click the **Fill** command to open the Fill dialog box.

9. Set Use to **50% gray**, set the opacity to **10%**, and click **OK**.

10. Play the action. You can watch the edits being performed. The action calls another action, which contains a stop. Click **Continue**.

11. Save the image as **fish3.jpg** in a new folder named **project_8-2**.

12. Select **Revert** from the **File** menu.

13. Double-click the second **Fill** command to open the Fill dialog box.

14. Set Use to **white**, set the opacity to **50%**, and click **OK**.

15. Play the action again to see the difference.

16. Save this image as **fish4.jpg** in the project_8-2 folder.

Project 3: Recording an Action in Photoshop

You want to create a simple action in Photoshop to create thumbnail images that are no taller than 36 pixels.

Complete these steps:

1. In Photoshop, click the **New Set** button at the bottom of the Actions palette.
2. In the dialog box, enter **Thumbnails** as the name of the set.
3. Open image file **fish.tif** on the Data Disk. You must have an image open to record an action.
4. Click the **New Action** button, name the action **36 pixels high**, and click **Record**. The Record button will turn red.
5. Click the **File** menu, point to **Automate**, and then click **Fit Image**.
6. In the dialog box, enter **36** for the height and **144** for the width. Click **OK**. You will see the image shrink to 36 pixels in height.
7. Click the **Stop** button.
8. Select the set you created.
9. In the Actions palette menu, select **Save Actions**.
10. Save **Thumbnails.atn** to a new folder named **project_8-3**.

Project 4: Recording an Action in ImageReady

You want to create a simple action in ImageReady that lets you create high-contrast thumbnail images.

Complete these steps:

1. In ImageReady, open image file **fish.tif** from the Data Disk.
2. Click the **New Action** button at the bottom of the Actions palette. Name the action **50 pixel.gif** and click **Record**.
3. Click **Image** on the menu bar, and then click **Image Size**.
4. Set the Width to **50** pixels.
5. Select **Action Options** at the bottom of the dialog box.
6. Click the **Fit Image By** list arrow, and then click **Width & Height**. Click **OK**.
7. Click the **Image** menu, and then click **Canvas Size**. Set the Height and Width to **50** pixels.
8. Click the **Stop** button at the bottom of the Actions palette.
9. Open the Actions palette menu and select **Insert Set Optimization Settings to GIF89a**.
10. Select the **Resize Image** command.

11. Click the **Record** button.

12. Click **Image** on the menu bar, point to **Adjust**, and then click **Auto Levels**. The new command appears between the two others. Click the **Stop** button.

13. Double-click the **Resize Image** command in the action. Set the Height to **50** pixels.

14. Open **stein.tif** from the Data Disk.

15. Play the action you created.

16. Save the optimized image as **stein.gif** in a new folder named **project_8-4**.

Project 5: Processing a Batch of Image Files in Photoshop

You have a folder of several images to process with your new action. Use the Batch command to automate the procedure.

Complete these steps:

1. Create a new empty folder named **project_8-5**.

2. In Photoshop, click the **File** menu, point to **Automate**, and then click **Batch**.

3. Click the **Set** list arrow, and select the set named **Thumbnails** you created in Project 3. This set has only one action, which appears in the Action list.

4. Click the **Source** list arrow, and select **Folder**, if necessary. Click the **Choose** button and locate and select the folder named **source_images** on the Data Disk. This folder contains several images.

5. Leave the remaining selection boxes in the Source area unselected.

6. Click the **Destination** list arrow and choose **Folder**. Click the **Choose** button and locate and select the new project folder you created.

7. In the File Naming area, click the **first** list arrow and select **yyyymmdd (date)**.

8. Type **thumbnail** in the second text box in the File Naming area. (This text box is to the right of the one where you selected yyyymmdd (date).)

9. Click the **third** list arrow and select **2 Digit Serial Number**.

10. Click the **fourth** list arrow and select **extension**. (This list is to the lower-right of the one where you selected yyyymmdd (date).)

11. Make sure the **Windows, Mac OS**, and **UNIX** boxes are all checked in the Compatibility section. The operating system you are using will be grayed out.

12. Click the **Errors** list arrow, and select **Stop For Errors**, if necessary.

13. Click **OK**. You will see each original image open, shrink, and close again.

14. Open the **project_8-5** folder. You should see several images with names like 20011025thumbnail03.jpg.

Project 6: Processing a Batch of Image Files in ImageReady

You have a folder of several images to process with your new action. Use the Batch command to automate the procedure.

Complete these steps:

1. Create a new empty folder named **project_8-6**.
2. In the Actions palette in ImageReady, select the action named **50 pixel.gif** you created in Project 4.
3. Open the **Actions palette** menu and select **Batch Options**.
4. Deselect the **Original** check box in the Save area of the Batch Options dialog box.
5. Select **Optimized** and select an output folder in which to save the images. Select **project_8-6** as the destination folder.
6. Make sure all three operating systems are checked for compatibility.
7. Under Playback, select **Display Images**.
8. Be sure the action stops on errors. Click **OK**.
9. Open the **Actions palette** menu and select **Create Droplet**.
10. Save the droplet to the **project_8-6** folder with the name **50 pixel gif.exe**.
11. Locate the folder named **source_images** in the Data Disk. Drag the folder onto the new droplet.
12. Open the **project_8-6** folder. You see several new thumbnail images.

Project 7: Creating a Thumbnail Page with the Web Photo Gallery Command

You want a thumbnail gallery. Use the Web Photo Gallery command.

Complete these steps:

1. Create a new empty folder on your desktop named **project_8-7**.
2. In Photoshop, click **File** on the menu bar, point to **Automate**, and then click **Web Photo Gallery**.
3. Click the **Styles** list arrow, and select **Simple**. You see a preview of a sample simple style in the right of the dialog box.
4. Set the Options to **Banner**, and type the text that will appear at the top of the gallery page.
5. Set the Options to **Gallery Images** and deselect **Resize Images**.
6. Set the Options to **Gallery Thumbnails**. Click the **Use Filename** check box to select it.
7. Set the Size to **72** pixels.

8. Set the Columns to **3** and the Rows to **4**.

9. For the Source directory, select the folder named **source_images** in the Data Disk.

10. For the Destination directory, select the folder named **project_8-7**.

11. Click **OK**. You see the images being processed.

12. Look in the new folder and preview the HTML pages in a browser. You have a basic Web gallery.

Project 8: Using Additional Automate Commands

You need another action that controls the color depth of the input image files and the size of the output image files. You want this action to be an all-purpose thumbnail generator.

Complete these steps:

1. In Photoshop, open file **stein2.tif** from the Data Disk.

2. In the set named **Thumbnails** in the Actions palette, create a new action named **thumbnail maker**.

3. In the palette menu, select **Insert Menu Item**. A dialog box opens telling you that you have selected nothing.

4. Click the **File** menu, point to **Automate**, and then click **Conditional Mode Change**. Click **OK** in the dialog box, and then click the **Stop** button.

5. Double-click the new command and set the Source Mode to **All** and the Target Mode to **RGB Color**.

6. Select **Insert Menu Item** again.

7. Click the **File** menu, point to **Automate**, and then click **Fit Image**. Click **OK** to close the dialog box.

8. Double-click the new command and set the Width to **96** pixels and the Height to **72** pixels.

9. Click the **Record** button and set the Background color to **white**.

10. Click **Image** on the menu bar then click **Canvas Size**. Set the dimensions to **96** pixels wide and **72** pixels high, with the anchor point in the center.

11. Click the **Image** menu, point to **Mode**, and then click **Indexed Color**.

12. Click the **Palette** list arrow, and select **Local (Selective)**.

13. In the Colors text box, type **64**, and then set Dither to **None**. Click the Stop button to stop recording.

14. Save this action in a new folder named **project_8-8** as a droplet named **thumbnail.exe**.

CASE PROJECT

Your ongoing project is to create an online portfolio.

Find at least three Web sites that contain picture galleries. Note how the images are displayed. Design a gallery of your own, keeping in mind the total size and number of files the user will have to download in order to see the gallery pages.

Generate the gallery pages and images for your portfolio, either by using the Web Photo Gallery command, or by creating thumbnails and HTML pages yourself.

Include links between these pages and the other pages you have created so far for your portfolio.

8

CREATING ANIMATION FOR THE WEB

Creating Animated GIFs

Animation is an optical illusion that you take advantage of every day. If objects had to move so that your eyes could see them as moving, there would be no film or television industry. Fortunately, when you look at sequences of still images you can perceive motion. For the purposes of this chapter, any Web-based motion is referred to as animation, whether it is cartoon-like or photographic.

You can use many file formats to create animation on the Web, but the most common is the GIF format. This chapter explains how to use ImageReady to create and use animated GIF images.

ImageReady, like most other Web animation programs, lets you create a sequence of images that appear as an animation when played in quick succession. However, ImageReady allows more control over the images than do many other tools, and offers additional features that make it easier to create animated GIF files. This means that ImageReady also has more options for you to understand and explore.

One of the most common uses for animation on the Web is in banner advertising. This chapter covers everything you must know to create and use animated GIFs, whether for advertising or other use.

UNDERSTANDING ANIMATION

Animation literally adds another dimension to Web graphics. Instead of having only three dimensions—width, height, and (color) depth—animation provides a fourth dimension of time. Several image formats support animation, but most require sophisticated authoring or programming and force the end user to play the animation in a special player or plug-in. The only format that supports animation and can be displayed in all browsers is the Graphics Interchange Format (GIF).

The following sections offer guidelines for using the illusion of animation, creating animated content, and creating animated GIFs.

Using the Illusion of Animation

Animation works because of a phenomenon called persistence of vision. When you view a quick succession of still images, persistence of vision makes you think you see motion. There is no real motion in an animation, film, video, or paper flip-book. In all cases, a set of static images is shown sequentially. If the sequential display of the images is fast enough, you experience the illusion of motion.

You can see an example of the illusion of motion by opening file 9-1.gif on your Data Disk in a Web browser. This animation has only two frames and lasts one second before repeating. Although it is simple, it does create the illusion that the red bar is flipping up and down, rotating around the lower-left end of the line. The only difference between this motion and the motion in video or film is the speed.

All animation media have a standard **frame rate**, measured in **frames per second**, or **fps**. Film has 24 frames for every second, but each frame is shown three times, making an effective frame rate of 72 fps. Partially to save film and partially because the equipment was not as sophisticated as today, moviemakers from the early part of the twentieth century used a frame rate of only 16 fps. This slow frame rate creates a jumpy quality and the motion is not smooth.

Video has 30 frames in each second, but each frame is divided into two fields, so the effective frame rate is 60 fps. When video is shown on the Web, it might have a frame rate as fast as 30 fps, although it is more common to cut the rate to 15 fps. This slow frame rate makes the frames flicker visibly during playback, but it also halves the memory and download time required to play video online.

Creating Animated Content

If you want sophisticated animations in your Web pages, you should use a video-creation program such as Adobe AfterEffects to generate QuickTime or Moving Picture Experts Group (MPEG) animations. You then can create video-quality animations at 30 frames per second, which is fast enough to show smooth motion with no flicker. While these animations can be impressive, the file size is often at least one megabyte for a brief half-screen animation.

Animations this long are not practical on the Web, however. The time it takes to download a video with a file size of 1 MB will probably discourage users from viewing your work. Because of time and bandwidth constraints, you need to use animation files that can be downloaded quickly. The format of choice for Web animation is GIF. Unlike the JPEG and PNG formats, GIF supports animation. The main advantage of GIF animations over other formats is that it is the only one supported natively in all browsers. Every other animation format requires a plug-in or external player to view the animation.

Because GIF animations use bitmaps, longer animations result in larger file sizes. You should use GIF only for short, simple animations. If you want longer animations, create MPEG or QuickTime movies that download separately. Because GIF supports only 8-bit color, photographic images often appear banded. QuickTime and MPEG are good choices if you want photographic-quality video.

If you want more complex online animation that does not have to be downloaded separately, consider creating a vector-based animation such as a Flash movie. Because they are vector-based, Flash movies cannot be photorealistic. Flash animations have smaller file sizes and are faster to download than QuickTime movies.

ShockWave movies are similar to Flash movies, but can include complex interactivity. Similarly, Java applets can be very interactive, but require high levels of programming to create.

So, for Web animations, use animated GIFs. For slightly more complex animations, use a Flash Movie. If you need the animation to be interactive, consider using ShockWave or Java. For photorealistic movies, such as video clips, use QuickTime or MPEG. Table 9-1 details the comparative strengths of different Web animation formats.

Table 9-1   Comparison of Web animation formats

Format	Works without plug-in or special coding on all browsers	Supports sound	Interactive	Supports high-color photographic video animation
GIF	Yes	No	No	No
QuickTime	No	Yes	No	Yes
MPEG	No	Yes	No	Yes
Flash	No	Yes	No	No
ShockWave	No	Yes	Yes	No
Java	No	Yes	Yes	No

If none of these formats suits your needs, consider streaming video. Streaming video formats, such as those available for RealMedia's RealPlayer and the Microsoft Windows

Media Player, have all of the features and advantages of a QuickTime or MPEG movie, but can be played before they are completely downloaded. Normally, a large video or animation clip, such as a QuickTime movie, must be downloaded completely before you can play it. Streaming audio and video allows you to start playing the file before it has finished downloading. It uses a **buffer** of a few seconds which causes the playback to lag behind the download. If the playback catches up to the data currently downloading, the stream ceases and the playback pauses until more of the file has downloaded.

Most of these sophisticated and streaming video animation formats and their creation are specialized subjects, requiring books and classes of their own. Some people devote their entire careers to specific formats such as Flash or streaming video.

Because GIFs are the most common animation format, the rest of this chapter covers creating animated GIFs.

Creating Animated GIFs

Animated GIFs have several advantages over other animation formats. They require no special coding, are supported by all browsers without requiring a plug-in, and support transparency. The restrictions of animated GIFs are that they cannot be interactive, other than being used as a button users can click like any other Web graphic, and they cannot include sound.

An animated GIF image is like any other GIF image except that one animated GIF file contains multiple individual GIF images, which then are displayed in order like a slide show. Each image includes information about how long it should play before the next image is shown. The file also includes information about whether to repeat the sequence after the last frame is displayed, and if so, how many times.

The specification for animating GIF images is called GIF89a, but you do not need to refer to the exact name when creating animated GIFs or using them in Web pages. You can just use the .gif file extension as you would with any GIF image.

Unlike almost everything else related to the Web, the specifications for animated GIFs have not changed in over 10 years. The new programs that create animated GIFs have the same basic functions as GIF animation programs from the mid-1990s. The ImageReady interface makes creating animated GIFs easier than some other tools, but the final product is the same.

This chapter assumes you are using ImageReady for the exercises. However, you can use many other freeware and commercial applications instead of ImageReady to create animated GIFs.

WORKING WITH THE ANIMATIONS AND LAYERS PALETTES

When creating animated images, ImageReady is not as intuitive as other animation programs. Most tools work by taking a set of images you have created, and then converting them into an animated GIF. ImageReady also uses this basic approach, but in addition lets you insert different images or modify single images over multiple frames. There is no limit to the number of frames in an animated GIF.

Creating animated GIFs in ImageReady requires using the Animation palette and the Layers palette. Both can be tricky to work with because you must always be aware of which frames and layers are selected. The Animation palette shows each frame in the animation in sequence from left to right. The Layers palette shows all the actual and potential image information in any of the frames. The use of layers differentiates ImageReady from many other GIF animation programs.

Like any other image composed in ImageReady, an animation can contain multiple layers, each of which can be moved and edited independently of the other layers. By default, any image opened or created in ImageReady is treated as an animation with only one frame, which is one way to describe a static image. As soon as you have at least two frames, the static image becomes an animation.

Using the Animation Palette

In the Animation palette, shown in Figure 9-1, you can add, delete, and modify frames. When you open any image in ImageReady, it is automatically displayed as the initial frame of an animation in the Animation palette.

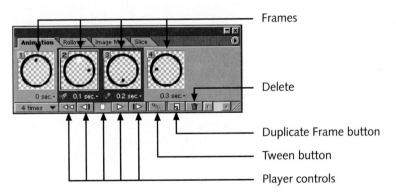

Figure 9-1 The Animation palette

To create a simple animation with the Animation palette:

1. In ImageReady, open the file named **snowman.gif** from the Data Disk.

2. If necessary, show the Animation palette by clicking **Window** on the menu bar, and then clicking **Show Animation**.

3. Add a frame by clicking the **Duplicate Frame** button at the bottom of the Animation palette, or by selecting **New Frame** from the Animation palette

menu. The new frame is added after the selected frame and retains all the properties of the selected frame.

4. Select the **new frame** in the Animation palette. The current frame opens in the Image window, and is indicated by a narrow white border around the frame. You can select multiple frames by holding down the Shift key or the Command key (Ctrl key in Windows) and clicking the other frames. Selected frames are indicated by a blue highlight around the frame in the Animation palette. When multiple frames are selected, only the current frame appears in the document window. Figure 9-2 shows selected frames in the Animation palette.

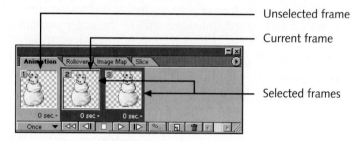

Figure 9-2   Selected frames in the Animation palette

5. Modify the duplicated frame. Use the Move tool to drag the image a few pixels to the right in the document window. Now each of the two frames shows a slightly different version of the same image.

6. Rearrange the frames by dragging them within the Animation palette.

7. Reverse the sequence of the frames by selecting multiple frames and selecting **Reverse Frames** from the Animation palette menu.

8. Add a third frame, and then delete it by selecting **Delete Frame** from the Animation palette menu, clicking the **trash can icon**, or dragging the **frame** to the **trash can icon**.

9. Click **File** on the menu bar, and then click **Save Optimized As** to save the animation to your Chapter 9 project folder as **snowman.gif**.

Choosing All from the Select menu selects all of the pixels in the image area, not all of the frames in the Animation palette.

Copying and Pasting Frames

Duplicating a frame creates a new frame that shows the same layers as the original frame. Copying and pasting a frame creates a new frame and also duplicates all the layers shown in the original frame. To copy and paste frames, select Copy Frame and Paste Frame from the Animation palette menu. When you use the Paste Frame option, you have a number of options:

- **Replace Frames** deletes the currently selected frame and replaces it with the copied frame.

- **Paste Over Selection** does not add or replace any frames. This option adds the copied layers to the currently selected frame.

- **Paste Before Selection** and **Paste After Selection** add a new frame with copied layers either before or after the selected frame.

You can delete an entire animation by selecting Delete Animation from the Animation palette menu. While this removes all but the first frame, it leaves all layers intact.

Playing Animations

9

The Animation palette contains playback buttons similar to those on any media device, as shown in Figure 9-3. Use these buttons to play the animation, which appears in the Image window. You also can stop the animation, step forward or backward a frame at a time, or rewind to the first frame. The animation plays at the speed determined by the delay settings for each frame. Timing of playback is covered in the next section.

You also can preview animations in a browser. This is recommended, as not all animation features work properly when previewed in ImageReady.

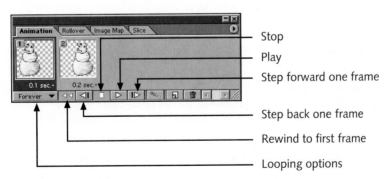

Figure 9-3 Player controls in the Animation palette

To preview an animation:

1. With snowman.gif still open, click the **Looping Options** list arrow, and then click **Forever**.

2. Click the **Play** button in the Animation palette. Note that each frame is selected in turn in the Animation palette as it appears in the Image window.

3. Click the **Stop** button to pause the playback.

4. To preview an animation in a Web browser, click the **Preview in Default Browser** button in the toolbox, shown in Figure 9-4. Alternately, click **File** on the menu bar, click **Preview In**, and then click the browser you want to use.

5. Click the **Stop** button in the browser or press **Esc** to stop the animation.

6. Click the **Refresh** or **Reload** button to begin playing the animation again.

7. Close the browser.

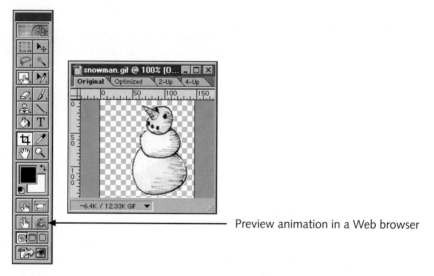

Preview animation in a Web browser

Figure 9-4 The Preview in Default Browser button

Previewing in a browser is important as the browser shows the true playback speed and transparency. The browser preview also shows the HTML code necessary to use an animation in a Web page. A sample preview window is shown in Figure 9-5.

Although you can view an animation file in Photoshop, you cannot see the animation. View animations in Photoshop to take advantage of filters or other tools not available in ImageReady, such as the Add Noise filter or Gradient tool. One task you can perform in Photoshop is editing individual layers. However, you should avoid adding or rearranging layers because this might ruin some of the animation effects when you view the animation later in ImageReady.

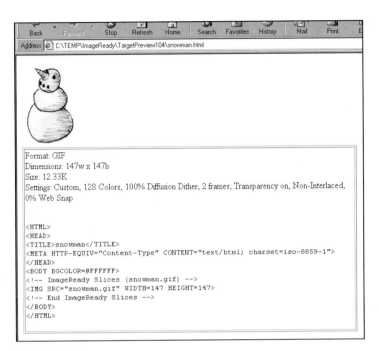

Figure 9-5   Previewing an animation in a Web browser

Using the Layers Palette

When creating animated GIFs in ImageReady, you do all of your work in the Animation and Layers palettes. Each frame in the animation is represented by one frame in the Animation palette. Each frame also has a number of layers associated with it, indicated by the visibility icons in the left column of the Layers palette, as shown in Figure 9-6. A layer, as defined in the Creating and Using Background Images chapter, is part of an image that can be moved in front of or behind other layers like sheets of clear plastic. When creating an animation, you can have multiple layers but only one frame, and you can have multiple frames but only one layer. A frame can include all the layers in an image, some of the layers, or no layers. Different frames can display the same layers.

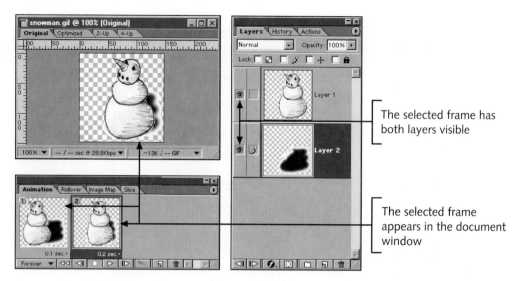

Figure 9-6 The Layers palette in ImageReady

Adding Layers

You often need to animate a specific element in an animation while keeping the background motionless. To do this, you need to place the moving element in a separate layer. When you add a layer to the Layers palette, the layer becomes visible in all frames in the animation.

To add a layer:

1. With snowman.gif still open, move the **snowman** in the second frame so it matches the position of the snowman in the first frame.

2. Select **Add Layer To New Frames** from the Animation palette menu. This causes ImageReady to automatically create a new layer for any frame you create.

3. Open **shadow.gif** from the Data Disk.

4. Select **All** from the Select menu and press Command + C (**Ctrl+C** for Windows) to copy the selected area.

5. Paste the selection into **snowman.gif**. A new layer is created for the shadow.

6. In the Layers palette, drag the **shadow** layer below the layer containing the snowman. Your work environment should resemble that shown in Figure 9-6.

Changing the Visibility of Layers

When you duplicate frames, all the aspects of the original frame are retained in the new frame, including which layers are visible. To control which layers are visible for a particular frame, first select the frame in the Animation palette, and then select and deselect the visibility icons in the Layers palette.

To change the visibility of layers of frames in ImageReady:

1. With snowman.gif still open, select the **second frame** in the Animation palette. In the Layers palette, deselect the **eye icon** next to the layer containing the shadow to make the shadow invisible.

2. Click the **Next Frame** button in the Animation palette to step through the animation sequence two or three times. The first frame of the animation contains the shadow and the second does not. As you play the animation, the shadow will blink on and off, and the visibility icon next to the shadow layer will turn on and off accordingly.

Figure 9-7 shows the Animation and Layers palette with visibility disabled for one layer.

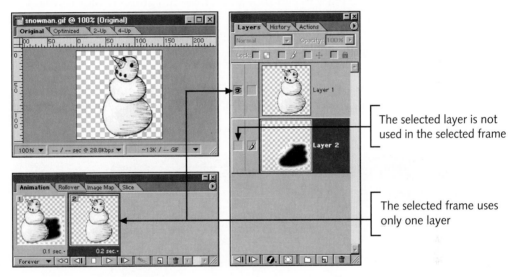

The selected layer is not used in the selected frame

The selected frame uses only one layer

Figure 9-7   Disabled visibility

Editing Layers

The key to creating animations with ImageReady is editing the layers in the Layers palette so that they change from one frame to the next. If the layers did not change, every frame in the animation would be identical.

At any time while editing an animation sequence, you will have one or more frames selected, and only one layer selected. Whenever you select a layer, it becomes visible in the selected frames. When editing a layer, your edits might affect only the current frame or a group of frames. Frame-specific changes affect only the current frame, even if other frames also show the layer. Adjusting a layer's opacity, position, or style changes those options for only the selected frame. Other frames that show the same layer do not register these edits. This allows you to animate single layers that change over time.

Global changes, however, affect all frames in an animation. These include any color changes, filters, type, and most other edits. All frames that show the layer will show global changes whether the frames are selected at the time or not.

To edit animation layers in ImageReady:

1. With snowman.gif still open, make both layers visible for both frames.

2. Select the **second frame**. Select the layer containing the shadow and set the opacity to **50%** in the Layers palette.

3. Step through the animation. The layer changes opacity across frames. This is a frame-specific edit.

4. Select the **Paintbrush** tool and set the foreground color to **black**, if necessary. In the layer containing the snowman, add **three coal buttons** to the front center of the snowman. This is a global change and affects all frames that display this layer.

5. Click **File** on the menu bar, click **Save Optimized As** to save the animation to your Chapter 9 project folder as **snowman.gif**, and then close snowman.gif and shadow.gif.

Figure 9-8 shows the Animation and Layers palette with these new changes.

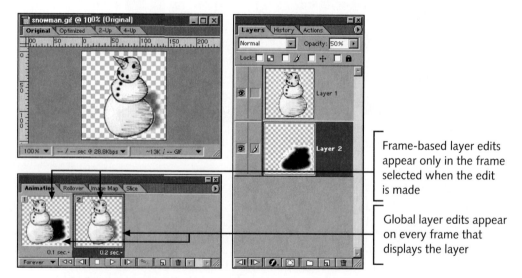

Figure 9-8 Global and frame-based changes

Frame-based layer edits appear only in the frame selected when the edit is made

Global layer edits appear on every frame that displays the layer

Editing Existing Animations

A good way to practice using the different animation features of ImageReady is to open and edit existing files. You can edit animated GIFs, QuickTime movies, and Photoshop images with multiple layers.

To open an animated GIF, click File on the menu bar and then click Open. The animation opens with a set of frames and layers where each layer corresponds to one frame. The visibility for all layers is turned off except for the corresponding frame, as shown in Figure 9-9. Frame 1 uses only the first layer, frame 2 uses only the second layer, and so on.

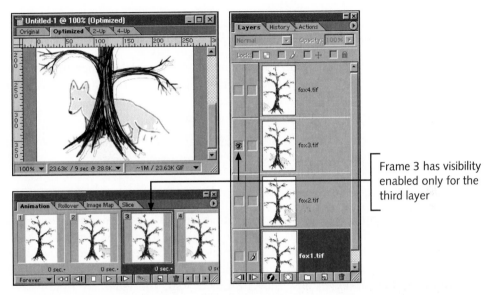

Figure 9-9   Selective visibility for individual frames

You also can create animated GIFs from Photoshop images that have multiple layers. In this situation, the Animation palette shows only one frame and the Layers palette shows all the layers or individual images. To convert these layers to animation frames, select Make Frames From Layers in the Animation palette menu. This creates one frame for each layer in the Layers menu, using the bottom layer as the first frame.

Additionally, you can create animations from folders of individual images. The images can be in any format. To import a folder of separate images, first place all the images for the animation in a folder. The images will be inserted into the Animation palette in alphabetical order, so name the images accordingly. You will get better results if the images are already sized identically. If the source images are of different sizes, the dimensions of the animation will be based on the dimensions of the first frame, and all other frames will be cropped or padded accordingly.

To import a folder of separate images:

1. In ImageReady, click **File** on the menu bar, point to **Import**, and then click **Folder as Frames**. Find and select the folder named **fox** on the Data Disk. Four image files are opened, appearing as four separate layers in the Layers palette. Four frames also are generated in the Animation palette, with each frame corresponding to one layer.

2. Step through the animation, noting the visibility icons in the Layers palette. For each frame, all layers are invisible except the associated layer.

3. Click **File** on the menu bar, and then click **Save Optimized As** to save the animation to your Chapter 9 project folder as **foxy.gif**.

CREATING ANIMATIONS WITH IMAGEREADY

Many programs can create GIF animation files. Most of these programs work by importing a folder of discrete files, as described in the previous section. ImageReady also allows you to create an animation from a single image file. To do so, duplicate the original frame and make frame-based changes to each new frame.

Whether you use ImageReady or another program, GIF animation allows you to set the duration of frames and to set how often the animation repeats.

Controlling the Timing of Animations

What makes animations different from static images is that an animation contains multiple images, appearing as separate frames. For each frame, you can adjust how long the images appear. Showing each frame for a few seconds creates a slide show; showing each frame for a fraction of a second creates the illusion of motion. Animated GIFs differ from traditional animations in how they are timed. Film and video are time-based and have strict frame rates that dictate how many frames are displayed in a second, and each frame appears only once.

In contrast, GIF animation is frame-based—each frame can appear for a different duration. The length of a GIF animation is set not only by the number of frames, but also by the display duration of each frame and the number of times the frame sequence repeats. For example, a two-frame animation where each frame appears for half a second creates a one-second animation. Adding two more frames and lengthening the display duration to one second per frame creates a four-second animation.

Adjusting the Delay

Film and video use a standard frame rate that affects all frames equally. Each frame of film appears on the screen for $\frac{1}{24}$ of a second, and each frame of video appears for $\frac{1}{30}$ of a second. Unlike film and video, the frames of a GIF animation can each have a different display time. You could set one frame to appear for $\frac{1}{100}$ of a second and another frame to appear for a few minutes.

The delay setting for each frame appears at the bottom of the frame below the thumbnail image in the Animation palette. Times are listed in seconds and fractions of seconds, which are shown as decimals. Select a frame or set of frames and click the delay value under one of the frames to open the Frame Delay menu, shown in Figure 9-10. The current delay time appears at the bottom of the list.

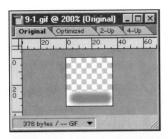

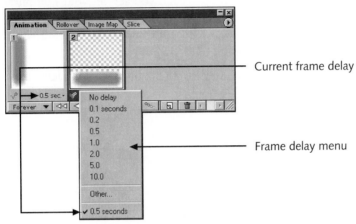

Current frame delay

Frame delay menu

Figure 9-10   Changing the frame delay

To change the frame delay:

1. Open **9-1.gif** from the Data Disk.

2. Click the **delay value** below frame 1 in the Animation palette. This displays the Frame Delay shortcut menu.

3. Click **5.0** to set the delay to five seconds. This corresponds to the length of time you want frame 1 to appear. You can select one of the preset times, No Delay, or Other to open the Set Frame Delay dialog box where you can enter another time.

4. Set the delay of the second frame to **2.0** seconds. Each frame in an animation can have a different delay.

5. Play the animation. The delay is so long that there is no appearance of motion.

6. Click **File** on the menu bar, and then click **Save Optimized As** to save the animation to your Chapter 9 project folder as **9-1a.gif**, and then close the image.

Delay times are set in increments of 1/100 of a second. The longest possible delay is 240 seconds, which equals four minutes. You seldom need to use such a long delay.

You could set each frame to delay for 0.03 seconds, which would result in a frame rate of 30 frames per second—equal to the frame rate for video. In this way, you can simulate standard video using GIF animation. However, to display even one second of video this way requires using an enormous file that would take a long time to download.

The shortest delay possible is No Delay. This means the computer displays the animation as quickly as it can. The speed of the playback then depends on the memory and processor speed of the computer on which it is played, rather than on your settings. If you choose this option, be aware that the playback you see on your computer does not always match what others see on their computers. If your computer is slow, the animation might play at an appropriate speed. But when a user views the animation in a Web page on a fast computer, it will play too fast.

You should always preview your animations in a Web browser. The delay times may not be accurate when viewing them in ImageReady.

Adjusting the Number of Loops

You can set the animation so that the sequence of frames plays only once, repeats indefinitely, or repeats for a set number of times.

Specify the looping of the animation by clicking the Looping list arrow in the lower-left corner of the Animation palette, as shown in Figure 9-11.

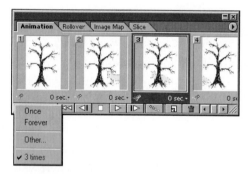

Figure 9-11   Looping options

Select Once to play the animation only one time. When finished, the last frame remains on-screen like a static image. Select Forever to repeat the animation indefinitely. In a Web browser, the animation will loop until someone clicks the browser's Stop button. Select Other to open the Set Loop Count dialog box. Enter the number of times you want the animation to repeat. The number of loops does not affect the size of the animation file.

The looping feature affects the entire animation—if you set the animation to loop once, it plays the entire sequence, from the first frame to the last, and then starts again with the first frame. Looping does not repeat individual frames or groups of frames within the sequence. To repeat frames within an animation, duplicate the frames and drag them to the proper position in the sequence. Although the information is duplicated, this still increases the animation file size.

To change the frame delay:

1. Open **foxy.gif** if it is not still open.

2. Click the **Looping** list arrow in the lower-left corner of the Animation palette, and select **Other**.

3. In the Set Loop Count dialog box, type **3** to specify that you want to play the animation three times and then stop.

4. Play the animation. It should cycle through three times, and then stop on the last frame.

5. Click **File** on the menu bar, and then click **Save Optimized As** to save the animation to your Chapter 9 project folder as **foxy_a.gif**, and then close the animation.

Using Frame Animation

The simplest type of GIF animation uses one image for each frame. In ImageReady, this is represented by a sequence of frames and a stack of layers where each frame corresponds to one layer and vice-versa. You can see this whenever you open an animated GIF in ImageReady.

Although the final animation will resemble a simple frame animation, with a different layer for each frame, you can reuse layers across multiple frames. You can create an entire animation out of a single layer by changing the position, opacity, or effects of the layer across multiple frames.

To create an animation using a single layer:

1. In ImageReady, open **ball.gif** from the Data Disk. This file contains one frame in the Animation palette and one layer in the Layers palette. Figure 9-12 shows the appearance of the Animation and Layers palettes.

2. In the Animation palette menu, deselect **Add Layer To New Frames**. You do not need any additional layers.

3. Click the **Animation palette menu arrow**, and click **Copy Frame**.

4. Click the **menu arrow** again, and choose **Paste Frame**. In the Paste Frames dialog box, click the **Paste After Selection** option button. Repeat this step to duplicate the frame. You should have three identical frames, but only one layer in the Layers palette.

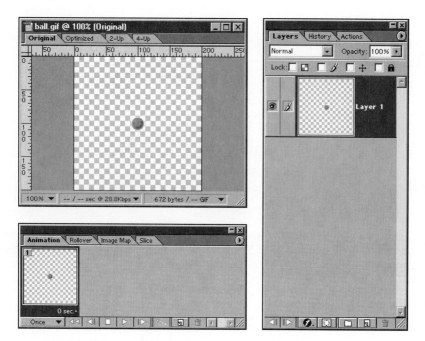

Figure 9-12 The Animation and Layers palettes before frame animation

5. Select the **first frame**, and then use the Move tool to drag the **ball** in the Image window to the top edge of the image area. This does not affect the position of the layer in the other frames.

6. Select the **third frame** and drag the **ball** to the bottom edge of the image area.

7. Select the **second frame** and drag the **ball** to about one-third from the bottom edge of the image area.

8. Duplicate the second frame, and then drag the **new frame** to the right of the Animation palette. The Animation palette should look like the one in Figure 9-13.

9. Click the **Play** button to see the ball bounce up and down in the image area.

10. Select the **first frame** again and set the opacity of the layer to **33%** in the Layers palette.

11. Select the **second** and **fourth frames** and set the opacity to **67%**.

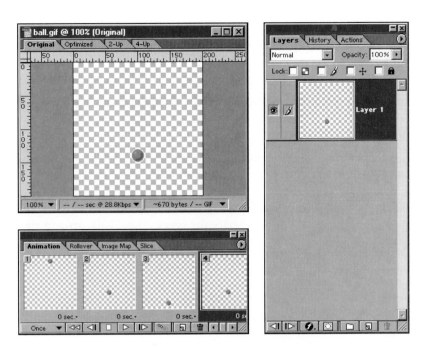

Figure 9-13   The Animation palette during frame animation

12. Click the **Play** button again to see the object fade in as it moves through the image area. The Animation palette should look like the one in Figure 9-14.

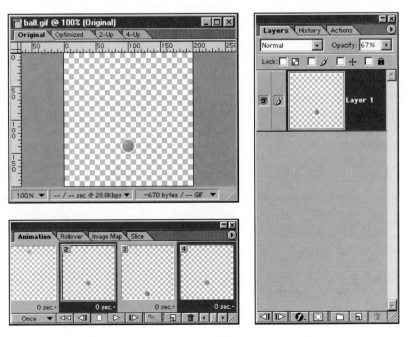

Figure 9-14   The Animation palette after frame animation

13. Click **File** on the menu bar, then click **Save Optimized As** to save the animation to your Chapter 9 project folder as **bounce.gif**, and then close the animation.

You can move single layers, or adjust opacity for single frames, but you cannot transform (scale, rotate, etc.) a layer without affecting every frame that calls it.

Tweening

Just as you manually modified position and opacity of a single layer across frames in the previous example, you can automatically modify multiple layers across frames with the **Tween** command. Tween is short for "in betweening," which is creating the intermediary frames that appear between two existing frames. For example, instead of having to manually position a layer and set the opacity for every frame, you can save time by making the adjustments for just the first and last frame and have ImageReady calculate the necessary frames between the first and last.

Use the Tween command to add or modify frames between two existing frames. Then set the position, opacity, or effect of the tweened frames to create the appearance of movement. For example, if you want to fade out a layer, set the opacity of the layer in the first frame to 100%; then set the opacity of the same layer in the last frame to 0%. When you tween between the two frames, the opacity of the layer is reduced evenly across the new frames.

The two existing frames are called **keyframes**, and act as reference points for the tweened frames. For example, you use tweened frames to fade out from one existing frame and then fade in to the next. You can apply the Tween command to a single frame, a set of frames, or any pair of adjacent frames. You also can tween the last and first frame, which are considered adjacent since the first frame follows the last frame when the animation loops. You cannot tween nonadjacent frames.

Tweening takes all the layer settings of the two keyframes and creates new frames between the keyframes, using an average of the keyframe settings. The new frames take the delay setting of the earlier frame. See Figure 9-15 for an example of tweening. In frame 1, the purple ball is at 50% opacity and is in the upper-left of the image. The black ball is at 100% opacity and is near the lower-left of the image. In frame 4, the balls are in opposite corners and their opacities have changed. Frames 1 and 4 are the keyframes. Frames 2 and 3 are tweened between the keyframes and modify the layers to show the intermediate positions and opacities of the layers. If one frame uses a layer with 100% opacity, and the next frame uses a different layer with 100% opacity, a tweened frame would use both layers at 50% opacity.

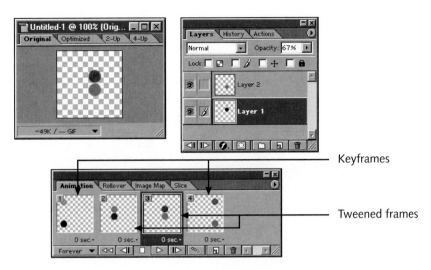

Figure 9-15   Tweening

Tweening adds frames to the animation, and increases the file size accordingly. Once you add frames by tweening, you can edit them like any other frames.

To use the Tween command:

1. In ImageReady, open **ball.gif** from the Data Disk.

2. Duplicate the frame in the Animation palette.

3. In the first frame, position the ball in the upper-left. In the second frame, position the ball in the lower-right. These are your keyframes.

4. Click the **Tween** button in the Animation palette or select **Tween** from the Animation palette menu. The Tween dialog box opens, as shown in Figure 9-16.

5. Make sure the All Layers option button is selected to include all layers visible in the keyframes. You also could click the Selected Layer option button to include only the currently selected layer. As there is only one layer, the choice does not matter here.

6. Make sure the Position, Opacity, and Effects boxes are checked. Selecting Position changes the position of layers across frames. Selecting Opacity fades layers in or out across frames. Selecting Effects has layer styles fade in or out. Here, only the position of the layer changes between the two frames, so tweening the opacity and effects will not affect the animation.

7. The Tween With text box can show First Frame or Previous Frame. In general, use this option to select whether to use the preceding or following frame as the other keyframe. If you already have both frames selected, you will not be given a choice here.

8. For Frames to Add, enter **3** to indicate the number of frames you want created between the selected keyframes.

9. Play the animation. You see the ball move smoothly from one corner to the other.

10. Click **File** on the menu bar, and then click **Save Optimized As** to save the animation to your Chapter 9 project folder as **bounce2.gif**, and then close the animation.

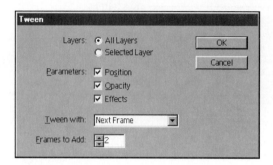

Figure 9-16   The Tween dialog box

OPTIMIZING AND SAVING ANIMATIONS

Animated GIF images are effectively multiple images in one file. An animation's file size can easily be several times larger than a similar static image with the same dimensions and color depth. Just as you can optimize a Web graphic by reducing extraneous colors from the color table, you also can optimize animated GIF images by reducing extraneous information that affects the animation. It is as important to optimize animated images as it is to optimize static ones, perhaps more so because animated image files can become very large. You can optimize animated GIF images the same way as normal GIFs, and use additional options specific to animations, including setting the frame disposal method and using the Bounding Box option.

Setting the Frame Disposal Method

When an animation plays, each frame appears in succession. The new frame either completely replaces the previous frame, or it covers only part of it so that other parts of the previous frame show through. Hold down the Ctrl key and click a frame (right-click in Windows) to display the Disposal Method shortcut menu, as shown in Figure 9-17. Here you can set an option called the **frame disposal method** for each frame. An icon under the frame indicates the method chosen for that frame. Select a disposal method when working with layers that include transparency. This specifies whether the current frame will be visible through the transparent areas of the following frames.

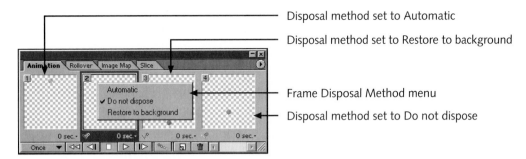

Figure 9-17   The Disposal Method shortcut menu

You can set the frame disposal method either to Restore to Background or to Do Not Dispose. In the first case, the new frame completely replaces the old one. In the second case, the new frame covers only part of the previous frame, allowing areas of the previous frame to show through the transparent areas of the new frame. Completely restoring frames results in larger files because the animation requires a full-size area for each frame. Choosing Do Not Dispose allows the animation to reuse parts of previous frames. This can result in smaller files.

In ImageReady you also can set the disposal method to Automatic, which finds the best combination of disposing and not disposing. You create the smallest files when not disposing frames, slightly larger files with the automatic method, and still larger files when restoring every frame. The drawback to not disposing frames is that information from previous frames might show through. The Automatic setting is required for the automated optimization in ImageReady.

To choose a disposal method, select one or more frames. Hold down the Ctrl key and click the frame for which you want to set a disposal method (right-click in Windows). You see the Disposal Method shortcut menu. Select one of the three options according to the following descriptions:

- The **Automatic** method disposes of the current frame if the next frame contains transparency, and keeps the current frame if the next layer is completely opaque. For most animations, this method produces good results.

- The **Do Not Dispose** method keeps the current frame and displays it through the transparent areas of the next frame.

- The **Restore to Background** method disposes of the current frame and displays the next frame over the background color.

To set the disposal method:

1. Open **ball.gif** from the Data Disk.

2. Duplicate the frame. Position the ball on the left in **frame 1** and position it on the right in **frame 2**.

3. Open the **Disposal Method context menu** for frame 1 (Ctrl+click in Mac, right-click in Windows).

4. Set the disposal method to **Do not dispose**.

5. Play the animation in ImageReady. You should not see any difference between the two frames.

6. Preview the animation in a browser. You should see the ball stay in place on the left and blink on and off on the right. The first frame is not disposed, and remains visible even when the next frame is shown.

7. Set the disposal method for the first frame to **Restore to background**. Set the disposal method for the second frame to **Do not dispose**.

8. Preview the animation in a browser. Each frame should appear in turn. Although the last frame is set to Do not dispose, all frames are disposed at the end of a loop, leaving an empty background when frame 1 appears again.

9. Make sure the Transparency box is checked in the Optimize palette, click **File** on the menu bar, and then click **Save Optimized As** to save the animation to your Chapter 9 project folder as **bounce3.gif**.

To take advantage of the different disposal types, use transparency when possible, and use only opaque pixels for new information and for blocking pixels in previous frames. For example, in Figure 9-18 you can see that in the second frame, eveything is transparent except for the new information and a small area that masks the information from the previous frame.

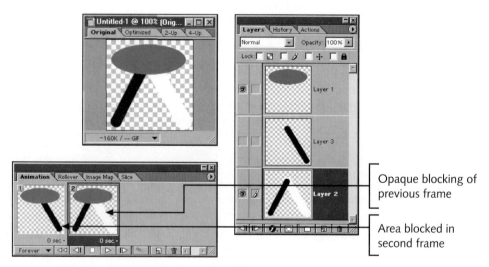

Figure 9-18   Blocking areas in layers

ImageReady does not show the results of not disposing of the frames. You must preview the animation in a browser to see how it is affected.

Optimizing Animations

You can optimize the layers of an animation the same way you would optimize any other image—by adjusting the settings in the Optimize palette to reduce colors or to set compression. You can also optimize frames to include only the areas that change between frames.

To optimize an animated image:

1. Open **bounce3.gif** if it is not still open.

2. In the Optimize palette, select the setting named **GIF 32 Dithered**.

3. From the Animation palette window, select **Optimize Animation**. This opens the Optimize Animation dialog box, as shown in Figure 9-19.

4. In the Optimize Animation dialog box that appears, check both the **Bounding Box** and the **Redundant Pixel Removal box**.

5. Click **File** on the menu bar, and then click **Save Optimized As** to save the animation to your Chapter 9 project folder as **bounce3a.gif**.

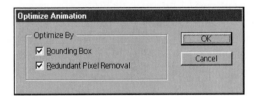

Figure 9-19   The Optimize Animation dialog box

Selecting the Bounding Box option trims each frame to the area that is different from the previous frame, and then displays a background color in place of the similar pixels. This helps reduce the file size of the finished animation. You can see the bounding box of an image by selecting the Move tool, and then selecting Show Bounding Box in the Options bar. You see a dashed line around the foreground pixels in an image. The bounding box is shown in Figure 9-20.

The Redundant Pixel Removal option takes all pixels that are identical between frames and makes them transparent. The frame disposal method must be set to Automatic for this option to have an effect. Removing redundant pixels eliminates unnecessary image data from the animation, creating a smaller file.

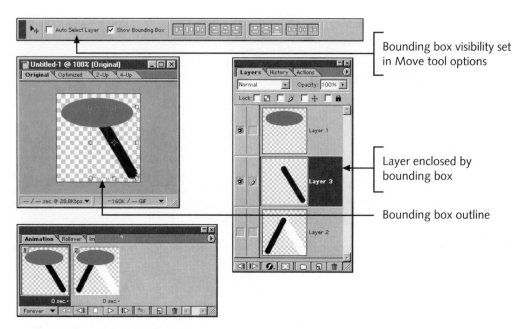

Figure 9-20   Bounding Box option

After optimizing the animation this way, use the Optimize palette to optimize the image as you would any other. Reduce the color and use dithering where appropriate. For most editing, you should use the Original view in the Image window because you can use all the layer-editing tools in this view. In the Optimize view, you can see the effects of different optimization settings, but some layer-editing tools are disabled.

When optimizing, make sure to use the Perceptual, Adaptive, or Selective color reduction method. This guarantees consistent color across the frames of the animation. Make sure also to use the GIF format optimization. Only GIF files support the animation discussed here, so optimizing the animation as a JPEG or PNG precludes the image from being used as an animation.

Designers used to optimize each frame individually, using a separate palette for each frame, and dither each frame slightly differently. This resulted in an unsightly flickering effect that detracted from the quality of the animation. Fortunately, in ImageReady there is only one palette used for all frames, and the dithering is automatically kept consistent across frames.

Saving Animations

You can save your animations as animated GIFs, QuickTime movies, or Photoshop files.

To save the file as an animated GIF, select Save Optimized As from the File menu and enter a filename. You can then use the image in a Web page as you would any other image.

In the HTML code, reference the image with an IMG tag. You can even use animated GIFs as background images, although this makes any text on the page difficult to read.

To save an animation as a QuickTime movie, select Export Original from the File menu to open the Export Original dialog box. Then click the Save as type list arrow and click QuickTime Movie. QuickTime must be installed on your computer for this option to work. Select a name and location, and adjust the compression settings. You can view the QuickTime movie in a special viewing application or in a browser that has the QuickTime plug-in installed. You also can import the animation into applications such as AfterEffects that support QuickTime.

Once the movie is in the QuickTime format, you can use software such as AfterEffects or Sparkle to convert the animation to other formats, such as MPEG. Users can view QuickTime movies in their browsers, but only if they have the proper plug-in installed. If they do not have the plug-in, they can download the movie and play it using any of a variety of free and commercial animation software.

You also can save the animation as a simple Photoshop (PSD) file. You cannot view the image in a browser, but you can preserve all layers and frames if you need to postpone completion of the project. Select Flatten Frames into Layers from the Animation palette menu. This creates a composite layer for each frame, containing all the layers visible for the frame.

9

Using Animation on the Web

Animated images can make a Web page dynamic without requiring interaction from the user. However, because animated images usually require a longer download time than do their static counterparts, you should use them only when the animation is necessary. For example, a good time to use an animated image is when you already have many colored images on a page and need to have one image in particular stand out from the rest. However, you use too many animated images, they will reduce the emphasis of the actual content of the page.

Animated images also draw more attention than do still images, which makes them distracting to some viewers. Animated GIFs are the graphical equivalent of the BLINK tag in HTML. Both flash and are very eye-catching, yet quickly become a nuisance. To avoid annoying your users, limit your animations to no more than one or two per page.

Creating Animated Icons

A colored graphical bullet has more impact than a bullet created in HTML. Similarly, an icon with the word "New!" has more impact than a bullet without any text. If you need bullets to draw attention to a specific piece of text, consider using an animated bullet.

A common animated bullet is an arrow pointing to the right, indicating that certain text is important. You should use such a bullet only when the text being emphasized is so important that merely a bright icon is insufficient. Use an animated bullet to guarantee that the user notices it.

Creating News Bulletins

You can create a type of news ticker with an animated GIF that displays headlines of news items in a rectangle on a page, and then updates those items every few seconds, cycling through all the frames. This is an effective way to display dynamic content that changes over time without having to use client-side programming such as JavaScript.

Create an animated GIF with at least two frames of text over a background. Set each frame to delay for four or five seconds—longer for a lot of text. Each frame should be different, so dispose of the frames to the background. However, when working with text you can use very low color depth, which results in small files. For simple black-and-white text, you can use one-bit color depth. For smooth, anti-aliased text, use two- or three-bit color depth.

Graphical news tickers are not often used because when the text is changed a new image file must be created. However, if you do not have the resources to implement a Java- or DHTML-based news ticker, this is a simple, effective solution.

Creating Banner Ads

Perhaps the most common use of animated GIF images is in advertising. Most commercial Web pages display a banner ad at the top of the page, and often use smaller ads on the side. In the mid-1990s there were no standards for advertising on the Web, but now all advertisers and sites that display advertising agree on at least some standards. Some of these standards still vary from site to site, but consistent standards make it easier to measure the value of ads. These standards are discussed in the following sections.

Advertising on Web sites should be prominent so that users see the ad. The advertiser also should be confident that the message is clear. On the other hand, if the ad is too visible and eye-catching, it will draw attention away from the content of the page.

Web sites usually develop a list of constraints for advertisements that limit the impact of the ads. The designers who work for advertising companies then have to create attractive, sophisticated ads that do not violate the parameters set by the hosting Web site.

Using Conventional Dimensions

There are several standard sizes for Web ads, but the most common is the banner ad, which is always 468 pixels wide and 60 pixels high. Web designers agreed on this size because on a standard 72-dpi monitor the ad appears as 6½ inches wide and ⅚ of an inch high. If the Web page is printed on a standard 8½ × 11-inch sheet of paper, the entire ad prints even if the page has a one-inch margin.

Most Web pages are about 600 pixels wide, which leaves enough room for a 1½-inch logo and a standard banner ad across the top of the page.

Another common standard is for the half-banner ad, which is 234 pixels wide and 60 pixels high. Some sites display two half banners across the top of the page instead of one full one.

A common size for ads positioned on the side of a page is 125 pixels square. Many commercial sites use the convention of placing a column along the left side of their pages to contain navigation elements. A common size for these columns is 125 pixels because it is wide enough to display a few words on the same line, but not so wide that it interferes with the appearance of content in the main area of the page. Ads for these columns need to be 125 pixels wide in order to fit.

Constraining File Size

The sites that display ads shoulder the burden for the file size of advertisements. Even if the ad is loaded from a server other than the one that serves the Web page, the contents of the page might not render completely until the ads have finished downloading.

Sites that accept advertising usually limit the size of ads to about 15 K. Files this size take about six seconds to download using a 28.8 Kbps modem. Ads with larger file sizes take longer to load, and further delay the display of the actual page content. This 15 K size constraint forces designers to optimize their animations and be prudent about the amount of animation and effects they include. Some sites require that ads be as small as 12 or even 10 K.

Limiting Visual Impact

Another concern for sites that host ads is how the presence of the ads affects their own page design and layout. It can be frustrating for Web designers to create a unified color scheme and style, only to have it dominated by an ad at the top of the page that uses conflicting colors, sometimes producing a garish effect. In some cases, the ad is the most colorful element on the page and the only animated one. When this occurs, readers are often distracted from the actual content of the page. Users also can find animated ads annoying, and avoid sites that use too many of them.

To control the flashiness of ads, many Web sites place restrictions on animation in advertisements. A common restriction is on the amount of looping. Some sites allow only one loop per ad; some allow up to three or four loops. Because your ad might loop only once or a few times, be sure to place all relevant information in the last frame. For example, show the name of the product being advertised and the URL of the site. This way, when the animation freezes on the final frame, it still provides important information. Set a longer delay for the final frame than for the other frames. While the ad loops, users need time to read the text you placed there. A general rule of thumb is to allow one second for each line of text, and a delay of one to two seconds for the final frame of a banner ad.

Some sites also restrict the number of frames in an ad to four or five. This forces the designer to use just a few frames with long delays rather than many frames with short delays. This also results in less flashy ads.

Evaluating the Effectiveness of Banner Ads

Web ads are sold in blocks of a thousand, at a rate determined by the Web site that is paid to display the ads. Ad rates are measured in **CPM**s, which stands for "cost per mille" or "cost per thousand." CPMs can range from $1 to over $100 per thousand ads displayed. This means that displaying a single ad can cost as little as a tenth of a penny or as much as a dime.

Web advertising is less expensive than most other forms of advertising because creating and displaying an animated GIF is much simpler than creating a radio or TV spot, or a full-page glossy ad for a magazine. However, advertisers still need to know if their investment is worth the cost.

The way to measure the effectiveness of an ad on the Web is to measure the **click-through-rate** (**CTR**) of the ad. If 1000 people visit a Web page which displays a particular ad, and ten people click the ad, then the CTR for that ad is 10/1000 or 1%.

In the early days of the Web, CTRs were sometimes as high as 25%, meaning that one out of four people clicked ads. In the late 1990s, average CTRs decreased to 1% or 2% as people began ignoring banner ads. Today the average CTR is under 1%. Some use this to argue that advertising on the Web is a waste of money. However, even if people do not click the ad, they still see it and are aware of it to some degree. Advertising on the Web is becoming more like advertising in traditional media such as magazines or television. In these media, viewers generally cannot interact with an ad, and an ad provides branding instead of an actual link. The same is true for Web ads.

Using Banner-Swapping Services

Most people with small Web sites cannot afford to buy advertising on larger sites, and cannot display ads themselves because their sites are not well-trafficked. This creates a problem because the owners of the sites cannot advertise their products or services. One solution is to use a link exchange service. These services are usually free and provide a way to promote small Web sites. Small Web sites agree to display other sites' banner ads on their site, and the other sites do the same. In addition to promoting a site, banner ads can add authority to that Web site. A site without advertisements may be cleaner and more attractive, but a site with ads is clearly business-oriented. Displaying banner ads on your site can help distinguish your site from the many nonprofessional personal Web pages. Link exchange services also let you test different ad prototypes to see which have the highest CTR. You then can introduce high-CTR ads into paid campaigns without having to guess whether they will be successful.

CHAPTER SUMMARY

❏ Animated Web graphics have four dimensions: width, height, (color) depth, and time.

❏ GIF animation displays a sequence of GIF images collected into one file. In ImageReady, you assign each image to a frame and organize the frames into a sequence.

❏ GIF animation has advantages over other formats because it does not require special plug-ins or coding to be displayed on Web pages.

❏ In ImageReady, each frame displays a combination of available layers. Each layer may be visible in multiple frames.

❏ Unlike most other animation formats, GIF animation is frame-based, not time-based.

❏ You can adjust the delay of each frame individually, and adjust how many times the sequence repeats.

❏ The frames and layers in an animation can be optimized like any other GIF image. You can optimize the animation by eliminating pixels that repeat across frames.

❏ Animation can easily be overused in Web pages; you should be discreet and use animation only when it serves a purpose.

❏ Most sites that accept advertising have strict guidelines about the banner ads they display.

9

REVIEW QUESTIONS

1. What would be an appropriate format to use if you had to have 30 fps photographic-quality video?

   a. Flash

   b. GIF

   c. JPEG

   d. MPEG

2. Which format is not vector-based?

   a. Flash

   b. Java

   c. ShockWave

   d. Streaming Video

3. Which frame rate creates the most flicker?

   a. 2 fps

   b. 15 fps

   c. 24 fps

   d. 30 fps

4. What animation format does not require a browser plug-in or separate viewing application?

   a. Flash

   b. GIF

   c. MPEG

   d. QuickTime

5. Which of the following sentences about creating animations in ImageReady is true?

   a. Duplicating a frame adds a new frame and new layers.

   b. Duplicating a frame adds a new frame but cannot add new layers.

   c. Pasting a frame adds a new frame and new layers.

   d. Pasting a frame adds a new frame but cannot add new layers.

6. What is NOT a reason to preview animations in a Web browser?

   a. Previewing in ImageReady does not always accurately display animation looping.

   b. Previewing in ImageReady does not always accurately display frame delay.

   c. Previewing in ImageReady does not display frame disposal.

   d. Previewing in ImageReady does not display optimization information.

7. What is NOT a way to prevent the contents of a layer from being displayed as part of an animation frame?

   a. Delete the layer.

   b. Deselect the layer.

   c. Deselect the visibility icon in the layer.

   d. Set the opacity of the layer to 0%.

8. Which of the following layer changes affect all frames that call the layer and cannot be used to animate across frames?

   a. Layer styles

   b. Opacity

   c. Position

   d. Scale

9. To what does frame delay refer?

    a. It is another name for frame rate.

    b. The number of frames per second

    c. The number of loops per second

    d. The number of seconds per frame

10. What is the fastest frame rate possible with GIF animation?

    a. 30 fps

    b. 72 fps

    c. 100 fps

    d. The processing speed of the computer

11. What is tweening?

    a. Duplicating keyframes and placing the new keyframes in between the new frames

    b. Duplicating intermediate layers

    c. Combining layers by averaging their settings

    d. Creating new frames that show the same layers as the keyframes, and then averaging the layer settings

12. What optimization settings are permitted for GIF animations?

    a. GIF only

    b. GIF or JPEG

    c. GIF or PNG

    d. GIF or PNG-8

13. Which frame disposal method produces the smallest files?

    a. Automatic

    b. Bounding Box

    c. Do not Dispose

    d. Restore to Background

14. What frame disposal method must you use to use the redundant pixel removal optimization?

    a. Automatic

    b. Bounding Box

    c. Do not Dispose

    d. Restore to Background

9

15. What color reduction method should you use when optimizing animated GIFs?
    a. Diffusion
    b. Perceptual, Selective, or Adaptive
    c. System colors
    d. Web palette

16. How do you display an animated GIF image in a Web page?
    a. By streaming the animation file
    b. With a browser plug-in
    c. With a separate image-viewing application
    d. With a standard IMG tag in HTML

17. What is an appropriate frame delay for graphical news tickers?
    a. Half a second per frame
    b. One second per frame
    c. Two seconds per frame
    d. Four seconds per frame

18. What are the dimensions of conventional banner ads?
    a. 460 × 68
    b. 468 × 60
    c. 480 × 60
    d. 488 × 68

19. What is NOT a typical constraint placed on banner ads?
    a. No larger than 12 K
    b. No looping
    c. No more than four frames
    d. No transparency

20. What is a typical click through rate (CTR) for banner ads?
    a. Below 0.1%
    b. Below 1%
    c. Below 10%
    d. Below 25%

HANDS-ON PROJECTS

Project 1: Creating an Animation from Multiple Images

You have a 3-D modeling and animation program that exports separate files for each frame of the animation. Collect these files and create an animated GIF from them.

Complete these steps:

1. On your hard drive, create a new folder named **project_9-1**.
2. In ImageReady, click **File** on the menu bar, point to **Import**, and then click **Folder as Frames**. In the Browse dialog box, locate and select the **cube** folder on the Data Disk and then click **OK**. This creates three frames and three layers in a new ImageReady file.
3. Select **frame 1** and make sure that the visibility icon is showing for only the bottom layer in the Layers palette.
4. Select **frame 2** and make sure the visibility icon is showing for only the middle layer.
5. Select **frame 3** and make sure the visibility icon is showing for only the top layer.
6. Make sure the Looping Option is set to Forever.
7. Select all **three frames** and set the delay value to **0.1** seconds.
8. In the Optimize palette, select the preset named **GIF 128 No Dither**.
9. Open the Animation palette menu and click **Optimize Animation**. Check both boxes in the Optimize Animation dialog box, if necessary, and click **OK**.
10. Preview the animation in a browser to check the optimization and speed.
11. Click the **File** menu, and then select **Save Optimized As**.
12. Save the animation as **cube.gif** in the project_9-1 folder.

Project 2: Animating Multiple Layers

Create an animation of a jittery house from a file with multiple layers.

Complete these steps:

1. In ImageReady, open image file **house.psd** from the Data Disk.
2. Create two new frames. Make sure the visibility for all layers is turned on for all frames.
3. Select **frame 1**. Select the layer named **door** and in the Image window, move it near the lower-left of the yellow square.
4. Move the **window** layer near the center-right of the yellow square. Move the **roof** layer near the top-center of the yellow square.

9

5. Select **frames 2** and **3** and repeat the process described in Step 4. Do not worry about placing the elements exactly as you did for frame 1. In frame 3, place the elements so that their edges line up exactly with the edges of the yellow square.

6. Select **all frames** and set the delay value to **0.1** seconds.

7. Set the looping to **5** times.

8. In the Optimize palette, select the preset named **GIF 64 No Dither**.

9. Open the Animation palette menu, click **Optimize Animation**, and accept both options.

10. Preview the animation in a browser to check the optimization and speed.

11. Click the **File** menu, and then select **Save Optimized As**.

12. Save the animation as **house.gif** in a new folder named **project_9-2**.

Project 3: Creating a Fading Text Animation

You want to animate a simple text image, but it needs to fade in and out, rather than move. You could use the BLINK tag in HTML, but you want a more subtle effect.

Complete these steps:

1. In ImageReady, create an image that is **125** pixels wide and **50** pixels high.

2. Use the Type tool to add the text **E-Mail Us!** in blue using a bold serif font, and using a size that fits within the image.

3. Click the **New Frame** button to duplicate the frame.

4. Select the **second frame** and set the opacity of the text layer to **40%**.

5. Click the **Tween** button. In the Tween dialog box, select **All Layers** and make sure Opacity is selected. Set the Tween with option to **Previous Frame**. Set Frames to Add to **2**.

6. Click **OK**. Two new frames are added that display the same layer at 80% and 60% opacity.

7. Select the **two middle frames** and click the **New Frame** button to duplicate the frames.

8. Drag these **new frames** to the far right of the Animation palette, reversing their order. The opacity of the frames should be, in order: 100%, 80%, 60%, 40%, 60%, 80%.

9. Select **all the frames** and set the delay value to **0.2** seconds.

10. In the Optimize palette, set the format to **GIF**, the Colors to **8**, and the dither to **Diffusion**.

11. In the Animation palette menu, select **Optimize Animation** and accept both options.

12. Preview the animation in a Web browser and make any changes, if necessary.

13. Click **File** on the menu bar, click **Save Optimized As**, and save the animation as **email.gif** in a new folder named **project_9-3**.

Project 4: Creating a Rotating Animation

You want to create another simple animation. This one will rotate rather than change position, so you need multiple layers.

Complete these steps:

1. In ImageReady, open image file **lightbulb.tif** from the Data Disk.
2. Duplicate the background layer and name the new layer **lightbulb 1**.
3. Create a new layer behind it and name this layer **glow**.
4. Set the foreground color to **pure yellow (#ffff00)**.
5. Select the **Paintbrush** tool and select a **feathered brush** of about **65** pixels in diameter.
6. Click once in the center of the glow layer to create a yellow spot behind the lightbulb image.
7. Select **Layer 1** in the Layers palette.
8. Click **Edit** on the menu bar, point to **Transform**, and then click **Rotate**. A transformation box appears around the lightbulb image.
9. Drag the **anchor point** so that it is over the center of the yellow spot.
10. Drag a **corner tab** of the transformation box to rotate the lightbulb image by about 10 degrees. Double-click **inside the box** to set the transformation.
11. Select the layer named **lightbulb 1** in the Layers palette and rotate it the same way as you did in Step 10, but in the opposite direction.
12. Create a new frame.
13. Select the **first frame** and deselect the **visibility icon** for the Layer 1 layer.
14. Select the **second frame** and deselect the **visibility icon** for the lightbulb 1 layer.
15. Click the **Play** button in the Animation palette. The lightbulb image swings back and forth centered around the yellow glow.
16. Select **both frames** and set the delay value to **0.3** seconds.
17. In the Optimize palette, select the preset named **GIF 64 No Dither**.
18. In the Animation palette menu, select **Optimize Animation** and accept both options.
19. Click **File** on the menu bar, click **Save Optimized As** and save the animation as **idea.gif** in a new folder named **project_9-4**.

Project 5: Simulating Acceleration

You want an animation of a ball bouncing, but you want it to accelerate as it rises and falls. You need to adjust the frames and layers to simulate acceleration.

Complete these steps:

1. In ImageReady, open image file **ball.gif** from the Data Disk.

9

2. Use the Move tool in the Image window to drag the **ball** to the bottom of the image.

3. Duplicate the frame in the Animation palette.

4. Select the **second frame** and use the Move tool to drag the **ball** to the top of the image.

5. Click the **Tween** button and add **3** new frames.

6. Select the **first** and **last frames**, but not the ones between them, and click the **Tween** button again to add **3** more frames at the end of the animation.

7. Play the animation. The ball should move up and down at a constant speed.

8. Set the delay of frame 1 to **No Delay**.

9. Set the delay of frames 2 and 8 to **0.1** seconds.

10. Set the delay of frames 3 and 7 to **0.2** seconds.

11. Set the delay of frame 5 to **0.5** seconds.

12. Delete **frames 4** and **6**.

13. Select **frame 1**. Click **Layer** on the menu bar, point to **Layer Style**, and then click **Drop Shadow**. In the Layer Style palette, set the Distance to **8**.

14. In the Optimize palette, select the preset named **GIF 32 No Dither**.

15. In the Animation palette menu, select **Optimize Animation** and accept both options.

16. Preview the animation in a browser. The ball should appear to move quickly near the bottom of the image and to move more slowly near the top.

17. Click **File** on the menu bar, click **Save Optimized As**, and save the animation as **ball_bounce.gif** in a new folder called **project_9-5**.

Project 6: Creating a Graphical News Ticker

You want to highlight some news headlines on your home page, but do not want to take up more than about one square inch to do so. Create a slide show of images containing text to use as a space-saving news ticker.

Complete these steps:

1. In ImageReady, create an image that is **96** pixels wide and **96** pixels high.

2. Select the **Type** tool and select a **serif font** of **14 p**. Set the foreground color to **black (#000000)**.

3. Click in the Image window and type **New software products in our reviews section!** Add blank lines to make the text fit on four lines. Use the Move tool to center the text layer in the image.

4. Open the Animation palette menu and make sure that the New Layers Visible In All Frames option is deselected. Also make sure the Add Layer To New Frames option is deselected.

5. Select the **frame** and duplicate it twice by clicking the **Duplicate Frame** button.

6. Select the **layer** and duplicate it twice by selecting **Duplicate Layer** in the Layers palette menu.

7. Select the **first frame**; only the bottom text layer should have visibility turned on.

8. Select the **second frame**. Set the visibility in the Layers palette so that only the middle text layer is visible.

9. Select the **middle text layer**, and select the **Type** tool. Edit the text in the middle text layer to read **New features added to our community forum!**

10. Select the **third frame**; only the top text layer should have visibility turned on.

11. Select the **top text layer**. Edit the text in the top text layer to read **New images in our image library!**

12. Select **all frames** and set the delay value to **3** seconds for each frame.

13. Set looping to **Forever**.

14. In the Optimize palette, select the preset named **GIF 128 No Dither**. Then reduce the colors to **8**.

15. In the Animation palette menu, select **Optimize Animation** and accept both options.

16. Preview the news ticker in a Web browser to make sure the animation plays properly.

17. Click **File** on the menu bar, click **Save Optimized As**, and save the animation as **news.gif** in a new folder named **project_9-6**.

Project 7: Creating a Banner Ad

Create a simple five-frame banner using text elements.

Complete these steps:

1. In ImageReady, create an image that is **468** pixels wide and **60** pixels high with a **white** background.

2. Convert the background layer to a normal layer by selecting **Layer Options** from the Layers palette menu. Change the name of the layer to **background**. Click **OK**.

3. Set the foreground color to **dark teal (#003366)**. Use the Paint Bucket tool to fill the layer.

4. Create four new layers. Name them **art**, **design**, **graphics**, and **url**.

5. Set the foreground color to **pure yellow (#ffff00)**. Select the **art** layer. Select the **Type** tool.

6. Use a **24 px bold serif font** and add the word **Art** to the layer.

7. Click **Layer** on the menu bar, point to **Rasterize**, and then click **Type**. This renders the vector-based text into pixels.

8. Move the text layer to the upper-left of the image.

9. Select the **design** layer. Add the word **Design** and rasterize the text. Drag the **text** to the top-center of the image.

10. In the graphics layer, add the word **Graphics** and drag it to the upper-right of the image. Rasterize the layer.

11. Set the foreground color to **pure red** (**#ff0000**). Using a sans serif text such as Arial or Helvetica, add the **URL** for your site or your class's Web site to the URL layer. Drag it to the bottom center of the image.

12. Duplicate the frame. Select the **first frame** and select the **background layer**. Set the opacity of this layer to **60%**.

13. Select **both frames** and click the **Tween** button to add **3** intermediate frames.

14. Select the **last frame** and set the opacity of the art, design, and graphics layers to **80%**.

15. Select the **first frame** and adjust the visibility icons in the Layers palette so that only the background and art layers are visible.

16. Select the **second frame** and adjust the visibility icons so that only the background and design layers are visible.

17. Select the **third frame** and adjust the visibility icons so that only the background and graphics layers are visible.

18. Select the **fourth frame** and adjust the visibility icons so that only the background and url layers are visible.

19. Select the **fifth frame** and make all layers visible.

20. Select the **first four frames** and set the delay value to **1** second.

21. Select the **last frame** and set the delay value to **2** seconds.

22. Set the looping to **4** times.

23. In the Optimize palette, select the preset named **GIF 128 No Dither**.

24. In the Animation palette menu, select **Optimize Animation** and accept both options.

25. Preview the banner in a Web browser to make sure the animation plays properly.

26. Click **File** on the menu bar, click **Save Optimized As**, and save the animation as **ad.gif** in a new folder named **project_9-7**. Also save the unoptimized file, including all layer information, as **ad2.psd** in the same folder.

Project 8: Manually Optimizing an Animation

All the previous projects for this chapter have used the default Automatic frame disposal method. This usually produces adequately small files. You can sometimes attain even smaller files by not disposing of frames and manually blocking out pixels that change between frames.

Complete these steps:

1. In ImageReady, create an image that is **60** pixels square.

2. Set the foreground color to **black**.

3. Use the Elliptical Marquee tool to create a circular selection area that fits the edges of the image area.

4. Stroke the edges with **black** to make a **2-pixel-wide black ring**.

5. Create four empty layers. Name them **12**, **3**, **6**, and **9**.

6. Duplicate the frame so that you have a total of four frames.

7. Select the **first frame** and set the visibility so that only the background and the 12 layer are showing. Select the **12 layer**.

8. Select the **Paintbrush** tool and select a **nonfeathered brush** that is about **5** pixels in diameter.

9. Draw a **short, black, vertical line** inside the ring near the top of the image.

10. Select the **second frame** and set the visibility so that only the background and the 3 layer are showing. Select the **3** layer.

11. Draw a **short horizontal line** inside the ring near the right side of the image.

12. Select the **third frame** and set the visibility so that only the background and the 6 layer are showing. Select the **6** layer.

13. Draw a **short vertical line** inside the ring near the bottom of the image.

14. Select the **fourth frame** and set the visibility so that only the background and the 9 layer are showing. Select the **9** layer.

15. Draw a **short horizontal line** inside the ring near the left side of the image.

16. Select **all frames** and set the frame disposal method to **Automatic**.

17. In the Optimize palette, select the preset named **GIF 128 No Dither**.

18. In the Animation palette menu, select **Optimize Animation** and accept both options.

19. Preview the animation in a Web browser. The file size of the animation will be a few kilobytes.

20. You can reduce the file size. Select **all frames** and set the frame disposal method to **Do Not Dispose**.

21. Preview the animation in a Web browser. The size of the animation file will be about half its original size. However, the four lines persist when their frames appear.

22. Set the foreground color to **white** and select a **Paintbrush tool brush** that is slightly larger than the one you used before.

23. Select the **second frame** and select the **3** layer. With the Paintbrush, paint over the area occupied by the vertical line in the 12 layer. Temporarily make the 12 layer visible so that you can see what you are doing. But make sure to paint inside the 3 layer.

24. Select the **third frame** and select the **6** layer. With the Paintbrush, paint over the area occupied by the lines in the 12 and 3 layers.

9

25. Select the **fourth frame** and select the **9** layer. With the Paintbrush, paint over the area occupied by the lines in the 12, 3, and 6 layers.

26. Preview the animation in a Web browser. The size of the animation file will be larger than before, but it will be still about two-thirds of the file size using automatic optimization.

27. Click **File** on the menu bar, click **Save Optimized As**, and save the animation as **clock.gif** in a new folder named **project_9-8**.

CASE PROJECT

Create two animated ads for your Web site. One should be 468 × 60 pixels, and the other should be 125 × 125 pixels. Both should be under 10 K each. They can have as many frames as you need, but should loop a finite number of times. The last frame in both animations should contain all the important information about your Web site, including a very brief description and the URL. The last frame of each animation should have a delay of at least a second and a half.

10

CREATING IMAGE ROLLOVER EFFECTS

Using JavaScript to Control Image Display

In this chapter, you will:

♦ Learn about rollover effects

♦ Create rollover effects with ImageReady

♦ Create rollover effects with JavaScript

♦ Optimize rollover effects with JavaScript

A nyone who surfs the Web is familiar with rollover effects—one image swaps with another when you point to an object with the mouse. These effects are sometimes also referred to as image swaps or mouseovers, though in this chapter they are simply called rollovers. Almost every professional Web site uses rollovers in some way. Rollovers can be functional, and provide the user with extra information when the mouse is rolled over a link. Rollovers are usually decorative, however, and reinforce that the mouse is pointing to a link.

The most basic rollover is one where moving the mouse pointer over an image replaces the current image with another. You can enhance the rollover to include a third image for when the user actually clicks the current image. Another type of rollover swaps a secondary image with a separate image when the user points to the image that initiates the rollover effect.

You can create rollover effects by hand-coding the necessary JavaScript, or by using software such as ImageReady, Fireworks, or many other available programs. These programs create the JavaScript for you, making the process easier. However, relying on the code generated by these tools limits what you can do. If you learn the basics of JavaScript, you can edit the code generated by these programs to create any effect you want.

Whether functional or decorative, mouseovers can add professional polish to a Web page. In this chapter, you learn to create simple and complex rollover effects using JavaScript, coding by hand, and using ImageReady.

UNDERSTANDING ROLLOVER EFFECTS

In addition to creating graphic files, you can use ImageReady to generate the HTML and JavaScript for creating basic rollover effects.

Creating rollovers with ImageReady is very similar to creating animations with ImageReady. Instead of creating multiple animation frames, you create multiple rollover states. Each rollover state you create results in a separate image file, which is associated with a specific position of the user's mouse relative to a hyperlink. The hyperlink is usually an image, but does not have to be. Possible rollover states include: Over, when the pointer is over the link on the screen, Down, when the user actually clicks down on the image, and a few others, which are covered in later sections.

Instead of playing in sequence, the different states appear only when the user initiates them, either by rolling over or clicking an image. Like animation frames, rollover states in ImageReady are composed of one or more layers with various settings for opacity, position, and style.

Each rollover state requires its own image. Using several rollover states with a link requires that the user load additional graphics files.

Unlike creating animations, you can create rollover effects without any special software by creating the images for each rollover state, and manually coding the necessary JavaScript and HTML. For complex rollover effects, such as having a rollover effect swap an image elsewhere on the page, you must produce the code manually. For most rollover effects, however, you will find it easier to use ImageReady.

A key advantage to creating rollovers with ImageReady is that you create images for all rollover states at the same time, using the same layers. This ensures that the rollover effects perfectly match across different states.

Before you start creating rollover effects, you need a better understanding of them.

Designing a Basic Rollover

Rollovers are commonly used to show the selected button in a navigation bar. In this usage the rollover image is usually a highlighted version of the initial image, as in Figure 10-1.

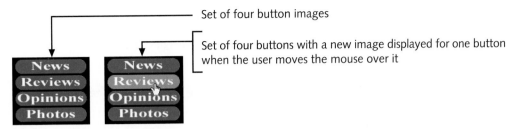

Set of four button images

Set of four buttons with a new image displayed for one button when the user moves the mouse over it

Figure 10-1   An image and its rollover version

The highlighted version serves only to indicate that the user's pointer is over a link. This is usually just a decorative effect, but can also let users know which link they are about to click. If you use many small buttons near each other, you may want to use rollover effects to make the navigation easier.

Some designers use a blurred image as the initial image, requiring the user to point to it to see the in-focus version, as shown in Figure 10-2.

Figure 10-2   A rollover effect where only the rollover version is clear

Avoid the blurred image technique because it hinders the usability of the site more than it helps. It forces users to search for the identity of the links, rather than making the identity obvious. Instead of making the navigation easier, using rollover effects this way actually makes the navigation more difficult.

A more elaborate type of rollover effect includes three images: one image in its normal state, a different graphic when the pointer is over a link, and a third graphic for when the user actually clicks down on the link. This sort of rollover typically uses a button image for the initial state and a more brightly colored or highlighted version of the same button for the Over state. For the Down state, the Over button can be inverted or rotated 180 degrees. This causes the 3-D effects to invert, as shown in Figure 10-3, enhancing the effect of the button being pushed down.

10

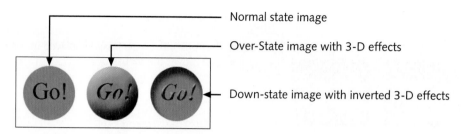

Normal state image

Over-State image with 3-D effects

Down-state image with inverted 3-D effects

Figure 10-3   Three states of a rollover

The benefits of using a three-state rollover effect are that the buttons seem more realistic and more similar to buttons on physical devices. Using the Down state also can help reinforce the idea that the user successfully clicked the link.

While using three images makes using a button seem more realistic, it also forces the user to download more image files, and can increase the download time. On the other hand, rollover images are usually used in navigation, so the same images are used on every page and need to be downloaded only on the first visit to a site, after which point they are cached. When deciding to use rollover effects, make sure that the benefits of using rollovers outweigh the drawback of the extra download time. While a few graphical rollovers help make a site look more professional, too many make the site look amateurish.

Image swaps that use multiple images can be used for instructional purposes. Mousing over a link or image can cause an informational text image to appear. For example, an educational resource site might have images of human anatomy where mousing over specific parts of the image causes the definition of that part to appear in a separate area on the page.

Like most other types of Web graphics, image rollovers can be overused. Therefore, you should use rollovers only when they provide a useful function for the Web page.

Using the Rollover Palette in ImageReady

When you create rollovers in ImageReady, you work primarily with the Rollover palette and the Layers palette. The Rollover palette is found next to the Animation palette, as shown in Figure10-4.

When you create or open an image, it appears in the Rollover palette in the Normal state—the initial image as it appears before the user points to it. When you have more than one state for a rollover, you can select only one state at a time. The selected state has a black outline around its thumbnail preview in the Rollover palette, and appears in the document window. Each state is treated as a separate image, using one or more layers in the Layers palette.

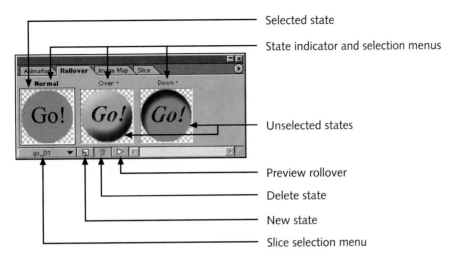

Selected state

State indicator and selection menus

Unselected states

Preview rollover

Delete state

New state

Slice selection menu

Figure 10-4   The Rollover palette in ImageReady

The Rollover palette includes buttons at the bottom of the palette. These include:

- **Slice selection bar.** You can use slices to make complex layouts of images using HTML tables. This book covers slices in detail in the Creating Sliced Images chapter.

- **New state button.** This adds a new state to the rollover. The first state is always the Normal state. Each new state takes the layer properties of the preceding state, so the second state has the same layer properties as the initial image. You can then use the Layers palette to make changes to the image in the new state.

- **Trash.** Delete rollover states as you delete animation frames. Select the state, then click the Trash button in the Rollover palette, drag the state to the Trash button, or select Delete State in the Rollover palette menu.

- **Preview.** Click this button to preview the rollover in ImageReady. Although it resembles a Play button, clicking Preview does not play a sequence of states. It allows you to roll over and click the Image window to view the rollover effect.

You also can preview the rollover in ImageReady by clicking the Rollover Preview button in the Toolbox, shown in Figure 10-5.

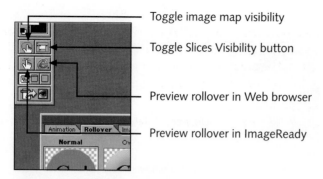

Toggle image map visibility

Toggle Slices Visibility button

Preview rollover in Web browser

Preview rollover in ImageReady

Figure 10-5   Preview buttons

You should preview the rollover in a browser to make sure it functions as you intended. Even after you have successfully viewed the rollover on your computer, you should view it on other systems as well. Rollover graphics might appear as you intended on one computer, but not appear at all on another. Rollover effects rely on simple JavaScript programming. A browser that does not support JavaScript or that has JavaScript capabilities disabled cannot display rollover effects.

Creating Rollover States

In ImageReady you can create rollovers from one layer or a set of layers. Each state uses some or all of the layers. There is one state for each type of mouse action. The available states are:

- *Normal:* This is the initial image displayed in the Web page.

- *Over:* The image displayed when the mouse rolls over the link. This is similar to using the Hover attribute in CSS.

- *Out:* The image displayed when the mouse rolls off the link. Normally this will be the same image as the Normal state.

- *Down:* The image displayed when the mouse button is pressed over the image. This is similar to using the Active attribute in CSS, or the ALINK attribute in HTML.

- *Up:* The image displayed when the mouse button is released. This is usually the same image as the Over state. This is similar to using the Visited attribute in CSS, or the VLINK attribute in HTML.

- *Click:* This is like the Down state, except the state reverts to Normal when another state is initiated.

- *Custom:* This state is reserved for uses that don't apply to creating rollover states.

- *None:* This creates an image that will be preloaded but will not appear in the Web page, so you do not need this state for Web graphics.

You probably will work with the Normal, Over, and Out states most often. The Down, Up, and Click states are used when you have separate images appear at the moment the user clicks a link. In the time it takes the user to click a link, the browser will display the image for the Click state or the images for the Down and Up state. These images appear so quickly that they are seldom worth the extra download time.

You cannot create a customized state, because JavaScript can deal only with the existing states. A state of None means the image will not be displayed at any time as part of a rollover effect.

Create rollover states in ImageReady:

1. Open **fox.tif** from the Data Disk.

2. Show the Rollover palette by selecting **Show Rollover** from the Window menu. You will see a thumbnail of the new image.

3. Click the **New state** button at the bottom of the Rollover palette. A second state of the Over type is added to the palette.

4. Click the word **Over** to display a menu of options listing all the available states. Select **Down**.

5. Leave this file open.

During rollovers, images are swapped depending on the state of the mouse and browser. Entire images are replaced, so you do not need to set the frame disposal method or the delay as you do with animations.

CREATING ROLLOVER EFFECTS WITH IMAGEREADY

Creating and editing rollover states is similar to creating and editing animation frames. Each state is composed of one or more layers, as indicated by the visibility icons next to the layers in the Layers palette. You can select only one state and one layer at a time.

Using Layers to Create Rollover Effects

As with animations, layer changes such as opacity, position, or style affect only the selected state. Other changes, such as using filters or brush tools, affect all states that display the layer.

To create rollover effects by changing opacity:

1. With fox.tif open, select the **first frame**.

2. In the Layers palette, set the opacity to **50%**.

3. Preview the rollover effect in ImageReady by clicking the **Preview** button in the Rollover palette or the **Rollover Preview** button in the toolbox.

4. Click the **image**. The image should be faint until you click it, at which time it appears brighter.

5. Preview the animation in a browser. You should see the same effect. Note the JavaScript code used to create the rollover effect. This will be explained later in this chapter.

6. Save this image by setting an appropriate optimization setting in the Optimize palette, then selecting **Save Optimized As** from the File menu. You will be asked to save an HTML file named fox.html. This file contains the HTML and JavaScript necessary to display the rollover images. Save this file in a folder named **chapter10-1**. ImageReady will automatically create a folder named images that contains the actual graphic files. The details of saving rollover files in ImageReady are covered later in this chapter.

Layer changes involving opacity and position affect only the selected state. You can apply changes to all states by selecting the layer, and then selecting Match Layer Across States in the Rollover palette menu.

Because layer edits using filters or tools from the toolbox affect all states that display that layer, you often need to create multiple layers for an image in order to use these tools.

To create rollover effects with multiple layers:

1. With fox.tif open, select the **layer** in the Layers palette.

2. Select **Duplicate Layer** from the Layers palette menu.

3. With the new layer selected, use the Hue/Saturation dialog box and boost saturation to **100%**.

4. In the Layers palette, set the opacity to **100%**.

5. Create a new state in the Rollover palette. Set the state to **Over**.

6. Select the **Normal** state and make the new layer invisible.

7. You should now have three states: Normal, Down, and Over. The order in which the states appear in the Rollover palette does not matter. Select each state in turn and make sure the proper layers are displayed for each state. The Rollover and Layers palettes should look like those in Figure 10-6. The Normal state should display only Layer 1 at 50% opacity. The Down state also should display only Layer 1, but at 100% opacity. The Over state should display the new layer, Layer 1 Copy, at 100% opacity. It does not matter if this state displays both layers or only the top one because Layer 1 Copy completely occludes Layer 1.

8. Preview the rollover in a browser. The image should get much brighter when you mouse over it, and somewhat dimmer when you click it.

9. Save the HTML and images in a new folder named **chapter10-2**. Close **fox.tif**.

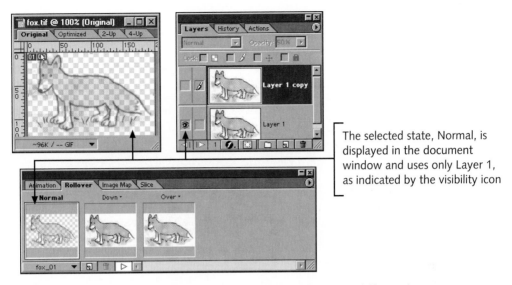

Figure 10-6 The Rollover palette with three states displaying different layers

The selected state, Normal, is displayed in the document window and uses only Layer 1, as indicated by the visibility icon

You can copy and paste rollover states just as you can copy and paste animation frames. In fact, you can copy rollover states and paste them into animations, and vice versa. When pasting, make sure to use the Paste Rollover State command from the Rollover palette menu. Selecting Paste from the Edit menu will paste the contents of the Clipboard into the current layer. When you paste a state, the existing state is replaced with the layer visibility options of the copied state.

Using Styles to Create Rollover Effects

One advantage to using ImageReady for creating rollovers is the convenience of using styles to create the rollover states. A style is an effect or combination of effects applied to a layer. In previous chapters, you applied layer effects such as Drop Shadow or Bevel and Emboss. ImageReady offers many preset combinations of multiple layer effects in the Styles palette, shown in Figure 10-7. For example, the Meshed Gradients style is a combination of the Outer Glow, Inner Glow, Bevel and Emboss, and Gradient Overlay layer effects.

Figure 10-7 The Styles palette in ImageReady

You can edit a style by clicking it in the Layers palette. The Layer Options palette then displays the style options. Figure 10-8 shows the Styles, Layer Options, and Layers palettes when editing a style.

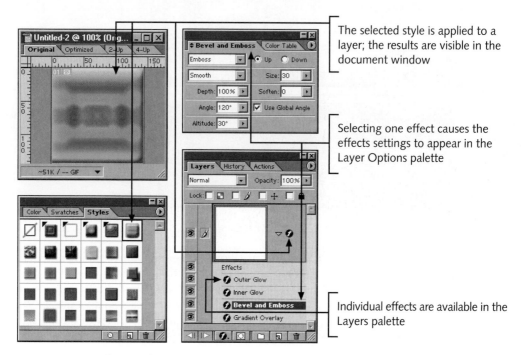

The selected style is applied to a layer; the results are visible in the document window

Selecting one effect causes the effects settings to appear in the Layer Options palette

Individual effects are available in the Layers palette

Figure 10-8   Editing a style

The selected style is applied to a layer and the results are visible in the document window. Specific effects are available in the Layers palette, where they can be enabled or disabled individually by clicking the visibility icons. Selecting an effect causes the Effects settings to appear in the Layer Options palette. There, you can edit the Effects settings.

To apply a style to a layer:

1. Create a **100 × 100-pixel image** with a **transparent** background.

2. Show the Styles palette by selecting **Show Styles** from the Window menu.

3. Locate and select the style named **Button–Up**. You should not see any changes to the image in the document window. Layer styles need image data to have any effect.

4. Select the **Paintbrush** tool and set the foreground color to **black**.

5. Draw a **star** in the document window. Instead of a normal black line, the drawn line will have a beveled, 3-D effect, as shown in Figure 10-9.

6. In the Layers palette, click the right-pointing **triangle** next to the effects icon in Layer 1. This expands the list of layer effects used in the style.

7. Hide the Drop Shadow effect by deselecting the **visibility icon** for the Drop Shadow effect in the Layers palette.

8. Save the optimized image as **style.jpg**.

Figure 10-9   An image with applied style

Some styles not only combine multiple layer effects but also automatically create multiple rollover states. When you select a style, you automatically create a full set of rollover images. This is a quick way to get immediate results. For most professional jobs, however, you need to control the images yourself, and you will not use styles.

Rollover styles are indicated by a black triangle in the upper-left corner of the style thumbnail, as shown in Figure 10-10.

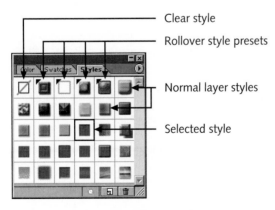

Figure 10-10   Layer rollover styles

Some styles generate many states, and others just one or two. You can add more states if you want, and edit the layers to create additional effects.

Create a rollover in ImageReady using styles:

1. Create a new image in ImageReady by clicking **New** on the File menu. Set the size to **72 × 72 pixels** and make the background **transparent**.

2. Fill the layer with **white** using the Paint Bucket tool.

3. Click the **Wood 3-state Rollover** style in the Styles palette.

   In the Rollover palette you see the three states for this style of rollover, as shown in Figure 10-11.

4. Click the **Preview in Default Browser** button. The three rollover images and all necessary HTML and JavaScript are generated and displayed in your browser.

5. Roll over and click the **image** in the browser to see the effect.

6. Save this optimized set of rollover images with an HTML file named **wood.html** in a new folder named **chapter10-3**.

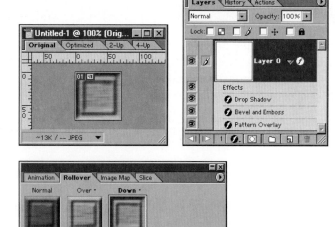

Figure 10-11   Creating a rollover effect using a rollover style

In addition to the default rollover styles in the Styles palette, you can load additional styles from the Styles palette menu.

Using Animation in Rollover Effects

When designing rollover graphics, you normally use a plain image for the initial state, and a highlighted image for the Over state. One way to highlight an image is to animate it. To animate a state in a rollover, select the state you want to animate in the

Rollover palette, select the Animation palette, and then create the animation. For more information on animating images, see the chapter on Creating Animated Graphics. You can create an animation for every state in a rollover, but this can lead to large files. Whereas one static image with no rollover effects might be 10 KB, a rollover effect with a similar design but three animated states might be 60 KB.

Create an animated rollover:

1. Open **fox.tif** from the Data Disk.

2. In the Rollover palette, create a new **Over** state.

3. With the Over state selected, show the Animation palette.

4. In the Animation palette, create a **second frame**.

5. With the second frame selected, use the Move tool to move the contents of Layer 1 in the Layers palette. Move the layer **10 pixels** to the right.

6. In the Animation palette, set both frames to delay for **0.2** seconds and set the looping to **Forever**.

7. Preview the file in a Web browser. You should see a static version of the fox. When you move your mouse over the image, the fox should move back and forth.

8. Save the optimized file as **fox.html** in a new folder named **chapter10-4**. This creates two images—the second image is animated.

It can be confusing to generate rollover states and animations at the same time from the same set of layers. You may find it is easiest to set up your layers for the rollover states, and edit the rollover state images first. Then use the same set of layers to animate individual states.

Saving HTML Files in ImageReady

When you save an image with rollover states, each state is saved as a separate image file. The names of the images are based on the name of the slice used in the image. **Slices** are sections of images, and are covered in detail in the Creating Sliced Images chapter. In this chapter, all rollovers use one slice that fills the entire image. Sometimes you will see outlines over the image with a blue box containing the number 01, as shown in Figure 10-12. This number displays the slice information about the image. You can hide the slice information by deselecting the Toggle Slices Visibility button in the Toolbox, shown in Figure 10-5.

Figure 10-12   Slice information about an image

The JavaScript generated by ImageReady must be able to refer to separate rollover images by name. By default, the image names are based on the name of the original image, plus an extension describing the rollover state. For example, if you create an image and build three rollover states from it, the images might be named Untitled_1.jpg, Untitled_1-over.jpg, and Untitled_1-down.jpg.

You can give the images other names if you wish. This will not affect the rollover effects, but may make managing your image files easier. When your image is open in ImageReady, you can name it using the Slice palette, shown in Figure 10-13. Show the Slice palette by selecting Show Slice from the Window menu.

Figure 10-13   The Slice palette in ImageReady

In the Name field you can name the slice. This name then determines the names of the images generated as part of the rollover. In the URL field you can enter the address of the page to which the rollover should link. You also can edit this information directly in the HTML file after it is generated.

Save rollover effects by selecting Save Optimized As from the File menu. Make sure you have selected appropriate optimization settings for the rollover images. Unlike animation files, rollover graphics can be saved as GIF, JPEG, or PNG. In the Save Optimized As dialog box, you have the option of saving images only, HTML only, or image and HTML files both. Make your selection in the Save as type field in the dialog box. Choose HTML and Images (*.html). In the File name field, choose a name for the HTML file.

Once you save the rollover images and have the HTML file, you can make multi-image rollovers more sophisticated by adding images and changing and adding names in the HTML code. You often will have to manually edit the JavaScript generated by ImageReady, because the software cannot create every effect you might need. To do so, you need to understand how to create rollover effects manually with JavaScript.

CREATING ROLLOVER EFFECTS WITH JAVASCRIPT

Until very recently all client-side effects, including rollovers, had to be coded by hand in JavaScript. Now many WYSIWYG HTML editors and some image editors, such as ImageReady, write JavaScript code for rollovers that you can use in Web pages. To create certain complex rollover effects, however, you must modify this code or create new JavaScript code yourself.

You do not need to understand every aspect of JavaScript to implement JavaScript rollovers. However, a lack of understanding might result in rollovers that work only on some browsers. Most browsers support JavaScript rollovers, but the oldest browsers cannot display any rollovers at all. Netscape version 4 and higher, and Internet Explorer version 4 and higher both display JavaScript rollovers.

Before continuing, locate the file named fox.html that you created in the last section, or find fox.html in the Data Disk. Open the file in a text or HTML editor so that you can see the code. The code will be explained in detail in this section.

Working with JavaScript

HTML is a markup language—you use it to control the display of text and graphics in a Web page. JavaScript is a programming language—you use it to write scripts that take inputs and produce corresponding output. Every program in any language must be run, or **executed**, in a specific environment for it to work. A program written in C can be compiled into a standalone application that runs on your desktop. A droplet created in Photoshop or ImageReady is similar, and also runs on your desktop. A CGI script written in Perl runs on a Web server. A Java applet runs within the browser in an application called a Java Virtual Machine (JVM) that works like a plug-in. JavaScript runs directly in the browser, needing no plug-in.

Java and JavaScript have a few similarities, but are otherwise unrelated. Both are based on the C programming language, and both are used primarily for Web-based applications. Java, however, is a complete, complex language which can be difficult to learn, but can be used to create server-side or desktop applications in addition to the applets used in Web pages. JavaScript is not as robust as Java and can be used only in Web pages. However, it is easy to learn and use.

JavaScript manipulates elements of the browser window and pieces of Web pages. For example, you can use JavaScript to print the current date to the screen or to control the size of the browser window. JavaScript is written directly into a Web page, so you can view and copy the source as you would with HTML or CSS. Like CSS, which is not a programming language, JavaScript can be written using any of three conventions:

- **inline**, meaning the code is placed within an HTML tag
- using **SCRIPT** tags elsewhere in the same HTML document
- in an **external file** that can be accessed by any other HTML file

10

Using Inline JavaScript

An example of inline JavaScript is:

```
<BODY BGCOLOR=#FFFFFF ONLOAD="preloadImages();">
```

The BODY tag takes a JavaScript attribute called ONLOAD, which takes the value preloadImages(). ONLOAD describes the state of a Web browser when all elements of a Web page have been downloaded. The onMouseOver attribute, which you use in rollovers, describes the state of a Web browser when the mouse pointer is directly over a particular link. You can see the onMouseOver and onMouseOut attributes within the A tag near the bottom of fox.html. These attributes are flags for the browser.

Essentially, the example above tells the browser "when all elements have been downloaded, execute the following script, named preloadImages()". In the example, preloadImages() is a **function**, which is a list of instructions. A function is a self-contained sequence of commands that can be called by other functions or called from an attribute such as onMouseOver. Some functions are included with the JavaScript interpreter that is part of the Web browser. You also can write your own functions.

Using the SCRIPT Tag

The following JavaScript example is not inline, and instead relies on the SCRIPT tag in HTML.

One of the simplest JavaScript codes displays text on the screen. The traditional first program in any programming language writes the message Hello World! to the screen:

```
<script>
document.write("Hello World!");
</script>
```

The above script can be placed anywhere in a Web page, and displays the text on the screen.

Here, write() is a JavaScript function included in the standard JavaScript function library. It takes the value specified in parentheses and displays it in the document, which is another term for the Web page. The JavaScript code in the preceding example writes Hello World! in the current document.

This script requires the use of the SCRIPT HTML tag. Most tags instruct the browser how to display the text that follows the tag. The SCRIPT tag, however, tells the browser that what follows is an executable command.

In fox.html, SCRIPT tags are used to contain three functions. These functions call each other, and are called by the onMouseOver and onMouseOut attributes.

In JavaScript, spaces, tabs, and carriage returns are all treated as equivalent white space. It does not matter if you use one space, ten spaces, a few tabs, or several carriage returns; they are all treated as a single space. You can format JavaScript using tabs, spaces, and carriage returns as you would in HTML, though you need to indicate the end of a line in JavaScript with a semicolon (;). Every distinct line of JavaScript code must end with a semicolon.

Using JavaScript in an External File

An external JavaScript might look like the following, and would be placed in a separate file. You can choose any name you want for the file. The following code is the same as the previous example.

```
document.write("Hello World!");
```

This JavaScript does not need the SCRIPT tag around it. However, to access the script in an external file, you must use the SCRIPT tag, indicating the filename. If the script above were saved in a file named image.js, you would access it using the following code:

```
<script src="image.js"></script>
```

You can write the simplest JavaScript inline. If you know you will use the same function in many places, you should use an external file.

Creating Simple JavaScript Effects

Using JavaScript to write text on the screen is not useful, because you can simply write the text directly in HTML without using JavaScript. If you want to do something more dynamic, however, JavaScript is much more useful than HTML by itself. The following JavaScript code displays the date and time in a Web browser:

```
<script>
document.write(Date());
</script>
```

Date() is another JavaScript function that reads the date and time from the clock on the computer where the Web browser is running, and then writes the information on the screen. In this case, the write() function is **calling** or **invoking** the Date function. The Date function does its job, and passes the information back to the function that called it. The write() function then takes the information and displays it as it would any text.

To display the date in a Web page:

1. Use a text editor such as Notepad to copy the code above (for displaying the date and time) into a text file. You can reformat the spacing and indenting of the code, but match the case of the JavaScript exactly.

2. Save the text file as **js-test.html** on your desktop.

3. Open the page in a Web browser to see the current date and time.

Creating Simple Rollovers

Some JavaScript rollovers require using separate functions. The simplest rollovers, however, can be written entirely inline. All JavaScript rollovers involve using JavaScript attributes with A tags. These attributes describe different browser states, similar to the anchor tag attributes in CSS. The most common browser state used for rollovers is the Over state.

In JavaScript, the onMouseOver attribute instructs the browser to do something, such as display a rollover effect, when the pointer moves over the link containing the attribute. It is similar to the anchor tag's HOVER attribute in CSS. The onMouseOver attribute is the core of any JavaScript rollover effect. In the following steps, you will set the onMouseOver attribute to a value which is itself a command. The command tells the browser to display certain text in the status bar at the bottom of the browser window.

To display text in the status bar when users point to a link:

1. Open a text editor such as Notepad and type the following JavaScript code:

   <a href="#" onMouseOver="status='Hello World!'">Roll Over Me</a>

 JavaScript rollovers require using links. However, if the rollover effect is not intended to be used for a link, you can set the URL to "#".

2. Save the text in a file named **js-test2.html**.

3. Open **js-test2.html** in a Web browser.

4. Point to the link that reads **Roll Over Me** and look to see Hello World! in the status bar, as shown in Figure 10-14.

Figure 10-14 Using JavaScript to display a message in the status bar

JavaScript includes additional attributes that describe other possible states:

- **onMouseOut** instructs the browser to do something when the pointer moves off the link. You could have the status bar display one message when the Web page loads, a second message when the mouse is over the link, and a third message when the mouse leaves. You also can use onMouseOut to return a rollover effect to its initial state when the user no longer points to a link or button. If you do not set this attribute, a rollover effect stays in place once it occurs. For example, if you create a rollover effect that highlights a button when the user points to it, unless you set the onMouseOut attribute, the button remains highlighted even when the user points to another area of the page. With CSS, the HOVER attribute has an implicit definition to return the link to the initial state when the mouse is pulled away. In JavaScript, you must explicitly define this with the onMouseOut attribute.

- **onMouseDown** instructs the browser to perform a task when the mouse clicks the link. The task can be anything from displaying text, to changing color, to opening a new browser window. This is similar to the ALINK attribute in HTML or the ACTIVE anchor tag attribute in CSS.

- **onMouseUp** instructs the browser to perform a task when the mouse button is released after clicking. Again, the task can be anything. This attribute is usually used to return rollover effects to their initial state after being clicked. Links return to the onMouseOver state by default, so use onMouseUp only when you want to display different images.

- **onClick** is similar to onMouseDown, but the effect of this attribute remains in place until the user activates a different rollover state on the page.

In fox.html, the onMouseOver attribute calls a function named changeImages, which swaps the initial image with a second image. The onMouseOut attribute calls the same function to again swap the second image with the initial image.

Creating Graphical Rollover Effects

Recall that you create most rollover effects by swapping one image for another. A basic image swap in JavaScript looks like this:

```
<a href="http://www.course.com"
onMouseOver= "document.image1.src= 'sheep.gif';"
onMouseOut= "document.image1.src= 'dog.gif';">
<img src= "dog.gif" name="image1">
</a>
```

Note the similarities to the anchor tag at the bottom of fox.html.

This JavaScript code initially shows an image of a dog. When the user moves the mouse over the image, the JavaScript replaces the dog image with a sheep image. When the user moves the mouse off the image, the JavaScript replaces the sheep image with the initial dog image.

A key concept is the difference between the document image name and the filename. A filename is associated with exactly one image file, but the file can be displayed multiple times in a Web page. A document filename, such as "image1", is associated with exactly one IMG tag and one place in a Web page, but can display different image files at different times.

The IMG tag is named image1 and the SRC attribute is set to display an image file named dog.gif. The onMouseOver attribute is set to "document.image1.src= 'sheep.gif';". This finds the element in the document with the name image1 (the dog image) and resets the source to a different image file, named sheep.gif. The onMouseOut attribute is set to "document.image1.src= 'dog.gif';". This finds the same element and resets the source back to the original image. On the Data Disk, open the file named 10-1.html in a Web browser to see the above example. The final effect also is illustrated in Figure 10-15.

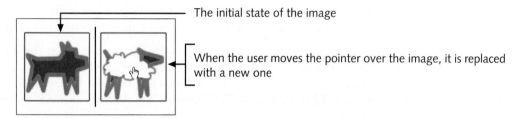

The initial state of the image

When the user moves the pointer over the image, it is replaced with a new one

Figure 10-15   A simple rollover effect using onMouseOver and onMouseOut

Creating Multi-Image Graphical Rollover Effects

Every IMG tag on a page can have a name, which then can be controlled by JavaScript. Not only can you create rollover effects to swap the image used as the link, you also can create rollover effects to swap other images on the page.

The following example swaps images for a different IMG tag:

```
<a href="#"
onMouseOver= "document.image2.src= 'sheep.gif';"
onMouseOut= "document.image2.src= 'frog.gif';">
<img src= "dog.gif" name="image1">
</a>
<img src= "frog.gif" name="image2">
```

The onMouseOver and onMouseOut attributes are set to affect the image named image2, which is the frog image. Moving your mouse over the dog image affects the frog image, but leaves the dog image alone, as shown in Figure 10-16. The frog image is not set to invoke a rollover, so nothing happens when you mouse over it.

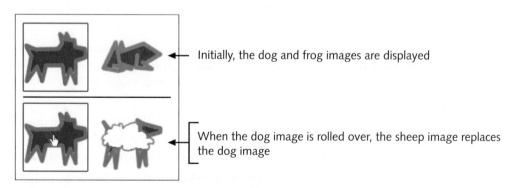

Initially, the dog and frog images are displayed

When the dog image is rolled over, the sheep image replaces the dog image

Figure 10-16   A rollover that affects a secondary image

On the Data Disk, open the file named 10-2.html in a Web browser to see the previous example.

You can even set up the JavaScript to swap two images at once:

```
<A HREF="http://www.course.com"
onMouseOver= "document.image1.src= 'sheep.gif';
document.image2.src= 'sheep.gif'"
onMouseOut= "document.image1.src= 'dog.gif';
document.image2.src= 'frog.gif'">
<img src= "dog.gif" name="image1">
</a>
<img src= "frog.gif" name="image2">
```

In the above example, the onMouseOver and onMouseOut attributes both are set to perform two actions, separated by semicolons. Moving the mouse over the dog image sets both image1 and image2 to the sheep image file. Moving the mouse back returns the images to their original states, as shown in Figure 10-17. On the Data Disk, open the file named 10-3.html in a Web browser to see the effect.

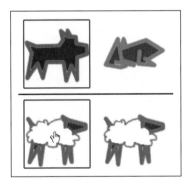

Figure 10-17   A rollover that affects both the activated and the secondary images

Although you can use ImageReady to create rollover effects that swap the image being moused over, you must edit the HTML manually, or use a WYSIWYG HTML editor to create multi-image swaps.

The examples given so far have left out a few elements that are necessary for them to work as well as they can. The following section explains how to optimize rollover effects to make them more efficient.

OPTIMIZING ROLLOVER EFFECTS

You optimize graphics by selecting their format, color depth, and compression level and method. When you optimize JavaScript code, you make the code work more quickly with fewer errors. If you create JavaScript by hand, you can assign different optimization settings and formats to the images used as different states in rollovers. For example, you might use flat initial-state images and save them as low-color GIFs, and use images with high-color gradations saved as JPEGs for the rollover images. If you use software such as ImageReady to create the rollovers, you must save all states in the same format with the same optimization settings. Then you can edit the JavaScript and again optimize the graphics separately.

The rollover effects used in the past few examples work, but have limitations. Fortunately, you can optimize them to work better. One limitation is that because of the way the JavaScript rollover effects have been written, they must always be written within the anchor tag. If you have many rollover effects, it can be more efficient to write a single JavaScript function to control all rollover effects. The Using Functions section, which follows, explains how to do so.

A second limitation is that the images called by the onMouseOver attribute do not load until the user points to the link. Only then does the browser make a request to the Web server to download the image. If the connection is fast, users might not notice the interruption, but if the connection is slow or if the browser must load many rollover images, users have to wait. To avoid a delay, you can preload the rollover images so that they are already in the cache by the time the user points to a link. The following Preloading Images section explains how to preload images with HTML, JavaScript, and JavaScript functions.

A third limitation is that not all browsers support graphical JavaScript rollovers. Some browsers display the JavaScript code directly in the page, or cause an error when they encounter a rollover. To avoid these problems, you can write the code so that older browsers ignore JavaScript and rollover effects they cannot process. The Making Cross-Browser Rollover Effects section later in this chapter tells you how to hide JavaScript and rollover effects from older browsers and how to specify the script language you want the browser to use.

The remedies for these three limitations are described below:

Using Functions

Instead of writing all of the JavaScript rollover code in the anchor tag, you can write a general-purpose function to swap any image for another. Following is an example of a simple JavaScript rollover function. It can appear anywhere in an HTML page, or can be included in a separate file:

```
<script>
function swapImage(imageName,imageFileName)
{
document[imageName].src = imageFileName;
}
</script>
```

This is a simplified version of the changeImages() function used in fox.html.

The above code defines a new function called swapImage that replaces one image with another. The first line defines the new function and its arguments. The word function indicates that a new function is being defined and its name is swapImage. After naming the function, the code defines the two **arguments** or **parameters** the function uses. The arguments or parameters are always in parentheses and are separated by a comma. Once you define the function name and the arguments it uses, you can use these elements to specify what the function does. The instructions of the function are between the curly braces ({ and }). In this code, the instruction is to take any document image name that is passed to it, and assign to it whatever image filename is passed to it. Thus, a document image, such as "image1", can be assigned to an image filename, such as "frog.gif", and the image of a frog is displayed wherever there is an IMG tag with the name image1.

The following is an example of the swapImage function being called in HTML. Initially, users see the image of a sheep. When users point to the image, it is replaced with the frog image. When they move the pointer away from the link, they see the sheep image again.

```
<a href="http://www.course.com"
onMouseOver="swapImage('image5','frog.gif')"
onMouseOut="swapImage('image5','sheep.gif')">
<img src="sheep.gif" name="image5">
</a>
```

In this example, the onMouseOver attribute calls the swapImage function and passes it two arguments. The first argument is the name of the IMG tag, and the second argument is the image filename that is to be placed in that position. The onMouseOut attribute also calls the swapImage function, setting the source of that image back to the sheep image.

On the Data Disk, open file 10-4.html in a Web browser to see this example.

Functions make multi-image swaps easy. In any anchor tag, include a call to the function, passing the name of the image you want to swap, and the name of the file you want to use.

You can write functions to do almost anything you want. In addition to making the JavaScript more efficient by using less code, you can use functions to improve speed by preloading images.

Preloading Images

Rollover images should swap immediately when the user points to a link. This can happen only if the images are already stored in the browser cache. If they are not, the user has to wait while the images download from the server. You can preload the rollover images to place them in the browser cache before they are needed.

When any Web graphic is downloaded for the first time, it is stored in the Web browser's cache. If the graphic is used again, the browser loads it from the cache instead of downloading it. Preloading images means downloading them and storing them in the cache without displaying them first. You can preload images using HTML or with JavaScript.

Preloading Images with HTML

The easiest way to preload images is to display them on the Web page, using dimensions so small that the user does not notice them. You can use a normal IMG tag and set the WIDTH and HEIGHT attributes to 1 or even 0. Then the image appears as a small dot. If you use this technique, position the reduced images where they will not be noticed, such as at the bottom of the page.

```
<img src="rollover5.gif" width="1" height="1">
```

Although this method works, it shows dots on the page, which might be an effect you don't want. You also can preload the images using JavaScript. Then the images never appear on the page until they are used in a rollover effect.

Preloading Images with JavaScript

To preload images using JavaScript, first specify which image file the browser should load and with what name it should be associated. Following is an example of JavaScript code to preload images:

```
<script>
var image1=new Image();
image1.src="dog_glow.gif";
var frog=new Image();
frog.src="frog_glow.gif";
</script>
```

This code sets two variables and assigns each of them a particular image file. A **variable** is a placeholder. To create JavaScript rollovers, you use the term "var" to the left of the name of the image you are preloading. The first line declares a variable of the name image1 and defines it as an image by calling the Image() function. The second line takes the image name and sets the source to the image file named dog_glow.gif. When the browser reads this line, it requests the file from the Web server. The third and fourth lines do the same thing, preloading the image file named frog_glow.gif. You can use any variable names you want. In the anchor tag, you can refer to the original image filenames.

When you preload images this way the user does not have to wait for the rollover images to download when the mouse moves over the link. The rollover images are downloaded with all of the other page elements. However, the whole page takes longer to load as it preloads the rollover images. You can use JavaScript functions to preload the rollover images before the images are accessed by a rollover, but only after the rest of the page has finished loading and rendering.

Preloading Images with JavaScript Functions

To preload images with JavaScript functions, your first step is to make a function to pre-load the images. In the following code, two document images (image1 and frog) are each assigned to an image file (dog_glow.gif and frog_glow.gif):

```
<script>
var image1=new Image();
image1.src="dog_glow.gif";
var frog=new Image();
frog.src="frog_glow.gif";
</script>
```

To convert this code to a function, add the word "function", choose a name, and enclose the instructions in curly braces, as in the following code:

```
<script>
function preLoadImages()
{
      var image1=new Image();
      image1.src="dog_glow.gif";
      var frog=new Image();
      frog.src="frog_glow.gif";
}
</script>
```

This function takes no arguments, as indicated by the empty parentheses after the function name. Your second step is to call this function only after the rest of the page has loaded. To do so, you use a special JavaScript attribute, called onLoad for the BODY tag. This instructs the browser to do something only after all the elements in the body of the Web page have loaded.

Following is an example of a BODY tag calling the preLoadImages function after the other page elements have loaded:

```
<body onLoad="preLoadImages()">
```

Compare the code in the above example with the code in fox.html. Both use preloading functions called by the onLoad attribute in the BODY tag.

You cannot see the advantage of preloading images if you view these examples on your desktop. If you have access to a Web server, try using a graphical rollover effect with and without preloading. The preloaded rollover images appear without making you wait.

In addition to preloading the images, you can optimize your rollovers by making the scripts backward-compatible.

Making Cross-Browser Rollover Effects

There are two ways a browser might have trouble interpreting a JavaScript rollover. An older browser might support some JavaScript features, but does not support setting

10

sources for images. Alternately, an older browser might not support JavaScript at all, or the user might have turned off JavaScript in the Web browser, disabling it.

If a browser has only limited support of JavaScript, it might not be able to display rollover effects properly. It might display a JavaScript error instead. If a browser does not support JavaScript at all, it will not interpret the SCRIPT tag and will display all the JavaScript code in the page as if it were normal text.

When creating Web pages, you always need to consider just how many users will actually be able to see your work. The percentage of users with JavaScript-incompatible browsers is lower every year as people upgrade to the newest Web browsers. Still, you need to make a few additions to your JavaScript code to make sure that no problems are caused if the JavaScript does not work in a browser. These additions are described in the following sections.

Hiding JavaScript from Older Browsers

To make sure JavaScript code is not displayed in older Web browsers, use comments within the SCRIPT tags just as you do with style sheets. JavaScript comments are the same as CSS comments: two slashes at the beginning of the line.

Following is the sample code that assigns two filenames with two document images, with comment tags added:

```
<script>
<!--
function preLoadImages()
{
    var image1=new Image();
    image1.src="dog_glow.gif";
    var frog=new Image();
    frog.src="frog_glow.gif";
}
//-->
</script>
```

Note how comment tags are used in fox.html. Some comment tags hide text that is intended only for people editing the code, but the comment tags between the SCRIPT tags hide the JavaScript code from noncompliant browsers.

HTML comments frame the code itself, hiding it from the browser. A JavaScript comment to the left of the HTML comment at the bottom prevents a browser that supports JavaScript from interpreting the HTML comment as a JavaScript command.

Another way to prevent the JavaScript from being displayed in older browsers is to place it in the HEAD tag rather than in the BODY tag. Text in the head of a Web page does not appear in the page. If you use comments, it does not matter where you put the JavaScript code, although it is conventional practice to place it at the top of the file.

Specifying Language

JavaScript is not the only language you can use between SCRIPT tags to add function-ality to a Web page. You also can use VBScript, which is similar to JavaScript but is based on Visual Basic. To make sure the browser understands which language you are using, you should specify the language using the LANGUAGE attribute of the SCRIPT tag.

Following is the preload script again, with the script language explicitly stated:

```
<script language="JavaScript">
<!--
function preLoadImages()
{
     var image1=new Image();
     image1.src="dog_glow.gif";
     var frog=new Image();
     frog.src="frog_glow.gif";
}
//-->
</script>
```

Most browsers assume the language is JavaScript, but it is safer to state it directly.

Hiding Rollover Effects from Older Browsers

The oldest browsers that support JavaScript support only basic functions, and do not support working with images. You can test whether the browser interpreting the script can work with images. If you include this test in the script itself, it runs whenever a browser reads the script.

The test uses the if statement in JavaScript. This tells the browser that if the condition inside the parentheses is true, continue, otherwise stop. In this case, the condition for which you are testing is whether the browser can work with images in JavaScript.

Following is the preload example with the test for image capability in JavaScript:

```
<script language="JavaScript">
<!--
function preLoadImages()
{
if (document.images)
     {
     var image1=new Image();
     image1.src="dog_glow.gif";
     var frog=new Image();
     frog.src="frog_glow.gif";
     }
}
//-->
</script>
```

10

After the HTML comment, include the name of the function, followed by an if statement with document.images as the condition. When a browser begins reading the script, it reads the SCRIPT tag and the comments. If it is an older browser, it stops reading until it gets to the end comment tag. If it is a browser with some JavaScript support, it continues reading. When it processes the line "if (document.images)" and its JavaScript support allows it to correctly interpret document.images, it continues through the script, executing all the remaining instructions. If it cannot interpret document.images, it skips the remaining instructions.

In fox.html, each of the three functions tests for this condition.

Most browsers can work with images in JavaScript, so this code is for a minority of users who still use browsers from around 1996.

The JavaScript generated by ImageReady uses functions and preloads the images. Many designers prefer to use the prewritten rollover code from ImageReady or DreamWeaver instead of writing it themselves. The code generated by these programs works across browsers and includes the preloading function described earlier. If you want to create more-sophisticated effects, such as multi-image swaps, generate JavaScript code using ImageReady, and then edit the JavaScript to fit your particular needs.

CHAPTER SUMMARY

- Rollover effects reinforce users' actions by changing the appearance of images or links when users point to or click them.

- Rollovers can be overused, distracting the user and causing extra downloads. Use rollovers only when they serve a purpose.

- Creating different rollover states in ImageReady is very similar to creating different frames for animations.

- Styles are preconfigured combinations of multiple layer effects.

- You can use layer styles to automate the creation of simple JavaScript rollovers.

- Most rollover effects can be created with tools such as ImageReady. For more complex effects, you must edit the JavaScript code manually.

- Unlike HTML, the JavaScript programming language displays output that depends on its input.

- JavaScript can be written inline or in separate functions. Often you will use both procedures to create rollover effects.

- You should preload the images used in rollover effects so the user does not have to wait for them to download.

- You should hide JavaScript code from browsers that cannot interpret it, and test to make sure that JavaScript-compatible browsers can display the rollover effects.

REVIEW QUESTIONS

1. How many images in total are needed if you use Over and Down states with an image?

   a. 1

   b. 2

   c. 3

   d. 4

2. What HTML tag must be used with every rollover effect?

   a. A tag

   b. IMG tag

   c. P tag

   d. SCRIPT tag

3. What states do people use most often for rollover effects?

   a. Click and None

   b. Down and Up

   c. Normal, Over, and Out

   d. Normal and Over

4. Which of the following statements is true?

   a. The Custom state allows you to create additional rollover states.

   b. The names of rollover image files are set in the Name field in the Slice palette.

   c. The None state defines the image shown in the initial state, before the user mouses over it.

   d. You can select multiple states to adjust their layer properties at the same time.

5. Why should you preview a rollover in a browser?

   a. To make sure the frame disposal method works properly

   b. To make sure the images actually swap

   c. To make sure the delay times are accurate

   d. To make sure the looping works properly

6. What changes to a layer do not have to appear in all rollover states?

   a. Applying filters

   b. Applying layer styles

   c. Changing opacity

   d. Changing position

10

7. In what palette do you choose the names for rollover images?

    a. Animation palette

    b. Layers palette

    c. Rollover palette

    d. Slice palette

8. What files are created in addition to the actual images when you save a rollover in ImageReady?

    a. An HTML file only

    b. An HTML file, a JavaScript file, and a folder named images

    c. An HTML file and a folder named images

    d. An HTML file and a JavaScript file

9. How do you add animation effects to a rollover image?

    a. Create the animation file separately and manually insert it into the HTML file.

    b. Create the animation using the Animation palette, then import it into the Rollover palette.

    c. It cannot be done.

    d. Select the state in the Rollover palette, then create the animation in the Animation palette.

10. Which of the following statements is false?

    a. JavaScript is not the same as VBScript.

    b. JavaScript ignores white space.

    c. Lines of JavaScript code must end in semicolons.

    d. JavaScript must always be written inside SCRIPT tags.

11. Because it includes parentheses at the end of its name, what is rollover()?

    a. an argument

    b. a function

    c. a state

    d. a variable

12. Where would this code be placed in a Web page?

    ```
    onMouseOver="document.a.src='b.gif'; document.c.src= 'd.gif'"
    ```

    a. between STYLE tags

    b. between SCRIPT tags

    c. between A tags

    d. inside an IMG tag

13. What do we know from looking at the code in question 12?

    a. The number of images swapped by this rollover

    b. What happens when the mouse clicks down on the image

    c. What happens when the mouse rolls off the image

    d. What image is being rolled over

14. What does the following code contain?

    ```
    language="JavaScript"
    ```

    a. an HTML attribute and value of the SCRIPT tag

    b. an HTML attribute and value of the STYLE tag

    c. a JavaScript attribute and value of the SCRIPT tag

    d. a JavaScript attribute and value of the STYLE tag

15. What is the purpose of the code in question 14?

    a. It tells the browser that the rollover is not CSS-based.

    b. It tells the browser that the rollover is not HTML-based.

    c. It tells the browser that the rollover is not Java-based.

    d. It tells the browser that the rollover is not VBScript-based.

16. What browser will not display JavaScript rollovers?

    a. IE 4

    b. Netscape 3

    c. Netscape 4

    d. Netscape 6

17. What is the difference between Java and JavaScript?

    a. Java does not run in the browser.

    b. JavaScript can be run only in a Web browser.

    c. JavaScript is not a programming language.

    d. They are two names for the same thing.

18. What would this script do?

    ```
    if (document.images) {document.write("Success")}
    ```

    a. cause an error

    b. do nothing

    c. write the word Success on the Web page

    d. write the word Success on the Web page, only if the browser supports JavaScript rollovers

10

19. What would this script do?

    ```
    var foo=new Image(); foo.src="bar.jpg";
    ```

    a. It cannot be determined.

    b. Preload an image file named bar.jpg

    c. Preload an image file named foo

    d. Swap an image named foo with one named bar.jpg

20. How can you create rollover effects that will work in every browser?

    a. This cannot be done.

    b. The JavaScript must be hand-coded.

    c. The rollover state images in Photoshop must be edited.

    d. The code generated in software such as ImageReady must be used.

HANDS-ON PROJECTS

Project 1: Analyzing Rollover Effects on the Web

You want to incorporate rollover effects on your Web site, but first you want to see what other designers are doing with them.

Complete the following steps:

1. Using your Web browser, find at least three Web sites that use rollover effects.

2. Move your pointer over the images.

3. Are the images preloaded? You can tell by rolling the pointer over the images, and noticing whether there is a delay. If the rollover images are preloaded, there should be no delay.

4. How many states are used? Do the images use only Normal and Over, or do the effects include additional images for Down and Up?

5. Do any of the sites use rollover effects for instructional purposes, such as swapping in explanatory text messages? Or, are the effects only for navigation buttons?

6. Look at the source code used on the pages. Are the rollover effects created with a JavaScript function? Can you tell what the script does?

Project 2: Using Animation in a Rollover in ImageReady

You want a simple rollover effect, but do not want to do more than change the colors of the initial image. Animate the MouseOver state image so that it rotates when the mouse is over it.

Complete the following steps:

1. In ImageReady open the **house.gif** file from the Data Disk.

2. Select **Duplicate Layer** two times from the Layers palette menu.

3. Select the **top layer**.

4. Select the **Edit** menu, point to **Transform**, then click **Numeric**.

5. In the dialog box, type **10** under Rotate and click **OK**.

6. Select the **middle layer** and rotate it by **–10** degrees.

7. Open the **Rollover palette** and duplicate the **Normal** state. Make sure it is of type Over.

8. Select the **Over** state and open the **Animation palette**.

9. Click the **Duplicate Frame** button at the bottom of the Animation palette.

10. Select the **second frame**, and then deselect the **visibility icons** for the middle and bottom layers.

11. Select the **first frame** and deselect the **visibility icons** for the top and bottom layers.

12. Set the delay for both frames to **0.1** seconds and set the looping to **Forever**.

13. Play the animation to confirm that the house rocks back and forth.

14. Open the **Rollover palette** again.

15. Select the **Normal** state and deselect the **visibility icons** for the top and middle layers.

16. Preview the rollover in a browser. The house should be straight. When you roll over the house it should wiggle back and forth.

17. Optimize and save the rollover images and HTML in a new folder named **project_10-2**. Save the HTML file as **house.html**.

Project 3: Use Styles to Automate Rollover Creation in ImageReady

You want a quick, simple rollover effect. Use layer rollover styles to quickly make a three-state rollover effect.

Complete the following steps:

1. In ImageReady, create a new **36-pixel square image** with a **transparent** background.

2. Use the Paint Can tool to fill the layer with any color.

3. Show the **Styles** palette.

4. To make sure you have the default style set displayed, select **Reset Styles** from the Styles palette menu.

5. Click the style named **3-state Gradient** from the Styles palette.

6. In the Optimize palette, select the preset named **JPEG High**.

7. Show the **Slice** palette.

8. In the Name text box, type **button**.

9. In the URL text box, type **next.html**.

10. Preview the rollover in a browser.

11. In ImageReady, click the **File** menu, click **Save Optimized As**, and save the HTML file as **button.html** in a new folder named **project_10-3**.

Project 4: Using Different Optimization Settings for Rollovers in ImageReady

In ImageReady, all layers and states must be optimized using the same settings. This is inconvenient when the states require different settings. You can create a rollover using weaker optimization, then later you can further optimize specific states.

Complete the following steps:

1. In ImageReady, create a new **image**, **50** pixels high and **100** pixels wide with a **transparent** background.

2. In the Rollover palette, create an **Over** state.

3. In the Layers palette, duplicate the layer.

4. Select the **lower layer**.

5. Use the Paint Can tool to fill the layer with **white**.

6. Select the **Buttons** style set from the Styles palette menu.

7. Click the style named **Clear Embossed**.

8. Select the **upper layer**.

9. Using **red** text, type the word **Vote!** with the Type tool. Center the text.

10. Select the **Over** state and select **Match Layer across States** from the Rollover Palette menu.

11. Select the **Normal state** and make sure only the upper layer is visible.

12. Select the **Over state** and make sure both layers are visible.

13. Open the **Optimized tab** in the image window. In the Optimize palette, adjust the settings to **8-color GIF**.

14. Select each of the **states** to view in the Image window with the Optimize tab selected. The Normal state should look fine, but the Over state will look banded.

15. In the Optimize palette, select the preset named **JPEG High**. Both states should look fine with this setting, but the first state could be optimized much more.

16. Save the optimized files and HTML file in a new folder named **project_10-4**. Name the HTML file **vote.html**.

17. Find the image used for the Normal state, open it in ImageReady and reoptimize it again with **8 colors** as a **GIF**.

18. Save the image as **vote_01.gif**.

19. In a text editor, edit the HTML file to reflect the new name.

Project 5: Create a Secondary-Image Rollover with ImageReady

Edit the HTML from Project 3 to create a rollover effect that affects a secondary image. You cannot create the rollover for this exercise with ImageReady alone. You must edit the rollover's HTML code.

Complete the following steps:

1. Open the file named **button.html** from Project 3 in a text editor.
2. Save the file as **button2.html** in a new folder named **project_10-5**.
3. Copy the **images** folder from project_10-3 to project_10-5.
4. Add the following IMG tag to the bottom of the page, above the </BODY> tag:

   ```
   <IMG NAME="button2" SRC="images/button-down.jpg">
   ```

5. Edit the values of the attributes of the A tag so that the four calls to the changeImages() function use **"button2"** as a parameter instead of using "button".
6. Edit the line beginning with ONMOUSEUP to use **"button.jpg"** as a parameter instead of using "button-over.jpg".
7. Save the HTML file and open it in a browser. Rolling over and clicking the button on the left should cause the image on the right to swap.

Project 6: Create a Simple Rollover in JavaScript

You are creating another Web site and want the rollover effect to be visible by as many users as possible. However, you need to create the page as quickly as possible. Knowing you can use a more-sophisticated method later, use inline JavaScript to create the rollovers.

Complete the following steps:

1. In Photoshop or ImageReady, create **three round buttons 72** pixels high and **72** pixels wide with **transparent** backgrounds.
2. In **black** text, type the words **one**, **two**, and **three** on the buttons.
3. Optimize and save the images as **one.gif**, **two.gif**, and **three.gif** in a new folder named **project_10-6**.
4. Select the **Paintbrush** tool and set the foreground color to **yellow**.
5. Select each **image** in turn, and add a new layer behind the text. Use a **65-pixel feathered brush** to add a **faded yellow spot** behind the text.
6. Save these new images as **one_glow.gif**, **two_glow.gif**, and **three_glow.gif**.
7. Open a new text file and save it as **rollover.html** in the project folder.

10

8. Copy the following HTML into the file:

```
<a href="one.html"
        onMouseOver= "document.one.src='one_glow.gif';"
        onMouseOut= "document.one.src='one.gif';">
<img src="one.gif" name="one" border="0"></a>
```

9. Duplicate this code twice, changing every reference of "one" to **"two"** and **"three"**, respectively.

10. Save the file and view it in a browser. Test to make sure the three images change as you mouse over them, and change back as you roll away from them.

Project 7: Create MouseDown Rollovers with JavaScript

You have a next button that is too plain. Make it more interesting by using ImageReady to add a second image for the MouseDown state.

Complete the following steps:

1. In ImageReady, create a **50-pixel square image**.

2. Make the foreground **green (#009900)** and select the **Line** tool.

3. Select the **Create filled region** box. Set the Weight to **5**. Select an **arrowhead** at the end of the line. Set the shape to **500%** width and **250%** length.

4. Draw a **line** from left to right across the middle of the Image window. Hold down the **Shift** key to keep the line horizontal.

5. Select **Duplicate Layer** from the Layers palette menu.

6. In the lower layer, turn the arrow **black** by using the Hue/Saturation window and setting the Lightness to **−100**.

7. Select the **Gaussian Blur** filter and blur the layer at a radius of **2** pixels.

8. Open the **Rollover palette** and click the **New** button at the bottom of the Rollover palette to duplicate the state. Change the type of the new state to Down by holding down the **mouse** button over the state name and selecting **Down**.

9. Select the **Normal** state in the Rollover palette. Select the **upper layer** in the Layers palette.

10. Select the **Move** tool. Press the **up arrow** key four times and the **left arrow** key three times. This should move the green arrow up and to the left of the black arrow.

11. Click the **Rollover Preview** button in the toolbox or in the Rollover palette.

12. The arrow should appear to float above its shadow. Click the **image** in the Image Window. The arrow appears to be pressed down.

13. Click the **Preview in Default Browser** button in the toolbox. You should see the arrow and all necessary JavaScript below it, including all preloading functions.

14. Select **Save Optimized As** from the File menu. Save the HTML page as **arrow.html** in a new folder named project_10-7.

Project 8: Create Image Swaps Controlled by Text Links

Rollover effects do not have to involve rolling over images. Create images containing text that describes the links used to display those images.

Complete the following steps:

1. In Photoshop or ImageReady, create three **100-pixel square images**.

2. Use the Type tool to add text messages to each image. In the first, write **The latest news about graphics on the Web**. In the second, write **See sample images in our photo gallery**. In the third, write **Biographies of our staff**.

3. Optimize and save the images as **text1.gif**, **text2.gif**, and **text3.gif** in a new folder named **project_10-8**.

4. Create a **1-pixel transparent image**. Save it as **clear.gif**.

5. Open a new text file and save it as **text.html** in the project folder.

6. Copy the following code into the text file. The swapImage() function needs only one argument, since it will be making changes to only one IMG tag.

```
<script language="JavaScript">
<!--
function swapImage(imageFileName)
{
        document.textImage.src = imageFileName;
}
//-->
</script>
<img src="clear.gif" name="textImage" height="100" width="
100">
<br>
<a href="news.html"
  onMouseOver="swapImage('text1.gif')"
  onMouseOut="swapImage('clear.gif')">News</a>
```

7. Duplicate the anchor tag twice and edit the link text to read **Gallery** and **Who's Who**.

8. Edit the name of the image file used for the MouseOver states to **text2.gif** and **text3.gif**.

9. Save the HTML file and open it in a browser. Rolling over the three links displays the relevant text image above each link. Rolling off the links returns the image to the blank, transparent image.

10

Case Project

By this point, your portfolio should almost be finished. It should contain pages for your gallery and pages for your resume and biography. The pages should be linked together using a navigation bar with buttons. Now you should add rollover effects to the buttons in the navigation bar.

❏ You created a set of navigation buttons for the chapter on buttons. Create duplicates of these to use as rollover graphics. The rollover versions should change color in a way that highlights the text and distinguishes them from the nonrollover buttons.

❏ Use JavaScript from ImageReady or from one of the examples in this chapter to create the effect.

❏ In addition to the buttons, create 150-pixel square graphics with text descriptions of the different sections in your site.

❏ When the user rolls over a navigation button, the rollover image should appear, and the related text image should also appear on the side.

11

CREATING SPLASH SCREENS

Creating Image Maps

> **In this chapter, you will:**
> ◆ Design splash screens
> ◆ Use guides
> ◆ Create image maps with ImageReady
> ◆ Create image maps manually

Splash screens are often used on the Web to introduce sites. Unlike magazines, Web sites have no front cover that quickly establishes the identity of the site. Most sites have a unique logo and color scheme, but many use the same layout and end up looking almost exactly alike. Designers of some sites choose to use a large graphic on the home page to introduce the site to visitors and to help distinguish the home page. These splash screens might be only a large static graphic, or also can link to other parts of the site.

You can use any type of graphic for splash screens, but a common one is an image map, which is a single graphic that can link to multiple destinations. Image maps do have some limitations, so you might prefer to lay out your splash screen using tables in HTML and multiple small image files instead of one large image map.

This chapter covers creating image maps and using graphics to lay out Web pages.

DESIGNING SPLASH SCREENS

Not every site is appropriate for using splash screens. Web page design often involves a compromise between speed and graphics; most sites need to focus on being fast rather than being attractive, if they want to retain users who are reluctant to wait for pages to download. Design is, of course, more than just making things attractive. It also is about making the interface more useful by helping to identify content and by making navigation clear. A well-designed splash screen, therefore, should be more than something pleasing to the eyes. It can establish the identity of the site as well as all of the content and features available on the site. It also can be functional, and provide clear navigation to the rest of the site. Many sites can benefit from using splash screens, as long as they do not take too long to download.

If you decide to use a splash screen, it will probably be the largest image on the site, with a few hundred pixels on each side. Most Web graphics have tight constraints of dimensions, file size, and purpose, so creating images such as buttons, bullets, and animations is more craft than art. Splash screens provide the biggest opportunity for artistic expression and require the most creative design skills of any type of Web graphic.

You can create splash screens using image maps (described later), or using multiple pieces of a larger image positioned in the cells of HTML tables. You also can use Flash or other animation formats.

Splash screens are normally used on the home page of a site and are the users' first introduction to the style of the rest of the site. The splash screen sets the mood for all the pages to follow. If the splash screen takes a few minutes to load completely, the user may suspect the rest of the site will also load slowly. If the navigation is unclear and requires hunting for the proper link, the user may suspect that the rest of the site also has an unintuitive architecture. If the splash screen is attractive and useful, however, the user probably will have high expectations for the other pages.

The design of a splash screen has to be as creative and interesting as possible, without compromising the needs of quick downloading.

Selecting a Format

If you look around the Web, you will see that only certain types of sites use splash screens. Most commercial sites make money from displaying ads or by collecting commissions from online purchases. The producers of these sites normally want the content or services to be available to users as quickly as possible, and splash screens can represent barriers that users must cross before they can begin engaging with the site. The style of most commercial pages is to provide the user with as much content and as many links as possible at all times, encouraging them to click to additional pages. Commercial sites usually have no blank space and fill every inch with information, navigation buttons, or advertisements. Commercial sites rarely use any extraneous design or graphics. Their business relies on pages loading quickly, and they do not use elements that slow down the loading of a page.

A better candidate for splash screens is a promotional site. Promotional sites range from personal sites (that promote a person or hobby), to portfolio sites that promote an artist and his or her work, to corporate sites that promote a product or image. The purpose of these sites is to define the brand, image, and mood of a person or product and to provide information or services. Splash screens are appropriate for these sites because the graphical display of information and navigation allows the designer to evoke a feeling, instead of merely listing text links.

Another type of site that can benefit from splash screens is one that requires users to open an account before accessing the site. Such sites include online banking or stock trading sites. The producers of these sites usually want to provide information only to users who do have accounts on the site. The front page of these sites requires only an identity, a login box, a signup box, and information about the site. This often leaves plenty of room for a splash screen. Without one, the page would be nearly empty. So, in addition to helping brand the site, splash screens can help fill a page.

If you choose to create a splash screen for a site, you have several choices for implementation. You can create an image map, lay out several small images in a table, or use an advanced technology such as Flash, which is a vector animation format requiring a plug-in.

Using an Image Map

If you have tried positioning buttons in tables, you know it can be difficult to use any layout other than a simple row or column. Image maps, on the other hand, allow pixel-perfect control over the positioning of your graphics. Instead of multiple images where each one links to a different page, an image map is a single image that can have links to many pages. The locations and sizes of the linked regions are defined in HTML code. The links in image maps are called **hot spots**. Recall that any image can be used as a hyperlink. Because Web graphics are always rectangular, the clickable area is always rectangular as well, even when the image contains transparency. With image maps, the hot spots can be rectangular, circular, or polygonal—having many sides. These are shown in Figure 11-1.

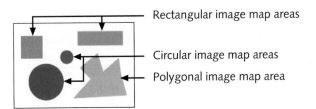

Figure 11-1   Different shapes of hot spots

Another advantage to image maps is that you can use soft, feathered gradations of color over textured backgrounds in an image map, as shown in Figure 11-2. This cannot be done with normal buttons, which always have hard edges.

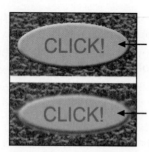

Button image placed over background image with hard edge

Button incorporated into image map with soft edge

Figure 11-2 Feathered edges over a background in an image map

Because image maps tend to be larger than other types of Web graphics, and have larger file sizes, it is worth creating an image map only when you have a complex design that cannot be easily implemented with multiple small images. Usually, the image maps take longer to download than anything else on a site. This is especially problematic because splash screen pages are almost always the first page that users see. It is crucial to not discourage users when they get to that first page. Everyone who has used the Web has had the experience of trying to view a page, becoming frustrated by how slowly the page loads, then clicking the back button and trying a different site. If users must wait more than several seconds for a page to load before they see anything, they will try another site. As with every Web graphic, you have to find the right balance between an attractive image and one that loads quickly.

Few site designers use image maps. They prefer to use several images positioned near each other in a grid. This type of image is called a sliced image. Other alternatives to creating an image map are to use a Flash animation or a 3-D graphic as a splash screen. These alternatives are discussed in the following sections. One reason for using image maps as opposed to these other options is that image maps are single images, and all links are available at the same time. If you use several buttons, or use individual images positioned close to each other in tables, users might have to wait and watch as each component image loads.

Using a Sliced Image

Image maps tend to be large, perhaps a few hundred pixels in each direction, and their files are large, too. Image maps must use the same optimization method for the whole image, even if large areas are solid color. When optimizing an image, whether through color reduction or compression, you must choose the appropriate optimization method, based on the highest color area of the image. Even if most of the image is blank, as long as a section of the image contains smooth gradients or photographic detail, the entire image must be optimized for these high-color areas. The image cannot be optimized fully; this results in a file that is larger than necessary. To solve this problem, break up the image map into several pieces, optimize each piece separately, and display them in a grid. This is similar to the tabbed interfaces discussed in the Creating Buttons chapter.

Slicing images allows you to compress each image slice separately. It also allows you to animate or swap specific regions in the splash screen, as you do with rollover effects, which are covered in the Creating Image Rollover Effects chapter. The disadvantage to using these presentations is that they can be very complicated to put together, even with the help of software such as ImageReady.

Another disadvantage is that you cannot use circles or complex polygons as clickable areas because the tables that contain them are rectilinear. All clickable images in a sliced image must be rectangular. This is not a problem for most projects, but if you have many small linked areas near each other in a sliced image, and the clickable areas are adjacent, the user can accidentally click the wrong link. Figure 11-3 shows the difference between image map hot spots and clickable sliced images.

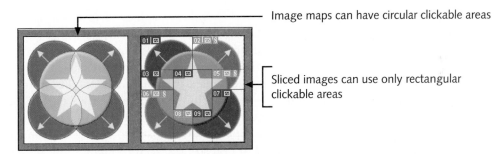

Image maps can have circular clickable areas

Sliced images can use only rectangular clickable areas

Figure 11-3   Clickable areas in image maps and sliced images

Still, because of the additional optimization control and the ability to animate and swap specific sections of the larger image, most sites use sliced images for their splash screens rather than image maps. Creating sliced images is covered fully in the Creating Sliced Images chapter.

Using Flash

You might want to use Flash to create animations for your splash screens instead of using image maps. Flash is actually perfect for splash screens because it can contain sophisticated animation and, as a vector file, the Flash movie loads quickly. Flash movies usually take more time to create than image maps or sliced images, so you would not use Flash to create small images such as simple buttons or logos. Because splash screens are larger and can showcase your work, the time it takes to create a Flash movie is worth the effort.

Splash screens are the first image users see at a site, and provide an opportunity for the designer to impress the user. An application such as Flash helps you create animations that are more sophisticated than the simple GIF animations discussed in the Creating Animation for the Web chapter. The main advantage of using Flash is that your sophisticated animations also will have a relatively small file size. On the other hand, animating an image map or table full of sliced images using ImageReady will produce files that are prohibitively large.

To view a Flash animation, users must have installed the appropriate version of the Flash plug-in in their browser. You cannot guarantee that all users will have the appropriate plug-in. According to Macromedia, the developer of Flash, over 90% of users have a Flash plug-in installed on their browser. However, many of these plug-ins are older versions, compatible with Flash versions 2 or 3. These older versions cannot display movies created with the latest version of Flash, which at this writing is Flash 5. If you do use Flash, you need to create a backup image that will display if the user's browser does not have the proper plug-in and the Flash movie does not play. So, even if you do not intend for most users to use your image map, you should create one as a backup.

Using 3-D Technology

In addition to a Flash animation, consider other graphics formats for splash screens. Formats such as Virtual Reality Markup Language (VRML), Java 3D, MPEG-4 and MPEG-7 (two multimedia formats from the Moving Picture Experts Group, the same organization that developed the MP3 audio format), and Extensible 3D with XML (X3D) are programming languages or complex markup languages. The tools to create images in these formats are almost as complex as the formats themselves. Also, other than the Java applets, all these formats require special viewing software that most users do not have. These formats all use vectors, as opposed to bitmaps, to encode information about images. The viewing software is used to rasterize the vector graphics into bitmap images that can be displayed on the screen. Choose these formats when you want to create a long-playing, high-color, complex animation or interactive environment.

You may have heard of VRML or Web3D, but you probably have never actually seen graphics in these formats. These technologies help create sophisticated, 3-D Web pages that look more like a 3-D space than the usual, magazine-like 2-D page. Unfortunately, the graphics files required to view these pages are so large that even users with fast connections have to wait several minutes before the page and all necessary files load.

You can use these technologies for tasks, such as demonstrating technical information, that you already perform with conventional Web graphics. For example, you could create a 3-D environment where the user flies through a model of a skeleton or car. Sites such as educational pages for a medical school course, or a demonstration at an automobile manufacturer's site might also need to display objects this way.

You can sometimes create these sorts of demos with simpler formats such as QuickTime Virtual Reality (QTVR). QTVR files are panoramic bitmap images that have their ends connected, allowing you to scroll seamlessly across the image. See Apple's Web site (*www.apple.com*) for more information on QTVR.

Although these advanced formats have many limitations, you may want to investigate them for specialty projects. For example, if you need to show all sides of a product, and want the user to be able to rotate the product on the screen, you may want to use a QTVR file.

Using Metaphors

In some ways, designing splash screens is like designing site logos, which are discussed in the Creating and Using Icons chapter. For both types of graphics you need to convey the attitude and style of the Web site. With logos, however, you are restricted to a small space, and cannot add many elements other than the site name, address, and a small graphical representation of the site. Splash screens give you much more room, the entire browser window if you want, and you can work with many more elements.

Splash screens will not always have links; you can use graphics that decorate the page but do not link to other pages. Most splash screens will be navigation tools as well, however, and need to represent not just the site as a whole, but also a collection of discrete pages or sections.

To get started creating a splash screen that doubles as a map to the site, sketch a schematic diagram of the site, such as the one in Figure 11-4, that shows the relationship between different areas of the site.

Figure 11-4   A simple schematic diagram of a Web site

After you sketch the site, find appropriate metaphors for the different areas. The most obvious use for an image map is when you actually need people to select a geographic region. Clicking an image that looks like a roadmap can be much more intuitive than selecting individual regions from a list of links or a selection menu.

The site content itself should suggest a metaphor. If the site is related to food, for example, you can use an image of a dinner table setting, a kitchen, or a restaurant. In a restaurant image, users click the kitchen to find recipes and food preparation tips, while they click the dining room to find information about creating table designs. If the site has more technical content, you can use a metaphor such as a circuit board or a car engine.

Although a metaphor related to the site content is effective because it reflects its subject and unifies the site, you can use a common metaphor that is not related to the subject matter. For example, a simplified city map and a house plan are common site metaphors.

Sometimes you want to evoke a feeling that transcends the actual content of your site. You might want to use an image of the solar system, for example, where the home page is represented by the sun and the other pages are represented by individual planets and moons. You also might want to just use textures, colors, and fonts that are reminiscent of specific movies or other cultural artifacts, and are appropriate for the site.

Once you have found an appropriate metaphor, sketch your diagram again, using simple pictures instead of words. Include text to reinforce the meanings of the pictures, but make sure the pictures are meaningful on their own. Then simplify the diagram and pictures, removing the inessential elements to create an abstract representation. You might want to make your splash screen photorealistic, but normally you should abstract the idea to make navigation easier to understand. An abstracted version of the solar system metaphor is shown in Figure 11-5.

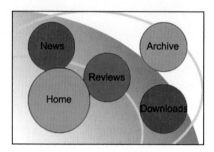

Figure 11-5   An abstraction of a solar system metaphor

Once you have a completed sketch, start creating the image in Photoshop or ImageReady.

Making the Functionality Clear

Not only do you have to make image maps functional by setting them to link to different pages, you also must make their purpose clear. You can add labels to the hot spots of image maps or to the individual slices of sliced images. While splash screens are an opportunity to be creative, the design should not overwhelm their purpose and usability. Also, splash screens are not always a substitute for text links. Make sure the users can navigate the site even if the splash screen cannot be displayed.

Using ALT Attributes

Whether you use image maps or sliced images in tables, you can add labels for the links that appear when the user rolls over them. These labels are created using the ALT attribute of the IMG tag for sliced images and the ALT attribute of the AREA tags used in image maps. Often the destinations of the links are not entirely clear. Use labels to describe the purpose of the links, reinforcing the information in the image itself. Also, users who cannot or choose not to display graphics in their browsers will not be able to navigate your site without the ALT text to help them know where the links lead. Figure 11-6 shows images with and without ALT text, as they appear in browsers, both those that can display images and those that cannot.

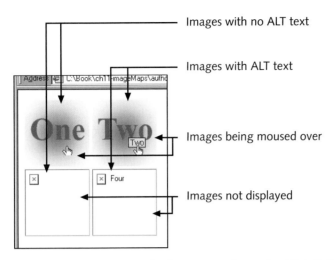

Figure 11-6   Browsers displaying text from the ALT attribute

Limiting Abstraction

Metaphors and abstraction make links more interesting than using text alone. For example, if you want to link to a section on your site containing news, you might use the image metaphor of a newsboy holding a newspaper. You could then abstract that image into just a stylized hand holding a newspaper with the word "Extra!" on the front. However, if the image maps are too abstract or the metaphors are not obvious, the images are unclear. Figure 11-7 shows a splash screen that uses too much abstraction. Although it is supposed to represent a map, that is not obvious. The metaphorical icons also are too abstract to have meaning. The graduation caps are meant to represent the locations of universities, but that also is unclear.

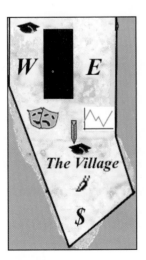

Figure 11-7   A splash screen designed with too much abstraction

Although you can be creative when designing splash screens, the links should be obvious. The users should not have to guess which areas are clickable. Game and novelty sites can encourage users to discover parts of the site on their own, and make them hunt for the part of the image that actually leads somewhere, but professional Web sites should have clear and easy navigation.

When designing splash screens, make sure that every link is well-defined graphically. You might want to have others test the interface to make sure it is clear, such as the one in Figure 11-8. This image is based on the same idea as Figure 11-7, but is more obviously a map, and uses text because graphical metaphors inadequately represent different geographic areas.

Figure 11-8   A well-designed splash screen

Controlling Navigation

If a splash screen is well-designed, the links will take the user anywhere he or she needs to go within the site. However, you probably will not want to use an image map or a set of sliced images on every page, as it would take up too much space. You also will need to construct a navigation bar for the other pages in the site. The navigation bar must contain the same links as the splash screen, but in a condensed shape. Figure 11-9 shows two navigation bars that reflect the colors used in the splash screen shown in Figure 11-8.

When designing the navigation bar, you should repeat the colors, lines, and textures used in the splash screen. When they match, they appear to be part of a larger design, rather than separate designs forced together. A simple navigation bar can contain only single words or phrases, while a splash screen can contain graphical representations of the links. If the designs of the navigation bar and the splash screen match, the user will be reminded of the graphical representations when using the simple text links. This helps to make the functions of the text links clear as well.

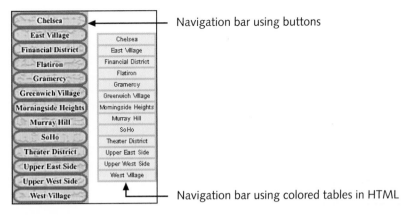

Navigation bar using buttons

Navigation bar using colored tables in HTML

Figure 11-9   A splash screen and a navigation bar that share a similar design

You should also include the navigation bar on the same page as the splash screen. Some users have the graphics display disabled in their browsers to speed the loading and rendering of pages. Some other users have text-only browsers. None of these users can navigate sites that have only graphical navigation.

When you create a splash screen with links, you plan which parts of the image users will click to perform tasks, such as going to other parts of the site. To make splash screens easy to use and navigate, you must be able to easily specify the clickable regions. Photoshop and ImageReady include a feature called guides that helps make this possible.

11.

Using Guides in Photoshop and ImageReady

Guides are thin vertical or horizontal lines that display over the image in the Image window. An example of an image with guides is shown in Figure 11-10. You use guides as an aid when laying out elements or slicing images to use later in tables. Like selection areas, guides are not saved or printed with the rest of the image when the image is saved in a Web format such as GIF or JPEG. However, they are saved in the PSD format, which is largely for saving temporary versions of files. Unlike selection areas, guides cannot be used as masks and do not constrain paint or filter effects to certain regions.

Figure 11-10   An image with guides showing

Creating Guides

The easiest way to create guides is to drag the pointer from the ruler in the Image window toward the image.

To create guides in Photoshop:

1. Open **blue_sky.tif** from the Data Disk.

2. If rulers are not visible, make them visible by selecting **Show Rulers** from the View menu.

3. Using any tool, drag the pointer from the left ruler into the image to create a vertical guide.

4. Drag the pointer down from the upper ruler to create a horizontal guide.

To see exactly where you are placing the guide, show the Info palette and watch the X and Y values in the lower-left of the Info palette. By holding down the Shift key as you drag from the ruler, you can force the guide to snap to the ticks on the ruler.

In Photoshop, you also can create guides by selecting New Guide from the View menu. In the New Guide dialog box, enter whether the guide will be horizontal or vertical, and enter the number of pixels away from the top or left side of the image to place the guide.

In ImageReady, you can create entire sets of guides at once. This is convenient for creating image maps and sliced images because you will probably want to use several guides.

Create a set of guides in ImageReady:

1. Create a 200 × 200-pixel image.

2. Select **Create Guides** from the View Menu. The Create Guides dialog box opens, as shown in Figure 11-11.

3. Select **Horizontal Guides** to create guides running across the page. Select the top radio button and enter the number **3**. This creates three guides that divide the image into four even rows.

4. Select **Vertical Guides** to create guides running from top to bottom. Select the middle radio button and enter the number **18**. This creates 11 evenly spaced guides. The guides count from the upper-left corner, so any remaining gaps will appear on the right or bottom edges if the spacing of the guides does not divide evenly into the dimensions of the image. This results in a leftover space on the right side of the image.

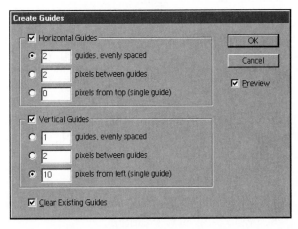

Figure 11-11   The Create Guides dialog box in ImageReady

If you want to create only one guide, select the bottom option button and enter the number of pixels from the top or left side of the image that you want the guide positioned. You also can select whether to clear the existing guides.

Viewing Guides

In ImageReady, guides always appear as light blue lines. In Photoshop, you can adjust the color and set the guides to display as solid or dotted lines. Change these aspects of your guides if they conflict with colors or textures in your original image. If the original image has areas of blue sky, for example, you might not be able to see blue guide lines over it.

To adjust the color and style of guides in Photoshop:

1. With blue_sky.tif open, create a vertical guide by dragging the pointer of any tool from the left ruler to the center of the image. Because the blue of the sky is similar to the blue color of the guide, the guide is difficult to see.

2. Click **Edit** on the menu bar in Photoshop, point to **Preferences**, then click **Guides & Grid** to open the Preferences dialog box.

3. Set the color to **Light Red**, the Style to **Dashed Lines**, and then click **OK**.

11

In both ImageReady and Photoshop, you can show or hide guides. When you hide guides, you remove them from view, allowing you to see the image unobstructed. Features such as guides and selection areas are called Extras and can be hidden all at once by deselecting the Show Extras item from the View menu.

To hide guides from an image:

1. With blue_sky.tif still open, and guides visible, click **View** on the menu bar, and then click **Show Extras** to deselect it. The guides should be invisible.

2. Click **View** on the menu bar again. Point to **Show**, and then click **Guides** to select it. The guides should be visible again.

The Show submenu includes other items such as Selection areas, Guides, and Slices. Next to each one is a space for a check mark. You can toggle the visibility of these items by selecting them from this submenu. You can also show or hide all items by selecting All or None.

Working with Guides

You can move, reorient, delete, or lock guides once they are created.

To work with guides:

1. With blue_sky.tif still open in Photoshop, create a horizontal and a vertical guide.

2. Move the vertical guide. Select the **Move** tool, position the pointer over the guide, and then drag the guide to its new location.

3. Reorient the horizontal guide. Hold down the **Option** key (for Windows, hold down the **Alt** key) and click the guide. This rotates the guide, turning it from vertical to horizontal or vice versa.

4. Remove one of the guides from the image by using the Move tool to drag the guide off the image.

5. Delete all guides by selecting **Clear Guides** from the View menu.

6. Create a new guide.

7. Lock the guide by selecting **Lock Guides** from the View menu. Once you are satisfied with the positions of your guides, you should lock them so you do not accidentally move them while editing other parts of the image.

Using Snap

The Snap feature allows you to precisely position selection areas, crops, slices and other extras without having to rely on your coordination with the mouse. When Snap is enabled, new selections and slices position themselves to your guides when you drag them within eight pixels of the guide. To enable Snap, click View on the menu bar, point to Snap To, and then click Guides.

You will use guides as you plan the layout of your splash screens. With Snap enabled for guides, setting image map regions and slices for sliced tables is easier.

CREATING IMAGE MAPS WITH IMAGEREADY

ImageReady provides several features you can use to create image maps. You can define the hot spots in an image map using the Image Map tools available in the toolbox. You also can define hot spots using layers.

Using the Image Map Tools

The Image Map tools are available in the toolbox, as shown in Figure 11-12. You also can open the Image Map tools in a separate palette by selecting the bottom row of the Tool menu. The first three Image Map tools create each of the three types of hot spots: rectangular, circular, or polygonal. Drag the tool over the area you want to define as clickable, or for polygonal areas, click once for each point that defines the area. The fourth tool is the Image Map Select tool. This lets you select and resize image map regions you have already defined.

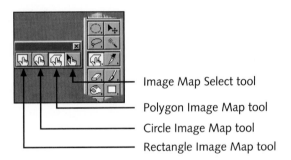

Image Map Select tool

Polygon Image Map tool

Circle Image Map tool

Rectangle Image Map tool

Figure 11-12   The Image Map tools in the ImageReady toolbox

You can constrain the Rectangle Image Map tool to create only perfect squares by holding down the Shift key as you drag. The Circle Image Map tool can be used only to create perfectly circular image map areas. You cannot create elliptical image map areas.

Create hot spots in ImageReady:

1. Open **us_map.tif** from the Data Disk.

2. Open the Image Map tools in a separate palette by clicking the **Image Map** tool area in the toolbox and selecting the bottom row.

3. Select the **Rectangle Image Map** tool from the Image Map tool palette and drag it over Colorado on the map to create a rectangular image map area.

4. Hold down the **Shift** key while dragging the pointer over North Dakota to create a square.

5. Select the **Circle Image Map** tool and drag it over Florida to create a circular image map area.

You can constrain the Rectangle Image Map tool and the Circle Image Map tool to a fixed size by selecting the Fixed Size check box in the Options bar. When this option is checked, you can enter the specific height and width you want for the rectangle, or the specific radius for the circle.

To use the Polygon Image Map tool, click anywhere in the image to create the first point. Click again to create more points; the polygon follows the path defined by the straight lines between the points you set. Hold down the Shift key to constrain the line to 45 degree increments. To finish the polygon, double-click the mouse at the last point. The line will then join the first and last point, closing the loop. You also can finish by holding the pointer near the first point you defined and clicking the mouse.

Create polygonal hot spots in ImageReady:

1. With us_map.tif still open, select the **Polygon Image Map** tool and create a polygonal image map area around California by clicking repeatedly around the perimeter. When you are finished, to complete the area click the first point you made.

To constrain all three shapes to any guides you have created, check the Snap option on the View menu.

You use the Image Map Select tool to adjust existing image map areas. First select an area with the tool; selected areas change to a new color. You can drag entire areas, or manipulate the anchor tabs on the sides and corners of the selected area. You can resize circle areas, and resize and reshape rectangle and polygonal areas.

Resize hot spots:

1. With us_map.tif still open, select the **Image Map Select** tool.

2. Select the image map area surrounding Colorado. The anchor tabs should become visible.

3. Drag the corner and side tabs to make the area fit more precisely around the state outline.

Setting Image Map Preferences

By default, the image map areas you define cloud the image below the area, making it easier to see where the hot spot is positioned. This clouding only helps you edit the image and does not affect the image itself.

To set image map preferences:

1. Click **Edit** on the menu bar, point to **Preferences**, and then click **Image Maps** to open the Image Maps dialog box, shown in Figure 11-13.

2. Select **Show Lines Only** to disable the clouding feature.

3. To adjust the clouding, enter **40%** in the Image Map Overlay text box. (0% is completely transparent and 100% is completely opaque.)

4. Set the color of the lines used to display the boundaries of image map areas to **Brick Red**.

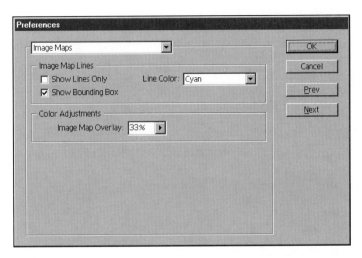

Figure 11-13   The Image Maps Preferences dialog box in ImageReady

You might want to hide the image map area outlines when editing the image. To do so, click the Image Map Visibility button in the toolbox, as shown in Figure 11-14. You also can hide the outlines by selecting Show Extras from the View menu, or by selecting Image Maps from the Show submenu under the View menu.

The Image Map Visibility button

Figure 11-14   The Image Map Visibility button

Using the Image Map Palette

You can view and set options for an image map's areas by using the Image Map palette, shown in Figure 11-15. When a rectangular or circular area is selected, the Image Map palette displays the X and Y coordinates of the upper-left corner of the area relative to the upper-left corner of the image. You can adjust these coordinates by clicking the arrows to the left of the numbers or by typing in new coordinates. In a similar way, you can edit the height and width of a rectangular area or the radius of a circular area.

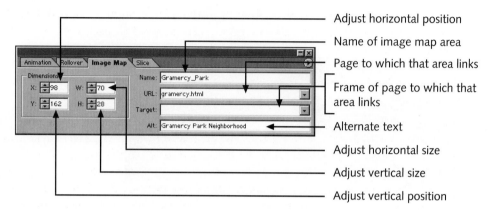

Figure 11-15 The Image Map palette in ImageReady

To adjust the dimensions of image map areas:

1. With us_map.tif still open, use the Image Map Select tool to select one of the rectangular image map areas.

2. Click **Window** on the menu bar, and then click **Show Image Map** to show the Image Map palette.

3. Click the **up arrow** next to the X value to translate the area to the right.

4. Click the **down arrow** next to the Y value to translate the area up.

5. Click the **up arrow** next to the W value to extend the right side of the area.

6. Select the circular area around Florida.

7. Click the **down arrow** next to the R value in the Image Map palette to decrease the radius of the area.

On the right side of the Image Map palette are text fields where you can enter values for an area. Each area is given a name, which is not used unless you create a rollover effect. Rollover effects and animations in image maps are not efficient because the entire image must swap or be animated, not just the selected area. In the Image Map palette, you also can set the destination URL for an area and the alternate text that will appear as a label over the area when the user's mouse is positioned there.

To set attributes for the image map area:

1. Select the image map area around California in us_map.tif.

2. In the Name text box of the Image Map palette, type **California**.

3. In the URL text box, type **cali.html**.

4. In the Alt text box, type **California. Capital: Sacramento**. This is the text that appears when a user rolls over the link.

When an image map area is selected, you can use features in the Image Map tool options or the Image Map palette menu to send the area forward or backward, or to the top or bottom of the stack of areas. The only time you will need to use this feature is when you have overlapping areas and need to define which area will take precedence. Areas in the front take precedence. You also can delete or duplicate areas by selecting those options from the Image Map palette menu.

You can select more than one area at a time by holding down the Shift key as you select areas with the Image Map Select tool. When multiple areas are selected, additional features become available in the Image Map tool options and the Image Map palette menu regarding alignment. If you wish, you can align the centers or edges of image map areas. When at least three areas are selected, you have more options for distributing the selected areas. You can evenly space the centers or edges of image map areas. You will seldom want to use the align or distribute features because normally you base the hot spots on the content of the image, instead of defining the hot spots in patterns.

Creating Image Maps from Layers

Depending on how you have constructed your splash screen, you might find it easier to define hot spots based on the layers in an image, rather than with the Image Map tools.

To create an image map area from a layer, first choose a layer that has areas of transparency. If you want the area to be based on multiple layers, you must first merge the layers. Then select New Layer Based Image Map Area from the Layer menu. This creates a **layer-based** image map area.

To create a layer-based image map area:

1. With us_map.tif still open, use the Canvas Size dialog box to pad an extra **100** pixels to the left side of the image.

2. Open **alaska.gif** from the Data Disk.

3. Click **Select** on the menu bar, and then click **All** to select the contents of the Alaska image.

4. Copy the selection and paste it into us_map.tif. Use the Move tool to position the Alaska image in the lower-left corner.

5. Make sure the new layer containing the Alaska image is selected in the Layers palette. Click **Layer** on the menu bar, and then click **New Layer Based Image Map Area**. Five new rectangular image map areas are created around the main part of the image and the clusters of islands.

11

6. In the Image Map palette, change the Shape to **Circle**. The image map areas turn into circles.

7. Change the shape to **Polygon**. The areas turn into polygonal areas.

8. Zoom in to the areas to see the multiple points.

9. Set the Quality option to **0**. This sets how many points are used to define the polygon that encloses the layer. Note how the outline is very crude and does not follow the outline of the layer very well.

10. Set the Quality to **100**. Note how the area selection more closely follows the outline of the layer. You also can see the difference in Quality settings in Figure 11-16.

11. Preview the image in a browser. Note all the coordinates required to define the polygonal coordinates of this area. Over 2,400 bytes are added to the HTML file.

12. In ImageReady, set the Quality to **60**.

13. If you edit the layer, the image map area changes accordingly to follow the new outline of the layer contents. Move the layer up with the Move tool. The image map area follows.

14. You cannot edit the individual coordinates of the area as long as it is layer-based. Click the **palette** menu in the Image Map palette, and then click **Promote Layer Based Image Map Area**. This converts the layer-based area to a tool-based area. Once a layer-based area is converted to a tool-based area it cannot be converted back.

15. Use the Image Map Select tool to edit the tabs on the polygonal image map area. Make the outline fit the shape of the state.

16. When a layer contains content separated by transparency, multiple image map areas are created. Sometimes, many small, insignificant areas are generated by this process, and are too little to be clicked by users. Select the small areas surrounding the islands and delete them.

For most layers you will want to use a polygon shape because it follows the outline of the layer more closely than do the other two shapes. The default setting for the Quality option is 80. This is a percentage of accuracy, not the number of points created for the polygon. You should use as low a value as you can to conserve the file size of the resulting HTML.

Sometimes you will want to define hot spots based on selection areas. Using the Magic Wand tool gives you more control over defining specific areas based on pixel color. To create image map regions from selection areas, copy the selection and paste it as a new layer. Then create the layer-based image map area as described in the preceding steps.

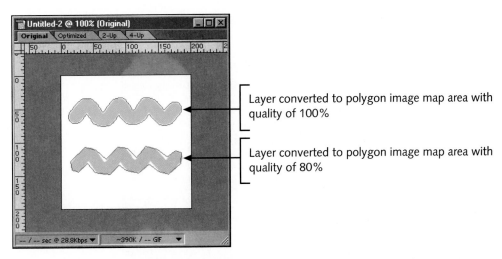

Figure 11-16   Layers converted to image map areas using different quality settings

Saving Image Maps

You save image maps as you would any other image in ImageReady. Optimize the image using the Optimize palette and select Save Optimized As from the File menu. This saves the image map image file as well as the HTML file that displays it. To incorporate the image map into a Web page, copy the necessary HTML from this file.

To save the image map:

1. Choose an appropriate setting in the Optimize palette.

2. Click **File** on the menu bar and then click **Save Optimized As**. Click the **Save as type** list arrow and then click **HTML and Images**. Save the image as **us_map.gif** in a new folder named **chapter11**. This automatically also saves an HTML file named us_map.html in the same folder.

3. Open **us_map.html** in a text editor to see the code. If you want to use the image map in a Web page, copy all the text between the comment tags and paste it into your page.

You have some control over the HTML that is produced. Click File on the menu bar, point to Output Settings, and select HTML. At the bottom of the Output Settings dialog box, shown in Figure 11-17, are two options for the HTML produced for image maps. Next to Type, make sure that Client-Side is selected. The other options are for creating server-side image map code and require a special script on the Web server. Next to Placement, select Top, Body, or Bottom to determine where the MAP tag will be placed in the created HTML file.

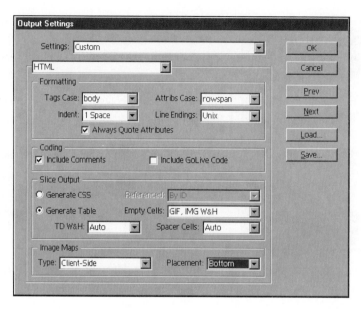

Figure 11-17   The Output Settings dialog box

CREATING IMAGE MAPS MANUALLY

Although you can easily create image maps with WYSIWYG HTML editors and tools such as ImageReady, often it is just as easy to code the HTML manually. Also, you may find yourself in a situation where you do not have access to software that can be used to create image maps, or where the software does not fully support all features of image maps. For example, some WYSIWYG HTML editors do not define polygonal hot spots. If you use one of these editors and you require clickable areas other than rectangular or circular, you must either find other software or code the HTML yourself.

In the early days of the Web, image maps were coded with server-side scripts. When the user clicked the image, a script on the Web server processed the coordinates of the place on the image the user clicked, the script looked up the appropriate destination in a list, and delivered that page to the user's browser. The drawback to this method is that server-side scripting requires additional work for both graphic designers and systems administrators. It is far easier to use the client-side image maps used today. Most browsers released after 1996 support client-side image maps.

The first step in creating a client-side image map is to define the image as an image map.

Defining an Image as an Image Map

You can use any image as an image map without editing the image file. The map itself is defined in the MAP HTML tag. This tag requires one attribute, NAME. It also requires a closing tag. Between the opening and closing tags are additional AREA tags. Each AREA tag defines one hot spot. An example MAP tag follows. It has the name *Manhattan* and contains one rectangular hot spot that links to a file named soho.html.

```
<map name="Manhattan">
<area href="soho.html" alt="SoHo" shape="rect"
coords="95,255,130,275">
</map>
```

To define an image as an image map, add the USEMAP attribute in the IMG tag. The value of the USEMAP attribute must be set to the name of the relevant MAP tag. The MAP tag does not have to be on the same page. You could have several image maps on different pages all referring to a single MAP tag. It is unlikely, but possible, that you will use more than one image map on a page. To guarantee that there is no confusion about which image uses which MAP tag, the names must be kept consistent. Here is the example again with an IMG tag accessing the map:

```
<map name="Manhattan">
<area href="soho.html" alt="SoHo" shape="rect"
coords="95,255,130,275">
</map>
<img src="manhattan.jpg" usemap="#Manhattan">
```

The USEMAP attribute must be set to the name of the map with a pound sign to the left of it. Notice that the IMG tag does not use an ALT attribute. This is unnecessary because the alternate text is defined in the ALT attribute of the AREA tag. The image tag also does not need to be wrapped in an anchor tag, because the AREA tag also contains the necessary HREF attribute to define the destination of the link.

Defining Hot Spots in an Image Map

The AREA tag requires two additional attributes, SHAPE and COORDS. The SHAPE attribute determines the shape of the hot spot and can be set to one of three possible values:

- RECT defines the hot spot as a rectangle.

- CIRCLE defines the hot spot as a circle. The circle must be symmetrical and cannot be an ellipse.

- POLY defines the hot spot as a polygon with any number of straight sides. The polygon does not have to be symmetrical and can wrap around regions in an image or even double back on itself.

11

The COORDS attribute determines the dimensions and position of the hot spot and requires numerical values, separated by commas. The values are X and Y coordinates of pixels in the image. Counting always starts at 0,0 in the upper-left corner of the image, and the numbers increase in value moving down and across. The COORDS attribute must be set for rectangular, circular, and polygonal hot spots as follows:

- For rectangular hot spots, the COORDS attribute requires four values. The first two numbers are the X and Y coordinates of the upper-left corner of the hot spot. The last two numbers are the X and Y coordinates of the lower-right corner of the hot spot. This is different from creating image maps with ImageReady, where you specify the height and width of the area, rather than the coordinates of the lower-right corner.

- For circular hot spots, the COORDS attribute requires three values. The first two numbers are the X and Y coordinates of the center of the hot spot. The last number is the radius, in pixels, of the hot spot.

- For polygonal hot spots, the COORDS attribute can take any number of pairs of values. Each pair represents the X and Y coordinates of a corner of the hot spot. The final shape is defined by the lines that connect each successive pair of coordinates. The point defined by the last pair of values connects back to the first pair. Because it is easy to get confused when typing or editing long strings of numbers, remember that there should always be an even number of values of the COORDS attribute for polygonal hot spots.

The following is an example using all three shapes of hot spots, as shown in Figure 11-18:

```
<map name="Manhattan">
<area href="gramercy.html" alt="Gramercy Park"
shape="rect" coords="93,165,    174,195">
<area href="financial.html" alt="Financial District"
shape="circle" coords="110,306,35">
<area href="theater.html" alt="Theater District" shape="pol
y" coords="7,106,    64,106,    64,123,    85,123,    85,165,
 13,169,    7,152">
</map>

<img src="manhattan.jpg" usemap="#Manhattan">
```

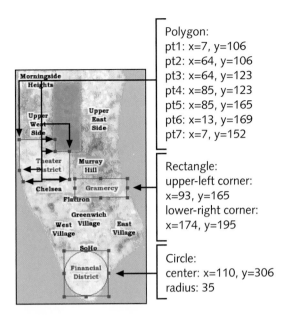

Polygon:
pt1: x=7, y=106
pt2: x=64, y=106
pt3: x=64, y=123
pt4: x=85, y=123
pt5: x=85, y=165
pt6: x=13, y=169
pt7: x=7, y=152

Rectangle:
upper-left corner:
x=93, y=165
lower-right corner:
x=174, y=195

Circle:
center: x=110, y=306
radius: 35

Figure 11-18   An image map with hot spots of different shapes

The hot spots are not outlined or indicated in any way on the image, other than that the ALT text appears when the pointer is over the hot spot. In the figure, the outlines are added for explanation. The spacing of the values for the COORDS attribute does not matter. You might want to add extra space to make the coordinates more readable.

Finding the Coordinates for Hot Spots

The only tricky part of creating image maps manually is finding the exact coordinates to use for the hot spots. Most image software has a feature that lets you know the exact position of any pixel in the image. In Photoshop and ImageReady, you use the Info palette. So, while you can create image maps manually, you still need to rely on graphics software to help find the coordinates. The Info palette always displays the position of the pointer relative to the rest of the image.

To find the values for a rectangular hot spot, position the pointer in the upper-left corner of the region you want to be linked. Look at the X and Y values in the Info palette and add them to your HTML code. Then do the same for the lower-right corner. You might find it easier to select the area with the Rectangular Marquee tool first.

To find the values for a circular hot spot, select the Elliptical Marquee tool and position the pointer over the center of where you want the hot spot. Note the coordinates in the Info palette and add them to your HTML. Hold down the Shift and Option keys and drag the pointer over the image to create a perfect circle selection centered around your

11

original coordinates. Note the Width and Height values in the Info palette. These are equal to the diameter of the circle. Because you want the radius, record half of the width.

If you're working in Windows and want to create a perfect circular selection, hold down the Alt key and then drag the pointer over the image.

To find the values for a polygonal hot spot, select the Polygonal Lasso tool and select the area you want as a hot spot. Then position the pointer over each corner and note the coordinates in the Info palette. Record the coordinates of each corner, in order, around the image. If you record the coordinates out of order, you might get hot spots that double back on themselves, as shown in Figure 11-19. These hot spots work, but might not produce the results you intend.

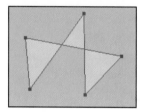

Figure 11-19   A polygonal hot spot that crosses over itself

If you define multiple hot spots that overlap each other, the browser gives precedence to the first area defined. You can use overlapping to create oddly shaped hot spots such as crescents.

CHAPTER SUMMARY

- Splash screens should establish the identity of the site, make the available content clear, and evoke a feeling about the site.

- Image maps are relatively easy to make, but tend to be large and have less flexibility than sliced images.

- Using Flash or other advanced technology requires more effort than creating image maps and the resultant images will not be supported by all users' browsers.

- Guides make it easy to plan where to place hot spots or make cuts for sliced images.

- Snap the edges of the image map areas to guides to keep them aligned.

- Hot spots in image maps can have three shapes: rectangular, circular, or polygonal.

- You can create hot spots for image maps in ImageReady with the Image Map tools, or by basing them on different layers in the Layers palette.

❏ A polygonal hot spot can be created to follow a complex outline exactly, but including every point may result in burdensome HTML. Use as few points as possible to minimize file size.

❏ You need to write the coordinates of the hot spots in the HTML file that displays the image map. These coordinates are available from the Info palette.

❏ ImageReady saves both the image and the HTML file necessary to display the image map. You can copy, paste, and edit the HTML in your own Web pages.

REVIEW QUESTIONS

1. Which of the following is true about image maps?

   a. They can have animations in specific regions.

   b. They can have circular hot spots.

   c. They contain complicated tables.

   d. They contain one image file for each area.

2. Which of the following is true about sliced images?

   a. They can have animations in specific regions.

   b. They can have polygonal hot spots.

   c. They do not contain complicated tables.

   d. They contain one image file.

3. What kind of site is not appropriate for splash screens?

   a. E-commerce site that requires user accounts

   b. Online magazine

   c. Online portfolio

   d. Promotional site

4. Which of the following is true about Flash and 3-D technologies?

   a. They have universal browser support.

   b. They are not good for specialty visualizing projects.

   c. They do not use vectors.

   d. They require a long development time.

11

5. Which of the following statements is false?

   a. Client-side image maps are obsolete.

   b. Server-side image maps are obsolete.

   c. Server-side image maps require a script on the server.

   d. Server-side image maps use the USEMAP attribute in the IMG tag.

6. Which of the following is a reason to use an image map?

   a. You want to animate certain areas in a graphic.

   b. You want to optimize certain areas in a graphic differently from other areas.

   c. You want to use HTML instead of graphical elements.

   d. You want to use polygonal hot spots.

7. Which of the following image formats can be used as image maps?

   a. GIF only

   b. GIF or JPEG only

   c. GIF, JPEG, or PNG

   d. JPEG only

8. Which of the following is not a way to use the Create Guides dialog box in ImageReady to create a horizontal guide that runs through the middle of an image that is 100 pixels high?

   a. Make one guide, evenly spaced

   b. Make 49 pixels between guides

   c. Make 50 pixels between guides

   d. Make a single guide that is 50 pixels from the top

9. Which of the following statements about guides in Photoshop or ImageReady is false?

   a. Guides are saved with PSD images.

   b. Guides can be saved with GIF and JPEG images.

   c. Guides do not affect edits made to an image.

   d. Guides do not print.

10. Which of the following is not a way to hide guides from view?

    a. Deselect Guides from the Show submenu.

    b. Deselect Show Extras.

    c. Double-click the guides.

    d. Select None from the Show submenu.

11. What happens when you hold down the Option key (Alt key in Windows) and click the guide?

    a. The guide is deleted.

    b. The guide is hidden.

    c. The guide is selected.

    d. The guide reorients from vertical to horizontal or vice-versa.

12. If you see that the Image Map palette includes options for Shape and Quality, what do you know about the currently selected image map area?

    a. It is a tool-based area.

    b. It is a layer-based area.

    c. It is a polygon.

    d. It is not a circle.

13. How would you create an elliptical hot spot in ImageReady?

    a. Overlap two circular hot spots.

    b. With the Circle Image Map tool

    c. With the Ellipse Image Map tool

    d. It cannot be done.

14. Which of the following options are available when two image map areas are selected in ImageReady?

    a. Alignment

    b. Changing the stacking order

    c. Conversion to layer-based hot spots

    d. Distribution

15. How do you numerically change the size of a circular image map area in the Image Map palette in ImageReady?

    a. Edit the H value.

    b. Edit the R value.

    c. Edit the W value.

    d. Edit the X value.

11

16. Why would you not use a Quality setting of 100 when converting a layer-based image map area to a polygonal tool-based one?

    a. A polygon set to 100% is the same as a circle.

    b. It generates too many coordinate points.

    c. The polygon will not follow the true outline of the layer.

    d. A setting of 100 should be used; it gives the best results.

17. Why do you need to include a NAME attribute in the MAP tag?

    a. A NAME attribute is unnecessary.

    b. So the AREA tag knows to which map it applies

    c. So the IMG tag knows which map to use

    d. So the MAP tag knows to what image it applies

18. Which of the following is not a valid value for the SHAPE attribute of the AREA tag?

    a. "circle"

    b. "poly"

    c. "rect"

    d. "square"

19. Which of the following statements is true?

    a. Circular hot spots always take four coordinates.

    b. Rectangular hot spots always take four coordinates.

    c. Polygonal hot spots can take any number of coordinates as long as the number is odd.

    d. Polygonal hot spots are defined by listing X/Y pairs with the radius to the next point.

20. Which of the following is a valid AREA tag?

    a. `<a href="net.html"><area shape="circle" coords="98,87, 76" src="map.jpg"></a>`

    b. `<area coords="13,24,35,46" shape="rect" href="next.html"> <img src="map.jpg"></area>`

    c. `<area shape="circle" href="next.html" coords="12,23,34">`

    d. `<area shape="poly" href="next.html" coords="12 23, 34 45, 56 67, 78 89">`

HANDS-ON PROJECTS

Project 1: Exploring Splash Screens on the Web

Many sites use splash screens, but others do not. In your Web browser, visit at least 20 Web sites and answer the following questions:

1. As a percentage, how many Web sites use splash screens of one kind or another?

2. What sorts of sites are these? Are they online magazines, service sites, retail sites, or promotional sites?

3. How many of these splash screens are created using Flash? How many use image maps? How many use images in tables?

4. How would you characterize these splash screens? Do they contain mostly text, some text, or no text at all?

Project 2: Designing a Splash Screen

You are part of a team of people developing the front end for a new Web site that sells children's toys. Design a splash screen to use on the home page of this site.

Complete the following steps:

1. In Photoshop, create a new image that is **320** pixels wide and **240** pixels high. There is no standard size for splash screens, but this is a common size.

2. The site contains six sections: Electronic Toys, Board Games, Dolls and Stuffed Animals, Educational Toys, Computer Games, and Infant and Toddler. Rather than list links to the different sections, create a single image that incorporates the six section names as well as icons for each section. For example, include an image of a teddy bear near the link to Stuffed Animals.

3. Use a large, simple sans serif font such as Clownface or Comic sans for the text containing the different section names.

4. Because the theme of the site is related to children, use bright colors for the text and background colors. Use pure black (#000000) and white (#ffffff), the paint primaries red (#ff0000), yellow (#ffff00), and blue (#0000ff), and the paint secondaries orange (#ff9900), green (#00ff00), and purple (#9900ff).

5. The background color of the home page is white. The edges of the image should also be white so that the screen blends with the background color.

6. Render the design in Photoshop, using layers to separate all the elements from each other.

7. Save the file as **toy_screen.psd** in a new folder named **project_11-2**.

11

Project 3: Designing Another Splash Screen

You need to create another splash screen, this time for an alternative music site.

The section names do not lend themselves to obvious iconography the way those of the toy site do. The metaphor for this image should evoke a feeling, rather than actually show pictures of the content.

Complete the following steps:

1. In Photoshop, create a new image that is **320** pixels wide and **240** pixels high.

2. The color scheme for this site is very dark. The background color of the home page is black. Make the image black.

3. Create a rough pattern to use as the background, using the Add Noise filter and at least one other filter to add texture.

4. Blur the image with a radius of **0.3** pixels.

5. Colorize the image to a Hue of **150**.

6. Use an ornate, highly serifed font such as Gothic or Frankenstein to label the sections of the site: **News**, **Reviews**, **Downloads**, **Interviews**, **Calendar**. Use subtle monochromatic text to reinforce each section. Use dark shades of alternative colors such as dark ochre (#666633), maroon (#660033), and dark teal (#00366).

7. Add an **Outer Glow** effect to each text layer to make it easier to read. Keep each piece of text for each link in its own layer.

8. Save the image with layers intact as **music_screen.psd** in a new folder named **project_11-3**.

Project 4: Creating an Image Map in ImageReady

You have a map of Manhattan that is to be used as a navigation tool for linking to pages about businesses in different New York City neighborhoods. Use ImageReady to create an image map so that any click on the land area takes the user to a destination.

Complete the following steps:

1. In ImageReady, open file **imap.gif** from the Data Disk.

2. Use the Rectangular Image Map tool to select the **green** area in the image.

3. Select the **Image Map Select** tool to adjust the area. Alternately, adjust the X, Y, W, and H values in the Image Map palette.

4. With the area selected, type **park.html** in the URL field in the Image Map palette and type **Central Park** in the Alt field.

5. Everywhere you see text in the image, create a polygonal hot spot around it. Adjust the points with the Image Map Select tool so that nearly every pixel of the image (other than the blue water) is covered by one of the hot spots.

6. For each area, add the text from the image to the URL and Alt fields in the Image Map palette, for example, **MurrayHill.html** and **Murray Hill**.

7. Preview the image map in your browser. Each area in the image should be a link to a different URL.

8. Save the HTML and image as **map.html** in a new folder named **project_11-4**.

Project 5: Creating an Image Map from Layers in ImageReady

Create an image map from one of your designs from an earlier exercise.

Complete the following steps:

1. In ImageReady open the file **music_screen.psd** you created for Project 3.

2. Select the **layer** that contains text for the News link.

3. Click **Layer** on the menu bar, point to **Layer Style**, and then click **Create Layers**. This creates a new layer from the effect. Merge this new layer with the news text layer.

4. Select **New Layer Based Image Map Area** from the Layer menu. You should see a new image map area selection around the contents of the layer.

5. Select **Polygon** for the Shape.

6. Set the Quality to as low a number as possible so that the basic outline is preserved without using too many points.

7. Select **Promote Layer Based Image Map Area** from the Image Map palette menu.

8. Edit the polygon points with the Image Map Select tool to more closely fit the outline of the text.

9. Enter appropriate entries for the URL and Alt fields in the Image Map palette.

10. Repeat steps 2 through 9 for each link in the image.

11. When you are finished, preview the image map in a browser.

12. Select **Save Optimized** from the File menu and save as **music_screen.html** in a new folder named **project_11-5**.

Project 6: Creating an Image Map Manually

Take one of the images from a previous exercise and code the necessary HTML to make it an image map.

Complete the following steps:

1. In Photoshop, open the image **toy_screen.psd** that you created for Project 2, flatten the layers, optimize and save as **toy_screen.jpg** in a new folder named **project_11-6**.

2. Use the Rectangular Marquee tool to select a **rectangular area** around one of the section names and icons.

3. Show the Info palette. Position the pointer over the upper-left corner of the selection area and note the X and Y values in the Info palette.

4. Position the pointer over the lower-right corner of the selection area and again note the X and Y coordinates. Write down the name of the link and the two pairs of coordinates on paper or in a text document.

5. Open a new text document and save it as **screen.html** in the project_11-6 folder.

6. Add the following HTML:

```
<img src="toy_screen.jpg" width="320" height="240"
usemap="#screen" border="0">
<map name="screen">
<area href="###.html" alt="###" shape="rect" coords="###">
</map>
```

7. Replace the three ### characters with the appropriate link, alternate text, and coordinates. (You can make up the link, as there is not really anything to link to.) The coordinates should appear as four numbers separated by commas, first the upper-left X coordinate, then upper-left Y, then lower-right X, and lower-right Y. For example: coords="12,23,34,45".

8. Duplicate the AREA tag and fill in the necessary links, alternate text, and coordinates for each hot spot.

9. Save the screen.html file and open it in a browser. Point to the different hot spots. You should see the alternate text appear over the proper hot spots and the link display in the status bar.

Project 7: Creating Overlapping Circular Image Map Hot Spots Manually

You have an image that needs to be used for navigation. Because of its shape it cannot be created as distinct buttons or as image slices in a table.

Complete the following steps:

1. In Photoshop, open file **arrows.tif** from the Data Disk. Save it as **arrows.jpg** in a new folder named **project_11-7**.

2. You need to create five circular hot spots so that the area for the green disc overlaps the blue areas. The hot spots for the blue areas will end up being crescents rather than circles.

3. Use the Elliptical Marquee tool to select the **green disc**. Note the coordinates of the center of the disc and note the width of the selection in the Info palette. (The coordinates do not have to be exact; estimate as well as you can.) (*Hint:* The center of the disc is in the exact center of the image). Write down the coordinates of the center and the radius of the selection.

4. Repeat Step 3 for each of the blue discs.

5. Open a new text file and save it as **screen2.html** in the project_11-7 folder.

6. Add the following HTML:

```
<img src="arrows.jpg" width="160" height="160"
usemap="#screen2" border="0">
<map name="screen2">
<area href="home.html" alt="Home" shape="circle"
coords="###">
<area href="nw.html" alt="NorthWest" shape="circle"
coords="47,47,41">
<area href="ne.html" alt="NorthEast" shape="circle"
coords="###">
<area href="sw.html" alt="SouthWest" shape="circle"
coords="###">
<area href="se.html" alt="SouthEast" shape="circle"
coords="###">
</map>
```

7. Replace all the ### characters with the appropriate coordinates and radii for each area. The numbers will be the X coordinate of the center of the circle, then the Y coordinate of the center of the circle, then the radius of the circle, separated by commas. To get you started, the first blue disc already has its coordinates in place.

8. Save the text file and open it in a browser. Although the five hot spots overlap each other, because the area for the green disc was defined first it takes precedence over the others.

Project 8: Creating Polygonal Hot Spots Manually

You have an arrow-shaped button that will be used near other small buttons. You want to make sure that only clicks on the arrow-shaped button take the user to the destination and stray clicks are ignored.

Complete the following steps:

1. In Photoshop, open file **right.jpg** from the Data Disk.

2. Position the pointer over each of the seven distinct corners of the green arrow, noting the coordinates in the Info palette.

3. Open a new text file and save it as **arrow.html** in a new folder named **project_11-8**. Also save **right.jpg** to this folder.

4. Add the following HTML:

```
<img src="right.jpg" width="160" height="120"
usemap="#arrow" border="0">
<map name="arrow">
<area href="next.html" alt="Next Page" shape="poly"
coords="###">
</map>
```

5. Replace the ### with each pair of coordinates, separated by commas. Make sure to list the pairs in order, clockwise or counterclockwise around the arrow. Save the image to the project folder, using the same name.

6. Save the file with the same name and in the same location, and open it in a browser. You should see the alternate text appear only when the mouse is over the arrow and nothing else.

Case Project

For the home page of your portfolio, create an image map to use as a splash screen. The map should contain links to all the main sections of the portfolio, and should use the same color scheme used in the navigation buttons and other images on the home page. Any text on the home page should be placed in a colored box with a different colored border that displays in both Netscape and IE. Try making the colored border one pixel thick.

12

CREATING SLICED IMAGES

Breaking Up Images for Display on the Web

In this chapter, you will:

♦ Create image slices
♦ Edit image slices
♦ Set image slice options
♦ Create sliced images manually

Sliced images represent the culmination of everything you have learned so far about Web graphics. They can contain backgrounds, buttons, rollover effects, and animation, and require knowledge of all these different types of Web graphics.

You can create slices manually with Photoshop or ImageReady. ImageReady has more features for working with slices than Photoshop, so this chapter focuses on using ImageReady to create image slices.

Designing and creating sliced images requires a deeper understanding of HTML and Web graphics than creating simple images such as buttons or backgrounds.

CREATING IMAGE SLICES

An image slice is a rectangular piece of an image to which you can assign links and apply rollover and animation effects. While any whole image can be used this way, using image slices allows you to link, animate, or use a rollover effect on individual areas of an image. Image maps allow you to link individual parts of an image, but you cannot animate or swap these parts; the image used as the map is one image. Images used as slices, however, are separate files that can be animated or swapped. You fit slices together on a Web page to reconstruct the original image. When you save a sliced image in ImageReady, each slice is positioned individually in the HTML file and can contain its own link and rollover effects.

Because they are saved as separate images, slices can have different optimization settings. You can save slices in different formats or as empty areas requiring no image. For example, the image shown in Figure 12-1 has some high-color, high-texture areas and some areas that are blank. The image would download more quickly if you replaced the blank areas with simple HTML color. You could also slice the image to isolate the high-color areas, and then save the remaining areas as empty slices so that the user does not have to download blank image files.

Create only as many slices as you need to achieve the desired optimization, rollover effects, and animation. Every file that you force a user to download is a separate request to the Web server, and requires at least a fraction of a second to transfer, even if it is well-optimized. Creating too many slices from an image can actually slow down the loading of the page.

For example, an image with a file size of 60 KB requires that the browser makes one request to the server. If you slice the image into 30 pieces and optimize each piece separately, the combined file size of all the slices might be only 40 KB, but would require that the browser make 30 separate requests from the server. While the actual amount of data is smaller with the sliced images, the load time might be longer because of the extra contacts with the server.

Types of Slices

You create different types of slices with the Slice tool in either Photoshop or ImageReady. The slices do not affect the image itself until you save the image with the Save Optimized As command. Doing so cuts the original image into smaller images, which fit together like pieces of a jigsaw puzzle to re-create the original image in a Web browser.

You can create three types of slices:

- User-slices
- Layer-based slices
- Auto-slices

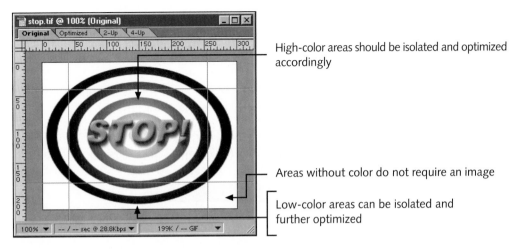

High-color areas should be isolated and optimized accordingly

Areas without color do not require an image

Low-color areas can be isolated and further optimized

Figure 12-1   An image with different optimization needs

Just as you can create image map areas with tools or from layers, you can also create slices with tools or from layers. Slices created with the Slice tool are called user-slices. Slices created from layers are called layer-based slices. When you create a new slice of either type, ImageReady fills in the remaining areas of the image with auto-slices. Whenever you add, delete, or modify slices in an image, the auto-slices automatically resize to fill the leftover area.

Figure 12-2 shows an image being sliced in ImageReady. The different types of slices are indicated by the icon in the upper-left corner of each slice and by the color of the slice border. User-slices and layer-based slices are defined by a solid line, while auto-slices are defined by a dotted line.

12

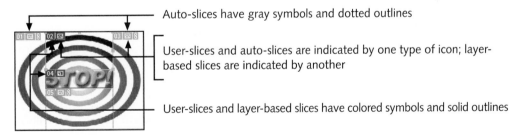

Auto-slices have gray symbols and dotted outlines

User-slices and auto-slices are indicated by one type of icon; layer-based slices are indicated by another

User-slices and layer-based slices have colored symbols and solid outlines

Figure 12-2   Types of slices

The distinction among the three types of slices only matters while editing slices. Once you save the image and the image slices are created as separate files, there is no difference between user-slices, layer-based slices, or auto-slices.

Creating User-Slices

You can create user-slices with the Slice tool. In ImageReady you can also convert selection areas or outlines defined by guides into slices.

To create a user-slice in Photoshop:

1. In Photoshop, open **apples.tif** from the Data Disk.

2. Click the **Slice** tool in the toolbox.

   Figure 12-3 shows the Options bar in Photoshop when the Slice tool is selected.

Figure 12-3   Slice tool options

3. In the Options bar, click the **Style** list arrow and then click **Normal**. All of the options are described in the following list:

   - Choose **Constrained Aspect Ratio** to set the proportions of the slice. For example, enter 1.5 in the Height text box and 3 in the Width text box. The width will always be twice as wide as it is high, regardless of the actual size of the slice.

   - Choose **Fixed Size** to set dimensions for the slice. You can use decimal values for the aspect ratio, but you must use whole numbers for the fixed size.

   - Choose **Normal** to have full control over the size and proportions of the slice.

4. Enable Snap by selecting **Snap** from the View menu. This forces new slices to justify their edges to the edges of adjacent slices.

5. Drag the Slice tool over the left-third of the image. Do not select the white area. As you drag, you can hold down the **Shift** key to force the aspect ratio to a perfect square. Hold down the **Option** key (**Alt** key in Windows) to draw from the center, rather than the upper-left. You see two slices, 01 and 02. Slice 01 is the selected slice and is fully transparent. Slice 02 is not selected and is grayed-out because it is not the current slice.

6. Click the Jump to ImageReady button at the bottom of the toolbox.

As in Photoshop, ImageReady lets you create a slice from an area you select in an image.

To create a slice from a selection in ImageReady:

1. Use the Rectangular Marquee tool to select the center-third of the image. Do not select the white area. Make sure the Feather is set to **0** px in the Options bar.

2. Click **Slices** on the menu bar, and then click **Create Slice from Selection**. You see four slices, 01, 02, 03, and 04. Slices 02 and 04 are auto-slices that fill the area left over by the user-slices.

You can also use the Lasso, Magic Wand, or Elliptical Marquee tool to select an area of the image. Although the selection can have an irregular shape, the resultant slice always is a rectangle. If the initial selection area is not rectangular, the generated slice is a rectangle large enough to cover the complete selection.

You often want to use the smallest slice possible that completely encloses an irregular area of pixels of a certain color. The primary way to select these pixels is with the Magic Wand tool.

To create a slice from an irregular selection:

1. Select the **Magic Wand** tool and set the Tolerance to **32**. Check both **Anti-aliased** and **Contiguous**.

2. Select part of the **blue tree** in the upper-left corner of the image.

3. Click **Slices** on the menu bar, and then click **Create Slice from Selection**. This creates a new slice based on the selection, as well as additional user-slices to fill in the remaining space. At this point your image should look similar to the one in Figure 12-4.

Figure 12-4   Creating a slice from an irregular selection area

Creating Slices from Guides

In ImageReady you can also create slices from an image containing guides. Recall that guides are thin lines that appear over an image in ImageReady or Photoshop, but do not appear over the final Web graphic. You often will want to establish the division of an image using guides before you actually implement the slices. Guides are less intrusive visually and allow you to see what you are doing as you edit and reposition elements in the image. For more on guides, see the Creating Splash Screens chapter.

To create slices from guides in ImageReady:

1. In apples.tif, create two guides in the open image by dragging the mouse pointer from the upper ruler in the document window down into the image area. Place the guides at ⅓ and ⅔ from the top of the image.

2. Click **Slices** on the menu bar, and then click **Create Slices from Guides**. This creates new slices based on the guides, deleting the slices you created earlier.

The preceding steps create as many user-slices as necessary for all the intersections of vertical and horizontal guides. If you move the guides after creating the slices this way, the slices do not resize to fit the new position of the guides. Creating slices from guides deletes any existing slices, so you should use this method only to create initial slices and not to add to existing ones.

Creating Layer-Based Slices

You can also create slices from layers. You often design images, especially large ones such as those used for sliced images, using multiple layers, with each separate image element in its own layer. It is convenient to use the layers as the basis for image slices, rather than having to create them with the Slice tool.

Figure 12-5 shows a slice created from a layer. When you move the layer or edit the transparency in the layer, the slice automatically resizes to fit the layer again. When creating a slice from a layer, the software uses the smallest rectangle it can to select the image information in the layer, and excludes all transparent pixels.

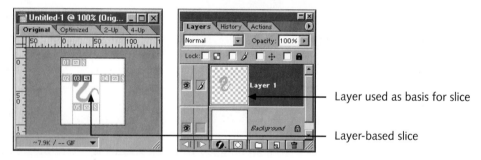

Figure 12-5   A slice created from a layer

To create a slice from a layer:

1. In apples.tif, create a new layer.

2. Use the Paintbrush tool to add a filled **blue circle** in the center of the image.

3. Choose **New Layer-Based Slice** from the Layer menu. This creates a new slice around the blue spot, and additional user-slices to fill the remaining area.

4. Use the Move tool to drag the **blue spot** to a new area on the image. The slices follow the spot, and are redrawn around the new location.

Once you have created your layer-based slices, you must convert them to user-slices before you can perform certain edits, such as combining them with other slices.

Converting Slices

User-slices have the most options for editing. If you need to manipulate an auto-slice or layer-based slice, you should first convert it to a user-slice.

Converting Auto-Slices to User-Slices

You can perform any type of edit on user-slices, including moving, resizing, and optimizing. Auto-slices, however, are linked to each other and they all must share the same optimization settings. You can convert auto-slices to user-slices to have more control over them. Once an auto-slice is converted to a user-slice, it no longer resizes itself based on the size and position of other slices.

If you try to set options for auto-slices, or if you try to divide, combine, or link auto-slices, ImageReady automatically converts them to user-slices before performing the edit. Almost anything you do to an auto-slice converts it to a user-slice. Once converted, it will not resize to fill in gaps left by other slices.

You can also convert auto-slices manually. In Photoshop, select an auto-slice, and then click Promote to User Slice in the Options bar. In ImageReady, you can select one or more auto-slices, then select Promote to User-slice from the Slices menu.

Converting Layer-Based Slices to User-Slices

Layer-based slices rely on the contents of the layers to determine their size and position. To edit a layer-based slice, edit the layer itself. You can combine layer-based slices by merging their layers, and you can move layer-based slices by repositioning the contents of their associated layers. When you are finished editing the layer, you might want to convert the layer-based slice to a user-slice to combine it with other user-slices. Once converted, the slice cannot become a layer-based slice again. You convert layer-based slices to user-slices the same way you convert auto-slices. In Photoshop, select a layer-based slice and click Promote to User-Slice in the Options bar. In ImageReady, select one or more layer-based slices and select Promote to User-Slice from the Slices menu.

Selecting Slices

Select slices in Photoshop or ImageReady with the Slice Select tool. The Slice Select tool is available with the Slice tool in the toolbox, as shown in Figure 12-6. To apply optimization settings to the different slices, you can also select slices in Photoshop in the Save for Web dialog box.

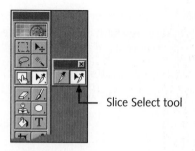

Slice Select tool

Figure 12-6 The Slice Select tool

In the Save for Web dialog box, you can select multiple slices by holding the Shift key while selecting, or by dragging the pointer over the slices you want to select. If slices overlap each other, use the Slice Select tool to select the underlying slice by clicking the part you can see.

In ImageReady, you can save slice selections to group slices into a single set.

To save a slice selection:

1. Select one or more slices.

2. Click **Slices** on the menu bar, and then click **Save Slice Selection**. The Save Slice Selection dialog box appears.

3. Assign a name to the selection and click **OK**.

You then can load the selection later and immediately select multiple slices without having to click each one separately. You can load or delete slice selections by selecting the appropriate options from the Slices menu. Deleting a slice selection does not delete the slices themselves.

Deleting Slices

You can delete user-slices or layer-based slices, and auto-slices will fill in the remaining area. First select the slice, and then press the Delete key or the Backspace key. In ImageReady, you can also delete slices by selecting Delete Slice from the Slices menu or from the Slice palette menu. To delete all slices, select Delete All from the Slices menu in ImageReady, or select Clear Slices from the View menu in Photoshop. Deleting all slices leaves one auto-slice covering the entire image. Deleting a layer-based slice deletes the slice but does not delete the associated layer. Deleting the layer removes both the layer and the layer-based slice. You cannot delete auto-slices.

Locking Slices

When you are finished making changes to your slices, you can lock the slices so that you do not inadvertently move or resize them while making changes to the image. You can lock slices only in Photoshop. To do so, select Lock Slices from the View menu.

Setting Slice Preferences

Recall that slices are indicated by colored outlines, numbers, and symbols in the upper-left corner of each slice. Sometimes these identifiers get in the way of editing the image. In this case, you can temporarily hide the slice outlines and symbols or adjust their appearance.

Hiding Slices

The easiest way to prevent slice outlines from blocking your view of the image is to hide the outlines. This does not delete the slices; it only makes the outlines invisible.

To hide all slices in either Photoshop or ImageReady, do one of the following:

- Deselect Show Extras in the View menu. This hides all guides and slices.

- Select Show from the View menu and deselect Slices. This hides all slices. Check boxes indicate which options are still visible.

- Select Show from the View menu and select None. This hides all guides and slices.

To show slices again, reverse one of the above steps, or simply click anywhere in the image with the Slice tool or the Slice Select tool.

Setting Preferences for Slice Outlines

You also can adjust the appearance of slice outlines, numbers, and symbols in ImageReady. User-slices, layer-based slices, and auto-slices are differentiated from each other by the color of their outlines. User-slices and layer-based slices have solid outlines and blue symbols. Auto-slices have dotted outlines and gray symbols. You can change these colors in ImageReady by setting preferences.

To adjust the preferences for slices in ImageReady:

1. Click **Edit** on the menu bar, point to **Preferences**, and then click **Slices** to open the Slices area of the Preferences dialog box, as shown in Figure 12-7.

2. Click the **Line Color** list arrow in the Preferences dialog box and select a new slice outline color.

To change the slice outline color in Photoshop, select a new color from the Line Color menu in the Options bar.

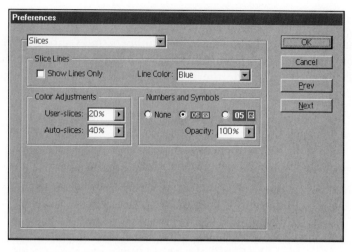

Figure 12-7 Setting slice preferences

Setting Preferences for Slice Outlines

In ImageReady, slices appear as slightly opaque areas over the image, as shown in Figure 12-8. Although the black ring in the image is actually the same color throughout the image, it appears slightly lighter where it is enclosed by a user-slice or layer-based slice, and much lighter where it is enclosed by an auto-slice. Only in the selected slice in the upper-right corner of the image is the actual image area fully visible. This shading does not affect the saved-image slices and serves only to help make the slices more visible during editing. By default, user-slices and layer-based slices are 20% opaque and auto-slices are 40% opaque. Selected slices are fully transparent (0% opaque). You can change the amount of opacity for slices.

To change slice opacity:

1. Open the Preferences dialog box again and view the Slices section.

2. In the Color Adjustments text box, type or drag the slider to enter an opacity value for User-slices and Auto-slices. The value you enter in the User-slices text box affects both user-slices and layer-based slices. A value of 0 means the slice will be fully transparent. A value of 100 means the slice will be completely opaque, unless it is selected.

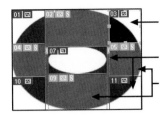 Selected slices are displayed fully transparent

User-slices and layer-based slices are displayed with 20% opacity

Auto-slices are displayed with 40% opacity

Figure 12-8   Slices with different opacity

Setting Preferences for Slice Numbers and Symbols

Slices are identified by the numbers and symbols that appear in the upper-left corner of each slice. The numbering always starts in the upper-left section of the image. As you create and move slices, the numbers change. The symbols indicate whether a slice is a user-slice, auto-slice, or layer-based slice, as shown in Figure 12-9. Symbols also indicate whether the slice contains a rollover effect, or is linked. (Linking is covered later in this chapter). You can change the display of numbers and symbols in slices. In the Slices Preferences dialog box, select one of the three size options under Numbers and Symbols:

- Select None to disable the display of numbers and symbols.

- Select the small icon to display numbers and symbols at their default size.

- Select the large icon to display numbers and symbols in an enlarged size.

Linked slices are denoted with chain symbols

12

Slices in the same selection set share the same symbol color

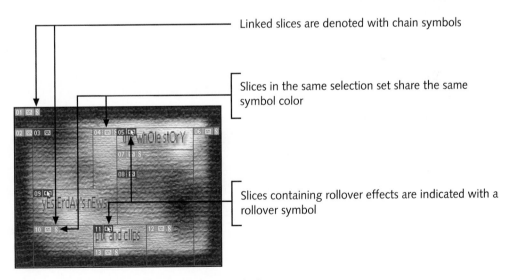

Slices containing rollover effects are indicated with a rollover symbol

Figure 12-9   Different types of slice symbols

You can also adjust the opacity of the numbers and symbols by entering a new value in the text field named Opacity. A value of 100% means the numbers and symbols are fully opaque, blocking the image behind them. Lower values make the numbers and symbols more transparent, allowing the image to show through. You can disable the display of slice numbers and symbols by selecting Show Lines Only. This causes slices to be shown with just the outlines and no symbols.

 To show or hide slice numbers in Photoshop, select Show Slice Numbers in the Options bar.

Once you have created some slices, you may need to edit them.

EDITING SLICES

The slices you initially create are usually not positioned exactly where you want them. Take some time to reduce the total number of slices, and reposition the slices so that they do not leave gaps. If you find that the auto-slices and layer-based slices need to be modified, convert them to user-slices before editing.

Creating Slices from Other Slices

Often it is easier to create slices from existing slices rather than to make completely new ones. You can duplicate the settings of an existing slice, divide a slice into two or more pieces, or combine multiple slices into one.

Duplicating Slices in ImageReady

When creating multiple slices, you may find it easier to duplicate existing slices. You can duplicate slices only when using ImageReady. Duplicated slices are always user-slices, and have the same optimization settings and dimensions of the original slice.

To duplicate a slice:

1. Open **apples.tif** on the Data Disk if it is not already open.

2. Delete all existing slices by selecting **Delete All** from the Slices menu.

3. Create a new slice with the Slice tool.

4. Select **Duplicate Slice** from the Slices menu or from the Slice palette menu. You can also duplicate slices by holding down the **Option** key (**Alt** key in Windows) and dragging the original **slice** to a new location. The new slice appears above the original, slightly lower, and to the right.

5. Drag the duplicated **slice** to a new position. Duplicated slices can be edited like any other user-slice.

You can also copy and paste slices. First select one or more slices, select Copy Slice from the Slice palette menu, then select Paste Slice from the Slice palette menu.

Dividing Slices

When you want to quickly create multiple slices, it is sometimes easier to split a slice into two or more pieces instead of creating new slices. For example, you can create a grid of slices from one large one. In ImageReady you can divide user-slices, but not layer-based slices. If you want to divide a layer-based slice, you must first convert it to a user-slice. You can divide auto-slices only when at least one user-slice also is selected. The new slices created by dividing are always user-slices.

To divide slices:

1. Create a new image in ImageReady that is at least **100** pixels high and wide.

2. All new images in ImageReady are by default one large auto-slice. You should see a slice number and symbol in the upper-left corner of the image. Convert the auto-slice to a user-slice by selecting **Promote to User-slice** from the Slices menu.

3. Select **Divide Slice** from the Slices menu or from the Slice palette menu. The Divide Slice dialog box appears, as shown in Figure 12-10.

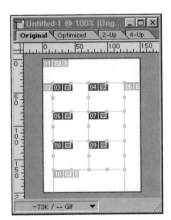 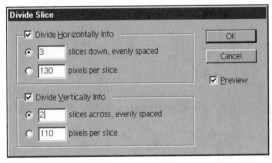

Figure 12-10   The Divide Slice dialog box

4. Click one or both of the checkboxes to divide the slice horizontally and/or vertically. Selecting both directions divides the slice into a grid of new slices.

5. Choose how to divide. Select the number in the top text field ("slices down, evenly spaced" or "slices across, evenly spaced") to divide the slice into a fixed number of new slices. A value of 1 creates no new slices. The combined height of all the new slices is the same as the height of the original slice, and is evenly divided by the number of slices. If you have more than one slice selected, each slice is divided separately.

Alternately, select the number in the lower text field ("pixels per slice") to divide the slice into slices of a fixed size. The number of new slices is determined by the size of the original. If the number in this field does not divide evenly into the dimensions of the original, the remaining space will be made into another user-slice of a smaller size. This might result in a very thin slice that is difficult to edit, so it should be eliminated. Simply deleting this thin user-slice leaves an auto-slice of the same size, so to remove the slice, expand the adjacent slice to fill the area.

Combining Slices

You might decide that you have too many slices. For example, you may notice that two adjacent slices use the same optimization settings, so there is no benefit in having them as separate slices. You can delete unwanted slices and resize existing slices to fill the space, or in ImageReady you can combine existing user-slices and auto-slices. You cannot combine layer-based slices. When you combine slices, the resulting slice is always a user-slice.

To combine slices, select two or more user-slices and select Combine Slices from the Slices menu.

If the edges of the slices are adjacent and aligned, the new slice is simply the combination of both slices. If the edges of the slices are not adjacent or aligned, the new slice is as large as necessary to completely enclose both original slices. This may result in overlapping slices, which creates extra, unnecessary image files. Eliminate slice overlap by transposing the slices, by moving, resizing or aligning them as described in the next section. The optimization settings of the new slice are those of the first slice selected. Figure 12-11 shows how two slices are combined into one larger slice. The two selected slices on the left are combined and result in the selected slice on the right.

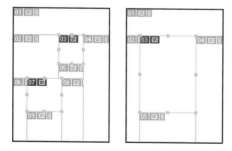

Figure 12-11 Combining slices

Transposing Slices

You can move and resize user-slices in Photoshop and ImageReady using the Slice Select tool, or by changing the numerical values in the Slice palette.

To move a layer-based slice, you move the contents of the associated layer, or convert the layer-based slice to a user-slice. Auto-slices automatically resize and reposition themselves to fit the remaining space when you move or resize user-slices or layer-based slices. To manually move or resize an auto-slice, first convert the auto-slice to a user-slice.

When the Slice Select tool is selected, the Options bar displays options for aligning, distributing, and changing the stacking order of slices. Figure 12-12 shows the Options bar when the Slice Select tool is selected.

Figure 12-12   Options for the Slice Select tool

Moving and Resizing with the Slice Select Tool

To move and resize slices in ImageReady or Photoshop with the Slice Select tool you first select a slice in Photoshop, or one or more slices in ImageReady. Then, with the Slice Select tool selected, drag the slice or slices to a new location in the image. You can hold down the Shift key to constrain the repositioning to vertical, horizontal, or 45-degree diagonal lines. To change the shape of the slice, drag one of the handles on the side of the slice. To change the size of the slice, drag one of the corner handles. You can maintain the aspect ratio of the slice by holding down the Shift key.

You can enable Snap to snap slices to guides or to the edges of existing slices. Click View on the menu bar, point to Snap To to see which Snap options are enabled, and then click a Snap option.

Moving and Resizing with the Slice Palette

When the Slice palette is expanded, you can resize and reposition slices. Expand the Slice palette to show the Dimensions area in ImageReady, or click the Slice Options button in Photoshop to open the Slice Options dialog box, shown in Figure 12-13. Both display the X and Y coordinates of the upper-left corner of the selected slice and the width and height of the slice.

To resize a user-slice using numerical coordinates:

1. Select a **slice**.

2. Show the Slice palette and make sure it is expanded by clicking the **palette tab**. The expanded Slice palette, shown in Figure 12-14, displays coordinates and dimensions for the selected slice.

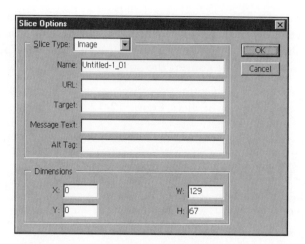

Figure 12-13 The Slice Options dialog box in Photoshop

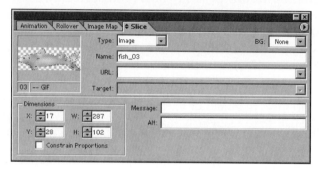

Figure 12-14 The Slice palette

3. Change any of the four values by clicking the arrows next to the text field or by typing directly in the text field. Raising the X value moves the slice to the right; lowering it moves the slice to the left. Changing the Y value repositions the slice vertically. Editing the W value expands the slice to the right. Editing the H value expands the slice downward. All auto-slices resize accordingly and the slices are renumbered automatically, if necessary.

4. Check the **Constrain Proportions** checkbox in the expanded Slice palette to force a constant aspect ratio for the width and height of the slice.

Aligning Slices in ImageReady

Often the slices you create will not line up in neat rows and columns. However, the final slices must be lined up neatly to create an efficient HTML file that does not include leftover slivers of slices. You cannot align slices in Photoshop, and you cannot align layer-based slices or auto-slices.

To align user-slices in ImageReady, select two or more slices with the Slice Select tool. Click one of the following Align buttons in the Options bar to align selected slices:

- **Align Top Edges** to move the selected slices vertically, so that their top edges are in the same horizontal line.

- **Align Vertical Centers** to move the selected slices vertically, so that their centers are in the same horizontal line.

- **Align Bottom Edges** to move the selected slices vertically, so that their bottom edges are in the same horizontal line.

- **Align Left Edges** to move the selected slices horizontally, so that their left sides are in the same vertical line.

- **Align Horizontal Centers** to move the selected slices horizontally, so that their centers are in the same vertical line.

- **Align Right Edges** to move the selected slices horizontally, so that their right sides are in the same vertical line.

You can also select Align from the Slices menu and select one of the six alignment options.

Distributing Slices in ImageReady

If the slices you create become so crowded that you cannot distinguish one from another, you can distribute them. **Distributing** spreads slices vertically or horizontally across the image. While aligning slices causes them to share common edges, distributing slices spaces the edges evenly from each other. Aligning slices usually results in fewer auto-slices, reducing the number of image files that must be downloaded. Distributing slices, however, sometimes produces extra auto-slices. You can distribute slices only in ImageReady; you cannot distribute slices in Photoshop. You can distribute user-slices only; you cannot distribute layer-based slices or auto-slices.

To distribute user-slices in ImageReady, select three or more slices. Then click one of the following Distribute buttons in the Options bar:

- **Distribute Top Edges** to vertically space apart the top edges of the slices.

- **Distribute Vertical Centers** to vertically space apart the centers of the slices.

- **Distribute Bottom Edges** to vertically space apart the bottom edges of the slices.

- **Distribute Left Edges** to horizontally space apart the left sides of the slices.

- **Distribute Horizontal Centers** to horizontally space apart the centers of the slices.

- **Distribute Right Edges** to horizontally space apart the right sides of the slices.

You can also select Distribute from the Slices menu and select one of the six distribution options.

12

Arranging Slices in ImageReady

As you create and modify slices, they might overlap each other. Each new slice appears at the front of the stack of slices. User-slices and layer-based slices are part of the slice stack, but auto-slices are not. When you save images with overlapping slices, underlying user-slices and layer-based slices are automatically divided and resized based on the slice or slices above them. You can change the stacking order of slices to change how underlying slices are divided and resized.

To change the stacking order of slices, select one or more slices. Then click one of the Arrange buttons in the Options bar:

- **Bring to Front** to move the selected slice or slices to the front of the stack.
- **Bring Forward** to move the selected slice or slices forward by one.
- **Send Backward** to move the selected slice or slices back by one.
- **Send to Back** to move the selected slice or slices to the back of the stack.

You also can select Arrange from the Slices menu and select one of the four arranging options.

Once the slices are positioned properly and are available for editing, you can set the options to control the display of the slices.

SETTING SLICE OPTIONS

Creating and positioning slices is only half your work; you still need to determine how the slices will appear in the final graphic. You use some slices as linked images, and others as empty space. Control the display of slices in HTML by deciding whether to use text or an image in the slice. Optimize the images and add effects such as rollovers or animation. Then save the images and HTML.

Controlling the Display of Slices in HTML

With the slices in position, for each slice determine whether to use an image or HTML color and text. Many slices will act as buttons, and need to be linked with HTML anchor tags. You can also add text that appears in the status bar when a user points to a slice.

Choosing a Content Type

Part of the advantage of using image slices rather than image maps or other large images is that you can replace portions of the sliced image with solid color or HTML text. This means users need to download one less file and can load the page faster. A slice contains either a piece of the original image or some combination of text, HTML color, and empty space. The content type of a slice—Image or No Image—determines whether the slice will be saved as an image or as text and color. Image is the default content type. ImageReady and

Photoshop save blank slices as images unless you specify that they are No Image content. Specifying the empty slices as Image content can be inefficient, as you might force the user to download several separate images that contain nothing but blank space.

To set slices as non-image slices:

1. Open **apples.tif** from the Data Disk.

2. Use the Slice tool to create slices around the three image areas. Do not select the white columns. You should see five slices: the three user-slices you defined, and two auto-slices around the white areas.

   You do not have to save the white areas as images because they contain no image information.

3. Select the two auto-slices and then select **No Image** from the Type menu in the Slice palette. To do the same in Photoshop, double-click the slice to open the Slice Options dialog box. Then select **No Image** in the Type list and click **OK**. Doing this means the HTML table that is generated to display the image slices will leave these areas blank.

4. Leave the apples.tif file open.

Photoshop and ImageReady do not display No Image slice content. To view No Image slice content, preview the image in a browser. Slice symbols indicate whether a user-slice is an Image or No Image slice.

Adding HTML Text to a Slice

When you choose a content type of No Image, the Slice Options dialog box in Photoshop and the Slice palette in ImageReady display a large text field where you can enter text and HTML that will appear in place of an image. This text field is shown in Figure 12-15.

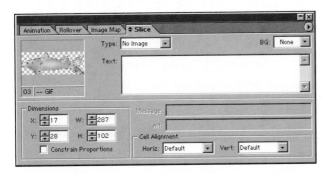

Figure 12-15   The Slice palette with Type set to No Image

You can use HTML tags to set the font and color of the text. You also can use IMG tags or add HTML tables, though the slice probably doesn't provide enough room to do so. If you add too much text, the slice expands to fit the text and pushes the adjacent slices

12

over, disturbing the layout, as shown in Figure 12-16. Because the text is in HTML, white space is ignored by the browser. If you want to include carriage returns in the text, you must explicitly define them with a P, DIV, or BR tag. Any carriage returns you simply type in the text field are ignored.

Figure 12-16   A sliced image with too much text in a No Image slice

When an image contains text in slices, you should preview it in a browser, not just in Photoshop or ImageReady. Different browsers display slice text at slightly different sizes. Any text you add could fit easily within the slice when viewed with one browser, but not in another. Preview sliced images in as many browsers and systems as possible. Although Netscape and Internet Explorer display text with only slight differences, Macs and Windows systems display text with major differences. Windows systems usually display larger text than do Macintosh systems. If you are using a Mac to create slices with text, be sure to preview the layout on a Windows computer.

In ImageReady and in the Save for Web dialog box in Photoshop, you also have the option of setting cell alignment for slices that do not contain images. After you save the slices, they are displayed in a normal HTML table in a Web page. You can set table cell attributes as you do when you create tables by hand or with a WYSIWYG editor. Under the Cell Alignment area of the Slice palette, select from the following options in the Horiz list:

- **Default** to use the browser's default for horizontal alignment. The default is usually to left-align the contents of table cells.

- **Left** to align the text at the left side of the table cell

- **Center** to align the text at the center of the table cell

- **Right** to align the text at the right side of the table cell

You also can align the text vertically by selecting an option from the Vert list:

- **Default** to use the browser's default for vertical alignment. In some browsers the default is to vertically align text in the center of a table cell. In other browsers the default is to align it at the top.

- **Top** to align the text at the top of the table cell

- **Baseline** is not supported in all browsers. It usually results in text being aligned at the bottom of the table cell.

- **Middle** to center the text vertically in the table cell
- **Bottom** to align the text at the bottom of the table cell

Specifying Slice Background Colors

If you choose a content type of No Image, you might want to set a background color so the slice blends in with the other slices. You also should set the background color for slices that contain transparent areas. You can change slice background colors in ImageReady and in the Save for Web dialog box in Photoshop.

To choose a background color in ImageReady:

1. Select both of the **white slices** in apples.tif.

2. Set the foreground color to **black**.

3. In the Slice palette, select **Foreground Color** from the Background menu. The list of options is described below:

   - **None** to set no background color and leave the slice transparent
   - **Matte** to use the Matte color specified in the Optimize palette
   - **Foreground Color** to set the background of the slice to the current foreground color
   - **Background Color** to set the background of the slice to the current background color
   - **Other** to open the Color Picker dialog box, from where you can define a specific color
   - One of the preset colors to assign a color

4. Preview the image in a browser. The white columns should appear black.

To choose a background color in the Save for Web dialog box in Photoshop, select a slice. Double-click a slice with the Slice Select tool to open the Slice Options dialog box and make a selection from the Background menu:

- **None** to set no background color and leave the slice transparent
- **Matte** to use the Matte color specified in the Optimize palette
- **Eyedropper** to set the background of the slice to the current color in the Eyedropper sample box
- **White** to use a white background
- **Black** to use a black background
- **Other** to open the Color Picker dialog box, from which you can define a specific color

You cannot preview the slice background color in either Photoshop or ImageReady. Preview the image in a browser to see the changes.

12

Assigning a URL to a Slice

To make a slice a link to another page, you need to assign a URL to the slice.

To apply a hyperlink to an image slice:

1. Select the **first slice** in apples.tif.

2. In the Slice palette, set the Type to **No Image**. Note that there is no URL text field available in the Slice palette. The hyperlinking option is not available for slices with a No Image content type. Slices that do not contain images can contain normal hypertext links, but you must type the HTML directly into the Text text box.

3. Set the Type to **Image**. Note that three text fields become available: Name, URL, and Target.

4. If you are adding rollover effects to a slice, the slice needs a name. Otherwise you can ignore this field. Slices have default names, such as Untitled-1_03 that are based on the number of the slice. You can use these names or assign new ones.

5. Type a URL into the URL field. The URL can take the form: "http://www.mysite.com" if you want to link to another Web site, or take the form "/index.html" if you want to link to another page on the same Web site. If you leave this field blank, the slice will appear as a normal, unlinked image.

6. Once you assign a URL to a slice, the Target field becomes visible. The target tells the browser where to open the page identified in the URL field. By default, the target field is left empty. This causes any URL to open in the same browser window or frame as the image slice. In addition to leaving the Target field empty, you can click the list arrow and choose one of four options:

   - **_blank** to open the new page in a new browser window. You also can type any other name to achieve the same effect.

   - **_self** to open the new page in the same window or frame as the location of the image slice. This is the same as leaving the target empty.

   - **_parent** and **_top** if you use HTML frames in your site. Choosing one of these options for the target causes all frames to be replaced with the new page.

7. Leave the apples.tif file open.

In general, you can leave the Target field empty, and edit the HTML after the file is generated.

Specifying Browser Messages

Image slices are separate Web images, and like any other graphics in a Web page they can display alternate text that appears if the image does not load or when the user rolls the pointer over them. Additionally, ImageReady includes a feature that displays a text message in the status bar of the browser.

To add alternate and message text for a slice:

1. Preview **apples.tif** in a Web browser. When you roll your mouse pointer over the left image slice, the URL you entered should appear in the status bar of the browser.

2. In ImageReady, expand the Slice palette if it is not already expanded by selecting **Show Options** from the Slice palette menu, or by clicking the arrows in the tab on the Slice palette. This exposes the Dimensions and message areas of the palette.

3. In the Alt text box in the Slices palette, type **blue tree**. This text is inserted as the value of the ALT attribute in the IMG tag used to display the image slice.

4. Preview the image in a browser again. In most browsers, a small text box should appear containing the words "blue tree" when you roll your pointer over the slice. This text will also appear in place of the image if it fails to load on the user's browser.

5. In the Message text box, type **Click here for more information**.

6. Preview the image in a browser again. This time when you roll your pointer over the slice, the status bar displays the message text instead of the URL.

By default, if the image slice has a link, the status bar displays the URL of the link. Photoshop and ImageReady can generate special JavaScript that displays a message in the browser's status bar when the user rolls over an image slice. When you include message text, the message is displayed instead of the URL. The slice does not need to have a link to use this feature. You may want to use this feature to add explanatory text for each image.

Any image can have the feature of displaying text in the status bar. However, in ImageReady only the Slice palette offers status bar messages as an option. If you want other images or even text links to have rollover messages, use the following HTML code:

```
<a href="http://www.course.com"
    ONMOUSEOVER="window.status='this is your message';
return true;"
    ONMOUSEOUT="window.status="; return true;"> </a>
```

Alternately, you can add a message to a slice in ImageReady, and then preview the image in a browser and copy the code that appears. This is a type of rollover effect. For more information on creating rollover effects, see the chapter on Creating Image Rollover Effects.

Working with the Images in Slices

Like other Web graphics, image slices need to be optimized and can contain the rollover and animation effects. If you have many similar image slices in one large graphic, you can link the slices together to share optimization and effects settings.

Optimizing Slices

One of the most important reasons to use image slices instead of large, single images is that you can optimize each image slice separately. You can optimize image slices such as photographic images so that they have low JPEG compression, and save other image slices as 8-bit GIFs, 1-bit GIFs, or with another optimization setting.

When you slice an image, every new slice inherits the optimization settings of the original image unless you specify different settings.

Because the original image files tend to be large, and because you normally use many image slices, the total file size for all image slices is often high. You should optimize each slice as much as possible. Before making any slices, optimize the original file with high JPEG compression. Any slice you make will also have that compression setting. If necessary, you can reduce the optimization settings.

You can optimize image slices like any other image. In Photoshop, use the Save for Web dialog box and in ImageReady, use the Optimize palette.

If you select multiple slices that have different optimization settings, some controls are disabled. Only the menus and text fields that apply to the settings for all selected slices are enabled.

In ImageReady, you can copy optimization settings between slices. Select the slice with optimization settings you want to copy. Find the droplet icon in the Optimize palette and drag it to the slice that you want to optimize.

Linking Slices in ImageReady

In ImageReady you can link slices together in the same way you link layers together in the Layers palette. Optimizing a linked slice applies the same settings to all other slices in the same link set. Although you cannot actually link slices together using Photoshop, you can optimize linked slices together in Photoshop using the Save for Web dialog box.

If you duplicate a linked slice, the new slice is automatically included in the same link set. Linking slices is not the same as combining them. Combining slices actually makes one new slice out of two or more slices. Linking slices leaves them separate.

One advantage to linking slices is avoiding the inconvenience of having to optimize individual slices. The main advantage, however, is that linked slices share the same color palette and dither pattern. If you optimize individual image slices as GIFs with reduced colors, each slice uses its own palette and dither pattern. This can result in visible seams between adjacent slices, as shown in Figure 12-17. Linking slices avoids this problem. In the top image, each slice is reduced to 12 colors. In the bottom image, the slices are linked and collectively reduced to 12 colors.

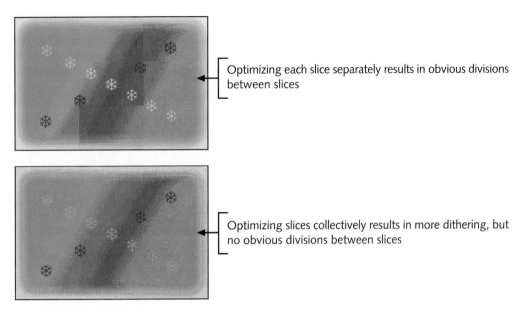

Optimizing each slice separately results in obvious divisions between slices

Optimizing slices collectively results in more dithering, but no obvious divisions between slices

Figure 12-17   Unlinked slices with different optimization settings

To link and optimize slices:

1. In apples.tif, select slices **01** and **03**.

2. Select **Link Slices** from the Slices menu.

3. To link slices, select two or more slices and select **Link Slices** from the Slices menu. The color of the slice symbols should turn red.

4. Select slice **01**.

5. In the Optimize palette, select the **JPEG Medium** setting. Because the slice is linked, slice 03 is automatically optimized the same way.

If you link user-slices and auto-slices together, the auto-slices convert to user-slices. Optimizing slices should be one of the last steps in preparing image slices, and you should link slices together only when you are ready to optimize them.

If you change your mind about linking a slice, you can unlink it by selecting Unlink Slices from the Slices menu. To unlink all slices in a link set, select Unlink Set from the Slices menu. To unlink all slices in an image, select Unlink All from the Slices menu.

Adding Effects to Slices

You can easily add rollover and animation effects to individual slices, though the file size increases with each effect you add. A sliced image with animations and rollover effects in every slice can easily develop such a large file size that you will not want to use it in a Web page.

12

It is easier to create rollovers and animations in image slices when you use layer-based slices. These types of slices automatically resize based on the contents of the layers. If you create animations or rollovers using user-slices, you will have to manually resize the slice if the animation or rollover effect extends beyond the area defined by the slice.

Before you create effects, make sure you have all the necessary layers prepared for the different rollover states or animation frames.

Copy the image selection for each rollover state or animation frame as separate layers, then create slices from those layers. Then edit the layer to include the rollover or animation effect. The slice automatically resizes if necessary.

The last step is to actually apply the rollover or animation. Adjust the visibility of the layers so that the overall image appears in its initial state. Select the slice where you want to add the effect. Then show the Rollover or Animation palette and create additional states or frames. With a new state or frame selected, make the appropriate layers visible.

To animate an image slice:

1. In apples.tif, select the **right-most slice** with the Slice Select tool.

2. The slice will be animated, so it must be saved as a GIF. Because the image has a lot of texture, you can use a lot of color reduction without any noticeable effect. In the Optimize palette, select the **GIF 64 Dithered** setting.

3. Click **Select** on the menu bar, then click **Create Selection from Slice**. This creates a rectangular selection area based on the selected slice.

4. Copy the selection and paste it in a new layer. If necessary, use the Move tool to position the new layer to the right of the image.

5. Use the Hue/Saturation dialog box to set the hue of the new layer to **120**.

6. Show the Animation palette and duplicate the first frame.

7. Make sure the first frame shows only the bottom layer and the second frame shows both layers.

8. Set the delay for both frames to **0** seconds and set the looping to **Forever**.

9. Preview the image in a browser. The right third of the image should appear to shimmer.

Saving the Images and HTML

More than with any other type of graphic created with ImageReady or Photoshop, sliced images rely on the HTML that is generated by the software. You copy this HTML into the final page after you save the image.

Before saving the image, adjust the output settings. Point to Output Settings on the File menu and select HTML. This opens the Output Settings dialog box, shown in Figure 12-18. From there select one of the submenus: HTML, Background, Saving Files, or Slices. Regardless of which you choose, you can access the other three from the same dialog box. Click the buttons marked Prev or Next to cycle through the four windows. The Settings menu at the top should be set to Custom. This allows you to edit the settings.

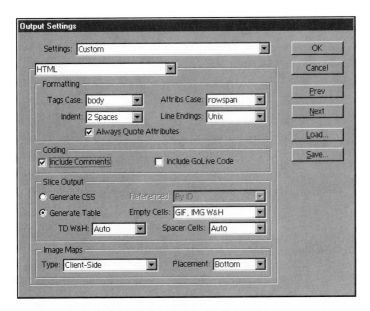

Figure 12-18   The Output Settings dialog box

Setting HTML Options

In the Formatting area of the dialog box,j you can choose the coding style for the final HTML. Different Web servers and browsers accept slightly different standards of HTML, so it is best to format the HTML to make it compatible across platforms. Next to the Tags Case you can choose BODY, Body, or body. This sets the code to uppercase, sentence-case, or lowercase, respectively. The latest specification for HTML requires lowercase for all HTML tags. You can also set the case of the attributes from the Attribs Case menu.

ImageReady can indent the generated HTML to make it easier to read. However, every character, including tabs and spaces, that you add to an HTML file increases its file size by one byte. Although browsers ignore this white space, it still contributes to file size. Next to Indent, you can choose how much to indent the HTML. Selecting Tabs or one of the spaces options makes the final code easier for you to read. However, choosing None creates a smaller file.

Most Web servers that serve your Web files use the UNIX operating system. To have your code be compatible with the UNIX system, select UNIX from the Line Endings menu.

If you select the Always Quote Attributes check box, the HTML will include double quotation marks around every attribute. This adds a significant number of extra characters to the HTML, but makes it more universally compliant, so even very old Web browsers will be able to display the HTML properly.

In the Coding area, you can choose to include HTML comments and GoLive code. Again, the comments make the HTML easier to read, but also increase the download time. You should include GoLive code only if you use Adobe GoLive to edit your HTML pages.

In the Slice Output area, you can choose to display the slices as positioned HTML layers or in a table. Select Generate CSS to lay out the image slices in separate HTML layers rather than in a table. Although most of the recent browsers support positioned layers, many older ones do not. To be compliant with older browsers you should select Generate Table. If any of your slices are set to a content type of No Image, you need to specify how those table cells will be filled. Under the Empty Cells menu, choose one of the first two options, either GIF, IMG W&H or GIF, TD W&H. These both place 1-pixel transparent GIFs in the cell, stretched to the appropriate size. The third option, NoWrap, TD W&H, uses a nonstandard attribute that is ignored in some browsers.

Some browsers do not align tables properly, even when you create them with standard HTML. Even if the final image looks fine on your browser, it might still split on others. The term breaking tables refers to tables with unwanted margins between rows or columns of image slices. This is more common with especially complicated layouts. To avoid broken tables, you should require the table cells to use WIDTH and HEIGHT attributes. Do this by selecting Always from the TD W&H menu. You can also select Auto to have ImageReady decide whether to add these attributes. Do not select None. You can also avoid broken tables by having ImageReady add invisible table rows and columns around the completed table layout. However, this can slow the rendering of the layout, and is often not necessary. Choose Auto to have ImageReady add these rows and columns only when necessary.

Setting Background Options

Click Next in the Output Settings dialog box to display options for saving backgrounds. You can define a background color or image to include in the body of the generated HTML. This color or image will show through any transparent areas in the image slices. The color appears in the body, not the table that controls the layout, however, so you will probably not want to use this option. If you do, click Choose to browse and select a GIF, JPEG, or PNG to use as the background, or choose a color from the Color list.

Setting File Options

Click Next on page 2 of the Output Settings dialog box or select Saving Files from the second list menu to set options for file naming. Information on how to save multiple files is provided in the chapter on creating thumbnail galleries. Choose names for the individual image slices based on the slice name, document name, date, number, or letter. You can also include information about the rollover state or trigger name. The trigger name refers to the image that, when rolled over, triggers a rollover effect.

To be as compatible as possible with all systems, select all available systems in the File Name Compatibility area.

In the Optimized Files area, select Put Images in Folder and type a name in the text field. The individual image slices will be saved in a folder with this name.

Select Include Copyright to include copyright information for images. You must add this information yourself using the Image Info or File Info dialog box.

Setting Slice Naming Preferences

Click Next in the Output Setting dialog box to display options for saving slices. You can specify the file naming conventions for slices in the Output Setting dialog box or the previous one. Setting options in one window overrides the settings from the other one.

When you save a sliced image, each slice is saved as a separate file, and the software produces HTML based on your chosen output settings. You often need to use a text editor or WYSIWYG HTML editor to edit the HTML produced by Photoshop or ImageReady.

To save apples.tif:

1. Review the options for saving sliced images and HTML.

2. Click **File** on the menu bar, and then click **Save Optimized As**. Make sure the format box or the Save as type box is set to HTML and Images (*.html) so that both the images and the HTML file are saved.

3. Create and select a new folder named **apples**.

4. Enter the filename **apples.html** for the HTML file and click **Save**. The images are saved and named, based on the slice numbers and the settings in the Output Settings dialog box.

12

CREATING SLICED IMAGES MANUALLY

If you do not have current versions of Photoshop or ImageReady, you might need to create sliced images by hand. You can split the images into several smaller ones and place them in a grid using HTML tables. This allows you to optimize each portion separately, and to animate or create rollovers for individual portions.

Most layouts require hand-tuning to keep the file sizes minimized. Even if you use Photoshop or ImageReady, you should understand how to slice images manually.

Slicing Images

Creating slices manually is similar to using ImageReady, but instead of relying on the Slice tool, you must crop each slice individually. Then you must also code the necessary HTML so that the images appear without gaps in a Web browser.

To prepare for slicing images, determine how many images you must create out of the original. To streamline the process of creating slices, create as few images as possible without sacrificing the benefits of using sliced images—being able to optimize, animate, and link pieces of a large image separately.

Use guides to plan where you will make the slices. Position the guides to surround important areas that will be used for rollovers or animations, or areas which require different optimization settings from the rest of the image. Also use the guides to exclude areas of solid color. These can be replaced by transparent images. You can use one small transparent image for all empty slices. Most designers have one image for every layout project, often named clear.gif, that is a 1 × 1 pixel GIF with no color, just transparency.

Cropping Slices

The next step is to use the Crop tool to save each piece as a separate image. To control the cropping, enable Snap under the View menu. Before cropping the first slice, save the image as a PSD file. This maintains all guides in place, even after closing and reopening the image. Choose a slice and crop it with the Crop tool. Then optimize it as necessary and save. You do not need to crop the empty corner pieces. Be careful not to vary the optimization methods too widely, and not to alter the appearance of the slices after they are separated. When put in place in the table they might not match.

Positioning Images in Tables

Unlike the areas in image maps, image slices can only be rectangular. The images inside individual table cells can have any shape, but the linked area is the full area defined by the cell.

When you put your slices in table cells in a table, the first thing you will see is that there is a margin surrounding every image. The following code produces the image in Figure 12-19:

```
<table>
<tr><!--row 1-->
<td colspan="3">
<img src="top_slice.gif">
</td>
</tr>
<tr><!--row 2-->
<td>
<img src="left_slice.gif">
</td>
<td>
<img src="center_slice.gif">
</td>
```

```
<td>
<img src="right_slice.gif">
</td>
</tr>
<tr><!--row 3-->
<td colspan="3">
<img src="bottom_slice.gif">
</td>
</tr>
</table>
```

Figure 12-19   A sliced image with visible margins

Just like when you created the tabbed interface in the chapter on buttons, you need to set the BORDER, CELLPADDING, and CELLSPACING attributes of the TABLE tag to 0. You also need to eliminate the spacing between the IMG tags and the TD tags. The proper code is shown below and makes the boundaries between the image seamless and invisible.

In the previous coding example, the empty corner images were left out. Sometimes extra space in table cells will force those cells to be taller or wider than you want. To prevent this, use transparent GIFs to fill the space.

The following code produces the image in Figure 12-20:

```
<table border="0" cellpadding="0" cellspacing="0">
<tr><!--row 1-->
<td colspan="3"><img src="top_slice.gif"></td>
</tr>
<tr><!--row 2-->
<td><img src="left_slice.gif"></td>
<td><img src="center_slice.gif"></td>
<td><img src="right_slice.gif"></td>
</tr>
<tr><!--row 3-->
<td colspan="3"><img src="bottom_slice.gif"></td>
</tr>
</table>
```

12

Figure 12-20 A sliced image with no visible margins

Some browsers may still add margins between or around the images. You should also specify the height and width of each sliced image. You can set the dimensions either in the IMG tags, in the TD tags, or both. This is especially needed if the images used are of different sizes. To be safe you should also define the height and width of the TABLE tag.

The following code contains additional safeguards to ensure the table does not break:

```
<table border="0" cellpadding="0" cellspacing="0"
height="240" width="320">
<tr><!--row 1-->
<td height="23" width="67"><img src="clear.gif"
height="23" width="67"></td>
<td height="23" width="167"><img src="top_slice.gif"
height="23" width="167"></td>
<td height="23" width="66"><img src="clear.gif"
height="23" width="66"></td>
</tr>
<tr><!--row 2-->
<td height="171" width="67"><img src="left_slice.gif"
height="171" width="67"></td>
<td height="171" width="167"><img
src="center_slice.gif" height="171" width="167"></td>
<td height="171" width="66"><img src="right_slice.gif"
height="171" width="66"></td>
</tr>
<tr><!--row 3-->
<td height="130" width="67"><img src="clear.gif"
height="130" width="67"></td>
<td height="130" width="167"><img src="bottom_slice.gif"
height="130" width="167"></td>
<td height="130" width="66"><img src="clear.gif"
height="130" width="66"></td>
</tr>
</table>
```

Note how all cells and images in a row must have the same height, and all cells and images in the same column must have the same width.

One drawback to using ImageReady to make slices is that it is not intelligent enough to use HTML sparingly. A complex table may have a few kilobytes of HTML just to position the slices. Every character takes up one byte of memory. The following line of code:

```
<img src="/images/blue_moon.gif" width="36" height="42"
name="blue_moon" alt="Blue Moon over Miami"
usesrc="moon2.gif">
```

Would take up 119 bytes on a Web page, about a tenth of a kilobyte. This may not seem like a lot, but you should always keep your graphics, and the HTML that displays them as lean as possible.

With the skills learned in this chapter, as well as those in the previous ones, you are ready to start looking for a job as a professional graphic designer.

CHAPTER SUMMARY

- Slices are rectangular pieces of an image that can be positioned in an HTML table to re-create the original image.

- Although you can create many slices from the original, too many slices will delay the loading and rendering of the layout.

- A slice can contain empty space or text instead of an image. Using empty spaces in a slice helps to minimize total file size.

- Each slice can be optimized separately, and can contain animation and rollover effects that are separate from the other slices.

- In Photoshop and ImageReady, you can create user-slices using the Slice tool, or layer-based slices from the contents of layers. User-based slices are easier to edit. Layer-based slices are better for adding animation or rollover effects to a slice. Layer-based slices resize according to the contents of the associated layer.

- ImageReady and Photoshop automatically fill in any remaining space with auto-slices. Auto-slices automatically resize if necessary whenever you change the size or position of other slices.

- Use the Preferences dialog box to adjust the appearance of slices in ImageReady.

- Edit existing slices by moving them, changing their size, or dividing them into smaller slices.

- Image slices are like other Web graphics and can be linked as well as display alternate text.

- When creating image slices manually, make sure to use proper HTML to ensure no broken tables.

12

REVIEW QUESTIONS

1. Which of the following statements is true?

    a. Slices can be a different format from the original image, and can have different optimization settings.

    b. Slices can be a different format from the original image, but must have the same optimization settings.

    c. Slices must be the same format as the original image, and must have the same optimization settings.

    d. Slices must be the same format as the original image, but can have different optimization settings.

2. How do you convert a user-slice to an auto-slice?

    a. First convert it to a layer-based slice, then to an auto-slice.

    b. Use the Convert to Layer-Based Slice command.

    c. This cannot be done.

    d. This is unnecessary because auto-slices are a specific type of user-slice.

3. Which of the following is *not* a way to promote an auto-slice to a user-slice?

    a. Dividing the auto-slice

    b. Selecting the auto-slice

    c. Setting options for the auto-slice

    d. Using the Promote to User Slice command

4. Which of the following statements is true?

    a. Creating a slice from a selection creates a user-slice surrounded by auto-slices.

    b. Creating a slice from a selection deletes any existing slices.

    c. Creating slices from guides creates a user-slice surrounded by auto-slices.

    d. Creating slices from guides deletes any existing slices.

5. Which of the following determines the numbers in the upper-left corner of slices?

    a. The order in which the slices were created

    b. The size of the slices from largest to smallest

    c. The stacking order of the slices

    d. Numbering is from left to right and from top to bottom of the image.

6. Which of the following is never a way to reduce the number of auto-slices in an image?

    a. Aligning slices

    b. Arranging slices

    c. Combining slices

    d. Distributing slices

7. What does the symbol in the upper-left corner of the slice *not* tell you about the slice?

    a. The content type

    b. The stacking position

    c. Whether it is a user-slice, a layer-based slice, or an auto-slice

    d. Whether it is linked to another slice

8. How do you divide a layer-based slice?

    a. First convert it to an auto-slice.

    b. First convert it to a user-slice.

    c. It cannot be done.

    d. Select Divide Slice from the Slices menu.

9. What happens when slices overlap?

    a. A new auto-slice is created in the overlapping area.

    b. A new user-slice is created in the overlapping area.

    c. The slice with the higher stacking order takes precedence.

    d. The slice with the lower stacking order takes precedence.

10. Which of the following is one way to move the left side of a user-slice farther to the left?

    a. Lower the W value in the Slice palette.

    b. Lower the X value in the Slice palette.

    c. Raise the W value in the Slice palette.

    d. Raise the X value in the Slice palette.

11. What command spreads slices to reduce crowding?

    a. Align

    b. Combine

    c. Distribute

    d. Divide

12

12. How do you add a hyperlink to a slice that does not have image content?

    a. These types of slices cannot contain links.

    b. Type the anchor tag manually.

    c. Type the URL in the URL field.

    d. Use the Link command.

13. Which of the following fields in the Slice palette contains text that appears in the browser's status bar?

    a. Alt only

    b. Message only

    c. URL only

    d. Either Message or URL

14. Which of the following is a way you can make the HTML that ImageReady creates easier to read later, but does not increase the size of the HTML file?

    a. Include comments.

    b. Indent text.

    c. Use uppercase tags and attributes.

    d. They all increase file size.

15. Which of the following is *not* a way to make the HTML compatible with most browsers and operating systems?

    a. Include GoLive code

    b. Quote attributes

    c. Unix line endings

    d. Windows, Mac, and UNIX filename-compatibility

16. Why should you *not* select Generate CSS in the Slice Output area of the Output settings dialog box?

    a. This causes the slices to be positioned in HTML layers, which are not supported by all browsers.

    b. This causes the slices to be positioned in HTML layers, which causes broken tables.

    c. This generates style sheets, which are not supported on all operating systems.

    d. This generates style sheets, which increase the HTML file size unnecessarily.

17. Which of the following is *not* a cross-browser way to avoid broken tables?

    a. Using HEIGHT and WIDTH attributes in the images

    b. Using HEIGHT and WIDTH attributes in the table cells

    c. Using spacer GIFs in empty table cells

    d. Using the NOWRAP attribute in table cells

18. What table does this line of HTML produce?

```
<table><tr><td colspan="2"></td></tr>
<tr><td></td><td></td></tr></table>
```

   a. Three cells next to each other, with the first cell from the left cell twice as wide

   b. Two columns, with one cell in the left column and two cells in the right column

   c. Two rows, with one cell in the top row and two cells in the bottom row

   d. Four cells in a 2 × 2 grid

19. What attribute of the TABLE tag must not be set to guarantee that the image slices are adjacent, with no breaks?

   a. WIDTH

   b. BORDER

   c. CELLPADDING

   d. CELLSPACING

20. What value for the CELLPADDING attribute of the TABLE tag helps guarantee no broken tables?

   a. 0

   b. 0%

   c. 1

   d. 100%

12

HANDS-ON PROJECTS

Project 1: Analyze Sliced Images Online

A good way to learn about Web graphics is to see what other designers are doing. Find examples of sliced images on the Web and compare them with what you want to do.

1. Find at least three Web sites that use a sliced image. Make sure it is not an image map or Flash movie.

2. View the HTML source of the pages and find the code for the image slices. It will be a table with many IMG tags in it. How much HTML code do they use to create the slices?

3. Download each image slice to your desktop and add up the file sizes. What is the total file size for each of the sites you found?

4. How many images are used in each project?

5. Do they incorporate rollover effects and animation?

6. Do they use different optimization settings for each slice?

7. Do they use HTML instead of images when possible?

Project 2: Slice an Image

Another designer has given you an image to slice. The layers have been flattened, so you have to use the Slice tool.

Complete the following steps:

1. In ImageReady, open **flowerShopNav.tif** from the Data Disk.

2. With the Slice tool, create a slice that completely encloses the gray rectangle and all the text.

3. Optimize the slice using high-quality JPEG compression.

4. From the Slices menu, select **Divide Slice**. In the dialog box, set the slice to divide **horizontally** into **3** slices down, evenly spaced.

5. Select the slice containing the word **Roses**. In the Slice palette, enter the URL **roses.html**. In the Message and Alt text fields, type **Roses**. Do the same for the other two user-slices, using the appropriate words.

6. Create another slice that completely encloses the flower.

7. Optimize the slice using medium-quality JPEG compression.

8. Optimize all the other slices by reducing colors to **3** bits.

9. Add an **Easter egg** by first selecting one of the thin slices. In the Message field of the Slice palette, type **Produced by:** and then type your name.

10. Preview the image in a browser and check to see that the links work and the messages display correctly.

11. Save the images and HTML in a new folder named **project_12-2**. Save the HTML file as **flowerShopNav.html**. The images will be named automatically.

Project 3: Slice an Image for Better Optimizing

You have an image that is too large. Optimizing it causes degradation of quality, however. Slice the image so that you can optimize certain areas with greater compression than others.

Complete the following steps:

1. In ImageReady, open **crossball.tif** from the Data Disk.

2. Select the **Magic Wand** tool. Set the Tolerance to **100**. Select the **ball**. You may have to [Shift + click] click a few times to select the whole ball.

3. From the Slices menu, select **Create Slice from Selection**. This creates a user slice that exactly fits the ball, and four auto-slices.

4. With the Magic Wand tool, select the **white area** in the upper-left corner. From the Slices menu, select **Create Slice from Selection**. Do the same for the other three corners.

5. The image should have nine slices. If you see more than nine, adjust the slice edges to reduce the number of auto-slices.

6. The four corner slices contain no image information. In the Slice palette, set them to the type **No Image**.

7. The four slices that contain only white, black, and green can all be reduced to just three colors. Select the slices and reduce their color table to **three** colors in the Optimize palette.

8. Select the **middle slice** containing the ball and set it to medium JPEG compression.

9. Preview the image in a browser and save the images and HTML to a new folder named **project_12-3**. Save the HTML file as **crossball.html**.

Project 4: Replace Graphical Text with HTML

You have an image that contains text as part of the graphic. Replace this text with regular text in HTML to reduce the file size.

Complete the following steps:

1. In ImageReady, open **stop.tif** from the Data Disk.

2. Create a slice surrounding the text. Enlarge the slice so that it is as large as possible without crossing the white stripe.

3. Select the **center slice**. In the Slice palette, set the type to **No Image**.

4. Set the background color to the same shade of **red** in the image.

5. In the area labeled Text, type the following HTML:

```
<font color="white" face="arial">
<font size="5"><b>STOP</b></font>
<br>
<font size="6">Please Read Before You Continue</font>
</font>
```

6. Set the horizontal cell alignment to **Center**. Set the vertical cell alignment to **Middle**.

7. Select the surrounding auto-slices and optimize them as reduced-color GIFs. The total file size for the image should be under 1 KB.

8. Preview in a browser. The text causes the table to break. Reduce the lower font size to **3** and preview again.

9. Save the images and HTML in a new folder named **project_12-4**. Save the HTML file as **stop.html**. The images will be named automatically.

Project 5: Animate an Image Slice

You have a simple drawing to which you want to add some animation. The moving area is only in one part of the image. Animating the entire image would produce a large file. Create a slice for the area where the animation takes place and animate only that slice.

Complete the following steps:

1. In ImageReady, open **fish.tif** and **bubbles.tif** from the Data Disk.

12

2. Copy all pixels in bubbles.tif and paste as a new layer in fish.tif. Position the bubbles near the mouth of the fish.

3. Select the layer containing the bubbles. From the Layer menu, select **New Layer Based Slice**. This generates a layer-based slice around the bubbles, and four auto-slices.

4. Show the Animation palette. Duplicate the first frame. Select the **duplicated frame**.

5. Select the **Move** tool. Move the bubbles about **40** pixels up so that the top of the slice is above the top fin.

6. Set the opacity of the bubbles to **0**% for the second frame. Disable visibility for the layer.

7. Set the opacity of the bubbles to **100**% for the first frame.

8. Click the **Tween** button on the Animation palette. Select **All Layers**, all **parameters**, and add **2** frames. The two intermediate frames should show opacity of 67% and 33% for the bubbles layer.

9. Set the delay of the first three frames to **0.1** second. Set the delay of the fourth frame to **2** seconds.

10. Select **slice 01**. In the Slice palette, select **No Image** as the type. Do the same for slices 02 and 05.

11. Select **slice 03**. In the Optimize palette, choose the preset named **GIF 32 No Dither**.

12. Select **slice 04**. In the Optimize palette, choose the preset named **JPEG Medium**.

13. Preview the image in a browser. You should see bubbles appear at the fish's mouth and disappear as they float upward.

14. Save the images and HTML to a new folder named **project_12-5**. Save the HTML file as **fish.html**.

Project 6: Edit an Existing Sliced Image

Another designer created a sliced image for a Web project, but did not quite finish. Edit the project.

Complete the following steps:

1. In ImageReady, open **screen.psd** from the Data Disk.

2. Preview the image in a browser to see its functionality.

3. The white squares do not have the same texture as the rest of the image and should be edited. Find the layer containing the white squares in the Layers palette. Select it and make it visible.

4. Click **Filter** on the menu bar, point to **Distort**, and then click **Ripple**.

5. Set the Amount to **100**% and the Size to **Large**.

6. Click **Filter** on the menu bar, point to **Texture**, and then click **Craquelure**.

7. Set the Spacing to **15**, the Depth to **6**, and the Brightness to **9**.

8. Select all the slices that contain some text. Optimize them with medium JPEG compression.

9. Select all the slices that do not contain text. Optimize them with high JPEG compression (low quality).

10. Preview the sliced image in a browser.

11. Save the images and HTML to a new folder named **project_12-6**. Save the HTML file as **screen.html**.

Project 7: Manually Edit a Sliced Image

When using a background, ImageReady forces every slice to contain a piece of the background, even if there is no other image information. You can manually edit the resultant HTML to add a background image to the whole table, allowing many slices to contain nothing, thus saving file size.

Complete the following steps:

1. Open **undersea.tif** from the Data Disk, optimize it as a 5-bit GIF, and save it in a new folder named **project_12-7**.

2. Follow the steps in project 5 again, saving the images as GIF to maintain transparency.

3. When optimizing the slices containing the fish and the bubbles, set the Matte color in the Optimize palette to a **blue** color similar to the blue used in undersea.tif.

4. Add an additional slice along the bottom of the image where there is just white space.

5. Save the HTML and image files to project_12-7. Save the HTML file as **fish.html**.

6. Open **fish.html** in a text or HTML editor and set the table to use undersea.gif as the background image.

7. Preview in a browser. In some versions of Netscape, the background image will be reset for every table cell. This effect is unintentional, but acceptable.

Project 8: Find Jobs on the Web

The best place to look for Web graphic design jobs is on the Web, either through recruiting agencies or newsgroups, or sites such as hotjobs.com. Many cities have special sites for new media professionals in that area. In New York City, for example, many jobs are posted at nynma.org. To prepare yourself for professional Web graphic design jobs, you need to know what companies are looking for.

1. Find at least three Web sites that have postings for jobs in Web graphic design. These might be the classified ad section of the online versions of a local newspaper, a newsgroup on deja.com, a national site such as monster.com, or any similar site.

2. On each site, find at least three postings that interest you.

3. What are they looking for? Is it a full-time or part-time position? Is it permanent or freelance?

12

4. Can you work from home or do you need to work in their office?

5. What skills are required? Do they expect you to know print-related software such as Quark and Illustrator, or just Web-related software?

6. Would you be expected to use related Web technology such as Flash and JavaScript? Or would you only create GIF and JPEG images?

7. Visit the sites that placed the ads. What is the style of graphics used there? Do you think you would enjoy working on projects with similar styles?

8. If you can, gauge the size of the company. Is it a big office where you will have many colleagues? Or will you be the only person creating graphics?

CASE PROJECT

By now, you should have a complete portfolio of all your graphics work. Redesign your home page to include a sliced image. Either create a new image, or take the image map you created for the last chapter and slice it into separate images. Include at least one animation and rollover effect. You might not want to use the button navigation bar on the home page, and use it only on the other pages. Use the same color in both the background of the home page and the background of the sliced image so the slices will blend in with rest of the page.

Appendix

THE 216 WEB-SAFE COLOR PALETTE

The colors in the Web-safe color palette produce consistent colors both for graphics and for colors produced with HTML. You can use any of the 16,777,216 possible colors available with hexadecimal notation, although the colors in the graphics and in the HTML might not match exactly. See the Displaying Web Graphics chapter for more information.

Eight Web-safe colors can be expressed using names instead of hexadecimal notation. Table 1 shows these color names along with the associated hexadecimal code.

Table A-1   Color names for eight Web-safe colors

Color Name	Hexadecimal Value
Black	#000000
Red	#FF0000
Yellow	#FFFF00
Lime	#00FF00
Cyan	#00FFFF
Blue	#0000FF
Magenta	#FF00FF
White	#FFFFFF

The 216 Web-safe colors are shown in the following figures. Figure 1 shows the first 108 Web-safe colors, and Figure 2 shows the other 108 Web-safe colors. On your Data Disk is an HTML file called web-safe.html that you can load in your browser to see how these colors appear on your computer monitor. The colors that appear in Figure 1 and Figure 2 probably do not match the colors on your screen because of the difference between printer inks and monitor colors.

#000000 black	#330000	#660000	#990000	#CC0000	#FF0000 red
#003300	#333300	#663300	#993300	#CC3300	#FF3300
#006600	#336600	#666600	#996600	#CC6600	#FF6600
#009900	#339900	#669900	#999900	#CC9900	#FF9900
#00CC00	#33CC00	#66CC00	#99CC00	#CCCC00	#FFCC00
#00FF00 lime	#33FF00	#66FF00	#99FF00	#CCFF00	#FFFF00 yellow

#000033	#330033	#660033	#990033	#CC0033	#FF0033
#003333	#333333	#663333	#993333	#CC3333	#FF3333
#006633	#336633	#666633	#996633	#CC6633	#FF6633
#009933	#339933	#669933	#999933	#CC9933	#FF9933
#00CC33	#33CC33	#66CC33	#99CC33	#CCCC33	#FFCC33
#00FF33	#33FF33	#66FF33	#99FF33	#CCFF33	#FFFF33

#000066	#330066	#660066	#990066	#CC0066	#FF0066
#003366	#333366	#663366	#993366	#CC3366	#FF3366
#006666	#336666	#666666	#996666	#CC6666	#FF6666
#009966	#339966	#669966	#999966	#CC9966	#FF9966
#00CC66	#33CC66	#66CC66	#99CC66	#CCCC66	#FFCC66
#00FF66	#33FF66	#66FF66	#99FF66	#CCFF66	#FFFF66

Figure 1 The first 108 Web-safe colors

A

#000099	#330099	#660099	#990099	#CC0099	#FF0099
#003399	#333399	#663399	#993399	#CC3399	#FF3399
#006699	#336699	#666699	#996699	#CC6699	#FF6699
#009999	#339999	#669999	#999999	#CC9999	#FF9999
#00CC99	#33CC99	#66CC99	#99CC99	#CCCC99	#FFCC99
#00FF99	#33FF99	#66FF99	#99FF99	#CCFF99	#FFFF99

#0000CC	#3300CC	#6600CC	#9900CC	#CC00CC	#FF00CC
#0033CC	#3333CC	#6633CC	#9933CC	#CC33CC	#FF33CC
#0066CC	#3366CC	#6666CC	#9966CC	#CC66CC	#FF66CC
#0099CC	#3399CC	#6699CC	#9999CC	#CC99CC	#FF99CC
#00CCCC	#33CCCC	#66CCCC	#99CCCC	#CCCCCC	#FFCCCC
#00FFCC	#33FFCC	#66FFCC	#99FFCC	#CCFFCC	#FFFFCC

#0000FF blue	#3300FF	#6600FF	#9900FF	#CC00FF	#FF00FF magenta
#0033FF	#3333FF	#6633FF	#9933FF	#CC33FF	#FF33FF
#0066FF	#3366FF	#6666FF	#9966FF	#CC66FF	#FF66FF
#0099FF	#3399FF	#6699FF	#9999FF	#CC99FF	#FF99FF
#00CCFF	#33CCFF	#66CCFF	#99CCFF	#CCCCFF	#FFCCFF
#00FFFF cyan	#33FFFF	#66FFFF	#99FFFF	#CCFFFF	#FFFFFF white

Figure 2   The other 108 Web-safe colors

Index